FROM WELFARE TO CHILD CARE

What Happens to Young Children When Single Mothers Exchange Welfare for Work?

FROM WELFARE TO CHILD CARE

What Happens to Young Children When Single Mothers Exchange Welfare for Work?

Edited by

Natasha J. Cabrera
University of Maryland

Robert Hutchens
H. Elizabeth Peters
Cornell University

LAWRENCE ERLBAUM ASSOCIATES, PUBLISHERS
2006   Mahwah, New Jersey   London

Copyright © 2006 by Lawrence Erlbaum Associates, Inc.
All rights reserved. No part of this book may be reproduced in
any form, by photostat, microform, retrieval system, or any other
means, without the prior written permission of the publisher.

Lawrence Erlbaum Associates, Inc., Publishers
10 Industrial Avenue
Mahwah, New Jersey 07430
www.erlbaum.com

Cover design by Tomai Maridou

**CIP information for this book can be obtained by contacting
the Library of Congress**

ISBN 0-8058-5513-0 (cloth : alk. paper)

Books published by Lawrence Erlbaum Associates are printed on acid-free paper,
and their bindings are chosen for strength and durability.

Printed in the United States of America
10 9 8 7 6 5 4 3 2 1

Contents

Contributors   ix

Introduction   xiii

PART I.   THE LANDSCAPE OF CHILD CARE
IN THE POST-WELFARE REFORM ERA

1   Child-Care Arrangements and Help for Low-Income
       Families With Young Children: Evidence From the
       National Survey of America's Families   3
       Linda Giannarelli, Freya L. Sonenstein, and Matthew W. Stagner

2   Welfare-to-Work Transitions for Parents of Infants:
       Employment and Child-Care Policy Implementation
       in Eight Communities   19
       Christine Ross and Gretchen Kirby

3   Infant and Toddler Care After Welfare Reform:
       A Cross-State Comparison   51
       Ann Dryden Witte and Magaly Queralt

**PART II.   GOVERNMENT POLICIES AND THE NATURE
             OF CHILD CARE**

4   Welfare and Child-Care Policy Effects on Very Young
        Children's Child-Care Experiences   77
        Lisa A. Gennetian, Danielle A. Crosby, and Aletha C. Huston

5   Work, Welfare, and Child-Care Choices Among Low-Income
        Women: Does Policy Matter?   101
        Carlena K. Cochi Ficano and H. Elizabeth Peters

6   Nonstandard Work and Child-Care Choices:
        Implications for Welfare Reform   129
        Jean Kimmel and Lisa M. Powell

7   Low-Income Families' Child-Care Experiences: Meeting
        the Needs of Children and Families   149
        *Rebekah Levine Coley, Christine P. Li-Grining,
        and P. Lindsay Chase-Lansdale*

**PART III.   GOVERNMENT SUBSIDIES AND THE NATURE
             OF CHILD CARE**

8   The Dynamics of Child-Care Subsidy Use: A Collaborative
        Study of Five States   173
        *Marcia K. Meyers, Laura R. Peck, Elizabeth E. Davis,
        Ann Collins, J. Lee Kreader, Annie Georges, Roberta Weber,
        Deanna Schexnayder, Daniel Schroeder, and Jerry A. Olson*

9   Child-Care Subsidies and Low-Income Parents—Policies
        and Practices That Affect Access and Retention   199
        Gina Adams, Kathleen Snyder, and Analysis Team

10 Child-Care Subsidies and the Transition From
        Welfare to Work   225
        *Sandra K. Danziger, Elizabeth Oltmans Ananat,
        and Kimberly G. Browning*

PART IV.   IMPLICATIONS AND FUTURE DIRECTIONS

11   Child Care as Risk or Protection in the Context
of Welfare Reform   251
Deborah Phillips

12   Child-Care Subsidies, Quality, and Preferences Among
Low-Income Families   261
Margaret Burchinal

Author Index   267

Subject Index   273

Contributors

Natasha Cabrera is Assistant Professor in the Department of Human Development at University of Maryland.

Robert Hutchens is Professor in the School of Industrial and Labor Relations at Cornell University.

H. Elizabeth Peters is Professor in the Department of Policy Analysis and Management at Cornell University.

Gina Adams is Senior Research Associate in the Center on Labor, Human Services and Population at the Urban Institute.

Kimberly G. Browning is Research Associate at High/Scope Educational Research Foundation in Ypsilanti, Michigan.

Margaret Burchinal is Senior Scientist at the Frank Porter Graham Child Development Institute and Research Professor of Psychology at the University of North Carolina at Chapel Hill.

P. Lindsay Chase-Lansdale is Professor in the School of Education and Social Policy, and Faculty Fellow in the Institute for Policy Research at Northwestern University. She is also Chair of the Doctoral Program in Human Development and Social Policy in the School.

Carlena K. Cochi Ficano is Associate Professor of Economics at Hartwick College.

Rebekah Levine Coley is Associate Professor in the Developmental and Educational Psychology Program at Boston College's Lynch School of Education.

Ann Collins is Senior Associate, Education and Family Support, with Abt Associates Inc. in Cambridge, Massachusetts.

Danielle A. Crosby is Postdoctoral Scholar with the Center for Human Potential and Public Policy at the Harris School of Public Policy Studies at the University of Chicago.

Sandra K. Danziger is Professor of Social Work and Research Professor of Public Policy at the University of Michigan.

Elizabeth E. Davis is Assistant Professor in the Department of Applied Economics at the University of Minnesota, Twin Cities campus.

Lisa A. Gennetian is Senior Research Associate at Manpower Demonstration Research Corporation, New York, NY.

Linda Giannarelli is Senior Research Associate in the Income and Benefits Policy Center at the Urban Institute in Washington, DC.

Aletha C. Huston is the Priscilla Pond Flawn Regents Professor of Child Development at the University of Texas at Austin.

Jean Kimmel is Associate Professor in the Department of Economics at Western Michigan University.

Gretchen Kirby is Senior Researcher with Mathematica Policy Research, Inc.

J. Lee Kreader is Director of Outreach and Partnerships at the National Center for Children in Poverty at Columbia University.

Christine P. Li-Grining is a graduate student in the Human Development and Social Policy program in the School of Education and Social Policy at Northwestern University.

Marcia K. Meyers is Associate Professor at the School of Social Work and the Daniel J. Evans School of Public Affairs, and Director of the Institute on Inequality and Social Structure at the University of Washington.

Jerry A. Olson is President of Olson Research Services in Austin, Texas. He was formerly Chief Economist at the Ray Marshall Center for the Study of Human Resources, LBJ School of Public Affairs, at the University of Texas at Austin.

Elizabeth Oltmans Ananat is a doctoral student in the Department of Economics at Massachusetts Institute of Technology.

Laura R. Peck is Assistant Professor at the Arizona State University School of Public Affairs.

Deborah Phillips is Professor and Chair of the Psychology Department at Georgetown University.

Lisa M. Powell is Research Associate Professor in the Department of Economics and the Institute for Health Research and Policy at the University of Illinois at Chicago.

Magaly Queralt is Principal Investigator with the Wellesley Child Care Research Partnership & National Bureau of Economic Research.

Christine Ross is Senior Researcher with Mathematica Policy Research, Inc.

Deanna T. Schexnayder is Associate Director and Research Scientist, Ray Marshall Center for the Study of Human Resources, LBJ School of Public Affairs, at the University of Texas at Austin.

Daniel G. Schroeder is Research Associate, Ray Marshall Center for the Study of Human Resources, LBJ School of Public Affairs, at the University of Texas at Austin.

Kathleen Snyder is Research Associate in the Center on Labor, Human Services and Population at the Urban Institute.

Freya L. Sonenstein is Professor in the Department of Family and Health Sciences and Director of the Center for Adolescent Health at The Johns Hopkins Bloomberg School of Public Health.

Matthew W. Stagner is Director of the Center on Labor, Human Services, and Population at the Urban Institute in Washington, DC, and is Director of Social Services Research for the Urban Institute's Assessing the New Federalism project.

Roberta Weber is Director of Family Resources and Education at Linn-Benton Community College.

Ann Dryden Witte is Professor in the Department of Economics at Wellesley College and Research Associate at National Bureau of Economic Research (NBER).

Introduction

This book examines the accessibility, availability, and quality of child care for infants and toddlers from low-income families after the 1996 federal welfare legislation (PRWORA), which created Temporary Assistance for Needy Families (TANF). Under TANF, states received a block grant that, subject to broad federal guidelines, permitted them to run welfare programs that were of their own design. Among the federal guidelines were provisions that obliged welfare recipients to enter the workforce. In particular, work requirements were imposed on those who receive cash assistance for more than 2 years, and a 5-year lifetime limit was placed on eligibility for assistance.

The purpose of this book is to first describe what changes occurred in child care, and then to analyze how federal welfare and subsidy policies influence the availability, accessibility, and quality of child-care arrangements for single mothers with young children. These issues were the focus of the conference (held in Washington, DC, in May 2001) on which this collection of writings is based. Although there is a growing body of research that examines the impacts of the 1996 welfare reform and earlier state welfare waivers on maternal employment, economic self-sufficiency, and even outcomes for adolescents, there is little information on the child-care choices that mothers with young children who are required to work make, and how these choices affect the well-being of their children.

These topics were addressed by scholars from a variety of disciplines, including economics, developmental psychology, sociology, and public policy. The studies range from quantitative to qualitative using national, state, and local data. All examine low-income families with a child under 7, and some focus specifically on infants and toddlers. Some of the research featured here is emerging and reflects the unfolding nature of welfare reform. The effects of some of these policies on children will become clear in the near future as the children get older and effects can be measured and analyzed. However, these findings provide useful background information, anticipate some difficulties that single mothers may face, give insight into the system that mothers have to navigate to receive benefits, and provide a lens through which we can see what is happening to the children as their mothers are required to work. As such, the results provide information that is relevant to discussions of welfare reform at both the state and federal levels.

The audience for this book is policymakers and scholars interested in family and social policy issues. State and local policymakers should be especially interested. Much of the responsibility for implementing welfare reform lies at the state and local levels, and the bridge between policy and research is tenuous at best. This volume helps fill that void. Similarly, nonprofit organizations (e.g., the Children's Defense Fund, the National Governors Association, or the National Association for Education of Young Children) may find this volume useful in their efforts to promote child well-being. Finally, because the book includes chapters by scholars from a variety of disciplines (sociology, economics, child development, and psychology), it could serve as a text for a broad range of graduate-level courses dealing with welfare, poverty, children, and public policy.

The book is divided into four parts. The first part sketches the landscape of child care after welfare reform, addressing questions such as:

- When low-income single mothers work, who provides care for their children?
- Do most mothers receive some form of subsidy?
- To what extent do states differ in their answers to these questions?

The second part links welfare policies to the child-care choices that welfare mothers make as they enter the workforce.

- What effect do welfare-to-work programs have on the amount and type of child care received by the children?
- If a government policy of promoting work results in mothers taking jobs with nonstandard hours (e.g., a night shift), how does that affect child-care arrangements?

The third part focuses on child-care subsidies, which are a key federal policy that makes child care affordable and accessible to low-income children. It addresses the following questions:

- Who applies for and receives subsidies?
- Why are some types of families particularly likely (unlikely) to receive subsidies?
- Do subsidies actually affect whether people work?

The fourth part takes stock of the evidence presented and highlights important implications for future research and policy. Specifically, it discusses how the evidence presented in this volume fits into the ongoing debate about whether federal and state child-care policies support or undermine the fundamental goals of welfare reform. A key theme is that welfare policy affects the lives of two generations: parents and their children. Both are important.

SETTING THE STAGE

The Personal Responsibility and Work Opportunity Reconciliation Act of 1996 (PRWORA) was the most fundamental change in U.S. welfare policy since the Social Security Act of 1935. In place of Aid to Families with Dependent Children (AFDC), the 1996 federal welfare legislation created a block grant called Temporary Assistance for Needy Families (TANF), which provides funds to allow states to run welfare programs of their own design within broad federal guidelines. A central tenet of welfare reform is strict work requirements. In 1999, for example, 33% of welfare recipients were working, compared with only 11% in 1996 (Administration on Children and Families, 2000). Since 1996, welfare rolls fell by more than half, and studies show that 50% to 70% of mothers who left welfare are working (Schumacher & Greenberg, 1999). Overall, employment rates for single mothers with incomes less than 200% of poverty increased from 44% in 1992 to 57% in 1999 (Administration on Children and Families, 2000). As a result, demand for child care among low-income families skyrocketed. These statistics, however, do not show the level of unmet demand for child care, and we do not have good estimates of how much a lack of low-cost and high-quality child care has contributed to keeping low-income women out of the workforce. It is clear that child-care issues are central to understanding how low-income mothers can succeed in making the transition from welfare to work and to how children's outcomes are affected by welfare's work requirements.

Work requirements are not a completely new phenomenon. The 1988 Family Support Act (FSA) required some kind of work-related activity for AFDC recipients whose youngest child was age 3 or older. Required work-related activities included education, job search, and training, as well as subsidized or unsubsidized employment. In 1990, the year that the requirements of the FSA became effective, 29% of welfare recipients participated in some kind of work-related activity, but participation in education, training, and job search was more than three times higher than participation in employment (22% vs. 6.7% of welfare recipients; U.S. House of Representatives, 1996).

Work requirements for receipt of TANF are much stricter than the FSA requirements for AFDC receipt. Under TANF, welfare recipients with infants are often required to work, but states have some discretion to set their own work requirements. Five states have no work exemptions for recipients with young children regardless of age, 15 states require recipients with a 3- to 6-month-old child to work, and 26 states only exempt recipients with a child less than 1 year old (U.S. Department of Health and Human Services, 1999). In addition, states have increased the required hours of work activity. Many states require 30 or more hours of work per week and do not consider training, education, or job search alone to count toward the federally mandated participation rates. In 1998, 35% of welfare recipients were engaged in some work-related activity, with the overwhelming majority (28%) of this group being employed (U.S. House of Representatives, 2000). Thus, the proportion of welfare recipients engaged in work-related activities has increased, and work is a much larger share of all work-related activities.

These employment trends and welfare policies have clearly increased the demand for child care, but they may have also altered the demand for *specific types* of child care. For example, research consistently shows that infants are more likely to be in relative care compared with center or family day care (Smith, 2000; Giannarelli et al., chap. 1, this volume). In addition, low-income workers are often employed during nonstandard work hours, when formal modes of care are difficult to find (Kimmel & Powell, chap. 6, this volume). Thus, the stricter work requirement for TANF recipients with very young children is likely to increase the demand for relative care. Similarly, it has been shown that, compared with higher income families, low-income families are more likely to use parental care, relatives, and other informal modes of care. Increasing employment rates among low-income families are then likely to increase the demand for these informal modes of care.

However, other factors like the growth of child-care subsidies that accompanied welfare reform might lead to an increase in the demand for center care and a reduction in the use of parental care. Studies have shown that child-care subsidies are much more likely to be used for center care than for any other type of care (Cochi-Ficano & Peters, chap. 5, this volume; Witte & Queralt, chap. 3, this volume; U.S. House of Representatives, 2000), so the increase in subsidies may have led to an increase in center care. Also, Cochi-Ficano and Peters show that formal modes of care are more likely to be used by working mothers compared with those in job search or training activities. Thus, the fact that welfare recipients are now working rather than participating in these other work-related activities is likely to increase the demand for formal modes of care.

Although there are data on the amount of licensed family- and center-based care, the availability of informal child care is largely unknown. Several studies have shown that the growth in licensed care has been modest at best. The Children's Foundation (U.S. House of Representatives, 2000) estimated that the number of centers in the United States increased by 19% between 1991 and 2000, but data from the Economic Census show that the number of taxpayers who reported being a family day-care provider did not increase at all between 1992 and 1997 (O'Neill & O'Connell, 2001). More important, the General Accounting Office (GAO) found that the supply of licensed care relative to the demand for care was often smaller in poor areas compared with nonpoor areas (U.S. General Accounting Office, 1997).

Because type of care is influenced by several factors, some of which operate in opposite directions, it is difficult to predict the net effect of welfare reform on demand for specific types of care. Data from the Survey of Income and Program Participation (SIPP) show changes in the primary care arrangements for single mothers (see Table I.1) during the period just before and after the passage of PRWORA. The data show a striking decline in formal care—both center and family child care—and an increase in care by relatives. Thus, the factors that encourage the use of informal care (e.g., nonstandard work hours) appear to dominate the factors that encourage the use of formal care (increases in child-care subsidies).

Cost of care is another issue surrounding child care, child outcomes, and the work activity of low-income mothers. In 1995, 54% of employed mothers with income below the poverty level paid for child care, and these women paid, on average, 36% of their income for child care (U.S. House of Representatives, 2000). In part to address this problem, there have been large increases in government dollars both at the state and federal levels targeted toward supporting child care for low-income families. The 1996 Child Care Development

TABLE I.1

Distribution of Primary Child-Care Arrangements
for Children Less Than Age 5 With Employed Single Mothers[a]

Type of Care	1995	1997	1999
Center care (formal care)	36	28	26
Family day care (formal care)	16	8	9
Other nonrelative	14	13	9
Relative care	31	41	43
Parent care[b]	17	16	16

[a]The primary care arrangement is defined as the arrangement used the most hours per week while the mother was at work. Because of tied arrangements in greatest number of hours per week, percentages may exceed 100 percent.

[b]Includes families with an employed mother who report no regular arrangement and self-care.

Source: Authors' calculations from various years of U.S. Census Bureau, "Who's Minding the Kids?"

Fund (CCDF) is the major funding source for child-care assistance for low-income families. The CCDF replaced and combined funding from three previous low-income child-care programs: (a) AFDC Child Care, (b) Transitional Child Care, and (c) At-Risk Child Care. From 1992 to 1996, CCDF (and its predecessor programs) funding from federal and state governments grew at an average of 19% per year. From 1996 to 1998, this funding grew at an average of 34% per year. In 1998, CCDF funding was $5.2 billion. It is unclear, however, whether this increase was sufficient to meet the increased demand for care.

One way to assess the impact of the state and federal responses is to examine utilization rates for the subsidies. An analysis by the U.S. Department of Health and Human Services (2002) shows that only 12% of the 14.8 million children who were eligible for subsidies under federal regulations in 1999 actually received them. However, using state eligibility rules (which are generally less inclusive than the federal limits) and focusing on preschool children, utilization rates increase to 25% (U.S. Department of Health and Human Services, 2002).

THE VARIED LANDSCAPE OF CHILD CARE
IN THE POST-WELFARE REFORM ERA

It should be noted that the national trends described earlier mask significantly different state-level trends. Using multiple sources of data—qualitative, quantitative, and administrative—the three chapters in this section describe the type of child care available to mothers of young children, the patterns of child-care use among mothers who balance work and child care, and the manner in which subsidies are implemented in several communities. The picture that emerges is one of tremendous variation across states in how parents understand and use the subsidy system to pay for child care, the choices these women make in the context of particular markets, the patterns of care that children are in as a result of these choices, and the issues facing administrators who help women navigate the system.

Using a national sample of 42,000 households participating in the National Survey of America's Families (NSAF), Giannarelli, Sonenstein, and Stagner (chap. 1, this volume) report that, in 1999, 38% of single-parent families with children under 5 (and 50% of low-income single parents) received help paying for child care from a government agency or other organization. This rate is higher than what was reported from national administrative data and may reflect funding from sources other than the CCDF.[1] They also report that the

---

[1]Some child-care assistance is available from Title XX Social Services Block Grants, and some states help to pay for child care directly from TANF funds.

fraction of employed families with children under 13 years of age getting help from any source did not change between 1997 and 1999. This is despite the fact that the *number* of these families getting help actually increased by 9%. Because the denominator also increased (i.e., the number of employed families with children under 13 also increased), the fraction stayed the same. The share of low-income families getting help with child-care expenses is similar across most of the states that can be examined separately in the NSAF data; however, the type of care varies substantially across the states. Giannarelli and her colleagues show that the percentage of preschool children with a low-income employed parent who use center-based care ranges from a low of 10% in Michigan to a high of 37% in Alabama.

Ross and Kirby (chap. 2, this volume) take a qualitative approach to understand the variation in the child-care landscape after PRWORA. Using administrative records and qualitative data in eight communities, they identify promising ways to operate subsidy programs that can support low-income parents with infants in making a successful transition from welfare to work while also supporting the developmental needs of their children. One issue they examine is how subsidy policies, and particularly provider reimbursement rates, can affect child-care supply. To ensure that subsidy recipients have access to a reasonable quality of care, most states in their study set the reimbursement rate at the 75th percentile of the market rate for child care, with higher rates for infant care than for care for older children. However, states do not always adjust reimbursement rates to reflect changes in the market cost of child care. Even if updated, market rates may not reflect the cost of child care in the market for a particular family in a particular region of the state. To offset costs, providers can refuse care for children receiving subsidies or may charge parents the difference. In one of the study sites, Ross and Kirby found an unusually low proportion of infants cared for in centers. This finding was consistent with local respondents' comments that inadequate payment rates led many centers to refuse to accept subsidy families.

Another key problem that Ross and Kirby identify is that parents often have difficulty retaining their subsidies once they begin to work and leave welfare. To encourage retention, some states have set higher income eligibility cutoffs for recertification than for initial certification. This allows parents whose incomes increase with work to retain the subsidies for a time until they become better integrated into the labor market. Prior to 1996, a major difficulty in retaining subsidies was related to the fact that the child-care subsidy funding stream for welfare recipients (AFDC child-care assistance) was different from the funding stream for those who had left welfare (transitional child-care assistance). One goal of the 1996 CCDF was to unify several categorical child-care funding streams, in part, because program administrators believed that an integrated child-care system, where eligibility is based on income rather than on TANF status, would ensure that families continue receiving child care after they left TANF. According to Ross and Kirby, however, only three of the six states in the study have an integrated child-care system.

Using administrative records, Witte and Queralt (chap. 3, this volume) tell a tale of two geographic areas—Dade County, Florida, and Massachusetts—and highlight differences in how states implemented and markets reacted to welfare reform. They show that infant and toddler enrollment in subsidized care in Miami-Dade, Florida, increased by 150% as welfare reform unfolded, whereas in five representative areas in Massachusetts, the analogous increase was only 10%. They attribute this disparity to differences in the stringency of the Florida and Massachusetts rules regarding work by welfare recipients with very young children. Witte and Queralt also document important differences in the price and quality of care in the two markets. Prices were strikingly lower in Miami-Dade than in Massachusetts, and there is some evidence that lower quality of infant and toddler care accompanied this lower cost of care.[2]

GOVERNMENT POLICIES AND THE NATURE OF CHILD CARE

The chapters in Part II analyze how government policies affect the amount and type of care that children receive. There are several paths through which government policy can affect child care. Welfare policies that encourage mothers to work indirectly affect the quantity and quality of care received by their children. Similarly, when governments focus subsidies on formal as opposed to informal care, child-care arrangements are likely to change. It is important to understand such phenomena for at least two reasons. First, if welfare reform leads to greater demand for certain types of child care, to meet the goals of welfare reform, it is imperative that the supply of that particular type of care increase as well. Second, changes in child-care arrangements may affect the well-being of children and their parents, producing further instability to these already stressed family systems. In contrast to the prior section, the chapters in this section are less concerned with description and more concerned with analysis. The four chapters in this section make contributions to our understanding of links between government policy and demand for child care.

Gennetian, Crosby, and Huston (chap. 4, this volume) examine how welfare-to-work programs affect child-care arrangements for single parents with children under 6 and whether policies that reduce the cost of formal care increase the use of that care. The chapter is based on data from a series of experimental programs that were initiated during the late 1980s and mid-1990s.

---

[2]One way to address this methodological problem of generalizability of results versus more nuanced measures of the policy environment is to collect more detailed information (such as the information in chap. 8 by Meyers et al.) about various aspects of state child-care subsidy policies and outcomes in a parallel way for multiple states and to consider variables such as age of the child and the supply of care for different age groups.

Gennetian and her colleagues find policy components that encourage employment (e.g., earnings supplements and employment mandates) affect the *amount* of child care used by young children. When programs also offer policies that support paid or regulated child care (by making these forms of care affordable, accessible, or available), families use more center care and less home-based care. The authors argue that the existing studies that have measured quality of care find *on average* higher quality ratings for centers than for family day care. These authors then come to the controversial (but interesting) conclusion that subsidies which support paid or regulated child care *cause* families to get higher quality care on average.

Cochi Ficano and Peters (chap. 5, this volume) examine similar issues with statistical models estimated using nonexperimental data. They use data from the first half of the 1990s to analyze the extent to which welfare-to-work policies and stricter welfare eligibility requirements affected the welfare, labor supply, and child-care choices of low-income single mothers with young children. Their key conclusion is that the mother's work schedule and the supply of care are the primary determinants of the type of child care that mothers choose. In addition, their findings illustrate the importance of child-care supply for supporting mothers' work. They estimate that the probability that a mother with young children will be employed increases by 25% for every one additional center per 1,000 children less than 5 years of age in the respondent's state of residence. To put that estimate in context, the authors show that the number of centers per 1,000 children less than 5 years of age grew from 2.3 to 2.8 between 1991 and 1995. This 22% increase in center supply would imply a 12.5% increase in the likelihood a mother would become employed.

Kimmel and Powell (chap. 6, this volume) analyze a nationally representative 1992 to 1993 sample of low-income single mothers with at least one child under the age of 6. Fully 67% of the mothers work, with a majority working nonstandard hours (i.e., hours other than the standard Monday–Friday 8 a.m.–6 p.m.). This is, of course, a feature of the low-wage labor market; many of the jobs available to women leaving welfare or in welfare who have low levels of education involve nonstandard hours. They found dramatic differences in the type of child-care arrangements chosen by low-income single mothers who worked nonstandard versus standard hours. Those who worked nonstandard hours were less likely to choose center care (26% vs. 42%) and much more likely to use relative care (43% vs. 3%). Estimating statistical models that address reverse causation and controlling for factors that influence choice of child-care arrangements, they found that if a mother moved from a job with nonstandard hours to a job with standard hours, she would be more likely to use center and sitter care and less likely to use relative care. By implication, if the goal of public policies is to support work and increase the supply of quality child care for *all* women, then there is reason to encourage centers to provide quality care during nonstandard work hours.

In a related study, Coley and her colleagues (chap. 7, this volume) examine the difficulty parents have in finding child care that is reliable and flexible enough to support their work needs, yet of high enough quality to support their children's developmental needs. Their data come from interviews with 181 families in the 1999 wave of the Three City Study—a study of low-income families in Boston, Chicago, and San Antonio. Both the mother and (when appropriate) the child-care provider were interviewed regarding a 2- to 4-year-old "focal child." The authors used a battery of tests and assessment tools to measure how well child-care settings meet the developmental needs of the low-income children.

Their findings on quality of care echo similar findings in the literature (Cost, Quality, and Child Outcomes Study Team, 1995). Overall, nearly one quarter of child-care settings were rated as inadequate, one third were rated as minimally adequate, and 43% were rated as good. Moreover, these ratings differed by type of care. The majority of centers were rated as good; but only about one third of regulated home care was rated in the good range, and only a small percentage of unregulated settings were rated as good. In contrast, low-income parents who used unlicensed care (primarily relatives) reported being more satisfied with their arrangements presumably because they met their needs better than center care. Higher income mothers, in contrast, were more likely to find quality child care that met their working needs and their children's developmental needs.

GOVERNMENT SUBSIDIES AND THE NATURE OF CHILD CARE

For child-care arrangements to support working women and their children, they need to be affordable. The high cost of child care—especially care for infants—is at the core of child-care policies. Federal regulations require that states spend at least 70% of their CCDF funds on child-care assistance for low-income families. The aim of this assistance or subsidies is to offset the high cost of child care and thereby encourage work by low-income women. Given the devolution of welfare, states have a lot of freedom in designing plans, setting restrictions, and implementing policies to allocate subsidy dollars, hence the discrepancy between the national and state perspectives of subsidy application and receipt.

The chapters in Part III address questions about who receives child-care subsidies, the barriers to subsidy use, the dynamics and persistence of subsidy use over time, and the impact of subsidy availability on employment. Thus, unlike the previous section, this part analyzes one specific type of government policy. Child-care subsidies are the "carrot" in welfare-to-work policies, and funding for child-care subsidies increased dramatically following welfare reform in 1996. Despite their potential importance, we know very little about who receives subsidies and whether subsidies actually have their intended impact on employment. Such information can inform policymakers about which segments of the population may be having difficulty getting or retaining subsidies and what types of policies and practices can make it easier for mothers to use subsidies. The chapters in this section use data from a variety of sources to provide a more comprehensive picture of subsidies than has been hitherto available.

Meyers and her colleagues (chap. 8, this volume) use administrative data from five states (Illinois, Maryland, Massachusetts, Oregon, and Texas) to describe the characteristics of families and children who receive subsidies, the stability of child-care arrangements, and the continuity and duration of subsidy use. They found considerable variation across states in the characteristics of the families served. For example, the median subsidy recipient was much poorer in Texas than in Illinois, and the proportion of subsidized families that were mixing work and welfare ranged from 5% in Oregon to 71% in Illinois. The flexibility and generosity of child-care subsidies also varied across states. For example, 79% of subsidized children were in center care in Texas, compared with only 18% in Oregon, and the proportion of subsidized families that were exempted from copayments ranged from 10% in Illinois to 85% in Massachusetts.

The detailed nature of the data allowed them to examine the relationship between family characteristics and state policies on several child subsidy outcomes. They found that the duration of subsidy receipt was related to child-care subsidy and TANF policies and the interactions between those policies. Overall their data show that subsidy durations are short, ranging from a median of 3 months in Oregon to a median of 7 months in Texas. Moreover, subsidy duration was shorter in states that imposed higher copayments and in those that required families to recertify eligibility more often than every 6 months. These results suggest that subsidy durations are in part due to administrative barriers and policy practices, which reinforces concern about the extent to which the child-care subsidy system supports working mothers.

Adams and Snyder (chap. 9, this volume) help to shed light on why so few eligible mothers actually receive subsidies. They collected qualitative data from parents, providers, caseworkers, subsidy agency administrators, and other experts in a 1999 survey in 12 states. The authors document a complex system that at times inhibits mothers from moving into the workforce. For example, to apply for and receive benefits, mothers must sometimes appear at the local administrative agency for face-to-face interviews during regular working hours. In the words of a Florida mother, "[It is] almost like you have to be unemployed to be able to apply for all of these benefits, because if you were employed there would be absolutely no way the nicest employer would excuse all that time."

The concern over the impact of subsidies on employment is directly related to whether the availability of subsidies facilitates work. A substantial body of work examines the relationship between employment and child-care cost and subsidies for middle-class women, and this research consistently shows that employment and hours increase in response to lower child-care costs (Averett et al., 1997; Blau & Robbins, 1988; Connelly, 1992; Michalopoulos et al., 1992; Ribar, 1992). However, only a few studies have looked at this question for low-income families (Berger & Black, 1992; Child Care Bureau, 2002; Meyers et al., 2002; Witte et al., 2000), and the relationship between employment and subsidies for these families is not clear.

Danziger and her colleagues (chap. 10, this volume) directly address this issue in an analysis of data from the Women's Employment Study (WES), a multiwave survey of 753 women who had been welfare recipients in Michigan in February 1997. The study found that subsidy receipt increased employment and earnings among women who reported using care in the 1999 interview. Specifically, they show that women who used child care with a subsidy worked 85% of the weeks between the fall of 1998 and fall of 1999 and earned $966 per month compared with women who used care without a subsidy who worked 75% of the weeks and earned $884 per month. In a multivariate analysis that accounted for the likelihood that decisions to work and subsidy receipt are jointly determined, their results also showed a significant relationship between access to subsidies and work/earnings. The source of variation in access to subsidies that they exploit in this study is administrative differences across child-care offices in the likelihood of providing subsidies.

IMPLICATIONS AND FUTURE DIRECTIONS

One of the most anticipated findings of welfare reform studies is whether requiring welfare mothers to enter the workforce shortly after the birth of a child has any effects on the developmental outcomes of the child. On the one hand, the question of whether welfare reform via its impact on maternal choice of child care has any influence on children is somewhat misleading because welfare reform was designed more to influence parental behavior rather than children. On the other hand, since the 1930s, the well-being of children has been the driving force behind the federal government's involvement in providing assistance to single-parent families. The question is then one of whether imposing work requirements on mothers has indirect effects (positive or negative) on the well-being of children.

As we prepared for the workshop on which this volume is based, it became clear that studies looking at the effects of welfare reform on infants and toddlers were virtually nonexistent. This lack of data on how the youngest children are faring is an issue of great concern for policymakers and researchers. The major policy shift was in requiring mothers with infants to work. Some studies show that full-time work during the first year of a child's life is not beneficial (Baydar & Brooks-Gunn, 1991; Blau & Grossberg, 1992; Desai et al., 1989), but it is not known whether these results hold for welfare mothers. It is also important to understand how the stresses of finding appropriate child care impact women's ability to stayed attached in the workforce.

Burchinal (chap. 12, this volume), a developmental psychologist, views the issue of how maternal work affects child outcomes as tangential. What is important is quality of care—regardless of whether it occurs in the home or with a child-care provider. Additionally, Burchinal places the issue of quality of care at the center of government policy. She argues that if the goal of public policy is to both enhance school readiness of low-income children and encourage work by their mothers, then a good case can be made for a policy that provides for high-quality center care such as Head Start or public pre-kindergartens.

According to Burchinal, a complicating factor is the "contradiction between the types of settings that parents seem to prefer and the types of settings that appear to enhance child outcomes" (see Coley et al., chap. 7, this volume). Although Burchinal is somewhat skeptical about the evidence for this apparent contradiction, she sees lack of information as contributing to the problem: "The purchaser of the care (the parent) is not the person experiencing the care (the child), and the child is too young to communicate much about this experience to the parent." That is, parents may not have enough information about the quality of certain types of care.

A second complication in understanding how policies can improve child outcomes is the controversy in the statistical literature linking observed child-care quality and child outcomes. Burchinal provides a useful perspective on differences in the methodological approaches taken by empirical psychologists and economists. Echoing an issue covered earlier in this chapter, a third complicating issue is that of cost. High-quality child care is expensive. If we are to provide the requisite care to low-income children, then additional funds are necessary. Burchinal concludes that there is good reason to pursue the goal of enhancing the school readiness of low-income children.

Phillips (chap. 11, this volume) offers an integrative perspective on the effects of public policies on children's development. She argues that the influence of child care on children's development might be positive, negative, or neutral when examined in a larger ecology that includes family. If policies, such as welfare, are designed to affect income, but not necessarily education, then they are indirectly changing the home environment. In contrast, welfare policies for child-care environments emphasize access to care rather than quality of care. Lower quality care can have detrimental effects on children's development. Hence, policies that aim to protect children's development need to ensure that both home and child-care environments provide optimal care (Phillips; Burchinal, chap. 12, this volume). She then aptly summarizes the data presented in this volume to support the notion that welfare-linked child care is not protective of children and in some cases, because of its quality, may pose some risks to their development. She raises an important point that the chapters in this volume do not examine children's home environments. There is some evidence to suggest that welfare policies might have positive and negative effects on children's home environments. Echoing other authors' conclusions, Phillips argues that child-care policies and employment need to be aligned to meet both children's developmental needs and parents' needs to work. More important, Phillips makes a strong case for the need to conduct research within a two-generation framework. Such research would have the potential to "reframe the public debate" about how public policies should aim to help mothers become self-sufficient and at the same time have beneficial influence on children's environments.

CONCLUSIONS

Although federal and state support for child care has increased dramatically in response to welfare work requirements, low-income families are still facing difficulties balancing work and family obligations. There is wide variation across states in the strictness of welfare work requirements and in the generosity of child-care support. In addition, the level of copayments required and the flexibility to use subsidies for informal modes of child care differs across states and leads families to make different child-care and employment choices. The actual implementation of these policies at the level of the welfare or child-care office has also been shown to create problems in accessing and keeping subsidies.

By design, there are 51 welfare reform policies in place, each with its own set of rules and regulations and operating in different regional, political, economic, and cultural contexts. The dynamics of how welfare reform unfolds is dependent on the system in which families live, and the outcomes for their children and themselves are complex and difficult to discern. One of the important findings from our workshop is that the consequences of welfare reform for families and children do not simply depend on characteristics of welfare programs or the jobs available to low-skill workers; the availability and cost of child care is also of fundamental importance. A second recurring theme of the chapters in this volume is the difficulty in meeting both mothers' employment needs for flexible and reliable care and the needs of children for care that supports positive developmental outcomes. Many studies have argued that for women to stay in the workforce and out of poverty, employment needs to be meaningful and pay above minimum wage—the findings here suggest that for women to remain in the workforce, they have to have child care that is affordable, reliable, and flexible. In other words, child care should meet both the needs of the working parents and the needs of the child.

President Bush has declared that the 1996 welfare overhaul was a resounding success in ending generations of welfare dependency. He has called for even stronger work requirements, such as increasing the work requirement from 30 to 40 hours. If the goal of welfare reform is to increase employment rates among low-income mothers, then it is clear that welfare reform can be called a success. However, the papers in our workshop highlight the complexity of the interplay between mothers' needs in supporting work and children's needs for a safe and stimulating environment. From this perspective, the consequences of welfare reform are more equivocal. Questions remain about both the outcomes of welfare reform for children and the pathways through which child-care policies influence the provision of high-quality and reliable care.

ACKNOWLEDGMENTS

The chapters in this volume are based on a conference held in Washington, DC on May 17 and 18, 2001. We gratefully acknowledge sponsorship and funding provided by the National Institute of Child Health and Human Development Family and Child Well-being Network (grant number HD030944), the Cornell University School of Industrial and Labor Relations Pierce Memorial Fund, the Cornell University Institute for Labor Market Policies, and the Russell Sage Foundation. We appreciate the hard work of Christine Sanchirico on the logistical details of the conference. We also thank several people who played supporting roles at various points in the development of this book. Included are Francine Blau, V. Jeffrey Evans, Lori Stone, and Martin Wells. Finally, we are deeply indebted to Vered Kedar who not only handled the details, but kept us organized and on-task as this project reached fruition.

REFERENCES

Administration on Children and Families. (2000). *TANF third annual report to Congress: Introduction and Executive Summary.* Washington, DC: U.S. Department of Health and Human Services. http://www.acf.dhhs.gov/programs/opre/annual3execsum.htm

Averett, S. L., Peters, H. E., & Waldman, D. M. (1997, February). Tax credits, labor supply, and child care. *Review of Economics and Statistics, 79,* 125–135.

Baydar, N., & Brooks-Gunn, J. (1991). Effects of maternal employment and child-care arrangements in infancy on preschoolers' cognitive and behavioral outcomes: Evidence from the children of the NLSY. *Developmental Psychology, 27,* 932–945.

Berger, M., & Black, D. (1992). Child care subsidies, quality of care, and the labor supply of low-income single mothers. *Review of Economics and Statistics, 74*(4), 635–642.

Bianchi, S. M. (2000). Maternal employment and time with children: Dramatic change or surprising continuity? *Demography, 37.*

Blau, D. M., & Robbins, P. K. (1988, August). Child care costs and family labor supply. *Review of Economics and Statistics, 70,* 374–381.

Blau, F. D., & Grossberg, A. (1992). Maternal labor supply and children's cognitive development. *Review of Economics and Statistics,* 474–481.

Capizzano, J., Adams, G., & Sonenstein, F. (2000). Child care arrangements for children under five: Variation across states. *New Federalism: National Survey of America's Families,* Series B (No. B-7). Washington, DC: The Urban Institute.

Child Care Bureau. (2002). Access to child care for low-income working families. Washington: Author. http://www.scf.dhhs.gov/programms/ccb/research/ccreport/ccreport.htm

Connelly, R. (1992). The effect of child care costs on married women's labor force participation. *Review of Economics and Statistics, 74*, 83–90.

Cost, Quality, and Child Outcomes Study Team. (1995). *Cost, quality, and child outcomes in child care centers public report.* Denver: Economics Department, University of Colorado–Denver.

Desai, S., Chase-Lansdale, P. L., & Michael, R. T. (1989). Mother or market? Effects of maternal employment on the intellectual ability of four-year-old children. *Demography, 26*, 545–561.

Lemke, R. J., Witte, A. D., Queralt, M., & Witt, R. (2000, March). *Child care and the welfare to work transition.* Working Paper #7583. Cambridge, MA: National Bureau of Economic Research. Retrieved September 2, 2004, from http://www.nber.org/papers/w7583

Loeb, S., Fuller, B., Kagan, S. L., & Carrol B. (2004). Child care in poor communities: Early learning effects of type, quality, and stability. *Child Development, 75*, 47–65.

McCartney, K., Dearing, E., & Taylor, B. A. (2003). *Is higher-quality child care an intervention for children from low-income families?* Paper presented at the Biennial Meetings of the Society for Research in Child Development, Tampa, Florida.

Meyers, M., Heintz, T., & Wolf, D. (2002). Child care subsidies and the employment of welfare recipients. *Demography, 39*, 165–179.

Michalopoulos, C., Robins, P. K., & Garfinkel, I. (1992, Winter). A structural model of labor supply and child care demand. *Journal of Human Resources, 27*, 166–203.

Morris, P., Gennetian, L. A., & Knox, V. (2002, March). *Welfare policies matter for children and youth: Lessons from TANF reauthorization.* New York: MDRC.

NICHD Early Child Care Research Network. (1999). Child outcomes when child care center classes meet recommended standards for quality. *American Journal of Public Health, 89*, 1072–1077.

NICHD Early Child Care Research Network. (2001). Child care and the children's peer interactions at 24 and 36 months: The NICHD Study of Early Child Care. *Child Development, 72*, 1478–1500.

O'Neill, G., & O'Connell, M. (2001). *State estimates of child care establishments.* Working Paper Series No. 55, U.S. Bureau of the Census. http://www.census.gov/population/www/documentation/twps0055.html

Peisner-Feinberg, E. S., Burchinal, M. R., Clifford, R. M., Culkin, M. L., Howes, C., Kagan, S. L., & Yazejian, N. (2001). The relation of preschool child-care quality to children's cognitive and social developmental trajectories through second grade. *Child Development, 72*, 1534–1553.

Phillips, D. A., Voran, M., Kisker, E., Howes, C., & Whitebook, M. (1994). Child care of children in poverty: Opportunity or inequality? *Child Development, 65*, 472–492.

Ribar, D. C. (1992, Winter). Child care and labor supply of married women: Reduced form evidence. *Journal of Human Resources, 27*, 134–165.

Schumacher, R., & Greenberg, M. (1999). *Child care after leaving welfare: Early evidence from state studies.* Center for Law and Social Policy. http://www.claso.org/childcare/Child%20Care%20after%20Leaving%20Welfare.htm

Smith, K. (2000, October). Who's minding the kids? Child care arrangements: Fall 1995 (Current Population Reports, series P70, no. 70). Washington, DC: U.S. Census Bureau. http://www.census.gov/population/www/socdemo/childcare.html

U.S. Census Bureau. "Who's Minding the Kids? Child Care Arrangements." http://www.census.gov/population/www/socdemo/childcare.html

U.S. Department of Health and Human Services. (1999). *State implementation of major changes to welfare policies, 1992–1998.* Office of Human Services Policy, Assistant Secretary for Planning and Evaluation. http://aspe.hhs.gov/hsp/Waiver-Policies99/policy_CEA.htm

U.S. Department of Health and Human Services. (2002, April 8). Analysis of child care needs and enrollment. Mimeograph, Assistant Secretary for Planning and Evaluation, Income Security Policy.

U.S. General Accounting Office. (1997). *Welfare reform: Implications of increased work participation for child care* (HEHS-97-75). Washington, DC: Author.

U.S. House of Representatives. (1996). *1996 green book.* Washington, DC: U.S. Government Printing Office.

U.S. House of Representatives. (2000). *2000 green book.* Washington, DC: U.S. Government Printing Office.

Vandell, D. L., & Ramanan, J. (2002). Effects of early and recent maternal employment on children from low-income families. *Child Development, 63*(4), 938–949.

Walker, J. (1992). New evidence on the supply of child care services: A statistical portrait of family providers and an analysis of their fees. *Journal of Human Resources, 27*, 40–69.

Witte, A. D., Queralt, M., Witt, R., & Griesinger, H. (2000, April). *The policy context and infant and toddler care in the welfare reform era.* Cambridge, MA: National Bureau of Economic Research, Inc. Working paper #8893. Retrieved September 24, 2004, from http://www.nber.org/papers/w8893

PART ONE

The Landscape of Child Care
in the Post-Welfare Reform Era

Child-Care Arrangements and Help for Low-Income Families With Young Children: Evidence From the National Survey of America's Families

Linda Giannarelli
Urban Institute, Washington, DC

Freya L. Sonenstein
The Johns Hopkins Bloomberg School of Public Health

Matthew W. Stagner
Urban Institute, Washington, DC

Appropriate and affordable child care is crucial to the well-being of low-income families with young children. To understand the child-care issues these families face, it is important to examine the child-care arrangements they choose and the help they may receive in caring for their children. In this chapter, we present national and state data on the arrangements used by low-income families with young children and on their sources of help with child care. We examine differences by family structure, age of child, across states, and over time. For some issues, we compare low-income families with high-income families.

As we show, there is great diversity in the arrangements that low-income families use to care for their young children, and there is also great variation in how they get help with child care. Documenting this diversity provides an important backdrop for the consideration of policy and research issues. Recent and comprehensive information on these issues provides a context for policy-makers and researchers hoping to understand how child-care policies may affect low-income people.

To examine these issues, we use data from the 1999 National Survey of America's Families (NSAF) and compare some results to the 1997 NSAF. The

NSAF is a key element of the Assessing the New Federalism (ANF)[1] project at the Urban Institute. ANF is a multiyear project designed to analyze the devolution of responsibility for social programs from the federal government to the states, focusing primarily on health care, income security, employment and training programs, and social services such as child care.

The NSAF provides a comprehensive look at the well-being of adults and children at the national level and in 13 states studied in depth.[2] It is a comprehensive source of information on how American families use child care, what they pay for care, and whether and how they get assistance. The survey is representative of the noninstitutionalized, civilian population of persons under age 65 in the nation as a whole and in the 13 states. Together these states are home to more than half the nation's population. A "balance of nation" sample is added to provide unbiased national estimates. Through both the sampling procedures and the questions asked, the survey pays particular attention to low-income families.[3] Interviews in 1999 were obtained from over 42,000 households. The scope and design of the 1997 survey was similar, with over 44,000 households interviewed.

The NSAF allows us to examine child-care arrangements at the child level. We describe the child-care arrangements made for children ages 0 through 4 while their primary caregivers (usually their mothers[4]) were employed. We compare the primary arrangements made by low-income parents (those with family income below 200% of the federal poverty level) to higher income families (those with family income above 200% of poverty). Further distinctions are drawn between the arrangements made by single-parent and two-parent low-income families.[5] We also compare low-income families with a child un-

---

[1]The Assessing the New Federalism project is supported by the Annie E. Casey Foundation, the W. K. Kellogg Foundation, the Robert Wood Johnson Foundation, the Henry J. Kaiser Family Foundation, the Ford Foundation, the David and Lucile Packard Foundation, the John D. and Catherine T. MacArthur Foundation, the Charles Stewart Mott Foundation, the McKnight Foundation, the Commonwealth Fund, the Stuart Foundation, the Weingart Foundation, the Fund for New Jersey, the Lynde and Harry Bradley Foundation, the Joyce Foundation, and the Rockefeller Foundation.

[2]Alabama, California, Colorado, Florida, Massachusetts, Michigan, Minnesota, Mississippi, New Jersey, New York, Texas, Washington, and Wisconsin.

[3]Family income represents annual income for the year prior to the survey. Low-income families are those whose social family had income less than 200% of the federal poverty threshold in the calendar year prior to the survey. All other families are counted as higher income families.

[4]In the 1999 NSAF, 72% of those identified as the adult most knowledgeable about the child were mothers. In the 1997 NSAF, 74% were mothers. Throughout the chapter, we use the phrase *mothers* to refer to all most knowledgeable adults (MKAs).

[5]Single-parent families are those where the family head has no spouse or partner in the household. Some of the families we classify as single parent are in fact headed by a grandparent or other relative. Note that unmarried family heads with a partner in the household are classified as two-parent families.

der age 5 with those with no young children. Where we cite differences, they are statistically significant at the .10 level.

Information on whether and how families received help with child care was collected at the family level. Families were asked to report on the expenses for all children under 13 and were asked about various types of help they may have received for any child in the family. We present findings on the costs of child care for families, as well as the types and amount of help they receive. As with arrangements, we compare expenses and the sources of help for low- and high-income families with a youngest child age 5 or under with those with no children in this age group. As with arrangements, where we cite differences, they are statistically significant at the .10 level.

CHILD-CARE ARRANGEMENTS OF YOUNG CHILDREN
FROM LOW-INCOME FAMILIES

The NSAF gathers data on a variety of child-care arrangements for families with employed parents, including child-care centers, family child-care providers, relatives, and babysitters. Respondents discuss arrangements for "focal" children in two age groups (0–5 and 6–12).[6] If a family has more than one child in an age group, the focal child for that age group is selected randomly. Some families use multiple arrangements for the same child. *Primary* arrangement means the arrangement used for the most hours while the mother worked. In those cases where the mother does not report a child-care arrangement for the focal child, we code the child to be in "parent/other" care. For preschool children, the "parent/other" category may include parents who watch their children while at work or parents who arrange their work schedules around each other. Because we ask only about care that was used consistently over the past month, this category may also include children who do not have a regular and consistent child-care setting.

Primary Arrangements of Low-Income
Preschool Children

Figure 1.1 shows the distribution of primary child-care arrangements for children 0 to 4 years old with employed parents across all family types and incomes. The three most common forms of care are center-based care (28% of children), parent/other care (27%), and relative care (27%). Family child care is less common (14%), and use of a babysitter or nanny in the parent's home is the least common form of care (4%). The type of care varies by family income, household structure (two-parent families vs. one-parent families), and age, as

---

[6]We focus on children ages 0 to 4 because the transition of 5-year-olds into school creates unique child-care challenges.

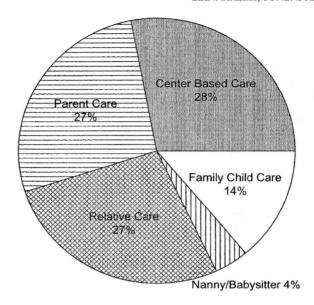

FIG. 1.1.   Primary child-care arrangements of preschool children (0–4) with
an employed parent, 1999.

we examine later, and there is variation across states in the arrangements for
young children from low-income families.

Differences by Family Structure
for Low-Income Families

The types of child care children use vary greatly by family structure (see Fig.
1.2). Looking just at low-income families, center-based care is more common
among children with single parents. Only 16% of two-parent low-income children are in center-based care, whereas 35% of children in low-income single-
parent families are in such care. Parent/other care, in contrast, is most common among children in two-parent low-income families. Forty-three percent
of children in two-parent low-income families are in this type of care, whereas
only 8% of children in single-parent high-income families are in parent/other
care. The low use of center-based care—and the high use of parent/other
care—in two-parent low-income families may reflect the high cost of center-
based care and the additional options available to families where two parents
can share child-care responsibilities. The use of other types of care does not
vary as greatly across family structure and income.

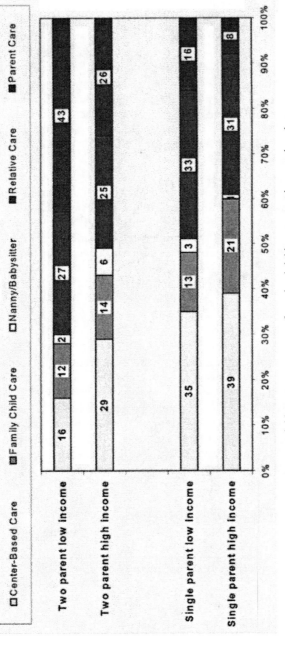

FIG. 1.2. Primary child-care arrangements of preschool children (0–5) with an employed parent by income and family structure, 1999.

Differences by Age of Child for Low-Income Families

Care arrangements of children in low-income families differ by age of child, as shown in Table 1.1. Infants are significantly less likely than 1- to 4-year-olds to be in center-based or family child care. They are significantly more likely to be in parent/other care. Three- to 4-year-olds are significantly more likely to be in center-based care than children 0 through 2 years old and are significantly less likely to be in relative care or parent/other care.

Differences by State of Residence for Low-Income Families

There are substantial differences among states in the types of care used for preschool children from low-income families. For example, differences are evident in the percentage of low-income children in center-based care (see Fig. 1.3). Twenty-three percent of low-income children were in center-based care nationwide in 1999. The proportion of low-income children in center-based care was significantly lower in Michigan (10%), New York (14%), and Texas (16%). It was significantly higher in Mississippi (32%) and Alabama (37%).

Changes Between 1997 and 1999 for Low-Income Families

Between 1997 and 1999, significant shifts occurred in the primary child-care arrangements made for low-income preschool children. We observe virtually no change between 1997 and 1999 in the pattern of arrangements for preschool children in low-income single-parent households. However, the primary arrangements among preschool children in low-income two-parent families shifted between 1997 and 1999 (see Fig. 1.4). Children in low-income two-parent families were significantly less likely to be in center-based care in 1999 than in 1997. Among these families, parent/other care increased significantly over the same period.

TABLE 1.1
Primary Child-Care Arrangements of Low-Income
Preschool Children by Age of Child (1999)

Type of Care	Less Than 1 Year Old	1 to 2 Years Old	3 to 4 Years Old
Center based	**8**	20	33
Family	**8**	14	13
Nanny/babysitter	1	2	4
Relative	32	31	**26**
Parent/other	**51**	34	**24**

Note. **Bold** indicates significantly different from other two age groups combined.

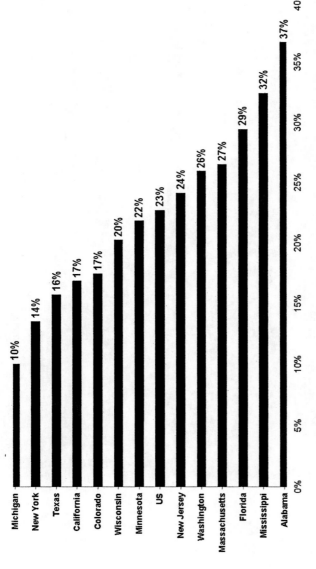

FIG. 1.3. Use of center-based care among preschool children (0–5) with a low-income employed parent by state, 1999.

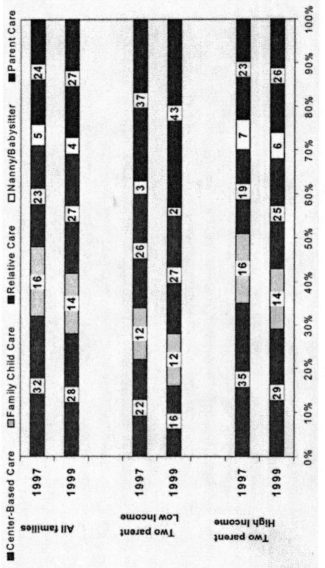

FIG. 1.4. Primary child-care arrangements of preschool children with an employed parent, 1997 and 1999.

TABLE 1.2
Child-Care Expenses for Working Families With Children
Under 13 Who Pay for Care by Whether They Get Help Paying (1999)

	United States	By Income	
		Low-Income Families	Higher Income Families
All Families			
Percent paying	48	42	51
Average monthly expenses (of those who pay)	304	232	332
Percent of earnings (of those who pay)	9	14	7

CHILD-CARE EXPENSES AND HOW LOW-INCOME FAMILIES GET HELP

Child care is expensive, and it can eat up a large share of a family's income. Some families bear this expense alone, but many receive help from relatives, government, other organizations, or employers.[7] The NSAF data allow us to look at child-care expenses of families with employed parents who have children under 13 and to examine how these families receive help with child care. (The 1999 and 1997 NSAF data do not allow us to examine these issues for the subset of families with younger children.) Looking at all employed families with children under age 13, over 48% have some child-care expenses (see Table 1.2). Those who have expenses paid an average of $304 per month out of pocket in 1999, which was 9% of monthly earnings. Higher income families who pay for care paid, on average, $332 per month for child care, or 7% of their monthly income. Low-income families who pay for care paid, on average, about $100 less—$232 per month—which represented 14% of their monthly income.

Sources of Help for Low-Income Families

Given the large portion of monthly salary that low-income Americans pay for child care, it is important to see where they get help with child care. This analysis uses a broad definition of nontax child-care help, including free child care provided by relatives, subsidies from the government or other organizations, government programs such as Head Start and state-funded pre-kindergarten, and assistance from employers, nonresident parents, and other individuals. The estimates of help come from two sources. In most cases, mothers specifi-

---

[7]Child-care expenses may also be defrayed through tax credits, tax deductions, or flexible spending plans, but the NSAF did not collect data on those types of assistance.

cally reported a type of nontax child-care help that was coded as either government/organization help or help from an employer, nonresident parent, or other individual. However, in some cases, mothers did not explicitly report getting help, but apparently received some type of help because the family used nonparental child care without paying for it. For these families, we were able to infer the source of help based on the type of care the family used. Possible sources of such help include care by relatives who did not charge the family and programs that did not charge a fee, such as Head Start, state-funded prekindergarten, or fully subsidized care by a local institution.[8]

The 1997 and 1999 NSAF data underestimate the actual incidence of nontax child-care assistance. First, these data cannot identify cases in which a family pays part, but not all, of the child-care bill unless the respondent reports it. Respondents may not know they do not pay the entire bill, or they may not choose to admit to receiving such help. Also, it is impossible in the 1997 and 1999 NSAF to identify where a family pays for at least one child-care arrangement, but another is provided for free.[9] For these reasons, we refer to the findings as *minimum* estimates of help being received.

In 1999, 29% of employed families[10] with children under age 13 received some sort of assistance with child care, considering all types of help (except that provided through the tax code; see Table 1.3). The percentage getting help was higher for low-income families, at 39%. The most commonly reported forms of help were free provision of child care by a relative and help from a government agency or other organization. As Table 1.3 shows, a minimum of 16% of low-income families received free care provided by a relative. A minimum of 21% of low-income families received government or organizational help, which could include child-care subsidies through the Child Care and Development Fund (CCDF) block grant, child-care subsidies through other federal funds or through state programs, or help provided by private organizations. Few families reported receiving help from a nonresident parent, employer, or any other source.

---

[8]These percentages understate the total percentage of families receiving child care without being charged a fee and without receiving an explicit subsidy because they exclude families that received this type of care for one child while paying for or reporting help for another child's care. Also our methods captured state-funded pre-kindergarten in this unspecified-free-care group only if the respondent reported that the child was in child care rather than in school.

[9]The 2002 NSAF identifies these cases and also allows us to link child-care expenses and child-care help with particular focal children.

[10]In general, the adult surveyed (who was reported to be most knowledgeable about the child) is either an unmarried parent or has an employed spouse. We analyze child-care assistance at the family level rather than at the child level because the 1997 and 1999 NSAF data do not allow child-care expenses and subsidies to be linked to individual children. Our definition of family is a narrow one that treats related subfamilies separately from a household's primary family.

TABLE 1.3

Percentage of Employed Families With Children Under 13 Using Different Forms of Help to Pay for Child Care by Income and Family Type, 1999

| Variable | United States | By Income | | By Family Type | | Single-Parent Families, By Age of Youngest Child | |
		Low-Income Families	Higher Income Families	Low-Income Single-Parent Families	Low-Income Two-Parent Families	Single-Parent Families With Children Under 5	Single-Parent Families With No Children Under 5
Minimum percentage of families getting any type of help	29	39	24	51	30	58	44
Minimum percentage of families with free care provided by a relative	14	16	14	18	13	15	21
Minimum percentage of families receiving help from a government agency or other organization	12	21	8	28	15	38	20
Percentage of families getting help from a nonresidential parent	2	3	2	5	1	7	2
Percentage of families getting help from an employer	<1	<1	<1	<1	<1	1	<1
Minimum percentage of families getting other forms of help	2	2	2	3	1	4	3

Source: National Survey of America's Families.

Note. Percentages in subcategories do not add to total because of rounding and a minimal amount of overlap between some categories. **Bold** indicates significant difference between low-income single-parent families and low-income two-parent families or between low-income single-parent families with children under 5 and low-income single-parent families with no children under 5.

Differences by Family Structure and Age of Child
for Low-Income Families

Among low-income families, 51% of single-parent families report help with
child care, whereas only 30% of low-income two-parent families report such
help (see Table 1.3). Low-income single-parent families with a child under age
5 are significantly more likely to report help than those with only school-age
children. Fifty-eight percent of low-income single parents with a child under
age 5 reported receiving any type of help, and at least 38% of low-income single parents with a child under 5 reported receiving government/organiza-
tional assistance—significantly more than those with only school-age
children. Low-income single-parent families with a child under 5 are *less* likely
than those with only school-age children to be identified as receiving free care
provided by a relative (15% compared with 21%).

Child Care Expenses for Those Who Do
and Do Not Get Help

Two thirds of families who receive help with child-care expenses pay nothing
for child care. Yet most subsidy programs require families to pay a copayment,
usually along a sliding fee scale that increases the payment as the family's income increases. Families may also get help for one child at the same time they
pay for care for another child.

Considering only low-income families with children under age 5 who pay
some child-care expenses, those who reported some sort of government/or-
ganization help paid an average of $108, compared with $257 among those
not receiving any help (see Table 1.4). Although the 1999 NSAF data do not
allow us to specifically examine payments relative to arrangements for particular children, there is some indication that the subsidized parents are paying somewhat less expenses while obtaining more hours of child care and
more center-based care. Among children under age 5 in low-income families
that paid for child care and reported some sort of help, 58% were in center-
based care, compared with 30% of the low-income children under age 5
whose parents paid for child care, but did not receive any help. Further, the
low-income children under age 5 whose parents received help and paid for
care were in care for more hours per week than the children whose families
did not receive any help (31 hours compared with 26 hours on average).[11]
The parents who needed more care or who preferred center-based care
might have been more likely to apply for subsidies, or the availability of

---

[11]These statistics are based on the focal children of mothers who received some sort of help paying for child care. The NSAF does not provide data on the child-care arrangements of nonfocal children.

TABLE 1.4
Selected Child-Care Characteristics for Low-Income Employed
Families With Children Under 5 Who Pay for Child Care
by Whether They Get Help Paying (1999)

	Family Reports Some Type of Help[a]	Family Does Not Report Help
Low-income families with children under age 5 paying for child care		
Average monthly child-care expenses	$208	$257
Children under age 5 in low-income families with some child-care expenses		
Percent in center-based care	58%	30%
Average hours in care	31	26

[a]The average non-$0 expense figure includes only those low-income families with children under age 5 who report government/organization help.

child-care help might have allowed some parents to choose center-based care who would otherwise have chosen less expensive types of care or allowed some parents to increase their hours of work.

Differences Among States for Low-Income Families

The share of low-income families getting help with child-care expenses is similar across most of the states that can be examined separately in the NSAF data. Looking at help received from government or other organizations, two states vary from the national average. The percentage of low-income families with such assistance is significantly higher than the 21% national average in Massachusetts (28%) and significantly lower in Mississippi (15%). Two substantive issues complicate the interpretation of these cross-state differences. First, variations in how subsidy programs operate might lead to more or less underreporting of government/organization help in different states. Second, there are many different types of government/organizational help, so a difference in the total cannot be traced to a difference in a particular type of government or organizational help through these data.

Two states differ from the national average of 16% in the percentage of families receiving free care. Significantly fewer low-income families receive free relative care in both California and Colorado (10%). States could vary in the incidence of free care because of differences in parental preferences for relative care, the costs or availability of other kinds of child care, the child-care needs of employed families, or the availability or willingness of relatives to provide this kind of child care.

Changes Between 1997 and 1999

We found that between 1997 and 1999, the national percentage of employed families with children under age 13 reporting getting help with child care from any source remained the same—at about 29%. NSAF surveys show no change in the percentage of families receiving government/organizational assistance between 1997 and 1999, but they do show an increase in the number of families receiving such assistance. The estimated number of families grew from 2.2 million in 1997 to 2.4 million in 1999—an increase of almost 9%. At the same time, the number of employed families with children also increased by nearly 6%.

The increase in the number of families with government/organizational help is due to an increase among higher income families. This increase is surprising given the growth in child-care subsidy programs in the late 1990s that targeted low-income families. It is possible that increases in government assistance were obscured by a lack of change or a countervailing change in help from other organizations. It is possible that the degree of underreporting of assistance changed during this period following changes in subsidy practices (such as changes from vouchers to direct payment of providers). It is also possible that gains in help for higher income families are primarily for families just above our low-income cutoff of 200% of the federal poverty line.

SUMMARY AND DISCUSSION

The national picture of child-care arrangements and help for low-income families is an important context for understanding policy issues. Data from NSAF provide an overview of the child-care arrangements for low-income families with young children and some insight into how these families get help with child care. Capturing the wide range of ways families arrange for child care and get help with child-care costs is difficult. Child-care arrangements include a range of settings and caregivers. Relatives, government, and, occasionally, employers can provide help in a variety of ways. Our survey captured the primary types of arrangements, but clearly does not fully explain how all parents arrange for child care, such as those we have categorized as using parent/other care. We also captured the major forms of help, but we found the full picture of help difficult to capture in a telephone survey with limited time to explore the issue. Our estimates of the percentages of families getting different types of help are minimums. In the third round of NSAF, administered in 2002, we revised the questions on help with child care, linking the types of help received with the arrangements of each focal child.

Families make a range of choices in determining child-care arrangements. There is variation in arrangements between low- and high-income families, as well as between single- and two-parent families, by age of child, across states, and across time. For example, low-income children are less likely than high-income children to be in formal child-care settings (center-based care and family child care). Child-care arrangements for low-income single-parent families are significantly different from those for low-income two-parent families. In single-parent families, parent availability is less, and the pool of relatives may be smaller. Therefore, although the resources for purchasing care are generally lower in single-parent families, family child care or center-based care may be the only available options for many single-parent families. Child-care arrangements appear to have changed somewhat for low-income Americans between 1997 and 1999. In particular, children in low-income two-parent families were significantly less likely to be in center-based care in 1999 than in 1997, and parent/other care increased significantly over the same period among this group of families. Policies to assist families with their care must take into account the implications of the differences across families and changes over time.

Child care takes a considerable percentage of low-income families' incomes. Forty-two percent of low-income employed families with children under age 13 have some child-care expenses, amounting to an average of $232 per month or 14% of monthly earnings.

Almost a third of all employed families with children younger than age 13 receive some sort of help paying for child care. Help with child-care expenses comes from a variety of sources, including government subsidies, help from noncustodial parents, and care provided for free by relatives or government programs such as Head Start. Low-income single parents are the most likely to receive help, with half of this group getting help, compared with a third of low-income two-parent families and a quarter of high-income families.

There is some evidence that families who receive help with child-care expenses pay lower expenses, but receive more care. Among low-income families who paid for child care and who had children under age 5, the average expense was $208 for those who reported government/organization help, but $257 for those who reported no help. However, the children under age 5 in low-income families paying for child care were more likely to be in center-based care and were in care for more hours when their families received some sort of help than when their families received no help. These findings may suggest that subsidies allow parents to make different child-care choices both in types of care and the number of hours of care purchased. Parents who need more care or who prefer center-based care may also be more likely to try to obtain subsidies.

From this analysis, it is clear that child care for low-income families with young children is a complex issue. There is diversity in the choice of child-care arrangements and in the forms and amount of help received. The arrangements used and the help received reflect interactions of parent preferences, income constraints, market forces, employment patterns, and public policies.

Yet this analysis highlights some clear themes. Child care plays a major role in the lives of low-income families, making it possible for them to work, but consuming a large share of income. Given the importance of child care for obtaining and retaining employment, it is crucial to examine policies that support low-income parents as they attempt to choose the best care for their children and themselves.

ACKNOWLEDGMENTS

The authors are grateful for research assistance provided by Sarah Adelman and Natalya Bolshun. The authors are also grateful for additional assistance and comments from Gina Adams, Jeff Capizzano, Gary Gates, Jason Ost, Stephanie Schmidt, and Sandy Hofferth. The analysis in this chapter was supported by funding from the Bulova Foundation.

## CHAPTER TWO

Welfare-to-Work Transitions for Parents of Infants: Employment and Child-Care Policy Implementation in Eight Communities

Christine Ross
Gretchen Kirby
Mathematica Policy Research, Inc.

This chapter reports findings from an implementation study that examined how welfare-related work requirements and child-care policies were applied to parents of infants in eight communities. Nearly half the states have used the flexibility provided under the federal welfare reform law to require parents of infants to work as a condition of receiving benefits, and nearly all states require teenage parents to return to school soon after the birth of a child. The study examined the policy environment (work and school requirements) and practical considerations (child-care and supportive services) that influence the timing and ease of the transition from welfare to work or school for parents of infants. The study is based on staff interviews and focus groups with key informants in eight communities: Bakersfield, California; St. Petersburg and New Port Richey, Florida; Waterloo, Iowa; Grand Rapids and Detroit (Warren-Conner District), Michigan; Nashville, Tennessee; and Milwaukee (Region 2), Wisconsin.

We found that case managers and program administrators did not view parents of infants as a group that had categorical needs substantially different from those of the broader Temporary Assistance for Needy Families (TANF) population. We also found that, in general, TANF policies regarding work requirements, sanctions, and time limits were applied in the same way to parents of infants as to other families. In contrast, *teenage* parents were viewed as a salient subgroup with special needs requiring comprehensive services and support. The study identifies several strategies that states and communities used to meet the challenges of helping parents of infants make the transition to school or work while promoting the health and development of their infants.

INTRODUCTION

The Personal Responsibility and Work Opportunity Reconciliation Act (PRWORA) emphasized moving families from welfare to work by introducing work requirements that specified the timing and level of work necessary among an increasing number of welfare families over time. This led many states to narrow significantly the exemptions from work requirements in their TANF programs. Federal law now requires that parents work when their youngest child reaches 1 year of age, and states can require that they work before that point. By October 1998, for example, 22 states required parents to work while their youngest child was less than a year old. These states have charted new territory in their efforts to move welfare recipients into work.

In addition, PRWORA guidelines increased states' scope for setting child-care subsidy policies and ended the entitlement to child-care assistance for families receiving Aid to Families with Dependent Children (AFDC) and those transitioning off AFDC. Four child-care subsidy programs were consolidated into a single program—the Child Care and Development Fund (CCDF)—and combined state and federal spending for child-care subsidies increased.[1]

This study provides a comprehensive picture of the experiences of parents of infants—both teenage and older parents—in meeting work participation or school attendance requirements as a condition of receiving welfare. Our findings extend beyond what can be discerned from information on state policies alone. Through an in-depth, qualitative approach, we examined how work requirements for parents of infants are implemented in local communities. In doing so, we considered both the interactions among welfare and child-care policies and the interactions among these policies, the local economy, and community support for low-income families. The study also takes a preliminary step in identifying strategies that may promote parental employment or school activities while supporting the development of very young children.

We begin by discussing the motivation for the study and providing background on work requirements for parents of young children in the 50 states. We then describe the study methods. We present our findings in four sections: welfare work requirements, comprehensive support for teenage parents,

---

[1]The child-care subsidy programs that were consolidated into the Child Care and Development Block Grant in 1996 were AFDC Child Care, Transitional Child Care, At-Risk Child Care, and the Child Care and Development Block Grant.

child-care support, and services to promote parenting and child development. We close with a summary of key findings and a discussion of policy implications and directions for research.

STUDY MOTIVATION AND BACKGROUND INFORMATION

Juggling work and family responsibilities is a challenge for many two-parent, middle-income families with young children, but it can be even harder for low-income single parents, who may lack both the financial resources and the help of another adult. Single mothers in low-wage jobs and mothers with a recent welfare history are more likely to be in jobs with inflexible schedules, without sick leave, and with limited or no vacation leave (Heymann & Earle, 1998; Presser & Cox, 1997).

Infants are of particular concern when their parents are required to work. Young children require stable, responsive, and intensive attention to meet their needs for physical care, emotional support, and cognitive stimulation (Beckwith, 1990; Berlin & Cassidy, 1999; Lally et al., 2003; NICHD Early Child Care Research Network, 1996; Raikes, 1993; Shonkoff & Phillips, 2000). Truly responsive caregiving is associated with lower child–staff ratios and highly trained staff (NICHD Early Child Care Research Network, 1996, 2000), which increase the cost of care (Cost, Quality, and Child Outcomes Study Team, 1995). The higher cost of quality child care naturally makes it more difficult for low-income families to afford. Young (15-month-old) children from families with incomes below the federal poverty line (FPL) received home-based care that was of lower quality than that received by children from higher income families (NICHD Early Child Care Research Network, 1997). Center-based care was of somewhat higher quality for young children from families with incomes below FPL, compared with that of moderate-income families, which likely reflects the effects of subsidies (NICHD Early Child Care Research Network, 1997; Phillips, Voran, Kisker, Howes, & Whitebook, 1994). Infants need stable care with a small number of primary caregivers, which may be difficult to ensure when job schedules change frequently. Infants' physical health is fragile compared with that of older children because infants have not been fully immunized, and chronic illnesses or disabilities needing special care or attention may not yet have been identified (American Academy of Pediatrics, 1997; McCormick, Kass, Elixhauser, Thompson, & Simpson, 2000; McCune, Kalmanson, Fleck, Glazewski, & Sillari, 1990). Children have more frequent illnesses when they are enrolled in child care than when they are cared for at home, with the greatest differences in the incidence occurring in the first 2 years of child care (Wald, Guerra, & Byers, 1991).

Many questions emerge as states tackle the challenges of supporting families with infants in their transition from welfare to work. What special challenges do these parents face in balancing their parenting activities with required work or school activities? What supportive services are critical to continued participation in work and school activities? Is continuous, reliable, affordable, and good-quality infant care available to these parents? Have states taken the opportunity to link these families with child care that can promote the health and development of infants?

Since states began to implement the TANF and CCDF programs, various organizations have collected a great deal of information on state-specific welfare and child-care program policies.[2] Nevertheless, the variation in the design of welfare and child-care policies makes it difficult to define consistent policy data across states or to understand how policy decisions interact. This qualitative study of eight communities examines how these policies were actually applied to parents of infants.

Nearly all states have some experience with the welfare-to-work or welfare-to-school transition for parents of infants (see Table 2.1). At the time of the study, 22 states required parents of infants to work as a condition of receiving welfare benefits. Twenty-three others required parents to work once the child reached its first birthday. Yet because federal law allows states to limit the exemption for the care of a young child to 12 months, an exemption may not be available for children born subsequently. Only 12 states exempted parents of infants from work with no restrictions for children conceived while on public assistance. Almost every state requires a fairly prompt return to school for unmarried teenage parents who have not completed school.

Among states that require parents of infants to work, the exemption period is set at about 3 months, which is consistent with the policy precedent for parental leave established by the Family and Medical Leave Act.[3] Only a few states allow longer periods of leave within the child's first year. In many states teenage parents must return to school within a shorter time, although in most states it is still by 3 months after the birth unless school is not in session.

---

[2]The most notable sources of information on welfare policy across states include the State Policy Documentation Project of the Center for Law and Social Policy and the Center on Budget and Policy Priorities [www.spdp.org]; TANF Program Annual Reports to Congress produced by the Office of Planning, Research, and Evaluation, Administration for Children and Families, U.S. Department of Health and Human Services [www.acf.dhhs.gov]; and the Assessing the New Federalism project of the Urban Institute [www.urban.org]. Information on child-care policies across states can be found in publications of the Child Care and Development Division of the Children's Defense Fund [www.childrensdefensefund.org]; the review of state CCDF plans produced by the Child Care Bureau [www.acf.dhhs.gov]; and the annual review of state child-care licensing policies published by the Children's Foundation [childrensfoundation.net].

[3]The Family and Medical Leave Act requires employers of 50 or more employees to provide up to 12 weeks of job-protected, unpaid leave for the birth and care of the newborn child of the employee.

TABLE 2.1

1999 Exemptions From TANF School, Training, or Work Activity Requirements Based on Youngest Child's Age

State	Teenage Parents			Older Parents				Limit Exemptions for Subsequent Births
	No Young Child Exemption	About 3 Months	Other Period	No Young Child Exemption	About 3–4 Months	Other Period Less Than 1 Year	One Year	
Alabama		√		√a				
Alaska[b]	√						√	√
Arizona		√					√	√
Arkansas		√			√			
California			√c			√d		
Colorado	√			√d				
Connecticut			√		√		√	√
Delaware			√		√		√	
District of Columbia			√					
Florida		√			√		√	
Georgia		√			√			
Hawaii			√	√a		√		
Idaho	√			√a				
Illinois	√	√					√	
Indiana	√	√			√e		√	
Iowa	√	√			√e			
Kansas	√	√					√	
Kentucky	√						√	√
Louisiana	√						√	√
Maine		√					√	√
Maryland		√					√f	√
Massachusetts		√						√

(Continued)

23

TABLE 2.1
(Continued)

State	Teenage Parents			Older Parents				Limit Exemptions for Subsequent Births
	No Young Child Exemption	About 3 Months	Other Period	No Young Child Exemption	About 3–4 Months	Other Period Less Than 1 Year	One Year	
Michigan		√			√			
Minnesota			√				√g	√
Mississippi		√					√	√
Missouri	√√						√	
Montana				√				
Nebraska		√			√			√
Nevada		√					√fd	
New Hampshire		√h	√h					
New Jersey		√			√			
New Mexico		√					√	√
New York		√			√d		√	
North Carolina	√				√			
North Dakota			√√		√√			
Ohio	√						√d	√
Oklahoma	√							
Oregon		√	√					
Pennsylvania		√					√	
Rhode Island		√					√	√

South Carolina						√
South Dakota	√		√			
Tennessee	√		√			√
Texas		√				
Utah		√		√		√[i]
Vermont		√				√[j]
Virginia	√		√			
Washington	√					√
West Virginia	√					√
Wisconsin	√					√[a]
Wyoming						

Note. State Policy Documentation Project (1999, 2000b); Gallagher, Gallagher, Perese, Schreiber, & Watson (1998); U.S. Department of Health and Human Services (2000, 2004a, 2004b).

[a] In 2002, the exemption period was 3 months (U.S. Department of Health and Human Services, 2004a, 2004b).

[b] Data on exemption policies for teenage parents unavailable.

[c] Postpartum period as prescribed by physician.

[d] Counties determine exemption period.

[e] In 2002, no automatic exemption period (U.S. Department of Health and Human Services, 2004a, 2004b).

[f] Exemption period is 2 years.

[g] No exemption period as of July 2004.

[h] Both 3-month and 6-month periods are specified; may indicate minimum and maximum exemption period.

[i] Exemption period in 1999 was 3 years, but in 2002 was 18 months (U.S. Department of Health and Human Services, 2004a, 2004b).

[j] Exemption period is 18 months.

The most recent report of state TANF policies indicates little change in the work exemptions for parents of infants. Our list of 22 states that require work while the youngest child is under age 1 remains unchanged, although the specific exemption period within a few of these states has been altered slightly. However, two additional states (Minnesota and Wyoming) have now joined this group.[4]

Work has clearly become the anchor of welfare policy. But the debate continues on how much work to require of whom. Although federal and state welfare-to-work policies continue to evolve, the experiences of the states and communities included in this study can provide valuable information about the challenges involved in requiring work of parents of infants and some potential strategies for meeting these challenges.

STUDY METHODS AND LIMITATIONS

Because our goal was to learn about the experiences of parents of infants making the welfare-to-work transition, we focused on states with greater experience working with such parents. Of the 22 states that required welfare-reliant parents of infants to work in 1998, we eliminated nine with small caseloads and one in the early stages of implementing TANF. Of the remaining states, we selected six that varied in their sanction and time limit policies and provided diversity in demographic composition, poverty level, teenage birth rate, child-care subsidy policies, and supportive service environments. We asked the TANF and CCDF administrators of the six states to identify potential communities for the study. To identify strategies that might help the transition of parents of infants from welfare to school or work, we sought communities that emphasized work support, parenting support, or good-quality infant care. In two states, we selected both an urban and a rural community to permit within-state comparisons of these different environments. Table 2.2 provides a brief description of the sites and our rationale for selecting them.

We collected the qualitative data for this study through semistructured interviews and focus groups conducted during one-person, 2-day site visits to each community during the spring and summer of 1999. Prior to site visits, we conducted telephone interviews with state TANF and child-care administrators to verify state policy information. During each visit, we spoke with administrators and staff of welfare, child-care, and supportive service agencies, including child-care resource and referral, early intervention programs, and other programs for parents of young children. We asked about the general policy and service environment in the areas of welfare, child-care subsidies,

---

[4]Wyoming had a 3-month work exemption for parents of infants in 2002 (U.S. Department of Health and Human Services, 2004a, 2004b). Minnesota had no young-child exemption as of July 2004 based on information gathered through a separate MPR study.

TABLE 2.2
Sites Included in the In-Depth Study

State	State TANF Families With an Infant (%)[a]	Community (County)	County TANF Caseload[b]	Rationale for Site Selection
California	10.2	Bakersfield (Kern)	19,039	California has a large population, and the work requirement for parents of infants is a county option. Kern is the largest county that requires parents of infants to work.
Florida	12.1	St. Petersburg (Pinellas)	4,275	Urban area with strong child-care licensing standards and innovative programs to support families with young children.
		New Port Richey (Pasco)	1,512	Rural county chosen to examine how a work-first approach to cash assistance is implemented in a rural area within a large state.
Iowa	15.9	Waterloo (Black Hawk)	1,652	Iowa implemented work requirements for parents of infants in 1993. This small city in a largely rural state was making a special effort to coordinate services for young children.
Michigan	10.3	Grand Rapids (Kent)	3,040	Mid-sized city with goal of reducing to zero the number of welfare households without earnings (Project Zero site).
		Detroit—Warren/Conner District (Wayne)	90,574 (1,793)[c]	Inner-city region with goal of reducing to zero the number of welfare households without earnings (Project Zero site).
Tennessee	13.0	Nashville (Davidson)	8,650	Tennessee has a high teenage birth rate. Nashville provides strong supportive services for teenage parents.
Wisconsin	24.4	Milwaukee—Region 2 (Milwaukee)	9,764 (1,245)[c]	Wisconsin has dramatically reduced welfare caseloads. Region 2 is an area with established community programs to support parents of young children in the state's largest city.

[a]U.S. Department of Health and Human Services (2000) and data provided by the study sites.
[b]Caseload numbers were provided by state welfare office staff in April–June 1999. Data represent February 1999 caseloads for Kern County, the two Florida counties, the two Michigan sites, and Milwaukee. Data represent May 1999 caseloads for Black Hawk County and Nashville.

and supportive services; child-care support, including quality of child care, supply of and demand for child care, and costs of and subsidies for infant care; and balancing work and family, including child-care arrangements for infants, TANF work requirements, work schedules, work supports, and living arrangements. To gain the perspectives and experiences of those affected, we conducted focus groups with TANF parents of infants identified by two or three community organizations in the sites: three with teenage parents of infants and four with older parents in six sites.[5] Topics discussed included the content and perceptions of self-sufficiency plans; understanding and perceptions of sanctions and time limits; selecting and arranging infant care; the quality, consistency, and flexibility of child-care arrangements; use of child-care subsidies; living arrangements; use of supportive services; and perceptions of gaps in support for work activities and family responsibilities. Site visitors took notes on the discussions and tape recorded the focus group meeting with parents. We compiled the information in site visit narratives, which we sent to state and local TANF and child-care administrators for review and comment. To supplement our qualitative data, we also obtained aggregate administrative data from the Child Care Bureau to analyze the type of child care that families with infants used in the sites we visited.

Key features of the in-depth study limit our ability to generalize the findings to all states that require parents of infants to work. First, we selected states and communities that we thought exemplified welfare-to-work experiences for parents of infants when TANF programs are fully implemented and, in some cases, when special work or parenting supports are available in the community. Therefore, the states and sites are not representative of all states and communities in which parents of infants are required to work. Second, the data we obtained from interviews and focus groups are necessarily subjective, influenced by the experiences, goals, and backgrounds of specific informants. Third, our informants are not fully representative of the population of agency front-line staff and TANF parents of infants because they were selected by local agency staff and showed a willingness to participate in the study. The parents of infants who participated in the focus groups may have been more organized and more able to access community service networks—and thus more able to cope with work requirements and family responsibilities—than those who did not attend. Finally, welfare and child-care policies continue to change as states modify their approaches to serving low-income families, and programs for young children are continuing to proliferate and expand, changing the level of support for welfare-reliant families with young children.

We offer one additional caution in interpreting our findings. We spoke with a range of stakeholders in the social welfare system, and there are times

---

[5]Focus groups that were planned in Nashville and New Port Richey were cancelled because of severe weather in one site and no one showing up in the other.

when their views differ based on their own experiences. Because of the nature of this nonrepresentative qualitative study, we cannot quantify responses or assign greater importance to one view over another. Rather, we present the range of experiences and opinions that we heard.

FINDINGS

Local Implementation of Welfare-Related Work Requirements

Low-income single parents of infants are likely to face challenges finding child care and participating fully in required work activities. Therefore, it seemed possible that, in practice, local welfare offices might permit a slower entry into work activities for parents of infants, excuse some of these parents from work requirements, or at least show flexibility in excusing absences or working through difficulties that arise while parents participate in work activities.

On the contrary, in the states and communities included in this study, welfare program administrators and front-line staff maintained that, except for the work exemption period just after the birth of the child, parents of infants were treated the same as all other parents with respect to work requirements, sanctions, and time limits. No special distinctions in policy or practice were made for parents of infants, and case managers and program administrators viewed them as no different than other welfare recipients.

One possible explanation for this is that most welfare recipients have some characteristic or circumstance that poses a challenge for employment, either temporarily or in the long term, and those barriers may be more significant inhibitors of work than having an infant. In 1999, four of every five welfare recipients had at least one barrier to employment, according to the National Survey of American Families (Zedlewski & Loprest, 2001).[6] Yet of new entrants to TANF in 1997, although 33% had an infant, smaller proportions of those who subsequently cycled on and off of welfare, or who stayed on welfare through 1999, had an infant in 1997. In contrast, the percentage of cyclers and stayers with other barriers was higher than their proportion among new entrants. Thus, caring for an infant does not appear to pose as great a challenge to employment as other barriers perhaps in part because the challenges of working and parenting a very young child ease as the child ages.

One important policy distinction that is permitted under federal law, but that we found was not uniformly practiced, is the option of requiring just part-time work of single mothers with children under 6. This policy recognizes that

---

[6]Barriers assessed were very poor physical or mental health, lack of a high school diploma or GED, no recent work experience, presence of an infant, presence of a child on Supplemental Security Income, and difficulty speaking English.

in society at large, most mothers who have young children and work hold part-time rather than full-time jobs so that they can balance their work and parenting responsibilities (Cancian, 2001). Federal law currently requires that welfare recipients engage in work or related activities at least 30 hours a week, but allows states to set a 20-hour minimum for parents with a child under 6 (Greenberg & Savner, 1996). Among the six states in this study, only Michigan had specified a lower number of required hours per week of work activity for single parents of children under 6 (20 hours) than for other TANF recipients (30 hours). At the time of the study, Florida required 25 hours a week of work activity for all recipients, but as of October 1999, the state increased the hours requirement to 30 to be consistent with federal requirements. The other four states required between 30 and 40 hours a week of all welfare recipients, including parents with young children (see Table 2.3).

The number of hours of required activities appeared to be balanced, however, by variation in the scope of activities that counted toward the participation requirement. Among the states in this study, those requiring fewer weekly hours of activity tended to count only work and closely related activities. States requiring more hours tended to allow a broader set of activities to count toward the requirement (for all welfare recipients), including postsecondary education; mental health, substance abuse, and domestic violence services; and parenting or early intervention program services.

Nevertheless, the ability to count a broader range of activities toward the participation requirement did not guarantee that parents of very young children would routinely combine part-time work with participation in parenting programs or early childhood services. In the sites where such services were available, there were few linkages between the welfare office and early intervention programs (except for teenage parents, as we discuss later), resulting in a lack of formal referral to such programs. Therefore, it was left mostly to parents to request that parenting or early childhood activities be included in their self-sufficiency plans, and very few parents exercised this option. It is possible that the welfare office did not explore linkages with early intervention programs because of concerns that parents earning the minimum wage would have difficulty escaping poverty by working part time.

Parents' Views of Work Requirements. Parents participating in the focus groups agreed that it was not particularly difficult to meet the required weekly hours of activity, but they expressed divergent views of the value of work requirements. Some believed it was a fair exchange for welfare benefits. Notably, these views about fairness were related to parents' beliefs that the activities would lead to economic advancement, which in turn was expected to benefit their children in the longer term. Those who expressed unfavorable views thought the work requirements were unlikely to lead to jobs with adequate wages, fringe benefits, and the opportunity for advancement. Many par-

TABLE 2.3
State TANF Work Requirements and Required or Allowable Work-Related Activities, Summer 1999

Site	Total Required Hours of Activity per Week for Parents of Infants	Required or Allowable Work-Related Activities									
		Mandatory Orientation	Up-Front Job Search (Work-First)	Unsubsidized Employment/Job Search	Work Experience/Subsidized Employment	Adult Basic Education/GED	Specialized Training Programs	Postsecondary Education	Life Skills Classes	Specialized Services (Mental Health, Substance Abuse, Domestic Violence)	Participation in Parenting/Early Intervention Programs
Bakersfield, CA (Kern County)	32	✓	✓	✓	✓		✓	✓[a]	✓	✓	✓
New Port Richey, FL (Pasco County)	25[b]	✓	✓[c]	✓	✓ (up to 6 months)	(In combination with community work experience)	✓				
St. Petersburg, FL (Pinellas County)	25[b]	✓	✓[c]	✓	✓ (up to 6 weeks)	(In combination with community work experience)					
Waterloo, IA (Blackhawk County)	No set number of required hours[d]	✓		✓	✓ (up to 6 months)	✓	✓	✓	✓	✓	✓
Detroit, MI (Warren/Conner District)[e]	20	✓	✓	✓				✓[a]	✓		
Grand Rapids, MI (Kent County)[e]	20	✓	✓	✓	✓ (1 month only)			✓[a]			

(Continued)

31

TABLE 2.3
(Continued)

Site	Total Required Hours of Activity per Week for Parents of Infants	Mandatory Orientation	Required or Allowable Work-Related Activities								
			Up-Front Job Search (Work-First)	Unsubsidized Employment/Job Search	Work Experience/Subsidized Employment	Adult Basic Education/GED	Specialized Training Programs	Postsecondary Education	Life Skills Classes	Specialized Services (Mental Health, Substance Abuse, Domestic Violence)	Participation in Parenting/Early Intervention Programs
Nashville, TN	40			√		Can meet required hours in full[f] √	√	√	√	√[g]	√
Milwaukee, WI (Region 2)	40[h]		√ (only when limited barriers exist)	√	√ (up to 2 years; max of 30 hours per week)	√	√		√	√	√

Note. From in-depth study phase of the Study of Infant Care under Welfare Reform.

[a] Activities could count toward work requirement only if the client was already enrolled in or nearing completion of the program at the time of entry into the employment-based program.

[b] Effective October 1999, required hours in Florida increased to 30 a week for all recipients.

[c] Since the time of the site visits, Florida discontinued the requirement of up-front job search.

[d] Iowa does not require a specific number of hours, but expects clients to participate in activities to their maximum capacity. On average, clients were considered full time if they were working 30 hours a week.

[e] Michigan allowed a client to be approved for 10 hours of educational activities, 10 hours of study time, and 10 hours of employment to meet the 30 hours of participation required of single-parent families with children ages 6 or older that became effective October 1, 1999. Clients could also be approved for 30 hours of vocational training without any hours of employment on a case-by-case basis.

[f] If a person read below a ninth-grade level, participation in 20 hours of Adult Basic Education could fulfill the full activity requirement. In Tennessee, for every hour of class, an hour of study time was allowed.

[g] At the time of the site visits, specialized services were not allowable work-related activities. However, these services were allowable as part of the required work hours since early 2000.

[h] Work-training activities, such as community work experience, could meet up to 30 hours of the 40-hour requirement. The state could not require more than 30 hours in work experience. Additional hours were comprised of education, training, and other activities as shown. Clients with significant barriers participated up to 28 hours a week in work training or other developmental activities up to their ability and up to 12 hours a week in education or training. These clients received a slightly smaller grant of $628, rather than the $673 provided to clients in the Community Service Jobs track.

ents across the sites were concerned that exclusion of postsecondary education as an activity that counts toward the work requirement would prevent them from obtaining better jobs.[7]

Views about combining work with parenting responsibilities also varied among the focus group participants, reflecting the divergent views that prevail among working mothers in society at large. In one site, several focus group participants expressed distress about leaving their children to attend work activities. These parents were sad about missing the milestones in their infants' lives and worried that their babies would become more attached to the child care providers than to them. In other focus groups, a few parents said that they were concerned at first about leaving their infants to attend work activities, but that these feelings had diminished over time. Nevertheless, in nearly all the focus groups, some parents expressed concern that their work and school activities left them with too little time and energy to play with their children and show patience toward them. Moreover, a few parents said that their work activities prevented them from addressing health or behavioral problems that they believed required more of their time and attention to resolve.

Comprehensive Support for Teenage Parents

Unlike parents of infants generally, teenage parents were viewed and treated as a group with special needs in learning to balance work or school demands with parenting responsibilities. In five of the eight sites, case managers worked specifically with teenage parents to develop their own self-sufficiency plans and to connect them with specialized case management and parenting services. Intensive case management services appeared to be offered uniquely to teenage parents, and they often had countable activities that were a mix of work or school and parenting activities in these sites. Nevertheless, such services were not offered in all sites.

Teenage parents in sites with intensive case management services specifically noted that such services were important in helping them stay in school and care for their infants. For example, case managers helped parents keep appointments with the pediatrician or find child care, and some of the teenage parent programs offered good-quality child care on site at the high school or at a residence facility for teenage parents.

Teenage Parents' Views of School Requirements.   Teenage parents, like older parents, expressed concern about time pressures they felt as they attended school while parenting an infant. Child care was typically provided during school hours, but in some sites it did not cover any additional time to

---

[7]In two study sites (Waterloo and Nashville), postsecondary education could count toward the participation requirement for any recipient. In Bakersfield, only parents already enrolled in postsecondary education could continue for a specific period of time.

study and prepare for class, which left the parent to fit these responsibilities in however possible while at home with the infant. Several parents noted that it is difficult to keep up with schoolwork and care for an infant, particularly when the child is sick or does not sleep through the night.

Financial Support for Child Care for Parents of Infants

Because subsidies can make infant care affordable to low-income families, state policies governing eligibility and the level of child-care subsidies can have an important effect on the infant care choices that facilitate welfare-to-work transitions. Regardless of whether parents of infants receive financial assistance, however, they are likely to need help finding child care both because of a lack of experience with it and because regulated infant care tends to be in shorter supply than care for older children (Fuller, Coonerty, Kipnis, & Choong, 1997). This section discusses policies and practices affecting the affordability of child care and the support that sites provided for locating it.

Affordability of Child Care.   State policy decisions regarding income eligibility, combined with state and local administrative practices, influence which families can access child-care assistance and the extent to which they can continue to obtain it as their welfare status and income change (Adams & Rohacek, 2002; Adams, Snyder, & Sandfort, 2002; Myers et al., 2002). Additional state policies setting provider reimbursement rates and required family copayments influence whether providers will offer subsidized care and the amount families pay for child care (Adams & Rohacek, 2002; Adams & Snyder, 2003). Together, access to child-care subsidies and the level of subsidies affect the affordability of child care for low-income parents.

Access to Child-Care Subsidies.   For TANF families, child-care assistance was nearly guaranteed in all the states included in the study. PRWORA ended the previous entitlement to child-care assistance for families receiving cash assistance and those leaving welfare because of employment. Yet because child-care assistance is a critical support for families that must meet work requirements, the states and sites we visited still functioned as if child-care assistance to TANF families was guaranteed. In sites that had waiting lists for child-care assistance, TANF families were given priority. Once families left the TANF program, however, it could be easy or difficult for them to continue receiving child-care assistance depending on income eligibility policies, procedures for recertification, and the level of state funding for child-care subsidies.

With CCDF dollars, states can provide child-care assistance to families with incomes of up to 85% of the State Median Income (SMI)—an increase from the cap of 75% prior to CCDF. Among the states in the study, California set the

TABLE 2.4
Income Eligibility Standards for Child-Care Subsidy
Programs in the Six Study States, 1999

State	Income Eligibility for a Family of Three			Income Eligibility for Recertification as % of the 1999 FPL
	Income Level	As % of the 1999 SMI	As % of the 1999 FPL	
California	$33,899	75%[a,b]	245%	245%
Florida	$20,820	55%	150%[a]	185%[c]
Iowa	$19,432	50%	140%[a]	140%
Michigan	$25,678	55%	185%[a,d]	185%
Tennessee	$22,804	60%[a]	165%	165%
Wisconsin	$25,678	55%	185%[a,e]	200%

Note. FPL = federal poverty level. SMI = state median income. From in-depth study phase of the Study of Infant Care under Welfare Reform. Updated with Schulman and Blank (2004).
[a]State income eligibility is determined using this standard.
[b]In 2004, income eligibility in California was set at 66% of SMI.
[c]In 2004, Florida's continued eligibility extends to 200% of FPL.
[d]In 2004, Michigan's income eligibility was set at 152% of FPL.
[e]Initial income eligibility in Wisconsin was 165% of FPL at the time of the site visit. Since that time, legislation for the 1999–2001 budget increased income eligibility to the level shown, and it remained at this level in 2004.

highest income eligibility limit—at 75% of SMI (or 245% of FPL).[8] The other states set limits at 50% to 60% of SMI, which ranged from 140% to 185% of FPL (see Table 2.4). Some states set two-part eligibility limits so that initial eligibility for child-care assistance required a lower income level, but families could continue to receive assistance until income reached a higher level. For example, Florida set an initial income limit of 150% of FPL, but families could continue to receive assistance until income reached 185%.[9]

By unifying several categorical child-care funding streams, PRWORA gave states the flexibility to create integrated child-care assistance programs that are based on income eligibility. Because they were based on families' welfare status, the separate funding streams had often made it difficult for families to retain child-care assistance after leaving welfare. Three of the six states—Iowa, Michigan, and Wisconsin—had moved to an integrated child-care subsidy system at the time of our site visits. Program administrators and staff in these sites maintained that an integrated child-care program that bases eligi-

---

[8]California's eligibility limit is still the highest among the study states, but by 2004 it had declined to 66% of SMI or roughly 224% of FPL. Families who were receiving assistance as of January 1998 maintain eligibility up to 75% of SMI.
[9]In 2004, families in Florida can continue to receive assistance until income reaches 200% of FPL.

bility on income without regard to current or recent TANF status helped families to continue receiving child care after they left TANF. To help ensure that families most in need of child-care assistance could receive it for as long as they were eligible, Wisconsin and Iowa had set income eligibility limits at a level that program administrators believed would enable them to provide a subsidy to all eligible families that applied. Michigan also appeared to have sufficient funding for all eligible applicants.[10] Nevertheless, longitudinal data that might show whether the integrated systems in these states actually promote greater continuity of subsidy program participation were not readily available. A recent study in five other states suggests, however, that subsidy durations tend to be short (median of 4–6 months) and are more closely related to parents' activities (employed parents had longer spells than TANF recipients) than to state policy choices (Myers et al., 2002).

The states that maintained separate child-care programs—California, Florida, and Tennessee—all had waiting lists for child-care funding at the time of our site visits, and they continued to in 2004 (Schulman & Blank, 2004). According to program administrators in the California site, families could obtain transitional child care (subsidies for families that left welfare because of employment) easily because the child-care resource and referral agency administered all three funding streams. Case managers in the Florida and Tennessee sites believed that most families did not continue to receive child-care assistance from the transitional child-care program. Respondents said that low-income families (neither TANF nor transitioning off TANF) in all three of these sites faced limited access to child-care subsidies because TANF families, and then those transitioning off TANF, were given priority.

Thus, although TANF families seemed to have had the greatest access to child-care subsidies in each of the sites, such access after leaving TANF was influenced by state policies governing income eligibility, the overall level of funding for child-care assistance (both state and federal), and the priority given to families transitioning off TANF.[11]

Affordability of Child Care for Families Receiving Subsidies: Family Copayment Rates.

Parents receiving child-care assistance are usually required to pay a portion of the cost of child care based on family income and size. In setting copayment levels, states try to balance the need to keep the copayment low enough to make child care affordable for families and high enough to spread the available funding among as many eligible families as pos-

---

[10]Unlike in Iowa and Wisconsin, policymakers in Michigan at the time of the site visit did not have the specific intent of creating universal access to child-care subsidies for eligible families. Nonetheless, none of these three states had waiting lists for child-care subsidies in 2004, and Michigan's income eligibility limit declined as a percentage of FPL, which suggests a more intentional approach to serving all those who are income eligible (Schulman & Blank, 2004).

[11]Because most focus group participants still received TANF, we could not gauge family experiences with maintaining child-care assistance as welfare status changed and as income increased.

sible. In designing the copayment schedule, states ideally would want to avoid cliff effects—large increases in child-care costs relative to earnings—that function as an implicit tax on earnings and can create disincentives to increase work hours (Adams & Rohacek, 2002; Ross, 1998). However, adopting a gradually increasing copayment schedule would require some states to make higher subsidy payments for families with income above FPL and possibly to set higher income eligibility limits—choices that can be difficult for states given the low levels of funding for child-care subsidy programs relative to the number of eligible families.

States have placed varying emphases on these goals as they set copayment policies. Before CCDF, welfare recipients were not required to make copayments toward the cost of child care. Under CCDF, states can waive contributions from families whose income is below FPL (which would include most TANF recipients). At the time of the site visits, California and Iowa waived copayments for families with income below FPL, Michigan and Tennessee waived them for TANF recipients, and none of the states set the copayment higher than 4% of income for families with income at 50% of FPL. Thus, many of the sites emphasized affordability for TANF recipients or, more broadly, for very low-income families. Beyond that point, California set very low fees throughout the income scale, requiring a copayment of 3% of income at 175% of FPL (see Table 2.5). Wisconsin set higher fees than other states in the study, requiring 7% to 11.5% of above-poverty income as copayment for child care. Of the four states that set fees in the middle range, Florida and Tennessee set gradually increasing fees as a percentage of income, whereas Iowa and Michigan set fees that increased sharply with certain changes in income. By 2004, these copayment patterns in the study states remained the same, although some of the states had made minor adjustments to their copayment schedules.[12]

Affordability of Child Care for Families Receiving Subsidies: Provider Reimbursement Rates.

Reimbursement rates influence providers' decisions about whether to accept children whose care is subsidized, the number of subsidized children to accept, and whether to charge parents more to cover their costs beyond the state's reimbursement rate (Adams & Snyder, 2003). Thus, how much providers are reimbursed also affects parents' choices of care and the affordability of care.

All the states in the study set the maximum reimbursement rate at the 75th percentile of the market rate for child care. This rate is intended to make at

---

[12]In 2004, Tennessee increased copayments such that families at 100% of FPL pay $39 (or 6% of income) toward child-care costs, and families at 150% of FPL pay $143 (or 7% of income). California now requires from families at 150% of FPL a copayment that amounts to 2% of income. Michigan also increased copayments for families at 150% of FPL to an equivalent of 7% of income (Schulman & Blank, 2004).

TABLE 2.5

Required Family Copayments Toward Child-Care Costs in Center-Based Care, 1999

State	Exemption of TANF Families From Copayments	Required Copayment When Family Income Is 100% of FPL		Required Copayment When Family Income Is 150% of FPL		Required Copayment When Family Income Is 175% of FPL	
		In Dollars	As % of Income	In Dollars	As % of Income	In Dollars	As % of Income
California	Families under 50% of SMI[a]	0	0	0	0	54	3
Florida	None	69	6	103	6	189[c]	9
Iowa	Families at or under 100% of FPL	22[b]	2	172[c]	10	237[c]	12
Michigan	All TANF families are exempt	25	2	25	1.5	200	10
Tennessee	All TANF families are exempt	39	3	112	6.5	138[c]	7
Wisconsin	Minor teenage parents in school and in the Learnfare program; families participating in the Food Stamp Employment and Training program	77	7	194	11	232	11.5

Note. FPL = federal poverty level. SMI = state median income. From state copayment schedules collected as part of the in-depth study phase of the Study of Infant Care under Welfare Reform. This table reflects monthly costs for a three-person household for the care of one child (an infant where fees vary by age of the child) in full-time center-based care. *Full-time care* is defined as care for 8 hours or full day, 5 days a week, 4.3 weeks per month. Fees in other forms of care are lower across the states.

[a] In California, 50% of SMI is equivalent to about 165% of FPL under the current fee schedule.

[b] Fee shown is for families with incomes of 101% of FPL. Families are exempt if their income is 100% of FPL.

[c] Only families with extended eligibility receive subsidized child care at this level.

least 75% of the available child care in a geographic area affordable to low-income families. Rates differ by the age of child, with higher rates for infant care than for care of older children.

Although these policies would seem to ensure that subsidy reimbursement rates are adequate, two common practices can reduce the reimbursement rate below the 75th percentile of the local child-care market that the parent encounters. First, although CCDF regulations require that states conduct market rate surveys on a regular basis, states may decide not to adjust reimbursement rates to reflect changes in the market cost of child care. For example, in 1999, Michigan was using market rates based on a 1994 survey.[13] Second, even if market rates are updated, they may not reflect the cost of child care relevant to a particular family if the geographic area over which rates are defined is large and diverse. For example, we found that in St. Petersburg and New Port Richey, Florida, which were in the same district with respect to defining market rates, the child-care rates were considered insufficient in St. Petersburg (an urban area with higher licensing standards), but very generous in New Port Richey (a rural area with lower licensing standards).[14] If reimbursement rates are lower than customary charges, providers have two or three options depending on state policies. One is to agree to the lower rate. Another is to refuse to care for a child receiving a subsidy or to restrict the number of subsidized children accepted. Some higher cost providers in a market area can be expected to do this if the rates are set at the 75th percentile. Finally, some providers may charge parents the difference between their cost and the reimbursement rate—a cost to parents that goes beyond the required copayment. This was a legal option in all the study states except Iowa. However, the contracts that two states (Tennessee and Wisconsin) had with providers discouraged such charges.

How family copayments and state market rates influenced the affordability of child care varied in the particular communities we studied. Many of the welfare and child-care staff and administrators in Bakersfield, New Port Richey, Waterloo, Detroit (Warren/Connor district), and Milwaukee (Region 2) reported that subsidy rates were adequate and that parents were rarely charged anything beyond the sliding fee. However, it appears that reimbursement rates either constrained child-care choices or increased costs for families receiving child-care subsidies in St. Petersburg, Grand Rapids, and Nashville. In these sites, it was not unusual for families to have to pay additional fees, beyond required copayments, to meet provider costs. Local program staff, particularly in Grand Rapids, repeatedly reported that the lack of affordability

---

[13]In 2004, four of the states based rates on surveys conducted since 2002. In contrast, 2004 payment rates were the 75th percentile of 1998 rates in Iowa and 1996 rates in Michigan.

[14]Effective July 1, 2000, Florida moved to a more localized market rate definition that was expected to address the problem of disparate prices within a single region.

was the greatest child-care challenge parents faced, and affordability was the greatest influence on parental choice of child care. TANF and other low-income families in Grand Rapids could not afford most center-based care, which suggests that rates based on the older market survey were not sufficient.

Parents, as reported in focus groups, were generally satisfied with the child-care subsidies they received and felt that without the subsidy system they would be forced to leave work and/or school. Even the groups in the two states that required copayments from TANF families did not specifically mention any difficulties in making these payments. We also did not hear about financial strains that any additional out-of-pocket expenses were creating for families, although in some sites respondents suggested that this was a problem. It is possible that in sites like Grand Rapids low rates affected child-care choices (such as limiting center-based care), but that there were other affordable options.

Arranging Child Care

Infant care may be particularly challenging for low-income single parents to find. Their jobs may provide little flexibility to respond to child-care or family emergencies, so child care may have to be particularly reliable and flexible (Emlen, Koren, & Schultze, 1999). Parents with less child-care experience may not know the range of options available to them or have accurate information on the advantages and disadvantages of each type of care. Yet the child-care arrangements that parents make are important—not just in making work possible, but in ensuring the health and development of infants.

TANF Penalty Exception for Inability to Locate Child Care. A persistent concern related to TANF work and school attendance requirements for parents of young children is the difficulty of arranging good-quality child care on short notice. Recognizing this concern, the designers of PRWORA incorporated a protection against sanctions for noncompliance with work requirements for parents who are unable to arrange adequate child care for any child under 6. Under PRWORA, TANF recipients may receive a penalty exception if they are unable to find appropriate and affordable formal or informal child care within a reasonable distance from their home or work site. States define terms such as *reasonable distance* and *appropriate and affordable care* to determine the circumstances under which the exception can apply (State Policy Documentation Project, 2000a, 2000b). In large measure, however, the state definitions are also vague, and the decisions on penalty exceptions are left for negotiation between case manager and client.

Although federal regulations instruct TANF and CCDF agencies to inform parents about the penalty exception to the TANF work requirement, this was not yet common practice in the sites, in part, because our visits took place just before or just after publication of the rule, so case managers may not yet have been aware of their responsibility. Only in Detroit did case managers discuss this policy with TANF recipients. In other sites, parents would learn about the policy only if they came back to the case manager to report that they could not find child care. In many sites, case managers withheld information about the exception because they felt that parents otherwise might not be as resourceful as possible in finding child care.

Provision of Consumer Information. To ensure that parents who need help finding child care can obtain assistance quickly, states and localities provide consumer information. Six of the eight sites provided free enhanced resource and referral services to TANF recipients who sought such assistance. These services included not only consumer information about choosing child care, but also a list of four or five providers who met the parent's criteria for location and type of care as well as other features, and who had openings.

Welfare administrators and staff reported that difficulties arranging adequate child care were rare and that whatever problems did arise were short-lived, although they felt the situation might be different if parents knew about the penalty exception for lack of child care. Welfare administrators and staff believed that their efforts to make child-care subsidies more accessible and to provide parents with child-care consumer information were sufficient to remove any obstacles to finding child care. Although TANF administrators, case managers, and child-care workers indicated that it was not easy to arrange child care, especially infant care, few had encountered any families with a child-care need that could not be met reasonably quickly.

There appeared to be a disconnect, however, between the perceptions of staff and the experiences of families. Except for teenage parents, focus group participants in most sites reported receiving little help in selecting a child-care provider for their infant. Only participants in Grand Rapids talked about receiving guidelines on how to judge the quality of a child-care arrangement, along with lists of providers from the Child Care Resource and Referral (CCR&R) agency. In Grand Rapids, CCR&R staff were on site at the TANF office and at the Work First program every day, actively distributing information to TANF recipients.

Even with such help, however, about half the participants in each of the seven focus groups felt that it was difficult to arrange care for their infants and said they did not always end up with the arrangement of their first or second choice. The types of concerns they raised included family child-care homes that were dirty and of questionable quality, difficulties placing three or more siblings in a single arrangement, and problems finding a center that could accommodate a child's special health care needs (e.g., asthma).

The disconnect between the perspectives of program staff and those of parents could have arisen because parents of infants arranged child care as necessary to respond to work requirements, but did not communicate to staff just how difficult the task could be. It is also possible that in assessing the task of arranging child care in the context of the full array of challenges that TANF recipients face, case managers did not hear that child care was any harder than others to overcome.

Child-Care Choices of Parents of Infants.   The patterns of child care chosen by parents of infants receiving subsidized care generally reflected the stringency of child-care regulations, the level of subsidized payment rates, and the extent of requirements (such as background checks) for unregulated providers of subsidized care. The proportion of families receiving subsidies who also used centers for their infants ranged from 10% to 74% (Table 2.6). The very low proportion of infants cared for in centers in St. Petersburg (10%) seems to confirm local respondents' comments that inadequate payment rates led many center-based providers to refuse to accept families receiving a subsidy, whereas the payment rates for centers in New Port Richey were more than adequate, and 74% of families used center-based care in this site. Similarly, the use of center-based care was low in Grand Rapids, where respondents said that low provider reimbursement rates shifted too much of the cost to families.

The relative proportions of infants in licensed and unlicensed home-based care in the sites reflects regulations governing the availability of the two types of care. In Florida and Wisconsin, home-based providers receiving a child-care subsidy must be licensed or registered, and we found that in New Port Richey, St. Petersburg, and Milwaukee, few if any families with a child-care subsidy were using unregulated home-based care. In contrast, home-based providers can care for several children without regulatory supervision in Iowa, Michigan, and Tennessee, and we did find that, among families with infants using home-based care in Waterloo, Grand Rapids, and Nashville, similar proportions reported using nonregulated and regulated care. In Detroit, a small proportion of families with infants was using licensed home-based care in comparison with care in the child's home and nonregulated home-based care, which may reflect the lack of supply of licensed home-based care in the site.

Care in the child's own home was relatively common in the two Michigan sites—a situation that reflects the state's policy not to place restrictions on use subsidies for such care. Florida and Tennessee also paid for subsidized care in the child's home. Although 17% of families with infants used this type of care in St. Petersburg (where center-based options were limited by their high price), smaller proportions did so in Nashville and New Port Richey, where subsidized center-based care was more affordable. In Milwaukee and Iowa, where in-home care was limited, no families (or very few) were using such care.

TABLE 2.6

Percentage of Infants With CCDF Subsidy by Type of Child Care, 1999

Site	Area Covered by CCDF Administrative Data	Child's Home	Licensed Family or Group Home	Nonregulated Family or Group Home	Center	Average Monthly Number of Infants
			Type of Care			
Bakersfield, CA (Kern County)	n.a.	n.a.	n.a.	n.a.	n.a.	n.a.
New Port Richey, FL (Pasco County)	Pasco County	3.1	19.1	3.4	74.4	94
St. Petersburg, FL (Pinellas County)	Pinellas County	16.7	73.2	0	10.1	397
Waterloo, IA (Blackhawk County)	State of Iowa	0.6	32.5	40.9	25.9	1,141
Grand Rapids, MI (Kent County)	Kent County	19.4	31.3	32.3	17.1	515
Detroit, MI (Warren/Conner District)	Wayne County	32.9	9.1	44.1	14.0	2,191
Nashville, TN	Davidson County	6.1	17.5	12.5	63.9	388
Milwaukee, WI (Region 2)	Milwaukee County	0	34.1	0	65.9	1,206

Note. Numbers and percentages are average monthly values. n.a. = not available (data were not available for California). From special analysis of the FY 99 CCDF case-level data submitted by states, conducted by Scott Spiegel, Anteon Corporation, for the Child Care Bureau.

43

Services to Promote Parenting and Child Development

Parents of infants and young children may need additional support to help them balance their intensive parenting responsibilities with those of work and/or school. Programs that provided parenting support and early intervention services to low-income families existed in all the study sites, but the degree to which these programs were viewed as part of the service network for TANF families with infants varied. Teenage parents were referred directly to parenting programs in five sites (Bakersfield, St. Petersburg, Waterloo, Grand Rapids, and Nashville). For teenage parents, each of these sites had in place intensive case management that typically included referrals to parenting support services. In four sites—Bakersfield, New Port Richey, St. Petersburg, and Waterloo—older parents could receive an informal referral to a parenting program if they requested it. The quality of these referrals varied with the case managers' knowledge of available programs. Only the Milwaukee site provided formal referrals to a parenting and family service program to all TANF parents of infants (under 10 months old). However, at the time of our visits to both Michigan sites, TANF administrators were in the preliminary stages of contracting with local service providers to offer parenting programs to TANF clients.

Parenting and early intervention services for teenage parents were usually available in school settings. All the sites had at least one high school that accommodated teenage parents in some fashion. At a minimum, this included offering on-site child care and parenting classes during the school day. In Bakersfield and the two Florida sites, the public school systems offered programs for pregnant and parenting teens. Through these programs, teenage parents were entitled to social services, child care, transportation, health services, and classes in parenting and child development regardless of family income. In each Florida site, teenage parents had three options. One was to attend a traditional high school, the second was to attend a vocational/technical school, and the third was to attend classes at an adult education center. All these sites provided child care. Grand Rapids was the only site with a school that served teenage parents from the 7th through the 12th grade exclusively. Any pregnant or parenting teen in the city could be transferred into this school.

Early intervention and parenting support programs were also available in the communities. These specialized programs tended to be small, and they conducted their own outreach to families. There were few linkages between these services and the TANF program offices, although the programs' focus on families with income below FPL led to varying degrees of overlap among the programs. In Grand Rapids, the Healthy Start program estimated that 90% of its clients were TANF recipients at the time of the site visit, and the Early Head Start program in Bakersfield estimated that 50% of those served at the time of the site visit were CalWORKs clients. In contrast, the Tri-County Hand-in-Hand Early Head Start program in Waterloo indicated that few of its clients received cash assistance. Instead a significant number were former TANF recipients who had had their benefits terminated because of either increased earnings or sanctions. Program staff reported that the Early Head Start program was one of the few that continued to serve these families, and they noted that these families' needs—for child-care assistance and other services—were extensive.

Overall, St. Petersburg appeared to have the richest array of programs available to low-income parents of infants. The Healthy Families program in St. Petersburg was the largest in the nation at the time of the site visit, serving 800 families throughout the city. In addition, the city had a number of home-visiting programs, including the Healthy Start program and Home Visitation 2000. The latter entailed home visits by skilled nurses to first-time, single mothers (Olds et al., 2002).

Although parents could receive referrals to early intervention programs in many sites, their work and related activities often left them with little time to participate in these programs. Time constraints for working single parents with young children are severe, and service providers reported difficulties in arranging services, including home visits. With less free time, parents are more likely to opt out of voluntary programs even if they believe the services are valuable.

SUMMARY OF KEY FINDINGS

Our findings on TANF policy, child-care options and choices, and supportive services create a picture of the environment in which parents of infants were expected to move from welfare to work in the eight sites we studied.

Welfare policy and practice, which provide the framework for work and cash assistance among TANF recipients, make few adjustments for parents of infants:

- Case managers did not view parents of infants as a group with categorical needs substantially different from those of the broader TANF population. Accordingly, TANF policies, including work requirements, sanctions, and time limits, were generally not modified for parents of infants once the exemption period ended.

- Under federal TANF law, states could require parents with children under age 6 to work 20, rather than 30, hours a week. Michigan was the only state that required this lower number of work hours of parents of infants.

Child care is a critical support for parents who have young children and must work or attend school, but the study found some gaps in this support:

• Parents of infants were not uniformly informed that they could receive a penalty exception to the work requirements if they cannot arrange child care, although this may have improved after our site visits because the requirement was at the early stages of implementation.

• There was a disconnect between the perceptions of case managers and the experience of families regarding the ease of arranging child care, which suggests that communication on child-care matters is not sufficient. Case managers did not perceive a problem, although about half the parents in our focus groups reported difficulty in arranging care.

• In most of our sites, parents reported never having received even basic child-care consumer information, although enhanced child-care referral services were available. In the one site where most parents appeared to receive information consistently, child-care counselors were on site at the TANF office every day.

• Most formal child-care arrangements were unaffordable in about half the sites because provider reimbursement rates were so much lower than the prices of formal care in the area.

Comprehensive supportive services were available in most communities, but the links between welfare parents of infants and these programs were uneven:

• Work-related supportive services provided through local TANF offices were generally strong, but the connections between local TANF offices and specialized services, including early intervention and parenting programs, appeared weak.

• Teenage parents in most sites were routinely linked with comprehensive case management services and often with parenting education and early intervention programs.

• In contrast, welfare case managers generally did not inform older parents of infants about parenting support and early intervention programs. Only in the Milwaukee site were referrals routinely made to all parents of infants.

DISCUSSION

Overall, based on the reports of parents in the focus groups and staff of the welfare and child-care agencies in the study sites, parents of infants appeared to be handling the dual responsibilities of work and parenting. However, the degree to which these parents were handling the pressures of work and family life well varied according to their individual circumstances. In many ways, TANF, child care, and supportive service policies, along with service delivery structures, were not focused on the needs of parents of infants largely because the system did not view them as a group with categorical and unique needs.

The in-depth study provided important information about how welfare and child-care policies interact to make it easier or more difficult for parents of infants to participate in welfare-to-work or welfare-to-school activities. Nevertheless, the study could identify only existing strategies and perceived gaps in service; future research is needed to evaluate the effectiveness of specific approaches. Therefore, we recommend that future research focus on a *representative* sample of parents of infants and toddlers in selected sites to document the characteristics and needs of these families, including risk factors; child-care challenges; welfare-to-work activities, hours, and sanctioning; the quality and stability of child care; and receipt of child-care subsidies.

We observed several policy alternatives and program strategies that could hold promise for helping welfare-reliant parents of young children with the transition to school or work while promoting the health and development of their children. For example, welfare-related work requirements were modified in several ways to improve the balance between work and family responsibilities. In Michigan, parents of young children were required to work 20 hours a week, which could help them gain labor market experience while still enjoying substantial time with their children. The states that required more hours of activity allowed parents to apply hours of early intervention program participation toward the weekly work requirement, although in practice this was not often implemented. Making these activities part of a parent's self-sufficiency plan whenever possible could also provide sufficient work experience while allowing the parent to spend more time with the child. Although parents working part time at minimum wage would not escape poverty, they would nevertheless acquire valuable job experience during the limited period of time while their children are young.

Child-care policies in many states made it difficult to continue receiving a subsidy beyond the period of TANF program participation and restricted the child-care choices of TANF recipients. Further progress by states toward integrated child-care systems that determine eligibility based on income without regard for TANF program status could help, but greater funding from federal, state, and private sources for child-care subsidies may be needed if states are to establish policies that would make it easier for families to keep child-care assistance while transitioning from welfare to work. In addition, up-to-date market rate surveys and smaller, more realistic geographic rate areas could help set reimbursement rates that would give TANF and other low-income families access to a broader range of providers.

CONCLUSIONS

Although balancing work or school responsibilities with parenting a young infant can be challenging, parents' achievements at work or in school can be valuable in the long term. This chapter identified the challenges involved in the transition from welfare to work for parents with infants and the strategies that some sites are using to meet these challenges. These strategies include comprehensive supportive services with parenting information and access to good-quality child care, a requirement to work part time rather than full time while children are young, assistance locating child care, subsidy policies that provide adequate support through the transition to employment, and referrals to early childhood education programs. These policies and programs merit further evaluation as welfare reforms encouraging work activity continue to involve parents with very young children.

ACKNOWLEDGMENTS

This chapter is based on research funded by the Office of Planning, Research, and Evaluation of the Administration for Children and Families, U.S. Department of Health and Human Services, through a contract to Mathematica Policy Research, Inc., and reported in Kirby, Ross, and Puffer (2001). The chapter was written after the contract ended. The contents of this chapter do not necessarily reflect the views or policies of DHHS, nor does mention of trade names, commercial products, or organizations imply endorsement by the U.S. government.

REFERENCES

Adams, G., & Rohacek, M. (2002). More than a work support? Issues around integrating child development goals into the child care subsidy system. *Early Childhood Research Quarterly, 17*(4), 418–440.

Adams, G., & Snyder, K. (2003). *Essential but often ignored: Child care providers in the subsidy system* (Occasional Paper). Washington, DC: Urban Institute.

Adams, G., Snyder, K., & Sandfort, J. (2002). *Getting and retaining child care assistance: How policy and practice influence parents' experiences* (Research Report). Washington, DC: Urban Institute.

American Academy of Pediatrics. (1997). Recommended childhood immunization schedule— United States. *Pediatrics, 99,* 136–138.

Beckwith, L. (1990). Adaptive and maladaptive parenting: Implications for intervention. In S. J. Meisels & J. P. Shonkoff (Eds.), *Handbook of early childhood intervention* (pp. 53–77). New York: Cambridge University Press.

Berlin, L. J., & Cassidy, J. (1999). Relations among relationships: Contributions from attachment theory and research. In P. Shaver & J. Cassidy (Eds.), *Handbook of attachment: Theory, research and clinical applications* (pp. 688–712). New York: Guilford.

Cancian, M. (2001). The rhetoric and reality of work based welfare reform. *Social Work, 46*(4), 309–314.

Cost, Quality, and Child Outcomes Study Team. (1995). *Cost, quality, and child outcomes in child care centers: Executive summary.* Denver, CO: University of Colorado at Denver.

Emlen, A. C., Koren, P. E., & Schultze, K. H. (1999). *From a parent's point of view: Measuring the quality of child care* (Final Report of the Oregon Child Care Research Partnership). Portland, OR: Portland State University. http://www.hhs.oregonstate.edu/familypolicy/occrp/publications.html

Fuller, B., Coonerty, C., Kipnis, F., & Choong, Y. (1997, November). *An unfair head start: California families face gaps in preschool and child care availability.* Berkeley, CA: PACE Center.

Gallagher, L. J., Gallagher, M., Perese, K., Schreiber, S., & Watson, K. (1998). *One year after federal welfare reform: A description of state Temporary Assistance for Needy Families (TANF) decisions as of October, 1997.* Washington, DC: Urban Institute.

Greenberg, M., & Savner, S. (1996). *A detailed summary of key provisions of the Temporary Assistance for Needy Families Block Grant of H.R. 3734: The Personal Responsibility and Work Opportunity Reconciliation Act of 1996.* Washington, DC: Center for Law and Social Policy.

Heymann, J., & Earle, A. (1998). The work–family balance: What hurdles are parents leaving welfare likely to confront? *Journal of Policy Analysis and Management, 17*(2), 313–321.

Kirby, G., Ross, C., & Puffer, L. (2001). *Welfare-to-work transitions for parents of infants: In-depth study of eight communities.* Washington, DC: Mathematica Policy Research.

Lally, J. R., Griffin, A., Fenichel, E., Segal, M., Szanton, E., & Weissbourd, B. (2003). *Caring for infants and toddlers in groups: Developmentally appropriate practice.* Washington, DC: Zero to Three.

McCormick, M. C., Kass, B., Elixhauser, A., Thompson, J., & Simpson, L. (2000). Annual review of child health care access and utilization: Annual report on access to and utilization of health care for children and youth in the United States: 1999. *Pediatrics, 105*(1), 219–230.

McCune, L., Kalmanson, B., Fleck, M. B., Glazewski, B., & Sillari, J. (1990). An interdisciplinary model of infant assessment. In S. J. Meisels & J. P. Shonkoff (Eds.), *Handbook of early childhood intervention* (pp. 219–245). New York: Cambridge University Press.

Myers, M., Peck, L., Davis, E., Collins, A., Kreader, L., Georges, A., Weber, R., Schexnayder, D., Schroeder, D., & Olson, J. (2002). *The dynamics of child care subsidy use: A collaborative study of five states.* New York: National Center for Children in Poverty.

NICHD Early Child Care Research Network. (1996). Characteristics of infant child care: Factors contributing to positive caregiving. *Early Childhood Research Quarterly, 11,* 269–306.

NICHD Early Child Care Research Network. (1997). Poverty and patterns of child care. In G. J. Duncan & J. Brooks-Gunn (Eds.), *Consequences of growing up poor* (pp. 100–131). New York: Russell Sage Foundation.

NICHD Early Child Care Research Network. (2000). Characteristics and quality of child care for toddlers and preschoolers. *Applied Developmental Science, 4*(3), 116–135.

Olds, D. L., Robinson, J., O'Brien, R., Luckey, D. W., Pettitt, L. M., Henderson, C. R., Ng, R. K., Sheff, K. L., Korfmacher, J., Hiatt, S., & Talmi, A. (2002). Home visiting by paraprofessionals and by nurses: A randomized controlled trial. *Pediatrics, 110,* 486–496.

Phillips, D. A., Voran, M., Kisker, E., Howes, C., & Whitebook, M. (1994). Child care for children in poverty: Opportunity or inequity? *Child Development, 65,* 472–492.

Presser, H. B., & Cox, A. G. (1997). The work schedules of low-educated American women and welfare reform. *Monthly Labor Review, 120*(4), 25–34.

Raikes, H. (1993). Relationship duration in infant care: Time with a high-ability teacher and infant–teacher attachment. *Early Childhood Research Quarterly, 8,* 309–325.

Ross, C. (1998). *Sustaining employment among low-income parents: The role of child care costs and subsidies. A research review.* Washington, DC: Mathematica Policy Research.

Schulman, K., & Blank, H. (2004, September). *Child care assistance policies 2001–2004: Families struggling to move forward, states going backward* (Issue Brief). Washington, DC: National Women's Law Center.

Shonkoff, J. P., & Phillips, D. (2000). *From neurons to neighborhoods: The science of early childhood development.* Washington, DC: National Academy Press.

State Policy Documentation Project. (1999, March). *School/training requirements: Exemptions.* Retrieved January 5, 2005, from http://www.spdp.org/school/exemptions.pdf

State Policy Documentation Project. (2000a, July). *The TANF child care protection: Definitions used.* Retrieved January 5, 2005, from http://www.spdp.org/tanf/CCDFDefinitions.PDF

State Policy Documentation Project. (2000b, July). *Work requirements: Exemptions.* Retrieved January 5, 2005, from http://www.spdp.org/tanf/exemptions.pdf

U.S. Department of Health and Human Services, Administration for Children and Families. (2000, August). *Temporary Assistance for Needy Families (TANF) program: Third annual report to Congress.* Washington, DC: Author.

U.S. Department of Health and Human Services, Administration for Children and Families. (2004a, October). *Child care and development fund: Report of state plans FY 2004–2005.* Washington, DC: Author.

U.S. Department of Health and Human Services, Administration for Children and Families. (2004b, November). *Temporary Assistance for Needy Families (TANF) program: Sixth annual report to Congress.* Washington, DC: Author.

U.S. Department of Health and Human Services, Assistant Secretary for Planning and Evaluation. (1997, June). *Setting the baseline: A report on state welfare waivers.* Washington, DC: Author.

U.S. Department of Health and Human Services, Child Care Bureau. (1999, October). *Access to child care for low-income working families.* Retrieved July 9, 2001, from http://www.acf.dhhs.gov/programs/ccb/reports/ccreport.htm. Available from U.S. Department of Education, Educational Resources Information Center, Inc. (Document No. ED 435 471).

Wald, E. R., Guerra, N., & Byers, C. (1991). Frequency and severity of infections in day care: Three-year follow-up. *Journal of Pediatrics, 118,* 509–514.

Zedlewski, S. R., & Loprest, P. (2001). Will TANF work for the most disadvantaged families? In R. Blank & R. Haskins (Eds.), *The new world of welfare* (pp. 311–334). Washington, DC: Brookings Institution.

## CHAPTER THREE

Infant and Toddler Care After Welfare Reform: A Cross-State Comparison

Ann Dryden Witte
Magaly Queralt
Wellesley College &
National Bureau of Economic Research

We provide descriptive evidence from Miami-Dade County, Florida, and from five representative areas in Massachusetts that government policies governing welfare reform, the child-care subsidy system, and minimum-standards regulations had considerable impact on the availability, use, quality, and price of infant and toddler care as welfare reform progressed from 1996 to 2000. During this period, we find a dramatic surge (more than a doubling) in the number of low-income infants and toddlers with child-care subsidies placed in formal (licensed) care in Miami-Dade County. This was likely related to a welfare reform policy in Florida requiring cash assistance recipients with children 3 months of age or older to engage in work-related activities. We also find evidence that, during this period, to meet state minimum-standards regulations, child-care centers in Miami-Dade County and Massachusetts must have had to find other sources of funding for their infant and toddler programs because neither the prices providers charged families nor the reimbursements providers received from the state covered the full costs of providing care for these age groups. This helps explain why it has been difficult to expand the amount of infant and toddler care available.

INTRODUCTION

We provide descriptive evidence from Miami-Dade County (MDC) in Florida (FL) and from five representative areas in Massachusetts (MA) that government policies governing welfare reform, the child-care subsidy system, and minimum standards regulations had considerable influence on the availability, use, quality, and price of infant and toddler care as welfare reform progressed from 1996 to 2000. We suspect that, in addition to the public policy environment, the different situations we observed for infant and toddler care in MDC and MA were influenced by the markedly higher proportion of the population that is foreign born in MDC, as well as by differences in income and educational levels between MDC and MA.

The period of our study—from February 1996 to March 2000—spans the period before and after welfare reform in FL (which started on October 1, 1996) and the period before and after December 1, 1996, the date when MA imposed time limits on welfare recipients. During this period, the budgets for child-care subsidies grew markedly in both MDC and MA.

In this chapter, we describe how child care and the use of child-care subsidies changed as welfare reform progressed in our research areas in FL and MA. We also provide background information about the policy and socioeconomic contexts in these areas of the country. The outline of the chapter is as follows. First we discuss major differences between the two markets we study in terms of policy and socioeconomic contexts. Then we describe our data. Next we discuss our findings as to what happened to child care for infants and toddlers following welfare reform in MDC and MA, with focus on the supply, use, quality, and price of care. In the concluding section, we summarize some of the main lessons from our study in terms of how government policies influence the quantity, price, and quality of child care for low-income families with very young children.

THE SOCIOECONOMIC CONTEXT

Our data from FL cover all of MDC. MDC, located in southern FL, is FL's most populous county and contains approximately 40% of the state's welfare population. The county has a population of 2,289,683. According to the 2000 census, of all the counties in the United States, MDC had the highest proportion (51%) of foreign-born individuals (U.S. Census Bureau, 2002). Fifty-seven percent of the population is Hispanic, 21% non-Hispanic White, 20% Black, and less than 2% Asian (U.S. Census Bureau, 2004b). Hispanics in MDC are predominantly Cuban, Puerto Rican, Colombian, and Nicaraguan. The county's non-Hispanic White population has been dwindling, particularly after Hurricane Andrew, in large part due to the arrival of continuous waves of immigrants from Latin America and the Caribbean. The Black population is split between African Americans and Caribbean Blacks. Haitians are the poorest and largest segment of the county's Caribbean Black population. According to the 2000 census, MDC's poverty rate was 18%, and for related children under the age of 18, it was 23%. The median household income for the county was $35,966. Sixty-eight percent of those in MDC age 25 and over had a high school diploma, and 22% had at least a bachelor's degree (U.S. Census Bureau, 2004b).

Our data for MA cover areas chosen by child-care experts in the MA's Executive Office of Health and Human Services to be representative of the Commonwealth's population. These areas comprise: (a) the Boston metropolitan area, (b) the area west of Boston from Lowell to Framingham, (c) Hampden County (Springfield, Chicopee, Holyoke, and surrounding areas), and (d) the New Bedford/Fall River/Taunton area. See Lemke, Witte, Queralt, and Witt (2000) for a list of MA townships included in our study.

According to the 2000 census, 12.2% of the population in MA was foreign-born (U.S. Census Bureau, 2003). Eighty-four percent of the population in MA is non-Hispanic White, 6% Hispanic (of any race), 5% Black, and 4% Asian. The 2000 census revealed a statewide poverty rate of 9.3%, and for related children under age 18, a poverty rate of 11.6%. Census 2000 median household income was $50,502. Eighty-five percent of those age 25 and over in MA had a high school diploma, and 33% had at least a bachelor's degree (U.S. Census Bureau, 2004a).

THE POLICY CONTEXT

We believe, based on the data we examine, that government policies governing welfare reform, the child-care subsidy system, and minimum standards regulations had considerable influence on the availability and use, quality, and price of infant and toddler care as welfare reform progressed from 1996 to 2000. In this section, we briefly highlight some relevant policies in each of these three areas.

Welfare Reform

Welfare reform started in FL in October 1996. One important aspect of the welfare reform legislation in FL is the requirement that, to receive cash assistance, adults must engage in approved work activities as soon as their youngest child is 3 months of age or older. For most recipients, welfare reform in FL also set a limit on the receipt of cash assistance to a maximum of 24 months in any 5-year period and a maximum of 48 months in the person's lifetime. These stringent time limits began to kick in for some recipients after September 1998.

The implementation of welfare reform in FL was associated with a dramatic increase in funding for child-care subsidies and, to a lesser extent, for other early childhood education (ECE) programs, such as Head Start, Early

Head Start, and public school pre-kindergarten programs. To be specific, during our study period, the budget for child-care subsidies in FL rose from $180 million in July 1995 to almost $450 million in July 1999.[1] This increased funding for child care and ECE programs was largely for the purpose of enabling poor and low-income parents to move from welfare to work, as required by the new law, and to maintain independence from the welfare system through employment.

MA requested a welfare reform waiver from the federal government in April 1995. The waiver was granted except for the time limits proposed. The MA reforms were initiated on November 1, 1995. After federal welfare reform, MA implemented its previously requested time limits as they became required for federal funding. Thus, cash assistance recipients in MA became subject to time limits beginning on December 1, 1996.

Anyone subject to the time limits in MA is permitted to receive Transitional Assistance for Families with Dependent Children funds (TAFDC, as the TANF program is referred to) for a maximum of 24 months in any consecutive 60-month period. Anyone subject to work requirements must be actively involved in some type of work for at least 20 hours per week. If the person fails to find a job, he or she is required to perform 20 hours of community service per week. However, the MA law is less stringent than the FL law when it comes to recipients with very young children. Specifically, a TAFDC recipient in MA is exempt from the time limits *and* from the work requirement if her or his youngest child is under the age of 2. The recipient remains exempt from work, but not from the time limits, until the youngest child is 6 years old.[2]

Spending on child-care subsidies in MA increased from $180 million in Fiscal Year (FY) 1996 (July 1, 1995–June 30, 1996) to $316 million in FY 2000.

The Child-Care Subsidy System

Client Eligibility.   FL law prescribes that every child younger than age 13 in an eligible family (i.e., a family with income below 150% of the Federal Poverty Level [FPL]) *may* receive subsidized child care.[3] Before welfare reform, child-care subsidies were an entitlement for cash assistance recipients engaged in work-related activities and for those income-eligible working recipients leaving the cash assistance program. However, after welfare reform was implemented on October 1, 1996, child-care subsidies became available in FL

---

[1]Additional funds for child-care subsidies came from local match (either cash or in-kind contributions), which is required to demonstrate local commitment to the subsidized child-care program.

[2]See Witte, Queralt, Witt, and Griesinger (2002, April) for further details on how the time limits and work requirement interact in MA.

[3]For example, in 1999, the maximum eligible income for a family of three was $20,082.

only if resources were available. In MDC, child-care subsidies are allocated on the basis of state-established priorities for participation, with highest priority allocated, in order of priority, to children at risk of abuse and neglect, the children of cash assistance recipients, and the children of families transitioning off cash assistance. Low-income working families that do not receive cash assistance and are not eligible for transitional assistance, called *income-eligible families*, have lower priority for subsidy receipt. However, waiting lists for subsidies for infants and toddlers were relatively small during the period of our study due to the rapid increases in funding.[4]

According to MA's law, all families with children under the age of 13 with incomes at or below 50% of the State Median Income (SMI)[5] can obtain child-care subsidies to the extent that funds were available. To facilitate welfare reform, MA offered child-care vouchers to all active recipients of cash assistance. MA also provided 1 year of Transitional Child Care (TCC) assistance to those leaving cash assistance. MA also made child-care subsidies available to former cash assistance recipients after they exhausted their TCC benefits for as long as they remained eligible (i.e., continued working and had gross monthly income at or below 85% of the SMI).

In MA, income-eligible low-income families that are not current or former cash assistance recipients are eligible for child-care subsidies only to the degree that funds are available. Unlike the situation in MDC, we observed throughout our study period that MA had a substantial waiting list for income-eligible child-care subsidies.[6]

Subsidized Providers.   In Florida, child-care providers may choose to enter into an agreement or contract with child-care subsidy agencies to accept children receiving subsidies. Child-care subsidy recipients who ask for help in finding a provider are referred to contracted providers by the subsidy management agencies, or they can elect to receive a voucher that can be used at any provider or to purchase informal care.[7] During the period covered by the MDC data (February 1996–March 2000), 95% of the child-care subsidies (i.e., vouchers) issued in MDC were to directly pay contracted providers. The remaining child-care subsidy monies (5%) were used to reimburse parents for the use of noncontracted providers and informal caregivers.

---

[4]The child-care subsidy administration files in MDC showed limited numbers of infants and toddlers waiting for care during the period of our study. The January 2001 files, for example, show 27 infants, 37 one-year-olds, and 40 two-year-olds from income-eligible families and 56 infants, 58 one-year-olds, and 68 one-year-olds from families receiving cash assistance waiting for care.

[5]For example, families with incomes below $23,172 in 1999 were eligible. This would be equivalent to 167% of FPL in 1999.

[6]In November 2000, for example, there were 2,412 infants and 3,602 toddlers (among children of other ages) from income-eligible families in MA on the waiting list.

[7]Informal care is unlicensed care provided by relatives, neighbors, or friends.

MA operates a mixed child-care subsidy system that provides current and former cash assistance recipients with child-care vouchers and income-eligible children with slots purchased directly by the state from selected licensed providers. As operated during our study period, the MA voucher program provided families with more choices than MDC's purchase of service contract system, but the MA contract system had a more extensive wait list.

Subsidized Provider Quality Incentives.   Under the Gold Seal Quality Care program established on July 1, 1996, FL providers accepting child-care subsidies may apply for Gold Seal designation. To qualify, providers must be accredited by a nationally recognized accrediting association whose standards substantially meet or exceed those of the National Association for the Education of Young Children (NAEYC), the National Association for Family Child Care, or the National Early Childhood Program Accreditation Commission. Beginning on July 1, 1998, Gold Seal providers have been receiving up to 20% higher reimbursements for providing subsidized child care as long as this higher rate does not exceed their private pay rate. During the period of our study, MA did not give subsidized providers financial incentives for accreditation.[8]

Subsidized Provider Monitoring and Assessments.   Both FL and MA have established elaborate ways to monitor and assess contracted providers participating in the subsidized child-care program. Space limitations do not allow us to describe these systems. One important difference is that MA uses the regular license monitoring system to identify contracted providers at risk due to minimum standards violations for more close follow-up and monitoring. In MDC at the time of our study, the county subsidy management agencies relied on the statewide Child-Care Program Assessments (a group of observational tools) to regularly assess contracted providers through observation (see Queralt, Witte, & Griesinger, 2000, for more details). They did not use the quarterly license monitoring reports issued by the district's licensing enforcement office to identify providers with frequent or serious minimum standards violations.

Payments (Reimbursements) to Subsidized Providers.   In FL, as well as in MA, state payments to providers vary depending on the age of the child in care, the type of care, and the area of the state. Federal regulations governing the CCDF child-care subsidy programs require states to set provider payments (reimbursement rates) at levels that offer equal access to children with child-care subsidies. States must justify that their reimbursement rates pro-

---

[8]However, MA providers were required to be accredited or to have applied for accreditation to participate in the MA Department of Education Community Partnership for Children (CPC) program, which provided substantial amounts of funding for the care of 3- and 4-year-old children.

vide equal access by referencing a market-rate survey no more than 2 years old. Rates set at the 75th percentile or higher of the local market price are presumed to provide equal access.

In FL, the Department of Children & Families (DCF) establishes procedures to reimburse providers at the prevailing market rate.[9] Rates cannot exceed the private pay prices a provider charges. The FL DCF contracts with the central agencies that manage the subsidized child-care program and provide local resource and referral (R&R) services to survey all providers in all areas in the spring of each year. In general, the R&Rs collect list prices, not market prices. During the period of our study, full-time reimbursement rates paid to center providers in MDC remained at $85 per week for infants and $80 per week for toddlers—until October 1997, when they were raised to $95 per week for infants and $90 per week for toddlers. There were no other increases in reimbursement rates.

During the period of our study, MA set provider reimbursement rates by periodically hiring outside contractors to survey providers to determine the "arm's-length" market price providers charged for care. This approach obtains prices for care that is actually purchased (not list prices) and requires that the care be unsubsidized and that the buyer and seller be unrelated. On July 1, 1996, the MA legislature approved reimbursement rates set at the 55th percentile of the local market price of care, determined by a 1994 market rate survey. From this time until October 1996, Boston area center weekly rates paid were $214 for infants and $185 for toddlers. Rates were increased in November 1996 to $215 per week for infants and $190 per week for toddlers. Once again the legislature increased reimbursement rates in September 1998. This was the last increase during the period of our study. For the Boston area, weekly rates for centers increased to $225 for infants and $200 for toddlers in September 1998.

Minimum Standards Regulations

Teacher Credentials. The FL child-care law requires that child-care personnel employed in a child-care facility be at least 16 years of age (unless the underage person is under direct supervision and not counted for the purposes of caregiver-to-child ratios). FL also requires that all child-care personnel hired on or after October 1, 1992, and all operators of family day-care homes take an approved 30-clock-hour introductory course in child care. Beginning on July 1, 1996, for every 20 preschool children enrolled in a licensed child-care facility operating 8 hours or more per week, the law requires that one of the child-care personnel in the facility must have a Child Development Associate (CDA) credential or an educational credential that is equivalent or higher.

---

[9]"Prevailing market rate," according to FL law, means "the annually determined 75th percentile of a reasonable frequency distribution of market rates in a predetermined geographic market at which licensed child-care providers charge a person for child care services."

The law in MA requires considerably higher minimum teacher credentials. Classrooms must have a teacher-qualified person present in the room who is at least 18 years of age and has a high school diploma. In addition, teachers must have completed three credits in a Child Growth & Development course, must have a CDA, or must have completed a 2-year vocational course in early childhood education approved by the Office of Child Care Services (OCCS). Assistant teachers must be at least 16 years old and must work at all times under a teacher-qualified staff person. Each provider site with at least 39 children must have a lead teacher and an additional lead teacher for every additional 40 children. Effective October 16, 1996, MA law required that lead teachers for infants and toddlers be at least 21 years of age and fulfill certain additional minimum education, training, and experience requirements. For example, either of the following combinations would qualify: (a) a high school diploma or equivalent plus 12 college credits, including credits in infant and toddler care plus 36 months of work experience; or (b) a BA or advanced degree in early education plus 12 college credits in infant and toddler care and 9 months of work experience.

Caregiver-to-Child Ratios.   FL and MA, like most states, require that centers maintain certain minimum caregiver-to-child ratios. Such minimum standards regarding caregiver-to-child ratios can have substantial impacts on prices. In FL, for infants (under the age of 1 year), the minimum caregiver-to-child ratio is 1 to 4, for 1-year-old children it is 1 to 6, and for 2-year-olds it is 1 to 11. FL does not regulate group sizes. MA's minimum ratio standards are more stringent than FL's, particularly for toddlers. In addition, the Commonwealth also sets maximum group sizes. This is an indication that public demand for quality child care may be higher in MA than in FL. The minimum caregiver-to-child ratio in MA for infants (ages 1–15 months) is 1 to 3 and the minimum ratio for toddlers (ages 15–33 months) is 1 to 4. In addition, there can be no more than seven children in an infant group and no more than nine children in a toddler group. This additional group size requirement in MA has an additional impact on prices.

DATA SOURCES

For MDC, our main sources of data are: (a) provider records maintained by the two R&R agencies serving the county; (b) Gold Seal accreditation records; and (c) administrative records for families with children receiving child-care subsidies.

The MA data we use come from three major sources: (a) provider records maintained by the five R&R agencies serving our study areas; (b) monthly voucher billing files received from OCCS, from which we obtained information on the use of and payments for child-care subsidies; and (c) child-care licensing lists received from OCCS, from which we obtained data on child-care capacities (slots).

The provider data we use for both MDC and MA contain information on all licensed centers and most license-exempt centers. Head Start providers are included in both the MA and MDC provider data. The data contain proportionally many more licensed family child-care homes in MA than in MDC because they are proportionally much more numerous in MA. Our provider data for MA and MDC do not contain information on informal (unlicensed) providers (which are not uncommon, particularly in MDC), although our subsidy databases do contain some information on families that use their child-care subsidies (vouchers) to purchase informal care from relatives, friends, and neighbors. In short, we base our findings on reasonably complete data for five representative areas in MA and for the entire metropolitan MDC for the period 1996 to 1999. Our data are not from a sample, but rather cover the universe of administrative records for the geographic areas covered in our study. These data include information on licensed providers—both centers and family child-care homes—as well as information on families that use their child-care subsidies (vouchers) to purchase informal care.

FINDINGS

In this section, we present selected findings arranged under three categories: those related to the availability and use of child care, those related to child-care quality, and those related to child-care prices.

Findings Related to the Availability and Use of Child Care

We found that the number of infants and toddlers in formal (licensed) care increased as welfare reform progressed in MA and MDC. Particularly in MDC, the increase was dramatic. As can be seen in Fig. 3.1, in March 1996, the number of infants from low-income families receiving care in MDC under the child-care subsidy program was slightly less than 400. By March 2000, almost 1,000 infants were in subsidized child care. This represents an increase of almost 150%. This increase in subsidized infant enrollments was particularly marked after September 1998.[10] The number of 1-year-olds in subsidized child care in MDC also grew rapidly during the period of welfare reform—from

---

[10]Only approximately 1,500 families statewide reached their 24-month time limit in September 1998. The dramatic increase in the use of child-care subsidies was probably largely due to the combined effects of increased work-related activity requirements for cash assistance recipients, particularly recipients with young children, and accelerated departures from cash assistance as the 24-month and 36-month time limits became more salient. The local Miami-Dade Wages Coalition that managed welfare reform became fully operational and focused on moving cash assistance recipients from welfare to work during the summer and fall of 1998.

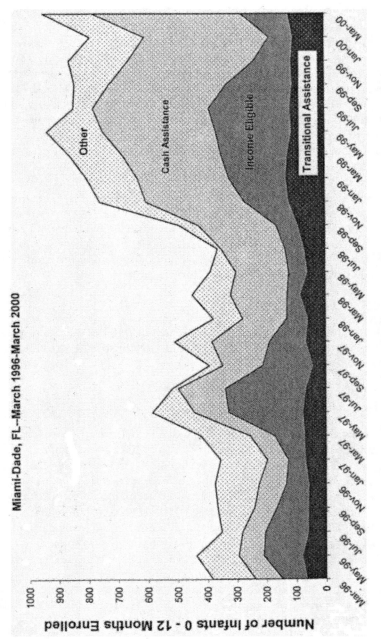

FIG. 3.1. Infant enrollment in subsidized child care—by program (Miami-Dade, FL—March 1996–March 2000).

slightly less than 900 in March 1996 to more than 2,000 by March 2000. This represents an increase of almost 125%. As for infants, this growth accelerated after September 1998. The number of 2-year-olds in subsidized care approximately doubled—from slightly over 1,100 in March 1996 to almost 2,300 by March 2000. The increase also accelerated after September 1998. However, the growth in enrollments of 2-year-olds in subsidized care was less rapid than that of infants and 1-year-olds probably because, prior to welfare reform, cash assistance recipients in FL were already required to participate in the JOBS program when their youngest child reached age 3.

Although the increase in the number of subsidies issued in MDC for infant and toddler care was dramatic, the growth in the full-time enrollment of infants and toddlers at centers accepting child-care subsidies was far less so. Figure 3.2 shows that full-time infant (i.e., age <12 months) enrollments in MDC at centers accepting subsidies increased only slightly from about 1,000 in February 1996 to about 1,150 by February 1999—an increase of 15%, compared with the over 150% increase in the number of child-care subsidy vouchers issued by the child-care subsidy agencies in MDC for infant care (see Fig. 3.1). During the same period, full-time infant enrollments at centers not accepting vouchers actually declined from about 1,160 to 1,000.[11]

There are a number of possible explanations for this discrepancy. For example, it is possible that many vouchers issued for infant care were for part-time care.[12] It is also possible that infants with child-care subsidies increasingly displaced other infants without subsidies, leaving enrollments largely unchanged. Another possible explanation, particularly for the income-eligible group, is that families that were initially paying the full cost of care were later receiving subsidies as funding was increased. The fact that the full-time enrollment of infants at providers accepting subsidies increased, whereas the enrollment of infants at unsubsidized providers declined, provides some support for this hypothesis.

Figure 3.2 also shows that the number of 1-year-olds and 2-year-olds in full-time care at subsidized providers increased at rates of 17% and 13%, respectively. In contrast, enrollment of 1-year-olds and 2-year-olds in full-time care at unsubsidized providers decreased by a similar amount.

In MA, as welfare reform unfolded, the increases in the use of subsidized care for infants and toddlers were much less dramatic and, particularly with respect to infant care, largely handled by the informal system (i.e., relatives,

---

[11]The reader should note that these enrollment-by-age figures reported by providers to the MDC R&Rs are not considered to be as reliable as the overall enrollments they report.

[12]During our study period, only 30% of cash assistance recipients with subsidies were working, and among those working only 23% worked 20 or more hours per week. In contrast, 93% of those receiving Transitional Child Care Assistance (TCC) were working (88% of those in this group were working at least 20 hours per week) and 99% of income-eligible subsidy clients were working (95% of those in this group were working at least 20 hours per week).

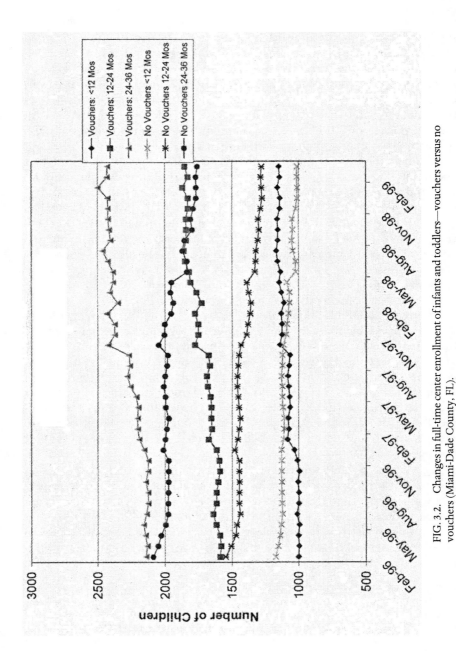

FIG. 3.2. Changes in full-time center enrollment of infants and toddlers—vouchers versus no vouchers (Miami-Dade County, FL).

neighbors, and friends). A review of the monthly billing files of three representative Child Care Resource Agencies (CCRAs)[13] for the month of May in 1997, 1998, and 1999 shows that the number of infants from low-income families receiving care under the voucher program in these three areas in MA increased by 10% between 1997 and 1999—from 1,157 to 1,277. During this period, the proportion of infants enrolled in centers declined from 44% to 34%, whereas the proportion of infants in informal care increased from 27% to 34%.

The proportion of vouchers issued by the same three CCRAs in MA and used by families for toddler care increased somewhat more rapidly (by 12%) between 1997 and 1999.[14] Around 45% of the vouchers for toddler care went to centers and 20% to informal caregivers. Throughout this period, the percentage of vouchers for the care of infants and toddlers in MA going to family child-care homes remained approximately the same.

Findings Related to Quality of Care. Quality child care and early education fosters children's intellectual, social, and emotional development; gets them ready for school; and puts them on the right path toward healthy and productive citizenship.

Staff Credentials. One recognized aspect of quality in the child-care and early childhood education world is the educational level of the staff.

In MDC, we find that, as welfare reform progressed, there was a decline in the average percentage of staff with a high school education or higher academic credential employed at centers with infant programs and participating in the subsidized child-care program—from 88% in 1997 to 85% in 1999. Similarly, the average percentage of staff with a high school education or higher at centers with toddler programs and accepting subsidies declined from 88% in 1997 to 86% in 1999. Centers that did not accept subsidies, with infant and toddler programs, had a higher percentage of staff with high school or higher credentials, but the proportion also decreased as welfare reform got underway—from 91% in 1996 to 86% in 1999 at centers with infant programs and from 92% to 88% at centers with toddler programs.

We observed improvement in MDC in relation to the proportion of staff with associate degrees and bachelor's degrees as welfare reform progressed. However, only a relatively small proportion of staff at child-care centers had these higher levels of education during our study period. Specifically, the aver-

---

[13]The three CCRAs are Child Care Choices of Boston, New England Farm Workers Council in Hampden County, and Child Care Works, which serves the Fall River/New Bedford/Taunton area of the state. We were not able to use data for our other two study areas because of a redefinition of their service boundaries.

[14]This greater increase was in accordance with the MA welfare reform time limits and work requirements, which become stricter when the youngest child turns 2.

age percentage of staff with an associate degree employed at centers accepting subsidies with infant programs increased from 33% in 1997 to 39% in 1999, and it also increased at similar facilities with toddler programs from 33% in 1997 to 37% in 1999. Centers not accepting subsidies made less progress in the hiring and retention of staff with an associate degree as welfare reform got underway—from 34% in 1996 to 35% in 1999 at facilities with infant programs and from 36% in 1996 to 38% in 1999 at facilities with toddler programs.

There was solid progress, during the early welfare reform years in MDC, in terms of the proportion of staff with bachelor's degrees at child-care centers. The average percentage of staff with a bachelor's degree employed at subsidized facilities with infant programs increased from 10% in 1997 to 14% in 1999, and it also increased at subsidized facilities with toddler programs from 9% in 1997 to 12% in 1999. Providers that did not accept subsidies made more limited progress during these years. Specifically, the proportion of staff with bachelor's degrees at facilities with infant programs increased as welfare reform progressed, but only from 9% in 1996 to 11% in 1999. Similarly, the percentage of staff with bachelor's degrees at unsubsidized facilities with toddler programs increased from 11% in 1996 to 13% in 1999.

Welfare reform was also associated with an increase in the proportion of staff with CDA credentials in MDC.[15] The average percentage of staff with a CDA employed at subsidized facilities with infant programs increased from 44% in 1997 to 49% in 1999, and at those with toddler programs it increased from 46% in 1997 to 51% in 1999. For unsubsidized providers, the increase was more limited—from 41% in 1996 to 44% in 1999 at facilities with infant programs and from 42% in 1996 to 44% in 1999 at facilities with toddler programs.

At the time of our study, MA's R&Rs did not collect data on the educational credentials held by staff employed at child-care centers. Therefore, we do not have parallel information to the data presented on MDC. We only have information on whether family child-care providers had an associate degree, a bachelor's degree, or a CDA credential.

As welfare reform progressed in MA, we observed a generally downward trend in the educational credentials held by family child-care providers, particularly among providers not taking children with child-care subsidies. The average percentage of family providers with associate degrees caring for infants with vouchers remained stable at 4% between 1997 and 1999, and the proportion of those caring for toddlers with vouchers also remained stable at 2% between 1997 and 1999. But the proportion of unsubsidized family providers with associate degrees caring for infants declined from 5% in 1997 to 4% in 1999, and the proportion of those caring for toddlers declined from 5% in 1997 to 0% in 1999.

---

[15] This was in accordance with recently instituted changes in the child-care regulations requiring a certain minimum number of staff with the CDA credential at each facility.

Family providers in MA are more likely to have bachelor's degrees than associate degrees, although the proportion with either degree is small. The average percentage of family providers with bachelor's degrees caring for infants with vouchers declined from 8% in 1997 to 6% in 1999, and the proportion of those caring for toddlers with vouchers also declined from 6% in 1997 to 5% in 1999. The proportion of unsubsidized family providers with bachelor's degrees caring for infants declined slightly from 15% in 1997 to 14% in 1999, and the proportion of those caring for toddlers declined dramatically from 15% in 1997 to 4% in 1999.

Few family providers in MA had the CDA credential during the period of our study. This is not surprising because MA law does not require the CDA, but rather accepts a reasonably wide range of early childhood education credentials and training. Yet we observe an increase in the proportion of family providers with the CDA caring for infants, both those with vouchers and those without, from less than 1% in 1997 to almost 2% in 1999. However, we found no family providers caring for toddlers who had the CDA credential.

Accreditation.   Accreditation by a nationally recognized professional organization is also widely recognized in the child-care field as an indicator of quality. To be accredited and re-accredited by an entity such as the National Association for the Education of Young Children (NAEYC), a child-care facility must pass periodic and extensive reviews of all aspects of its program.

Only a small fraction of the child-care and early childhood education facilities serving infants and toddlers in MDC were accredited during the 38-month period of our study. Two percent of centers that were not participating in the subsidized child-care program and that were offering infant care were accredited in February 1996, compared with 1.5% of centers offering infant care and participating in the subsidized child-care program. By March 1999, the level of accreditation in both sectors remained strikingly low, with only one additional provider in the subsidized sector and one in the unsubsidized sector becoming accredited.[16] Unsubsidized center providers serving toddlers were more likely to be accredited at both the beginning and end of our study period (approximately 3%). However, subsidized center providers serving toddlers were no more likely to be accredited than those serving infants.

It is interesting to note that, for the period of our study, the majority of accredited facilities in MDC were run by faith-based organizations. A handful of others were run by Head Start programs. The number of private, nonreligious, accredited providers in MDC was minimal both at the beginning and end of our study period.

---

[16]We used Gold Seal program accreditation records going back to the inception of this program in 1996. These records were kept by the state's R&R Network (The Florida Children's Forum). We also used the on-line NAEYC records.

In contrast, in the five representative areas of MA we studied, a much larger proportion of center providers (including Head Start providers) were nationally accredited. Yet the trend we observed in the proportion that were accredited during the early years following welfare reform was mixed, with subsidized providers improving their accreditation rate and unsubsidized providers losing ground on this measure. Specifically, for centers with infant enrollments and accepting vouchers, the proportion accredited was 18% in 1997, and it had increased to 22% by 1999. Similarly, for centers with toddler enrollments and accepting vouchers, the proportion accredited was 21% in 1997, and it had grown to 24% by 1999. In contrast, for centers with infant enrollments that did not accept vouchers, the proportion accredited declined from 24% in 1997 to 19% in 1999. Similarly, for providers with toddler enrollments that did not accept vouchers, the proportion accredited declined from 25% in 1997 to 20% in 1999.

We suspect that the substantially higher proportion of accredited providers in MA than in MDC is directly related to the substantially higher market prices for care and substantially higher reimbursements paid to subsidized providers in MA. In a subsequent section, we describe prices in both areas. For information on provider reimbursement rates, please refer to the Policy Context section. In contrast, in MDC, during the time of our study, many providers wishing to become Gold Seal accredited were unable, for financial reasons, to make the necessary changes in staff, facilities, resources, and programs. To overcome the financial barriers, the Miami Dade School Readiness Coalition, with child-care quality enhancement funds from the state, has been awarding a limited number of grants to providers wishing to upgrade to achieve Gold Seal-accredited status. This program has been successful, after the period of our study, in substantially increasing the accreditation rate of MDC providers. However, for providers to be able to retain their accredited status, they must be able to maintain quality and, to do so without government subsidies, they must be able to charge higher prices. Raising prices is harder in MDC than in MA given the lower median income of the population and higher levels of poverty of families with children. We also believe that MA has a substantially higher proportion of accredited providers because, compared with MDC, MA has a much higher proportion of the population that is native born and that has a higher level of education.

Findings Related to Price of Care.   Overall, we find that prices charged for infant and toddler care in MA during the period surrounding welfare reform were more than 2½ times the equivalent prices in MDC. We also find that, proportionally, prices increased slightly more during this period in MA than in MDC. In this section, we detail the price differences we found.

Figure 3.3 summarizes the weekly nonzero prices charged for full-time infant care in MDC from the first quarter of 1996 to the first quarter of 1999. As

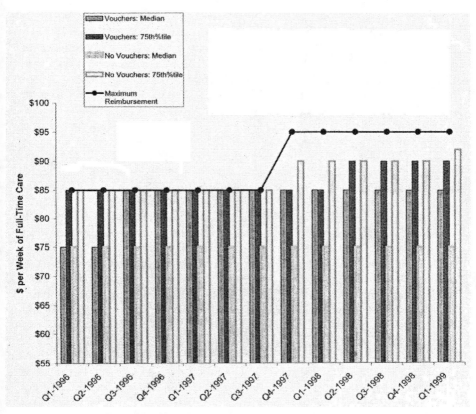

FIG. 3.3. Weekly full-time prices and reimbursement rates for infant care centers accepting and not accepting vouchers (Miami-Dade—February 1996–March 1999).

can be seen in this figure, median infant prices remained flat at $75 per week for unsubsidized care. For subsidized infant care, prices increased once (from $75 to $85 per week in the third quarter of 1996) and then remained at $85 per week until the end of our observation period. Similarly, the median weekly prices for full-time toddler care in MDC also remained largely unchanged—at around $70 during 1996 and 1997 and up to $75 by 1999 for unsubsidized care and at $79 for subsidized care for 1997 to 1999.

In contrast, weekly nonzero median prices for full-time infant care in MA increased from $205 in 1997 to $220 in 1999 for subsidized (voucher) care, although they decreased slightly from $232 to $230 for unsubsidized care. Median weekly prices for full-time toddler care in MA increased from $183 in 1997 to $200 in 1999 for subsidized (voucher) care, and they also increased from $195 in 1997 to $209 in 1999 for unsubsidized care.

Tables 3.1 and 3.2 provide descriptive statistics for the full-time prices of infant and toddler care in MA and in MDC for the period 1997 to 1999 as a whole. As can be seen in Table 3.1, the median weekly price of full-time infant care during the period 1997 to 1999 in MA was $218 for providers participating in the voucher program and $234 for providers not participating. By way of contrast, Table 3.2 shows that the median price of infant care in MDC for the same period (1997–1999) was $85 per week for providers participating in the child-care subsidy program and $75 per week for providers that did not participate. As per Table 3.1, in MA, the median weekly full-time price of toddler care was $194 for providers participating in the voucher program and $214 for nonparticipating providers. In MDC, as per Table 3.2, the median weekly full-time price of toddler (1-year-old) care was $79 for subsidized providers and $70 for unsubsidized providers.

In MA, prices charged by providers that did not accept children with child-care vouchers were significantly higher than prices charged by providers that did accept vouchers. In MDC, the situation was the reverse—that is, prices charged by providers participating in the child-care subsidy program were significantly higher than the prices charged by providers that did not participate.

As noted before, for the period 1997 to 1999, the median price of infant and toddler care in MA was more than 2½ times the median price of infant and toddler care in MDC. We computed that the costs of labor and other items needed to provide child care at the time was between 10% and 34% higher in MA than in MDC.[17] In addition, MA's more stringent minimum standards requirements meant that centers providing infant care in MA would have labor costs 32% higher than centers providing infant care in MDC. For children between 15 and 24 months old, minimum standards in MA caused labor costs that were 50% higher in MA than in MDC and labor costs that were 275% higher in MA than in MDC for children 24 months to 33 months old.

Computing the costs of meeting higher minimum standards requirements in MA than in FL explains most of the observed differences in the price of care for 24- to 33-month-old children in MA and MDC. But this only partially explains the differences in prices charged for the care of children less than 2 years old. The existing literature (see e.g., Vandell & Wolfe, 2000) suggests that the income and educational levels of the population are strongly related to the demand for higher quality child care. Accordingly, we suspect that the much higher educational and income levels in MA, as compared with MDC, likely account for much of the remaining price difference (after adjustment for costs) between MA and MDC with respect to the care of infants and 1-year-olds.

---

[17]For example, at the time of our study, the overall cost of living was 34% higher in Boston than in MDC and in the western part of MA it was 10% higher than the cost of living in MDC. The median child-care worker's wage in MA is approximately 10% higher in MA than in MDC ($8.59 per hour in MA and $7.79 per hour in MDC).

TABLE 3.1

Weekly Nonzero Prices of Center-Based Child Care and Early Childhood Education
Five Representative Areas of Massachusetts—1997–1999

	Prices of Programs Participating in Subsidized Center-Based Care					Prices of Programs Not Participating in Subsidized Center-Based Care[a]				
	#Obs.	Mean	Median	SD	CV	#Obs.	Mean	Median	SD	CV
Infant full-time (<15m)	535	$218.08	$217	45.30	0.21	157	$233.65	$240	54.01	0.23
Toddler full-time (15m–33m)	714	$194.12	$194	40.61	0.21	229	$210.66	$214	51.08	0.24

[a]The nonsubsidized market prices are the nonzero prices charged by providers other than FCCs, head start, public schools, nonpublic schools, and those centers participating in the subsidized child-care program.

TABLE 3.2

Weekly Nonzero Prices of Center-Based Child Care and Early Childhood Education
Miami-Dade County—1997–1999

	Prices of Programs Participating in Subsidized Center-Based Care					Prices of Programs Not Participating in Subsidized Center-Based Care[a]				
	#Obs.	Mean	Median	SD	CV	#Obs.	Mean	Median	SD	CV
Infant full time (<12m)	575–638	$84.92	$85	12.44	0.15	491–527	$78.60	$75	18.76	0.24
One-Year-Old (12m–24m)	700–746	$79.25	$79	11.09	0.14	620–654	$74.24	$70	17.63	0.24
Two-Year-Old (24m–36m)	784–842	$76.73	$76	12.16	0.16	932–1011	$72.00	$70	17.66	0.25

[a]The nonsubsidized market prices are the nonzero prices charged by providers other than FCCs, head start, public schools, nonpublic schools, and those centers participating in the subsidized child-care program.

We also find that the prices paid for the weekly full-time center care of infants and 1-year-olds in MDC are less than 10% apart, although the labor costs of providing infant care, given FL's minimum caregiver-to-child ratio requirements, should be about 50% higher than the labor costs of providing care for 1-year-olds. In addition, we find that the prices paid for the weekly full-time center care of infants in MA are approximately 12% more than prices paid for toddler care, although the labor costs of providing infant care, given MA's minimum caregiver-to-child ratio requirements, should be about 32% higher than the labor costs of providing care for 1-year-olds. We also find that the prices paid for the weekly full-time center care of infants and 2-year-olds in MDC are at most 32% apart, although the labor costs of providing infant care, given FL's minimum caregiver-to-child ratio requirements, should be about 175% higher than the labor costs of providing care for 2-year-olds. These price differences suggest that centers which comply with the state-promulgated minimum standards for infant care must be using funds from sources other than the prices paid by parents. For centers receiving child-care subsidies, the reimbursement rates paid by the state of FL for the care of infants in MDC are also only 8% to 12% higher than the reimbursement rates for 2-year-olds. Thus, the costs of providing infant care that is in compliance with state-imposed standards are not covered by the prices the state pays either.

The situation in MA, although not as stark, also indicates that centers which comply with the state's minimum standards must be using other sources of funding to subsidize the infant care they provide. As can be seen by comparing the price of infant and toddler care in Table 3.1, the price of infant care in MA is only approximately 12% higher than the price of toddler care. MA's provider reimbursement rates for infant care are 12.5% higher than the state's reimbursement rates for toddlers in Boston and 9% higher in the western part of the state. Yet minimum standards imply labor costs that are 32% higher. For more details on the relationship between infant and toddler care costs, provider reimbursements, and prices in MDC and MA, please refer to Witte, Queralt, Witt, and Griesinger (2000) and Queralt, Witte, and Griesinger (2000).

CONCLUSIONS

We provided descriptive evidence from MDC in FL and from five representative areas in MA that government policies governing welfare reform, the child-care subsidy system, and minimum standards regulations had considerable influence on the availability and use, quality, and price of infant and toddler care as welfare reform progressed from 1996 to 2000. We suspect that the markedly different sociocultural contexts in MDC and MA also had some influence on the very different situations for infant and toddler care in MDC and MA.

Our data suggest that child-care regulations, market prices, and provider reimbursements rates in MDC were out of synchrony in the period surrounding the passage of welfare reform. Specifically, the prices charged by providers in MDC for the care of infants and the reimbursements providers received from the state for infant care did not appear to be sufficient to cover the costs of providing infant care that met the state-imposed minimum standards. In the five areas of MA we studied, prices charged and reimbursements and regulations were more closely aligned.

We find that prices for infant and toddler care in MDC were uncommonly flat during the period of our study and strikingly lower than in MA, even after adjusting for the higher cost of living and for the more stringent regulatory environment in MA. We suspect, and provide some evidence, that this marked difference negatively impacted, at least in part, the quality of infant and toddler care in MDC as compared with MA. This is a concern given the rapid and dramatic increase (150%) in the number of low-income infants and toddlers that were placed in subsidized formal (licensed) care in MDC following passage of FL's stringent, work-first welfare reform. MA's less stringent welfare reform rules were associated with a much lower rate of increase (about 10%) in the number of infants and toddlers placed in formal care.

In MDC, enrollments at facilities with infant and toddler programs that accepted child-care subsidies increased moderately during the period of our study, whereas enrollments at providers that did not take children with subsidies declined. We suggest that the fact that the growth in the full-time enrollment of infants and toddlers at subsidized facilities was far less dramatic than the increase in the number of child-care subsidies issued for infant and toddler care may be indicative of a displacement of infants and toddlers from unsubsidized families by those with child-care subsidies.

With respect to quality of infant and toddler care, we find, as welfare reform progressed during the years of our study, there was some deterioration in MDC in the proportion of staff with a high school education or higher credential at subsidized centers (from 88% in 1997 to 85%–86% in 1999) as well as at unsubsidized centers (from 91%–92% in 1996 to 86%–88% in 1999). However, there was small but consistent improvement in the proportion of staff with associate and bachelor's degrees and with CDAs at both subsidized and unsubsidized centers serving both infants and toddlers. In MA, we find a generally downward trend with respect to the credentials held by family child-care providers as welfare reform progressed. There exist no equivalent MA data on centers.

National accreditation levels for centers with infant and toddler programs in MDC were flat and distressingly low (1.5%–3%) during the period surrounding welfare reform. These exceedingly low levels of accreditation in

MDC existed despite that, under FL's Gold Seal program, subsidized providers could receive up to a 20% increase in reimbursements if they became accredited. In contrast, the MA subsidized child-care program did not offer higher reimbursements to providers with accreditation. Yet accreditation levels grew during this period in MA—from 18%–21% to 22%–24% for centers with infant and toddler programs that accepted vouchers. However, for centers serving infants and toddlers that did not accept vouchers, accreditation levels decreased in MA from 24%–25% to 19%–20%.

ACKNOWLEDGMENTS

This chapter is a product of the Wellesley Child Care Policy Research Partnership and the Child Care Bureau's Child Care Policy Research Consortium. Our work was supported by Wellesley College under Grant #90YE0032 from the Child Care Bureau, Administration for Children and Families (ACF), Department of Health and Human Services (DHHS). The grant was awarded to the Wellesley Child Care Research Partnership through the National Bureau of Economic Research.

We are thankful to many people and organizations for their cooperation, feedback, and data. In particular, we wish to thank Ardith Wieworka, who was Massachusetts Commissioner of Child Care Services (OCCS) at the time of our study; Irene Taylor-Wooten, former Director of Miami-Dade County Child Development Services (CDS); and Barbara Weinstein (President of Family Central) for their support. We also would like to thank Rod Southwick (OCCS), Pilar Feldman (Miami-Dade County Information Technology Department), and Anita Platt (Resource & Referral Director at Family Central) for data and research direction. Finally, we wish to thank Pia Divine, Ivelisse Martinez-Beck, Robert Hutchins, Martha Moorehouse, Elizabeth Peters, and Karen Tvedt for their insightful comments on early drafts of this chapter. We also wish to thank Harriet Griesinger for collecting and setting up the Miami-Dade County Resource & Referral and subsidy databases and Dr. Robert Witt who provided help with analyses of the Massachusetts data.

The cooperation and support of our sponsors and of these individuals and organizations in no way indicate their concurrence with our analyses or conclusions. We alone are responsible for the views and opinions expressed in this chapter and for all errors and omissions.

REFERENCES

Lemke, R. J., Witte, A. D., Queralt, M., & Witt, R. (2000, March). *Child care and the welfare to work transition* (Working Paper #7583). Cambridge, MA: National Bureau of Economic Research. Retrieved September 2, 2004, from http://www.nber.org/papers/w7583

Queralt, M., Witte, A., & Griesinger, H. (2000, July). *Championing our children: Changes in the quality, price and availability of child care in the welfare reform era* (Working Paper #2000-07). Wellesley, MA: Department of Economics, Wellesley College. Retrieved September 2, 2004, from http://www.wellesley.edu/Economics/wkpapers/index.html

U.S. Census Bureau. (2002). *2002 American community survey. Table 2: County ranking—Percent of population that is foreign born.* Retrieved September 12, 2004, from http://www.census.gov/Press-Release/www/2003/ACSTables.html#tb2

U.S. Census Bureau. (2003, December). The foreign-born population: 2000. Census 2000 Brief #C2KBR-34. Retrieved September 12, 2004, from http://www.census.gov/prod/2003 pubs/c2kbr-34.pdf

U.S. Census Bureau. (2004a). *American fact finder. Census 2000 summary file 3 (SF 3)—Sample data. Quick tables for Massachusetts. General demographic characteristics (DP-1), selected social characteristics (DP-2), selected economic characteristics (DP-3).* Retrieved September 11, 2004, from http://www.census.gov/census2000/states/ma.html

U.S. Census Bureau. (2004b). *American fact finder. USA quick facts: State and county quick facts. Census 2000 summary file 1 (SF 1) 100-percent data. Quick tables for Miami-Dade County, FL. Profile of general demographic characteristics (DP-1.), profile of selected social characteristics (DP-2.), profile of selected economic characteristics (DP–3).* Retrieved September 11, 2004, from http://quickfacts.census.gov/qfd/states/12/12086lk.html

Vandell, D. L., & Wolfe, B. (2000, May). *Child care quality: Does it matter and does it need to be improved?* Washington, DC: Office of the Assistant Secretary for Planning and Evaluation, U.S. Department of Health and Human Services. Retrieved September 2, 2004, from http://aspe.hhs.gov/hsp/ccquality00/ccqual.htm

Witte, A. D., Queralt, M., Witt, R., & Griesinger, H. (2000, April). *The policy context and infant and toddler care in the welfare reform era* (Working Paper #8893). Cambridge, MA: National Bureau of Economic Research. Retrieved September 24, 2004, from http://www.nber.org/papers/w8893

PART TWO

Government Policies and the Nature of Child Care

Welfare and Child-Care Policy Effects on Very Young Children's Child-Care Experiences

Lisa A. Gennetian
MDRC

Danielle A. Crosby
University of Chicago

Aletha C. Huston
University of Texas at Austin

Using data collected from a diverse set of experimental programs for low-income parents that took place throughout the late 1980s to the mid-1990s, we examine how welfare and employment policies affect the child-care decisions of single parents with very young children. Policy components that encourage employment (e.g., earnings supplements and employment mandates) appear to affect the *amount* of care used for very young children, while policies designed to increase the access and affordability of care appear to affect the *type* of care. When programs offer more comprehensive, efficient, or generous child-care assistance, families use more center-based care and less home-based care. For several reasons, the majority of low-income working families rely on home-based arrangements. These findings suggest that expanded child-care assistance within income and employment policies can enhance the otherwise limited options available to low-income parents.

INTRODUCTION

Parents of children under the age of 6 constitute the largest proportion of families receiving public assistance distributed through the Temporary Assistance to Needy Families (TANF) block grants (U.S. House of Representatives, 2000). Both the Family Support Act of 1988 and the 1996 Personal Responsibility and Work Opportunity Reconciliation Act (PRWORA) imposed requirements that explicitly targeted mothers of very young children, allowing states to require women with children as young as age 3 years (under the Family Support Act) and then as young as age 3 months (under PRWORA) to participate in employment-related activities.[1] Although many states exempt work or work-related requirements for parents with infants under 6 months to 1 year of age, these parents are not exempt from other policies, such as time limits, that are also designed to increase employment and reduce dependence on welfare.

Child care is a key issue in understanding the effects of these new policies on families with young children; it serves a dual role as a support for maternal employment and an environment for children's development. Available, accessible, affordable, and quality care is essential for promoting sustained employment for low-income mothers and for the protection of their children. Securing child care for very young children poses particular difficulties for parents. Compared with available options for older children, care for infants and toddlers is harder to find; parents have more concerns about possible harmful effects on children. When care is found, it is often expensive (U.S. General Accounting Office, 1997). Moreover, research findings on the effects of infant child care show that extensive and early child care may interfere with the development of maternal sensitivity (see review by Lamb, 1998). High-quality care, however, may enhance maternal sensitivity, with possible long-term implications for children's social and emotional development (NICHD Early Child Care Research Network, 1996, 2002, 2004).

Recognizing that child care is necessary to enable welfare recipients to move into and remain in the labor force, federal and state governments increased investments in child care for low-income families by nearly double in the past two decades (Raikes, 1998). Federal child-care funds targeted to welfare and low-income families are now collapsed into one large fund—the Child Care and Development Fund (CCDF). With state contributions, child-care funds totaled $3.5 billion in 1996 and increased to more than $8.0 billion in 2000 (Greenberg et al., 2002). Estimates suggest that of the 1.18 million children who received federal child-care subsidies in 1995, approximately 20% were infants and toddlers and another 20% were school-age children (Raikes, 1998). Notably, the 1998 federal budget allocated $50 million for enhancement of the quality of care for infants and toddlers (Raikes, 1998). Despite the large increases in funding, only 15% of eligible children receive assistance (Mezey, Greenberg, & Schumacher, 2002), and in many states, reimburse-

---

[1]For 20 years prior to the 1988 Family Support Act (FSA), women receiving welfare who had children under age 6 generally were not subject to participation and work mandates. With the passage of FSA, women with children as young as age 3 (or as young as age 1, at state option) were newly designated as mandatory participants. However, FSA had also enacted a "child-care guarantee" applicable to the Aid to Families with Dependent Children (AFDC) Program, and a state imposing work-related requirements on families could not sanction a family if child care was among the reasons that constituted a good cause for noncomplying. In enacting TANF, Congress also repealed the child-care guarantee.

ment rates are low relative to the local child-care market (Schumacher & Greenberg, 1999). As states deliberate on future welfare and child-care policy, policymakers are especially struggling with how to structure child-care assistance policies to promote parental employment and improve developmental outcomes for children living in poverty.

In this chapter, we use data from five evaluations of experimental programs for low-income parents to examine how different welfare and employment policies affect the child-care decisions of single parents with very young children (less than age 3). Although these evaluations did not take place under the current welfare policy environment—particularly capturing stricter requirements for parents of very young children—the tested programs do represent a broad range of policies that are implemented in states today. Prior analyses of these experimental evaluations demonstrate that these programs generally increased employment and, in some cases, earnings for low-income parents (Bloom & Michalopoulos, 2001). It is likely that increased employment also increased the use of child care. By affecting the amount of employment, earnings, income, or dependence on welfare, other policy aspects of these programs might have also affected the type of care used, its stability, and its quality. For example, some programs might have enabled parents to use center-based care, which is more expensive than home-based care, if they preferred it. Center care often provides a better support than home-based care for regular employment because it is more reliable. There is also evidence that the average quality of center care is better than that of home-based arrangements that serve children from low-income communities (Coley, Chase-Lansdale, & Li-Grining, 2001; NICHD Early Child Care Research Network, 1997), and that children's cognitive and language development is enhanced when they experience center-based care from infancy onward (NICHD Early Child Care Research Network, 2000, 2002; NICHD Early Child Care Research Network & Duncan, 2003).

The programs being compared in this study differed not only on employment-related policies (e.g., whether parents were required to participate and whether they received earnings supplements), but also in the amount and types of child-care assistance offered. These treatment differences in child-care policies were designed to make child care more affordable, improve access by providing information, and, in one case, increase the availability of care. In this study, we asked whether "expanded child-care services" that were offered in conjunction with other employment-based policies allowed parents to overcome cost and other barriers in decisions about types of child-care arrangements. Using experimental studies, in which we compare the outcomes of individuals and families in a control group, under the then-current policy environment, with the outcomes of individuals and families in a program group, under a new policy environment, our analyses offer a test of the direct effects of programs on child-care outcomes.

We find that programs which require or encourage employment (e.g., earnings supplements and employment mandates) not only increased the employment of low-income parents, but also increased the total *amount* of child care used. The *type* of care used, however, depended on the child-care policies and practices included in these programs. Expanded child-care assistance enabled parents to use more center- rather than home-based care. If center care is more stable and reliable, and of a higher quality than home-based arrangements, these findings suggest that child-care policies which increase the accessibility and affordability of care, and serve the federal requirements to ensure parental choice, can play an important role in supporting the well-being of working low-income families and children.

The Role of Child-Care Assistance in the Lives of Low-Income Parents

Effects of Type of Care on Children's Development.   By allowing parents to purchase nonmaternal forms of care, especially center care, child-care assistance may alter the context of children's day-to-day environments. We distinguish broadly between center- and home-based arrangements. Center-based care takes place in group settings designed primarily for child care; it must be licensed by the state, and children are usually cared for in groups by multiple caregivers. Home-based care includes licensed and certified family child-care homes with multiple children as well as unregulated care by relatives or nonrelatives in the caregiver's or the child's home. Prior work on child-care use patterns suggests that children from poor families are less likely than children from nonpoor families to be in center-based care and more likely to be in home-based arrangements (e.g., Capizzano, Adams, & Sonenstein, 2000).

There is some evidence that center-based care can be a support for children's intellectual and language development. In observational studies, centers in low-income communities score higher than home-based settings on indicators of overall quality, particularly for cognitive stimulation and curriculum (Coley, Chase-Lansdale, & Li-Grining, 2001; Fuller, Kagan, Caspary, & Gauthier, 2002; Loeb, Fuller, Kagan, & Carrol, 2004). In the NICHD Early Child Care Research Network (1997) study, observations of infant care in home-based settings revealed that the quality of caregiver interactions and the child-care environment was significantly lower for children from low-income families than for high-income children. By contrast, the observed quality of center-based care received by very low-income children, many of whom were subsidized, did not differ significantly from the quality experienced by high-income children (NICHD Early Child Care Research Network, 1997). When these children reached age 3, those who had experienced center care in infancy performed better on measures of cognitive and language development than did children who had experienced home-based care of comparable quality (NICHD Early Child Care Research Network, 2000). Similar patterns occurred for a group of children whose mothers received welfare; those who attended early childhood programs performed better on cognitive assessments than did those who did not (Zaslow et al., 1999). The positive effects of stable center-based care endure into the first few years of school (Broberg et al., 1997; Yoshikawa, 1999).

Several features of center care may explain its contribution to cognitive and intellectual development. Although the quality of centers varies greatly, they are subject to licensing procedures that govern group size, adult–child ratios, and physical safety in all states. Compared with children who are cared for in homes, those who attend centers are more likely to be in licensed settings (Howes, 1983; NICHD Early Child Care Research Network, 1996), to encounter adults with advanced education and training in child development (NICHD Early Child Care Research Network, 2000), and to have caregivers who provide developmentally appropriate caregiving and activities (Kontos, Hsu, & Dunn, 1994).

Although centers appear to offer some advantages over other forms of child care for promoting children's intellectual development and school readiness, there is not comparable evidence for positive effects of center-based care on children's social behavior, social maturity, or behavior problems, and there is some evidence that center care increases the frequency of respiratory and gastrointestinal illnesses in the first year or two of life (NICHD Early Child Care Research Network, 2001; Zaslow et al., 1999). Although some small studies have shown associations between center care and more complex and competent social play (Kontos, Hsu, & Dunn, 1994), an extensive longitudinal survey found that children with a lot of center-care experience were rated by caregivers as having higher levels of externalizing behavior at age 4½ in comparison with children with little center experience (NICHD Early Child Care Research Network, 2004). The reasons for these differences are not clear, but experience with groups of same-age peers may lead children to become less conforming to adult expectations.

Employment and Child Care. Sweeping changes in the federal welfare system as a result of PRWORA have contributed to increases in the employment of single mothers. The influx of prior welfare participants into the workforce or work-related activities has been accompanied by an increased demand for child care, and this trend is expected to continue. Although not all welfare reform strategies institute a work-first approach, they do share such components as education, training, and job search activities, which require time away from home and away from children. There is some indication that the supply of child care has not increased at the same pace as the demand for child care, especially the supply of regulated care, care for sick or disabled children, and care during nontraditional hours (Collins et al., 2000).

For most families, and especially single-mother families, child-care costs comprise the largest proportion of the costs to employment (for reviews of the economic literature on the relationship between child-care cost and employment, see Blau, 2000; Chaplin et al., 1999; Council of Economic Advisers, 1997). Although low-income families are less likely to use paid arrangements than are families with higher incomes, those who do use market care expend from 18% to 20% of their incomes on child care, compared with 7% of total family income for nonpoor families (Casper, 1995; Smith, 2000). Care for infants and toddlers is often more expensive and harder to find than care for older children, and this is especially true for center-based arrangements (U.S. General Accounting Office, 1997).

Although typically more expensive than home-based arrangements, center care may be a better support for stable employment because of its reliability. Center-based care does not often fail unpredictably because of a caregiver's illness or decision to terminate caregiving, and it is less prone to problems that may force parents to miss or be late for work (Hofferth, 2001). Ethnographic work suggests that low-income parents like the stability and predictability of center care for employment purposes (Lowe & Weisner, 2004), but they also believe that home-based care provides the flexibility to care for sick children or accommodate employment that is erratic or during nontraditional hours (Emlen, Koren, & Schultze, 1999). Timing of employment hours is an important determinant of families' need for and use of child care. Low-income parents are more likely than higher income parents to work at more than one job and during nonstandard hours or weekends. Over half of the employed mothers of preschoolers with incomes below 200% of poverty work evenings, weekends, or rotating shifts (U.S. Department of Health and Human Services, 1999). Only 10% of centers and 6% of family child-care homes offer care on weekends (Phillips, 1995). Recent ethnographic studies highlight the unstable and shifting child-care arrangements that occur in correspondence with parents' irregular and changing work schedules (Knox, London, Scott, & Blank, 2003; Lowe & Weisner, 2004).

More important, parents' decisions about care reflect not only the fit of different arrangements with their employment situation, but also their beliefs about which settings will benefit their children. Parents who believe that their family should take priority over employment are less likely to use center care (or any care) than are mothers who believe that employment can be combined with family responsibilities (Huston, Chang, & Gennetian, 2002). Interviews with low-income single mothers highlight their concerns about the care and supervision of their children as they enter (or increase) employment, suggesting that parent preferences for different types of care change as children get older (Lowe & Weisner, 2004; Scott, Edin, London, & Mazelis, 2001). Parents frequently discuss the educational benefits of center-care arrangements. For very young children, however, many parents worry about whether centers or nonrelatives will provide the nurturance and attention needed by infants. They also have concerns about safety, particularly for children too young to communicate verbally (Lowe & Weisner, 2004).

Because they make nonmaternal child care more affordable, child-care subsidies play an essential role in allowing parents to go to work and use care they might not otherwise be able to afford. Given the complex and multiple determinants of parents' decisions about employment and child care, we examine whether experimental differences in child-care assistance policy, in the context of welfare and employment programs, were related to changes in the types of care arrangements experienced by very young children.

METHOD

The Studies and the Data

Using data from five experimental evaluation studies, we examine program impacts on patterns of child-care use for very young children. Although the effects of each program on child care have been examined in earlier reports, this study adds important information by focusing exclusively on samples of children who were less than 3 years old (and a small group who were less than 2 years old) when their parents were randomly assigned to a program or control group. By combining and comparing patterns across five studies testing different combinations of policies, our study overcomes many of the limitations in other studies that estimate the effects of a single policy on child-care use. The experimental evaluation studies examined for this chapter are:

> *Connecticut's Jobs-First Program (CT Jobs-First)* included the shortest time limit in the country on welfare receipt (21 months) and a generous financial incentive (see Bloom et al., 2000b).
>
> *Florida's Family Transition Program (FTP)* combined participation mandates, a small financial incentive, and a 2-year time limit and services (see Bloom et al., 2000a).
>
> *The New Chance program (New Chance)* emphasized integrated services, testing a mix of educational, personal development, employment-related, and support services aimed at helping 16- to 22-year-old mothers who dropped out of school and were on welfare become more self-sufficient (see Quint, Bos, & Polit, 1997).
>
> *Milwaukee's New Hope program (New Hope)* evaluated an antipoverty program with a financial incentive to work, including a generous child-care and health care subsidy for low-income parents who worked full time (see Bos et al., 1999).

The Canadian Self-Sufficiency Program (SSP) provided an earnings supplement to single parents who had been on public assistance for at least 1 year and who agreed to maintain full-time employment, tested in two Canadian provinces (British Columbia and New Brunswick; see Michalopoulos et al., 2000).

These studies were chosen because they had comparable information on child care for very young children and large enough samples for analyses; other experimental evaluations collected specific information about child care only for older focal children or, more generally, about child-care use at the family level. All of these studies share the common goal of moving welfare and low-income families into work, and some also share the goal of reducing poverty. The strategies to reach this goal, however, vary substantially from providing generous earnings supplements (e.g., New Hope and the Canadian Self-Sufficiency Project), to mandatory case management and work-first services (e.g., Florida's Family Transition Program), to imposing a time limit on the receipt of welfare benefits (e.g., Florida's Family Transition Program and the Connecticut Jobs-First Program), to providing basic education and other services (e.g., New Chance).

The studies collected three different types of data: demographic and socioeconomic characteristics at study entry from baseline information forms; longitudinal information on employment and welfare receipt from unemployment insurance records and public assistance records; and information about the characteristics of employment, child care, and other household and personal circumstances (sometimes including child well-being) from follow-up surveys. In the follow-up surveys, one or two children were identified as focal children; questions were asked about child care for that child. The age range of focal children varied across studies, but for this report only those children who were less than 3 years old at random assignment were included. The measures collected across these studies are roughly comparable, making a cross-study analysis such as a synthesis of program effects uniquely possible.

The adult samples for these studies were, for the most part, drawn from the local welfare populations. The exceptions are New Hope, which offered its benefits and services to all individuals who satisfied income eligibility requirements, and New Chance, which was designed to assist very young mothers on welfare. The target samples varied according to age of youngest child exemptions (keeping in mind that at a minimum all of them exempted parents with children under the age of 1) and other exemptions based on pregnancy, disabilities, welfare or work history, marital status, and educational level (details about target samples and baseline characteristics available on request). Nearly all of the respondents to the follow-up surveys that collected the child-care information were mothers, whose average age was roughly 30 (with the exception of New Chance, where the average age was 19). The majority of survey respondents were never married at study entry, had a high school or GED degree, and had been on welfare for 2 or more years prior to study entry. The racial/ethnic mix varied substantially by study, with the majority of survey respondents in New Chance, New Hope, and FTP being African American and the majority of survey respondents in SSP being non-Hispanic White.

Nearly all of these studies took place during the early to late 1990s—a time period that included vast changes in welfare policy (i.e., the passage of PRWORA), expansions in the Earned Income Tax Credit, expansions in child-care funding, and stable economic growth with low unemployment rates. Although these changing contexts may affect how successful these programs are in altering employment behavior (i.e., these changing contexts may interact with a program's effectiveness), the treatment difference is preserved because both program and control group members were exposed to (or embargoed from) the same levels of change in other welfare, employment, and income policies and economic growth.

Evaluating the Effects of Child-Care Policy Within Experimental Studies

The random assignment method used in these studies provides the strongest possible basis for causal inferences regarding program impacts on child care. On entering each of the studies, an individual or family was randomly assigned to a program group that was eligible for the benefits and subject to the requirements of the new welfare or antipoverty program, or a control group, that had access to the usual benefits and requirements available to low-income or welfare families in that locale. For some studies, families were recruited, and in most, welfare recipients were randomly assigned to either the experimental or control group when they applied for welfare or for their annual recertification of eligibility. Because individuals were assigned at random, any differences in outcomes during the follow-up between individuals in the program and control groups—the impact—can be attributed to the policy they faced.

Child-Care Use. The first step in our empirical analysis was to construct comparable measures of child-care use across these studies and then estimate program impacts on these outcomes. Impacts were estimated using a regression-based approach controlling for a number of prerandom assignment and baseline characteristics, such as whether ever married, number of children, race and ethnicity, and prior welfare and work history. For these analyses, *child care* refers to any nonparental (often nonmaternal) form of care that occurs on a regular basis (e.g., once a week for 10 hours or more during a specified time period). *Center-based care* refers to any care that takes place in a group setting outside of a home and includes programs that are designed to enrich or provide early education to young children (e.g., Head Start or preschool).

Home-based care refers to care by nonrelatives or relatives in the child's or care-giver's home. It includes licensed and certified child-care homes as well as more informal arrangements.

For each child, we coded (a) any child care—whether the child had experienced any nonparental care during the follow-up period, (b) any center care, and (c) any home-based care. Center and home-based care were not mutually exclusive (i.e., children could have experienced center care only, home-based care only, or both). These child-care outcomes were measured during periods of 18 months to 2 years before the follow-up interview. Because the time elapsed since random assignment varied across studies, the children who had been less than 3 at random assignment were roughly between 1 and 5 years old during the period sampled in the follow-up. For those who had been less than 2 at the study onset, the follow-up sampled the period roughly between 1 and 4 years. Hence, the child-care experiences sampled include both the toddler and preschool years.

Average quarterly employment rates are derived from state unemployment insurance records and, thus, exclude any self-employment or employment that is not reported to an unemployment insurance agency in that particular state. To preserve the experimental design of the study, all sample members, both employed and not employed, were included in the analyses of child-care use.

Expanded Child-Care Assistance.   Although individual experimental studies permit causal conclusions about a particular intervention, the interventions being tested in most studies included multiple components, making it difficult to attribute specific effects to specific policy components. By drawing from a variety of welfare and antipoverty programs that had similar objectives, and in many cases had broadly similar economic effects on families, the present analyses allow some inferences about which components of policy influence child-care outcomes.

The treatments are evaluated in comparison with a control environment that included some child-care assistance. Prior to 1996, in the United States, recipients of AFDC were entitled to some child-care subsidies; working poor families not receiving welfare also received some subsidized care. In most instances, the subsidies were low in comparison with market rates, and parents were reimbursed through earnings disregards on their welfare grant, requiring them to pay for care and wait for reimbursement. Many parents lacked information or referral sources, and the application and recertification processes were time-consuming. Since 1996, subsidies have been available to low-income working parents, but not as an entitlement. States are required to give some priority to parents receiving or leaving welfare.

Some of the experimental programs in the studies we evaluate included *expanded child-care assistance*—a range of economic and administrative means designed to address parents' child-care needs more effectively than the existing system did. A review of study reports, field notes, and discussions with project directors and state staff indicated that three of the programs in the current analysis (New Hope, New Chance, and FTP) provided some type of child-care assistance that differed from that available to control group families (Gennetian et al., 2001). This policy component of expanded assistance for child care is a broad characterization of any one or a mix of the following subcomponents: (a) programmatic promotion of center-based care (New Chance provided free center care for participants, and New Hope increased access to subsidies for licensed or certified care by providing assistance to all families with incomes less than 200% of poverty who met the program's full-time work requirements); (b) case management and support services for child care (FTP provided child-care resource and referral agents at the site of the welfare office); (c) restriction of subsidy to regulated care; and (d) seamless subsidy system for transitions on and off welfare (FTP extended the time limit for use of transitional child-care benefits). The remaining two programs, CT Jobs-First and SSP, did not include any treatment differences in child-care assistance. That is, they offered the same level of child-care assistance available in the locality to all low-income parents irrespective of the research group status.[2] The standard child-care assistance available to all parents in program and control groups consisted of subsidies that covered all or most of the cost of child care up to some limit.

Table 4.1 organizes programs according to whether they had a treatment difference in child-care assistance and identifies the other key policy components of these same programs that were used to differentiate effects on adult economic outcomes (such as earnings) and child outcomes. More important, this table shows that the child-care policy imbedded in these welfare and employment programs does not coincide exactly with the other program components (e.g., mandatory employment services and earnings supplements), and thus provides new information about how individual programs differ. For example, some programs with expanded child-care assistance (e.g., New Hope and FTP) included earnings supplements, but SSP, with no expansion of child-care services, also offered an earnings supplement. Sorting programs according to whether they had expanded child-care assistance may be empirically useful in differentiating program effects on child-care outcomes.

---

[2]Note that, "on paper," the CT Jobs-First program offered child-care assistance to program group members until they reached 75% of the median state income, whereas control group members had access to transitional assistance for 1 year. In practice, however, there is no measurable difference between these two groups because control group members who reached the end of the transitional child-care period moved directly into the child-care certificate program that serves low-income working parents. For this reason, we consider CT Jobs-First to have no treatment differences in child-care policy.

TABLE 4.1
Key Policy Components That Differed Between
Program and Control Group Families

Program	Mandatory Employment Services[a]	Earnings Supplements[b]	Time Limits[c]	Youngest Child Age Exemption[d]
Programs that expanded child-care assistance compared with the control group				
New Hope		X		
New Chance	X			
FTP	X	X	X	X
Programs that offered the same child-care assistance as the control group				
CT Jobs-First	X	X	X	X
SSP		X		

[a]Mandatory employment services are requirements to participate in work or work-related activities such as education, training, or job search.

[b]Earnings supplements allow welfare recipients to receive more money for paid work, either by allowing them to keep more of their welfare benefits as their earned income increases or receiving an earnings supplement outside of the welfare system.

[c]Time limits place a cap on the number of months a person can receive welfare.

[d]Women whose youngest child is less than a set age are not subject to the welfare program's participation mandate.

To the extent that differences in child-care policy and practice between program and control group members make more types of child care accessible, available, or affordable for working poor families, they may directly affect the types of care arrangements used by parents and experienced by children. Consequently, child-care assistance policies as a component of welfare and employment programs may have more direct effects than do employment and income policies on the type of child care used.

RESULTS

Sample and Natural Variation in Child Care

The analyses were conducted on samples of children ages less than 3 at study entry; these children were between 1 and 5 years during the period in which child care is measured, with most of them being ages 1 to 3. Within this group, we also analyzed children who were less than 2 years old at study entry, but the sample sizes in this age group were small. All studies included children between 1 and 3 years of age at study entry, but only some of them included infants less than 1 year old.

Table 4.2 presents descriptive statistics on employment and child-care usage across these studies and sites. Average quarterly employment rates for control group members varied considerably from a low of 20% in the Canadian SSP study to a high of 67% in the New Hope study. Recall that New Hope study includes all working poor adults (i.e., it is not limited to welfare recipients). Child-care usage corresponds with employment rates, with roughly half of the SSP sample and nearly the entire New Hope sample using some kind of care for very young children. Consistent with what has been found in other research (e.g., see Ehrle, Adams, & Tout, 2001), use of home-based care is almost always higher than use of center care for these young children, a large group of whom are infants and toddlers. Rates of center-care use among those who used any care varied from 29% (in CT Jobs-First) to a high of 76% (in New Hope).

Policy Effects on Child Care for Very Young Children

Effects of Policies on Employment and Use of Care.

Figure 4.1 presents program impacts on employment and use of any child care. Each bar in these figures represents the *difference* between the average outcome, such as use of child care, for individuals in the program group and the average of this same outcome for individuals in the control group. The remaining two programs that offered the same child-care assistance to program and control groups are presented on the right. Statistical significance of these impacts is noted at the tops of the bars.

As shown in Fig. 4.1, expanded child-care assistance does not appear to influence employment or use of any child care for parents with very young children. Programs without expanded child-care assistance—CT Jobs-First and SSP—produced significant increases in employment and significant increases in the overall use of child care, as did one program with expanded assistance, FTP. That is, other program components, such as mandatory employment services or earnings supplements, appear to influence employment and overall use of child care. In New Hope, very high rates of child-care use by control group members (99%) precluded any substantial impact on child care despite the impacts on employment. In New Chance, child care was provided during parents' participation in educational activities as well as employment, so child-care use increased without a corresponding increase in employment. This pattern of effects is essentially identical for parents of children ages less than 2 at study entry (not shown). The use of child care does not appear to be strongly related to specific policies that increase income (e.g., the earnings supplement in the New Hope and SSP programs), time limits (e.g., FTP and

TABLE 4.2
Impacts on Average Quarterly Employment and Child-Care Use

Outcome	New Hope Control Group	New Hope Impact	New Chance Control Group	New Chance Impact	FTP Control Group	FTP Impact	CT Jobs-First Control Group	CT Jobs-First Impact	SSP Control Group	SSP Impact
Employment										
Average quarterly employment	67.4	10.4	64.8	-3.0**	46.8	6.7*	45.0	4.6	20.4	8.4***
Child Care										
Percentage using any care	99.0	0.2	83.7	11.1***	64.3	8.0*	48.0	11.6**	51.8	11.0***
Percentage using formal care	75.1	5.1	36.7	30.9***	29.1	5.9	14.1	-1.2	23.3	8.3***
Percentage using home-based care	75.3	-9.8	74.4	1.4	47.5	6.4	35.0	13.5**	36.3	7.3**
Among those who used any care:										
Percentage using formal care	75.9	5.0	43.8	27.4	45.2	3.2	29.4	-7.7	45.0	5.4
Percentage using home-based care	76.1	-10.1	88.8	-31.9	73.9	0.6	72.9	8.5	70.2	-0.6
n	99	99	627	1,129	193	177	164	163	421	407

Note. Child-care type categories are not mutually exclusive and therefore do not add up to 100%. Children were less than age 3 at study entry. Each study had either an 18- or 24-month follow-up; children were between 2 and 5 years old at the end of the follow-up.

*p < .10. **p < .05. ***p < .01.

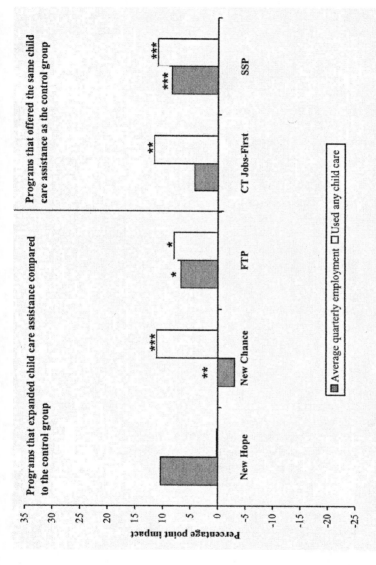

FIG. 4.1. Impacts on average quarterly employment and use of any child care.

NOTE: Children were less than age 3 at study entry. Each study had either an 18 or 24 month follow up; children were between 2 and 5 at the end of the follow up.

***p<0.01; **p<0.05; *p<0.10.

91

CT Jobs-First), or youngest child age exemptions (noting that parents of infants are universally exempted in these studies).

Effects of Policies on Type of Care Used and Other Characteristics of Care.
Figure 4.2 presents impacts on type of care used. The pattern of impacts in Fig. 4.2 somewhat supports the conclusion that programs with expanded child-care assistance increased the use of center care (relative to home-based care), whereas programs that offered no expansion of child-care assistance beyond that available to control group members show the opposite pattern. For children who were less than age 3 at study entry, this effect is particularly pronounced for the New Hope and New Chance programs, although impacts on center care were significant only for New Chance. Each of the New Chance sites that provided on-site care also showed a similar pattern of effects—increased center care and decreased or little change on home-based care. A site-by-site analysis of New Chance's effects shows that effects on center care were not as pronounced for those New Chance sites that offered only temporary on-site care or for those sites in which arrangements had to be made at a nearby child-care center (not shown). CT Jobs-First and SSP significantly increased home-based care, and these effects were larger than or almost as large as the effects on center care.

The lower graph shows an even cleaner pattern for children ages less than 2 at study entry. FTP significantly increased center care, and this effect was larger than the effect on home-based care.[3] In contrast, effects on use of home-based care were much larger than effects on use of center care in CT Jobs-First and SSP.

Duration and Stability.
Table 4.3 presents impacts on duration of care and stability of care based on information available in three of the studies with programs that had expanded child-care assistance. Although children in program group families were more likely than children in control group families to have spent at least some time in a nonmaternal care arrangement during the follow-up period, there are not consistent differences in the number of months children spent in care overall or in the stability of that care. Children in New Chance did spend 2.4 more months in a child-care arrangement over an 18-month period compared with children in the control group. Two of the three programs that had expanded child-care assistance—New Hope and New Chance—increased the number of months that very young children spent in center care, and New Hope decreased the number of months children

---

[3]The child-care outcomes constructed for FTP are derived from the child-care calendar collected during the 2 years prior to interview. Therefore, children who were less than 3 years old at study entry were, at a maximum, nearly 7 years old at the time of the interview (i.e., at the 48-month follow-up). Children less than 2 years old at study entry were, at a maximum, age 6 at the time of the interview, an age span that is closer in comparability to the other studies.

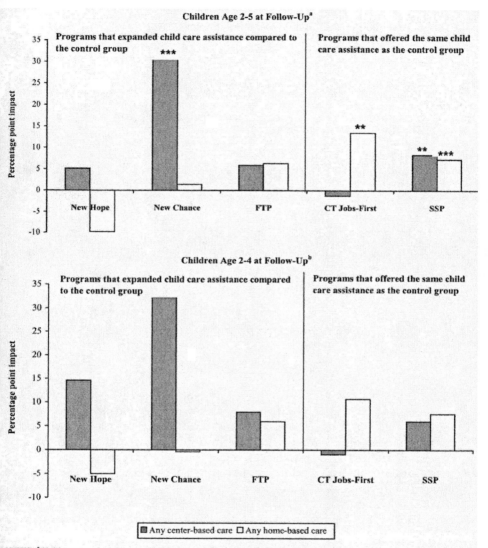

NOTES: [a]Children were less than age 3 at study entry. Each study had either an 18 or 24 month follow up; children were between 2 and 5 at the end of the follow up.

   [b]Children were less than age 2 at study entry. Each study had either an 18 or 24 month follow up; children were between 2 and 4 at the end of the follow up.

   ***$p < 0.01$; **$p < 0.05$; *$p < 0.10$.

FIG. 4.2.   Impacts on use of center- and home-based child care for very young children.

TABLE 4.3
Program Impacts on Duration and Stability

Outcome	New Hope Control Group	New Hope Impact	New Chance Control Group	New Chance Impact	FTP Control Group	FTP Impact
Number of months in any care	17.52	1.52	7.64	2.42***	12.80	1.53
Number of months in formal care	9.40	3.88***	2.54	2.54***	5.28	0.82
Number of months in home-based care	10.32	−2.45*	5.62	−0.05	8.62	0.42
In any care for 12 or more consecutive months (%)	—	—	—	—	54.98	−0.25
In formal care for 12 or more consecutive months (%)	—	—	—	—	18.8	1.94
n	204		1,673		370	

Note. Children were less than age 3 at study entry. Each study had either an 18- or 24-month follow-up; children were between 2 and 5 years old at the end of the follow-up.
*p < .10. **p < .05. ***p < .01.

spent in home-based care compared with children in control group families. There were no differences in impacts on our measure of stable care.

DISCUSSION AND CONCLUSIONS

Using data collected from a diverse set of experimental programs for low-income parents that took place from the late 1980s to the mid-1990s, we examine how welfare, employment, and child-care assistance policies affect the child-care decisions of parents with very young children. Comparing the outcomes of families in a control group, under the then-current policy environment, with the outcomes of families in a program group, under a new policy environment, offers a clean and direct test of the effects of policy. We expected that programs could affect child care directly via child-care assistance policies or indirectly via their effects on employment, income, or by affecting ties to the welfare system.

Although income and employment policies (e.g., earnings supplements and mandatory employment services) increased employment as well as the use of any child care, these same policies did not influence the type of care used by families. Rather, we find that it was the policies and practices specific to child care that affected parents' decisions to use center or home-based care for their very young children. None of these experimental evaluations of welfare programs was designed specifically to test child-care policies, but several of them included child-care policy features that went beyond the standard child-care assistance available to parents receiving AFDC/TANF or to other working parents with low incomes. These expanded child-care assistance policies included more generous subsidies, more convenient case work services, efficient reimbursement, restriction to regulated care, and seamless transitions in and out of the welfare system. Parents in programs offering such expanded assistance were more likely to use center-based care and less likely to use home-based arrangements for their toddlers and young preschool-age children.

The relation between expanded assistance and increased use of center care in welfare and employment programs has also been shown for children who were preschool age (3–5) or young school age (6–9) at study entry (Crosby, Gennetian, & Huston, 2005). Payment efficiency, supportive subsidies, seamless services, case management, and restricting subsidies to regulated care may have all contributed to the pattern of effects found in this study. By increasing parents' access to financial and nonfinancial supports for child care, expanded assistance policies expanded parental choices, making center care a more viable option, albeit not the only option. In fact it may be the presence of multiple care-related supports and services, including those that support employment and income in other ways besides child care, that led these programs to alter the types of care used for very young children. Additional analyses also show that these same programs did not increase the use of Head Start (Chang et al., 2001), suggesting that much of the increased use in center-based care was in day-care centers or, possibly, pre-K or nursery schools.

A complementary set of analyses further indicates that programs with expanded assistance increased the use of paid care and subsidies and decreased parents' out-of-pocket costs, particularly for families whose youngest child was less than age 3 at study entry (Gennetian, Crosby, Huston, & Lowe, 2004). That parents of very young children were somewhat more responsive to changes in child-care policy than parents of older children may reflect that center-based arrangements are more widely accessible and more commonly used for preschool- and school-age children (e.g., child-care centers, Head Start, state-sponsored pre-K, and afterschool programs) than for younger children, and that many parents believe center care is more appropriate for older children.

At the same time, there is little evidence to suggest that the welfare programs with expanded child-care assistance produced larger or more pronounced effects on employment, including more stable employment, as compared with the welfare programs that provided the same level of child-care assistance to program and control group families (Gennetian & Michalopoulos, 2003). With one exception, such programs also had few effects on child-care-related employment problems (Gennetian, Crosby, Huston, & Lowe, 2004). Broader and more generous targeting of child-care assistance may be important for achieving the goal of enhancing the stability of employment among low-income families. Furthermore, none of the expanded assistance policies in this set of programs was designed to help parents bridge multiple episodes of employment. Difficulty maintaining regular care arrangements because of features of the subsidy system (e.g., frequent recertification of eligibility), job loss, irregular work hours, or unreliable care arrangements may be particularly detrimental for the healthy development of very young children. Finally, center care does not fit the needs of many parents who work irregular and nonstandard hours.

What should we conclude from the fact that expanded child-care assistance policies *can* lead parents to use center care for their children while they are working? Is center care desirable? Both center and home-based care arrangements have possible advantages and disadvantages as supports for maternal employment and for children's well-being. Although parents might like the stability and predictability of center arrangements, these arrangements tend to be less flexible than home-based arrangements; centers typically do not offer evening or weekend hours, are less accommodating to schedules that fluctuate, and may not provide care for a child who is ill. Home-based care often plays an important role in families' efforts to piece together care that fits their needs (Lowe, Weisner, & Geis, 2003; Scott, Hurst, & London, 2003). A key challenge then is designing assistance policies that can accommodate families' diverse needs and preferences. At the same time, many of the informal and unregulated arrangements used by parents as a last resort may be inadequate or unsafe for children.

Unfortunately, the current data cannot adequately address whether children's increased exposure to center care resulted in higher quality arrangements. In recent work using sophisticated econometric techniques with the experimental data to estimate the effects of center care on children's well-being, we find that exposure to center-based care during a child's preschool years has a positive effect on school achievement in the early grades of elementary school (Gennetian, Crosby, Dowsett, & Huston, 2004). The limited number of studies with data on infants and toddlers prevents a similar analysis for this age group, highlighting the need for more research attention to the effects of child-care policy and different care arrangements on the development of infants and toddlers—particularly under the current welfare policy environment.

In designing child-care assistance policies, many policymakers have sought to facilitate parents' ability to work with less concern about supporting children's development. Supporting maternal employment and enhancing children's development are often competing policy goals, but low-income families and, by extension, all families would be best served if these were addressed in tandem (Huston, 2004). Parents seek arrangements that are affordable and can accommodate their employment situations, but they are also concerned about the effects of different employment and care situations on their children. Ethnographic data demonstrate that many parents do not hesitate to shift arrangements to meet their children's developmental needs (Knox et al., 2003; Lowe & Weisner, 2004). In the current study, increased resources and information enabled parents to select from a wider range of care options; for many, this translated into increased use of center-based care. Although further research (that includes direct tests of child-care policies) is clearly needed, our findings suggest that employment policies that include well-structured child-care assistance can help meet the needs of low-income parents, even those with very young children.

ACKNOWLEDGMENTS

This chapter is part of the Next Generation, a project that examines the effects of welfare, antipoverty, and employment policies on children and families. Many thanks to funders of these studies for access to the data and for providing feedback on earlier drafts of this chapter, in particular, Connecticut's Department of Social Services, Florida's Department of Children and Families, Human Resources Development Canada, Minnesota's Department of Human Services and the U.S. Department of Health and Human Services, Office of the Assistant Secretary for Planning and Evaluation (ASPE), and Administration for Children and Families (ACF). We also thank Dan Bloom, Hans Bos, Natasha Cabrera, Bruce Fuller, Irwin Garfinkel, Gayle Hamilton, Robert Hutchens, Sharon Lynn Kagan, Virginia Knox, Charles Michalopoulos, Pamela Morris, Elizabeth Peters, Phil Robins, Ruby Takanishi, and Marty Zaslow for helpful discussions and comments. An earlier version of this chapter was presented at "From Welfare to Child Care: What Happens to Infants and Toddlers When Single Mothers Exchange Welfare for Work?", a conference sponsored by Cornell University, The National Institute of Child Health and Human Development Family and Child Well-Being Network, and the Russell Sage Foundation.

REFERENCES

Blau, D. (2000). *Child care subsidy programs* (Working Paper 7806). Cambridge, MA: National Bureau of Economic Research.

Bloom, D., Kemple, J. J., Morris, P., Scrivener, S., Verma, N., & Hendra, R. (2000a). *The Family Transition Program: Final report on Florida's initial time-limited welfare program.* New York: MDRC.

Bloom, D., Melton, L., Michalopoulos, C., Scrivener, S., & Walter, J. (2000b). *Implementation and early impacts of Connecticut's welfare reform initiative.* New York: MDRC.

Bloom, D., & Michalopoulos, C. (2001). *How welfare and work policies affect employment and income: A synthesis of research.* New York: MDRC.

Bos, J., Huston, A., Granger, R., Duncan, G., Brock, T., & McLoyd, V. (1999). *New Hope for people with low incomes.* New York: MDRC.

Broberg, A., Wessels, H., Lamb, M. E., & Hwang, C. P. (1997). Effects of day care on the development of cognitive abilities in 8-year-olds: A longitudinal study. *Developmental Psychology, 33*(1), 62–69.

Capizzano, J., Adams, G., & Sonenstein, F. (2000). *Child care arrangements for children under five: Variation across states. Assessing the new federalism.* Washington, DC: The Urban Institute Press.

Casper, L. (1995). *What does it cost to mind our preschoolers?* (Current Population Reports, P-70, No. 52). Washington, DC: U.S. Bureau of the Census.

Chang, Y., Huston, A., Gennetian, L., & Crosby, D. (forthcoming). The effects of welfare and employment programs on children's participation in Head Start. *Economics of Education Review.*

Chaplin, D., Robins, P. K., Hofferth, S. L., Wissoker, D. A., & Fronstin, P. (1999). *The price elasticity of child care demand: A sensitivity analysis* (Working Paper). Washington, DC: The Urban Institute.

Coley, R., Chase-Landsdale, P. L., & Li-Grining, C. P. (2001). Child care in the era of welfare reform: Quality, choices, and preferences. *Welfare, Children and Families: A Three-City Study,* Policy Brief 01-4. Baltimore, MD: Johns Hopkins University.

Collins, A. M., Layzer, J. I., Kreader, J. L., Werner, A., & Glantz, F. B. (2000). *National Study of Child Care for Low-Income Families: State and community substudy interim report.* Washington, DC: U.S. Dept. of Health and Human Services, Administration for Children and Families.

Council of Economic Advisors. (1997). *The economics of child care.* Washington, DC: Author.

Crosby, D., Gennetian, L., & Huston, A. (2005). Child care assistance policies can affect the use of center-based care for children in low-income families. *Applied Developmental Science, 9*(2), 86–106.

Ehrle, J., Adams, G., & Tout, K. (2001). *Who's caring for our youngest children? Child care patterns of infants and toddlers* (Assessing the New Federalism Occasional Paper). Washington, DC: The Urban Institute.

Emlen, A., Koren, P. E., & Schultze, K. H. (1999). *From a parent's point of view: Measuring the quality of child care: Final report.* Portland, OR: Regional Research Institute for Human Services, Portland State University.

Fuller, B., Kagan, S. L., Caspary, G. L., & Gauthier, C. A. (2002). Welfare reform and child care options for low-income families. *The Future of Children, 12,* 97–119.

Gennetian, L., Crosby, D., Dowsett, C., & Huston, A. (2004). *Center-based care and the achievement of low-income children* (Working Paper). New York: MDRC.

Gennetian, L. A., Crosby, D. A., Huston, A. C., & Lowe, T. (2004). How child care assistance in welfare and employment programs can support the employment of low-income families. *Journal of Policy Analysis and Management, 23,* 723–743.

Gennetian, L., Gasman-Pines, A., Huston, A., Crosby, D., Chang, Y., & Lowe, T. (2001). *A review of child care policies in experimental welfare and employment programs* (Next Generation Working Paper). New York: MDRC.

Gennetian, L., & Michalopoulos, C. (2003). *Child care and employment: Evidence from random assignment studies of welfare and employment programs* (Next Generation Working Paper). New York: MDRC.

Greenberg, M. H., Levin-Epstein, J., Huston, R. Q., Ooms, T. J., Schumacher, R., Turetsky, V., & Engstrom, D. (2002). The 1996 welfare law: Key elements and reauthorization issues affecting children. *The Future of Children, 12,* 27–57.

Hofferth, S. L. (2001). Women's employment and care of children in the United States. In T. Van Der Lippen & L. Van Dijk (Eds.), *Women's employment in a comparative perspective* (pp. 151–174). New York: Aldine de Gruyter.

Howes, C. (1983). Caregiver behavior in center and family day care. *Journal of Applied Developmental Psychology, 4,* 99–107.

Huston, A. (2004). Childcare for low-income families: Problems and promises. In A. C. Crouter & A. Booth (Eds.), *Work-family challenges for low-income parents and their children* (pp. 139–164). Mahwah, NJ: Lawrence Erlbaum Associates.

Huston, A., Chang, Y., & Gennetian, L. (2002). Family and individual predictors of child care use by low-income families in different policy contexts. *Early Childhood Research Quarterly, 17*, 441–469.

Knox, V., London, A., Scott, E., & Blank, S. (2003). *Welfare reform, work and child care: The role of informal care in the lives of low-income women and children* (Next Generation Policy Brief). New York: MDRC.

Kontos, S., Hsu, H., & Dunn, L. (1994). Children's cognitive and social competence in child-care centers and family day-care homes. *Journal of Applied Developmental Psychology, 15*, 387–411.

Lamb, M. (1998). Nonparental child care: Context, quality, correlates and consequences. In I. E. Sigel & K. A. Renninger (Eds.), *Handbook of child psychology* (Vol. 4, 5th ed.). New York: Wiley.

Loeb, S., Fuller, B., Kagan, S., & Carol, B. (2004). Child care in poor communities: Early learning effects of type, quality and stability. *Child Development, 75*, 47–65.

Lowe, E. D., & Weisner, T. S. (2004). You have to push it—who's gonna raise your kids?: Situating child care in the daily routines of low-income families. *Children and Youth Services Review, 25*, 143–171.

Lowe, E. D., Weisner, T. S., & Geis, S. (2003). *Instability in child care: Ethnographic evidence from working poor families in the New Hope intervention* (Next Generation Working Paper). New York: MDRC.

Mezey, J., Greenberg, M., & Schumacher, R. (2002). *The vast majority of federally-eligible children did not receive child care assistance in FY 2000: Increased child care funding needed to help more families.* Washington, DC: Center for Law and Social Policy.

Michalopoulos, C., Card, D., Gennetian, L., Harknett, K., & Robins, P. K. (2000). *The Self-Sufficiency Project at 36 months: Effects of a financial work incentive on employment and income.* Ottawa: Social Research and Demonstration Corporation.

NICHD Early Child Care Research Network. (1996). Characteristics of infant child care: Factors contributing to positive caregiving. *Early Childhood Research Quarterly, 11*, 269–306.

NICHD Early Child Care Research Network. (1997). Poverty and patterns of child care. In G. J. Duncan & J. Brooks-Gunn (Eds.), *Consequences of growing up poor* (pp. 100–131). New York: Russell-Sage.

NICHD Early Child Care Research Network. (2000). The relation of child care to cognitive and language development. *Child Development, 71*, 960–980.

NICHD Early Child Care Research Network. (2001). Child care and common communicable illnesses: Results from the NICHD Study of Early Child Care. *Archives of Pediatrics and Adolescent Medicine.*

NICHD Early Child Care Research Network. (2002). Early child care and children's development prior to school entry: Results from the NICHD Study of Early Child Care. *American Educational Research Journal, 39*, 133–164.

NICHD Early Child Care Research Network. (2004). Type of child care and children's development at 54 months. *Early Childhood Research Quarterly, 19*, 203–230.

NICHD Early Child Care Research Network, & Duncan, G. J. (2003). Modeling the impacts of child care quality on children's preschool cognitive development. *Child Development, 74*, 1454–1475.

Phillips, D. A. (Ed.). (1995). *Child care for low-income families: A summary of two workshops.* Washington, DC: National Academy Press.

Quint, J. C., Bos, J. M., & Polit, D. F. (1997). *New Chance: Final report on a comprehensive program for young mothers in poverty and their children.* New York: MDRC.

Raikes, H. (1998). Investigating child care subsidy: What are we buying? *Social Policy Report, Society for Research in Child Development,* XII.

Schumacher, R., & Greenberg, M. (1999). *Child care after leaving welfare: Early evidence from state studies.* Washington, DC: Center for Law and Social Policy.

Scott, E. K., Edin, K., London, A., & Mazelis, J. (2001). My children come first: Welfare-reliant women's post-TANF views of work-family tradeoffs and marriage. In G. J. Duncan & P. L. Chase-Lansdale (Eds.), *For better and for worse: Welfare reform and the well-being of children and families* (pp. 132–153). New York: Russell Sage.

Scott, E., Hurst, A., & London, A. (2003). *Out of their hands: Patching together care for children when parents move from welfare to work* (Next Generation Working Paper). New York: MDRC.

Smith, K. (2000). *Who's minding the kids? Child care arrangements* (Current Population Reports P70-70). Washington, DC: U.S. Department of Commerce, Economics and Statistics Administration, U.S. Census Bureau.

U.S. Department of Health and Human Services. (1999). *Access to child care for low-income families.* http://www.acf.dhhs.gov/news/press/ccreport.htm

U.S. General Accounting Office. (1997). *Welfare reform: Implications of increased work participation for child care.* Report (HEHS-97-95) to the Ranking Minority Member, Subcommittee on Children and Families, Committee on Labor and Human Resources, U.S. Senate. Washington, DC: U.S. Government Printing Office.

U.S. House of Representatives, Committee on Ways and Means. (2000). *2000 Green Book.* Washington, DC: U.S. Government Printing Office.

Yoshikawa, H. (1999). Welfare dynamics, support services, mothers' earnings and child cognitive development: Implications for contemporary welfare reform. *Child Development, 70,* 779–801.

Zaslow, M. J., McGroder, S. M., Cave, G., & Mariner, C. L. (1999). Maternal employment and measures of children's health and development among families with some history of welfare receipt. In R. Hodson & T. L. Parcel (Eds.), *Research in the sociology of work: Vol. 7. Work and family* (pp. 233–259). Stamford, CT: JAI.

## CHAPTER FIVE

Work, Welfare, and Child-Care Choices Among Low-Income Women: Does Policy Matter?

Carlena K. Cochi Ficano
Hartwick College

H. Elizabeth Peters
Cornell University

Child-care policy has assumed national prominence both in response to the ongoing increases in labor force participation of low-income single mothers and as a result of the work requirements of the 1996 welfare reform and prior state welfare waivers. However, little is known about the extent to which welfare and child-care policies have affected change in child-care choice. The analysis in this chapter jointly models child-care, welfare, and employment choices among low-income single mothers with young children, controlling for child-care supply, state welfare and child-care policies, and child and maternal demographics. We specifically consider the time period from 1991 to 1995 when many states were experimenting with various welfare-to-work policies to capitalize on cross-sectional policy variation prior to the landmark 1996 Personal Responsibility Work Opportunities Reconciliation Act (PRWORA). Our data are drawn from the 1991 to 1993 panels of the Survey of Income and Program Participation. Our results show that policies matter only secondarily through work and welfare decisions. Our results also highlight the importance of child-care supply and work schedules in the child-care choices that mothers make.

INTRODUCTION

Child-care policy has assumed national prominence both in response to ongoing increases in the labor force participation of low-income single mothers (Blank et al., 2000) and as a result of the work requirements of the 1996 welfare reform and prior state welfare waivers. Between 1994 and 1998, labor force participation rates rose 25% for never-married mothers and 16% for mothers with an absent spouse (Bishop, 1998). By 2000, 73% of preschool-age children and nearly 80% of all children in female-headed households had a mother in the labor force (U.S. Department of Health and Human Services, 2001). At the same time, welfare rolls fell dramatically—from 14.1 million in 1993 to 7.3 million in 1999 (U.S. Department of Health and Human Services, 2000). An extensive literature is developing that analyzes the role of policies in changing welfare caseloads (Council of Economic Advisors, 1997, 1999; Figlio & Ziliak, 1999; Schoeni & Blank, 2000) and labor force participation (Bishop, 1998; Hotz, Mullin, & Scholz, 2000; Meyer & Rosenbaum, 1999; Nada & Lieberman, 1996; Schoeni & Blank, 2000). However, little is known about the extent to which welfare and child-care policies have affected behavioral change in child-care choice.

In this chapter, we address the question of how welfare work requirements and the welfare caseload decline have affected mothers' child-care choices. Both of these phenomena have increased the demand for child care and put pressure on the child-care supply. Because child care has important implications for child well-being, we are interested in exploring the child-care choices that low-income mothers made in response to the strict welfare-to-work policies for welfare recipients that began to be implemented in the early 1990s.

Our analysis jointly models child-care, welfare, and employment choices among low-income single mothers with young children. We control for child-care supply, state welfare and child-care policies and regulations, labor market policies such as the Earned Income Tax Credit (EITC), and child and maternal demographics. We specifically consider the time period from 1991 to 1995, when many states were experimenting with various welfare-to-work policies to capitalize on policy variation prior to the landmark 1996 Personal Responsibility and Work Opportunities Reconciliation Act (PRWORA). The data for our analysis are drawn from the 1991 to 1993 panels (covering the years from 1991–1995) of the Survey of Income and Program Participation (SIPP). The results show that welfare and labor market policies matter only secondarily through work and welfare decisions. We also find evidence that welfare and work status are endogenous, and that failing to model child-care, welfare, and work choices jointly will bias the estimated effect of AFDC on child-care choices. Finally, our results highlight the importance of child-care supply and work schedules in the child-care choices that mothers make.

Although in some ways the policy landscape and economic conditions have changed drastically since the time period covered in the data analysis, our results provide meaningful insight into contemporary child-care choice for a number of reasons. First, the 1996 welfare legislation that created the current Temporary Assistance for Needy Families (TANF) program incorporated many of the policy experiments that were in place in the early to mid-

1990s, including time-limited welfare benefits, substantially enhanced employment requirements, and extended transitional care. Second, the quantity and structure of child-care choices available to women today do not differ markedly from those available prior to the welfare overhaul. In general, local expansion in child-care supply has been slow and inconsistent (Ficano, 2004). Finally, despite a general upturn in economic conditions in the late 1990s, unemployment rates for low-income single mothers have remained at or above 10% since 1996 (Chapman & Bernstein, 2003). Like the individuals in our sample, low-income mothers today must negotiate the demands of welfare-work requirements in a context of limited employment opportunities and constrained child-care availability.

This chapter is organized as follows. First, it provides background on the policy and behavioral changes during the 1990s. Second, it outlines the theoretical framework and empirical model. Third, it describes the data. Fourth, it reports our empirical results. Finally, it presents our conclusions and directions for future work.

BACKGROUND

The policy environment facing low-income mothers with young children underwent major changes during the 1990s. The primary motivations for the policy changes were the intent to "encourage" employment among low-income mothers and reduce welfare dependency. Over 43 state waivers on AFDC policies were granted between 1990 and 1996, many of which limited exemption from work requirements (U.S. Department of Health and Human Services, 1997). In 1996, the system was completely overhauled with the landmark 1996 Personal Responsibility and Work Opportunities Reconciliation Act (PRWORA). In addition, the federal Earned Income Tax Credit (EITC) for the working poor expanded significantly over the same time period in an effort to make work pay. Some states also passed their own EITC to supplement the federal program. Finally, recognizing that the presence of young children represents an important barrier to successful, sustained employment, spending to support child care for those entering the job market increased from $1.7 billion to $5.2 between 1992 and 1998 (U.S. House of Representatives, 2000).

After changing very little during the preceding decade, in 1993, labor force participation rates among single mothers began to rise rapidly, increasing from about 65% in 1993 to more than 85% in 1998 (Blank, Card, & Robins, 2000). This increase in mothers' work activity also increased the demand for child care. In 1995, 57% of children less than age 5 were in some type of regular child-care arrangement while their mothers worked or attended school (Smith, 2000).

During the same time period (1994–1998), welfare participation rates declined by about 50% (Schoeni & Blank, 2000). The increase in labor force participation rates is partly related to the decline in welfare caseloads because employment is much more prevalent for those who are not on welfare. However, employment activities increased even among women on welfare. A report to Congress from the Administration on Children and Families documents a fivefold increase in employment activities of welfare recipients—from 7% of welfare recipients in 1992 to 33% of welfare recipients in 1999 (U.S. Department of Health and Human Services, 2000).

It is clear that decisions about welfare participation, work, and child-care use are linked, and policies that are directly targeted at one specific outcome have the potential to impact other outcomes as well. However, there is little research that analyzes the links among these three behaviors and policies.

A large literature examines the determinants of the welfare caseload decline (Council of Economic Advisors, 1997, 1999; Figlio & Ziliak, 1999; Schoeni & Blank, 2000). Although the numbers vary somewhat across the studies, Schoeni and Blank reported that about 15% of the decline can be explained by welfare policies and another 30% to 40% can be explained by the robust economy. Similarly, much of the research on the increase in single mothers' labor supply during the 1990s has focused on the role of the EITC (Hotz et al., 2000; Meyer & Rosenbaum, 1999; Nada & Lieberman, 1996). Meyer and Rosenbaum found that the EITC accounts for 37% of the increase in employment rates of single mothers from 1992 to 1996. Hotz et al. examined the effects of welfare policies and the EITC for California families on welfare. They found that these combined policies accounted for between 44% and 61% of the increases in employment for welfare recipients. Welfare leaver studies also document that the majority of those who exit the welfare rolls become employed sometime within a short period after leaving (Schumacher & Greenberg, 1999).

Until recently, the child-care literature has been largely separate from the welfare literature. Much of the research on child care and female labor supply has focused on middle-income women. There is a large literature that estimates the effect of child-care costs on female labor supply (Blau & Robins, 1988; Connolly, 1992; Heckman, 1974; Ribar, 1992). These studies all document that higher child-care costs significantly reduce the probability that a mother will work and the number of hours that she works. However, the magnitude of the effects differs substantially across the studies. There are several studies that examine the relationship between child-care costs and regulations and mothers' child-care choices (Blau & Hagy, 1998; Hotz, Kilburn, & Heeb, 2000). More closely related to the issues we address in this chapter is the research that examines the effects of child-care subsidies on female labor supply (Averett, Peters, & Waldman, 1997; Berger & Black, 1992; Blau & Tekin, 2000; Gelbach, 2002; Meyers, Heintze, & Wolf, 2002). This research generally finds that child-care subsidies increase employment.

As Blau and Tekin (2000) noted, methodological differences across studies have yielded a wide range of results. In particular, identification is difficult because labor supply depends on child-care availability and cost, and child-care choice depends on the same set of variables, so disentangling the causal pathways of these decisions is difficult.

One advantage of the welfare reform context is that it provides some leverage in trying to identify the causal links among labor supply, child-care costs, and choice of child care. Specifically, the EITC and welfare-to-work policies implemented in the 1990s provide strong incentives to work that are independent of child-care costs and availability. Other welfare eligibility rules have effects on the probability of welfare receipt, while the increase in child-care subsidies for the poor should affect child-care costs. These different policy levers provide plausible restrictions that allow us to identify the exogenous relationship among welfare receipt, labor supply, and child-care choice. Our approach in this chapter is unique in that we include welfare, labor market, and child-care policies, and environmental variables such as child-care supply and the child-care provider wages to estimate a model of the joint choice of welfare, employment, and child care.

EMPIRICAL MODEL

Although work, welfare, and child-care decisions are likely to be made jointly, to simplify estimation, we model the decisions as a recursive system in which work and welfare decisions are first made as a function of all exogenous variables. Child-care choices are then made conditional on welfare and work decisions, individual and child characteristics, child-care policies, and child-care costs. The exogenous variables include (a) family economic and demographic characteristics (X);[1] (b) child-care policies and regulations such as caregiver education requirements and adult–child ratios $(cc\ pol)$; (c) labor market policies and environment such as the EITC and the unemployment rate $(wrk\ pol)$; (d) welfare policies such as benefit levels, work requirements, and increased earnings disregards $(welf\ pol)$; and (e) characteristics of the child-care market such as center supply, state spending on child-care subsidies, and provider wages $(cc\ market)$. Documentation of the data sources for the policy and child-care market variables is available from the authors on request.

The structure we envision can be written as follows:

---

[1]Research shows that household living arrangements may be affected by policies (Moffitt, 1998), and these living arrangements can also affect the child-care choices of low-income women (e.g., through the availability of other adults in the household who could provide child care). It is beyond the scope of this chapter, however, to model these household structure decisions.

(1) Work   = f1(X, wrk pol, welf pol, cc pol, cc market)
(2) Welfare   = f2(X, wrk pol, welf pol, cc pol, cc market)
(3) cc choice = f3(X, wrk status, welf status, wrk schedule, cc pol, cc market)

Note that work and welfare are not mutually exclusive choices because some welfare recipients work and many nonworkers do not receive welfare. Welfare recipients have historically been much less likely to work partly because welfare income provides a substitute for earnings and partly because welfare rules traditionally discouraged work by taxing earnings at a high rate. However, recent welfare reforms have increased the likelihood that welfare recipients will work both by discouraging nonwork (e.g., reducing benefits for those who do not work) and encouraging work (e.g., allowing welfare recipients to keep a higher proportion of their earnings from work through an increase in the earnings disregard).

We expect the probability of welfare receipt to be positively related to welfare generosity and negatively related to restrictive policies that make welfare less attractive. Because those with high enough earnings become ineligible for welfare, receipt will also be negatively related to those individual, labor market, and policy variables that increase employment prospects and earnings. Similarly, the likelihood of employment will be positively related to the return from work (e.g., wage rates) and negatively related to the cost of work (e.g., child-care costs and availability). Work is generally negatively related to policies that make welfare more attractive, but, conditional on welfare, work is a function of welfare work-incentive policies.

Partly because of data limitations and partly for theoretical reasons, we estimate child-care choice only for working women.[2] This choice is modeled as a function of family economic and demographic characteristics, child-care policies, work schedules, and the child-care market. Welfare and labor market policies enter the child-care choice equation indirectly through their choice of work and welfare. However, it is likely that there are unmeasured characteristics that affect welfare, work, and child-care choice that we do not include in our analysis. For example, individuals with greater abilities or a great sense of responsibility may be more likely to work, less likely to be on welfare, and make better or different child-care choices. By not including those unmeasured characteristics in our analysis, the coefficients in the child-care choice model will be biased. To address this problem of endogeneity, we include predicted rather than actual welfare status. Problems of endogeneity or selection

---

[2]Hotz and Kilburn (1992) showed that child-care choices of workers follow a fundamentally different model from child-care choices of nonworkers. However, we cannot model the child-care choices of nonworkers because in all but the last wave of our data, child-care arrangements are asked only of women who are working, searching for work, or in school or training.

bias may also cause the estimated coefficients in the conditional child-care choice model to change as the sample of working women changes. We include predicted work status to account for selection effects.[3]

DATA DESCRIPTION

We use data from the 1991, 1992, and 1993 panels of the Survey of Income and Program Participation (SIPP). Each panel of SIPP is a nationally representative data set with sample sizes ranging from 14,000 to 20,000 households in the United States. The households are interviewed every 4 months over a 2½- to 3-year period (8–10 waves). Every household member 15 years and older is interviewed either by self-response or by proxy if that household member is not available. In addition to core information asked about household composition, demographics, income, labor force participation, and receipt of public transfers, each wave also includes additional modules that collect detailed information about specific topics (see http://www.sipp.census.gov/sipp for more information about SIPP). The topics covered by each module differ across waves, and some topical modules are repeated over time. The data used in this chapter come primarily from the child-care topical modules that were asked in Wave 3 of the 1991 panel, Waves 6 and 9 of the 1992 panel, and Waves 3, 6, and 9 of the 1993 panel. Our analysis treats the data as repeated cross-sections. The data from the three panels cover child-care choices made during 1991, 1993, 1994, and 1995. State- and time-varying measures of welfare, labor market, and child-care policies gathered from a variety of sources augment the individual-level SIPP data.[4] To account for inflation, all dollar amounts are converted to constant 1990 dollars.

We limit the analysis to a sample of low-income single mothers (or guardians) of a child less than age 5. We also eliminate cases in which the mothers or guardians are older than 55. Our *low-income* definition includes (a) households with income below 200% of poverty during the 4 months preceding the interview, or (b) households in which the mother (or guardian) is a current or former welfare recipient.

---

[3]Including predicted work status serves a similar purpose to the more standard Heckman selection correction term.

[4]We thank Ann Horvath-Rose and Joseph Hotz for their generous provision of welfare waiver and child-care regulation data, respectively. Ed Lazere and Nick Johnson of the Center on Budget and Policy Priorities were extremely helpful in providing data on state EITC policy. Additional EITC data were obtained from the Green Book (1998). We used information from (a) "Setting the Baseline: A Report on State Welfare Waivers" (U.S. Department of Health and Human Services, 1997) and supporting documents, (b) the Green Book (1992, 1994, 1996), and (c) "One Year After Welfare Reform" (Gallagher, Gallagher, Perese, Schreiber, & Watson, 1998) to code additional welfare waiver and child-care policy variables. Data on the supply of center care comes from the County Business Patterns data (U.S. Census Bureau, various years).

We divide the sample into *workers* and *nonworkers*. The working category includes households in which the mother (or guardian) reports that she is working, seeking work, or attending school in the reference period prior to the administering of the child-care topical module. The nonworking category includes a parallel set of low-income single mothers (or guardians) of children younger than age 5 in which the mother neither worked, attended school, nor looked for work in the reference period prior to the child-care topical module.

Child care is reported by mothers who were either working, in school, or searching for a job, and mothers are asked to report the primary child-care arrangement (i.e., the one used for the most hours) for each of their children in the household. Our analysis models the determinants of the primary child-care type that was reported for a child under the age of 5. If there is more than one preschool child in the household for which child care is reported, we randomly choose one of those children for our analysis. We classify child care into four different types: (a) center care (which also includes nursery school and head start), (b) family day care (which also includes any care outside the child's home by a nonrelative),[5] (c) relatives and inhome sitters, and (d) parental care (which includes both the mother caring for her child while she is at work and care by the child's father).

A central focus of our analysis is comparing the child-care choices of mothers with different AFDC statuses. We distinguish among (a) those who are currently receiving AFDC (*current recipient*); (b) those not currently receiving AFDC, but received AFDC within the past 2 years (*recent recipient*); and (c) those who never received AFDC or who received it more than 2 years before the interview (*not current or recent recipient*). We make these distinctions for two reasons. First, until 1996, there were separate child-care funding programs for each group. For example, current recipients were eligible to receive support from the AFDC child-care program, recent welfare recipients were eligible for transitional child-care money, while the at-risk child-care program provided funding for the nonwelfare working poor population. PRWORA combined those separate funds into one program—the Child Care Development Block Grant—in part to reduce disruptions that occurred when working mothers moved from one welfare status to another. However, although the welfare status distinctions are no longer explicit in child-care subsidy programs, studies have shown that states are most likely to target available funds to current welfare recipients (U.S. General Accounting Office, 1998). Thus, AFDC status may be an indicator for access to child-care subsidies.

---

[5]Except in 1993, the SIPP data do not allow us to distinguish between family day care (which is sometimes regulated) and other nonrelative care provided outside the child's home. We also include sitter care (nonrelative care in the child's home) in Category 3 because sitter care represents only about 2% to 3% of all care, which, given our sample size, is too low a frequency to be able to estimate with much precision.

Because child-care choices have important implications for child well-being (NICHD Early Child Care Research Network, 1999), we are interested in exploring the child-care choices that low-income mothers are making in response to the strict welfare-to-work policies for AFDC recipients that began to be implemented in the early 1990s. In addition, we want to understand the child-care consequences of the stricter eligibility requirements for welfare that pushed women off of welfare and into the labor force and contributed to the sharp decline in welfare caseloads during the 1990s.

The first panel of Table 5.1 reports the sample means by AFDC status. As expected, the data show that current welfare recipients are much less likely to work (13%)[6] than are recent recipients (71%) or not current or recent recipients (60%). Current recipients are, however, almost twice as likely to report being in school or undertaking job search activities (21%) than are women in either of the other two AFDC categories (11%). Conditional on working, the raw data do not show any large differences in child-care choices across the three groups, although there is some indication that women who are not current or recent recipients are a little less likely to use center care (30% vs. 33% and 35% for the other two groups).

Unfortunately, the 1991 to 1993 panels of SIPP do not provide any direct information about the use of child-care subsidies. However, when mothers report not paying for types of care that are generally paid care—specifically, center care and family day care—it may be reasonable to infer that the care is subsidized. The data show large differences across welfare status groups in degree to which mothers pay for center and family day care. Only 36% of current recipients who use center care pay any money for that care, compared with 69% and 75% of recent and never/not recent recipients, respectively. Similarly, 60% of current recipients who use family day care pay for that care, compared with 84% for the other two welfare status groups. These numbers provide evidence to support the common perception that, in the early 1990s, current welfare recipients were more likely to receive subsidies, and those subsidies were primarily available for center care use. More recent child-care policies in many states have removed some of the restrictions about the type of providers that parents can use to be eligible for subsidies. In addition, all three of our welfare status groups have, in theory, access to the same pot of child-care money, although Blau and Tekin (2000) found that in 1997, welfare recipients are still the most likely group to receive subsidies.

The economic and demographic differences across the three different AFDC categories are not surprising. Current recipients have slightly more and younger children. They are also more likely to be Black, have less nonearned

---

[6]This percentage is higher than what is reported in administrative data. However, other research has also found that survey reports of work by welfare recipients are higher than what is reported to welfare agencies (Harris, 1996).

TABLE 5.1
Weighted Sample Statistics by AFDC and Work Status

	AFDC Status			Work Status		
	Current Recipient	Recent[f] Recipient	Never/Not Recent Recipient	Currently Working	Job Search or School	Not in Labor Force or School
	Mean (SD)	Mean (SD)	Mean (SD)	Mean (SD)	Mean (SD)	Mean (SD)
Dependent variable—work:						
Working[a]	0.13	0.71	0.60			
Searching/school[a]	0.21	0.11	0.11			
Not working[a]	0.66	0.18	0.29			
Dependent variable—AFDC:						
Current recipient[a,f]				0.20	0.70	0.70
Recent recipient[a]				0.25	0.09	0.05
Not current or recent[a]				0.55	0.21	0.20
Dependent variable—child care:						
Center care[a]	0.35	0.33	0.30	0.34	0.30	
Center care paid[a,e]	0.36	0.69	0.75	0.71	0.31	
Family home/sitter care[a]	0.16	0.24	0.21	0.21	0.15	
Family home/sitter paid[a,e]	0.60	0.84	0.84	0.83	0.54	
Relative care[a]	0.41	0.37	0.42	0.38	0.46	
Relative care paid[a,e]	0.18	0.36	0.32	0.36	0.13	
Parental care[a]	0.08	0.06	0.07	0.07	0.09	
Household characteristics:						
# of other women > 18 in HH	0.58 (0.86)	0.77 (0.94)	0.65 (0.86)	0.59 (0.82)	0.74 (0.89)	0.58 (0.90)
# of other women > 65 in HH	0.04 (0.20)	0.05 (0.22)	0.05 (0.21)	0.05 (0.22)	0.05 (0.21)	0.04 (0.20)

Age of youngest child	1.94	2.15	2.08	2.30	1.89	1.94
	(1.32)	(1.28)	(1.34)	(1.30)	(1.27)	(1.31)
# of children ages 0–4	1.43	1.34	1.26	1.24	1.34	1.43
	(0.70)	(0.60)	(0.54)	(0.52)	(0.62)	(0.72)
# of children ages 0–18	2.82	2.56	2.55	2.37	2.71	2.82
	(1.51)	(1.52)	(1.51)	(1.38)	(1.54)	(1.57)
Household owns vehicle[a]	0.44	0.68	0.77	0.77	0.55	0.44
Nonlabor income ($000)[d,g]	2.23	2.75	2.75	2.16	3.02	2.23
	(3.91)	(3.95)	(3.30)	(3.30)	(4.36)	(3.80)
Mother's characteristics:						
Race = Not Black/Hispanic[a]	0.37	0.49	0.46	0.49	0.39	0.35
Race = Black Non-Hispanic[a]	0.42	0.34	0.35	0.36	0.45	0.40
Race = Hispanic[a]	0.21	0.17	0.19	0.15	0.16	0.25
Highest grade completed	10.97	11.60	11.74	11.99	11.34	10.97
	(2.13)	(2.12)	(2.26)	(2.08)	(2.06)	(2.20)
Mother's age	27.35	26.77	27.61	27.72	24.73	27.35
	(6.79)	(6.13)	(7.75)	(6.41)	(6.21)	(7.55)
Employment characteristics:						
Work part time (<20 hrs/wk)[a,c]	0.64	0.31	0.34	0.39		
Work traditional schedule[a,c]	0.63	0.68	0.69	0.67		
Weighted sample %	54.5	12.9	32.6	35.9	16.5	47.6
Sample size	1,193	298	743	811	364	1,059

[a]Dummy variable.
[b]Measured only for the working and school/job search sample.
[c]Measured only for the working sample.
[d]Reported in constant 1990 dollars.
[e]Proportion paying of those who use the specific type of child care.
[f]Did not receive welfare in current period, but did receive it within 24 months.
[g]Total income minus labor income minus welfare income.

income and education, and are less likely to have their own vehicle. In addition, conditional on working, they are somewhat less likely to work during traditional day-time hours (63% vs. 68%) and twice as likely to work part time.

The means by employment status, reported in the last three columns, are consistent with the large literature on female labor supply (Killingsworth, 1983). Single working mothers have fewer and older children and lower nonearned income. Two thirds of single working mothers work a traditional day-time schedule and only 39% work part time. Center and family day care are less likely and parental and relative care are more likely for single mothers who are in school or participating in job search, compared with those who are employed.

The period of our data is a time in which welfare and employment policies changed substantially. Because some states began to experiment with new welfare-to-work policies, the variation across states during that time period was also high. Figures 5.1a to 5.1d and Fig. 5.2 illustrate the changes in several of the policies we include in our analysis. The figures also show the amount of variation across states. Figure 5.1a shows that AFDC benefit levels declined slightly over time (primarily due to benefit levels being eroded by inflation). The variation across states in the maximum benefit guarantee is very large—ranging from over $900 a month in Alaska to less than $150 per month in Mississippi in 1990. This variation across states has remained fairly constant over time. The EITC, shown in Fig. 5.1b, is a national wage subsidy program for low-income workers. The figure shows large increases in the maximum EITC benefit over time—from $971 in 1990 to almost $1,800 in 1995. The variation across states is due to the few states that have their own EITC to supplement the federal program. The number of states with an EITC grew over time, increasing the cross-state variation in the late years.

Figures 5.1c and 5.1d show that child-care spending and center supply also increased over this time period. The number of centers per 1,000 preschool children increased by about 20%—from 2.3 to 2.8. The figure also shows sub-

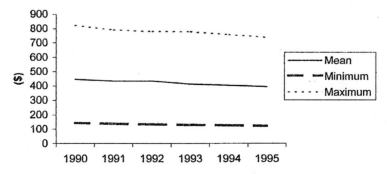

FIG. 5.1a.   Real maximum state AFDC guarantee, 1990–1995. *Source:* Green Book, 1998.

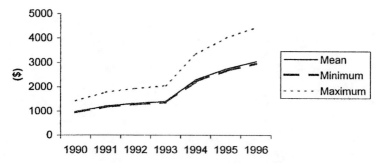

FIG. 5.1b.   Maximum combined state and federal EITC benefits (two children). *Source:* Green Book, 1998; Center on Budget and Policy Priorities.

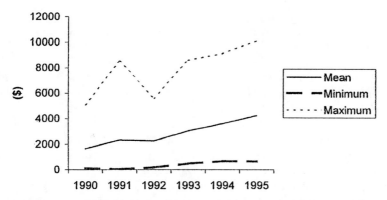

FIG. 5.1c.   Real child-care spending per child less than age 5 in poverty. *Source:* Green Book, 1998.

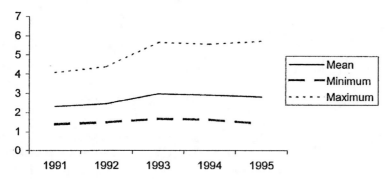

FIG. 5.1d.   Child-care centers per 1,000 children less than age 5. *Source:* County Business Patterns, various years.

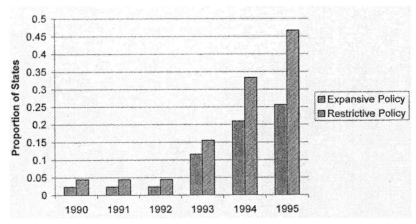

FIG. 5.2. AFDC policy variation, 1990–1995. *Source:* Author's calculation
from data available through U.S. Department of Health and Human Services
(see Appendix Table I for description of "expansive" and "restrictive" policy).

stantial variation across states, ranging, in 1995, from less than 1½ centers per
1,000 preschool children in Utah to almost 6 centers per 1,000 preschool children in Washington, DC. State child-care spending increased by about 150%
over the period—from $1,700 per 1,000 poor children less than age 5 in 1990 to
$4,200—and the gap between the highest and lowest states also increased.

This period was also the time when a large number of states applied for
waivers from federal AFDC rules. In an effort to encourage work, some
states made it more attractive to be on welfare by allowing workers to keep
more of their earnings without welfare benefits being lowered. Other states
took the "stick" approach and sanctioned (i.e., reduced benefits) recipients
who did not work after a specified period of time. Figure 5.2 shows the proportion of states with either expansive or restrictive welfare waivers (note
that a state could implement both restrictive and expansive policies). By
1995, there were twice as many states with restrictive policies as there were
states with expansive policies.

MULTIVARIATE RESULTS

As outlined earlier, the first step in our analysis is to estimate work and welfare
choices. Because we have classified each of these choices into three separate
categories, we use a multinomial logit model. Columns 1 and 2 of Table 5.2 report the results of the multinomial logit analysis of the outcomes *currently
working* and *job search / school* (the reference category is *not in the labor force or in
school*). The results are reported as exponentiated coefficients, where a value
greater than 1 indicates a positive relationship and a value less than 1 indicates

TABLE 5.2
First-Stage Work (Base = Not Working) and AFDC
(Base = Never or Not Recent Recipient) Multinomial Logit Equations
(Exponentiated Coefficients, e^{β}, presented)

	Work Equation		AFDC Equation	
	Currently Working	School/Job Search	Current AFDC Recipient	Recent AFDC Recipient
Household characteristics:				
# of other women > 18 in HH	1.08	0.94	0.94	1.22
	(0.92)	−(0.61)	−(0.74)	(1.92)
# of other women > 65 in HH	0.789	1.04	1.44	1.22
	−(0.95)	(0.16)	(1.49)	(0.61)
Age of youngest child in HH	1.33	1.17	0.96	1.10
	(6.55)	(2.98)	−(0.91)	(1.66)
Number of children ages 0–4	0.74	0.81	1.44	1.20
	−(3.27)	−(2.02)	(4.14)	(1.49)
Number of children ages 13–18	1.22	1.31	0.74	0.80
	(2.53)	(3.15)	−(4.43)	−(2.36)
Household owns vehicle[a]	4.55	1.53		
	(11.89)	(2.88)		
Nonlabor income ($000)[c]	0.92	0.99	0.97	0.98
	−(4.81)	−(0.41)	−(2.31)	−(0.89)
Mother's characteristics:				
Race = Black Non-Hispanic[a]	0.87	1.23	1.76	0.89
	−(1.01)	(1.26)	(4.48)	−(0.89)
Race = Hispanic[a]	1.15	1.103	1.11	1.08
	(0.83)	(0.48)	(0.67)	(0.34)
Highest grade completed	1.31	1.18	0.82	0.95
	(9.05)	(4.52)	−(7.54)	−(1.48)
Mother's age	1.16	0.88	0.99	0.98
	(2.50)	−(1.74)	−(1.50)	−(2.00)
Mother's age squared	1.00	1.00		
	−(2.93)	(0.69)		
Child-care regulations:				
Family child:caregiver ratio (infants)	1.15	0.94	0.89	0.93
	(2.21)	−(0.83)	−(1.92)	−(0.82)
Family home # of annual inspections	1.04	1.00	1.02	1.21
	(0.36)	(0.03)	(0.22)	(1.48)
Family home teacher required education ≥ 12 years[a]	0.69	1.26	1.27	1.48
	−(1.24)	(0.66)	(0.85)	(1.00)
Immunizations required: family home[a]	1.16	1.05	1.36	0.88
	(0.57)	(0.16)	(1.29)	−(0.37)

(Continued)

115

TABLE 5.2

(Continued)

	Work Equation		AFDC Equation	
	Currently Working	School/Job Search	Current AFDC Recipient	Recent AFDC Recipient
Child-care market/availability:				
Real child-care worker hourly wage[c]	0.99	0.85	1.10	1.04
	−(0.08)	−(1.74)	(1.27)	(0.40)
Centers per 1,000 children < 5	1.25	0.92	0.80	1.00
	(1.78)	−(0.55)	−(1.89)	−(0.03)
State CC spending per 1,000 children	1.00	1.07	1.08	1.08
< 5 in poverty ($000)[c]	−(0.05)	(1.03)	(1.51)	(1.22)
Welfare policy:				
Real maximum AFDC guarantee	0.84	1.42	1.44	1.29
($00)[c]	−(1.70)	(2.79)	(3.52)	(1.87)
State policy expansive[a,d]	1.38	1.34	1.16	1.26
	(1.55)	(1.18)	(0.73)	(0.84)
State policy restrictive[a,e]	1.00	0.88	0.78	0.72
	−(0.03)	−(0.60)	−(1.53)	−(1.47)
JOBS draw down[f]	1.00	1.00	1.00	1.00
	(0.90)	−(0.61)	−(0.59)	(0.73)
Economic conditions/policy:				
Maximum combined state/federal	1.00	1.00	1.00	1.00
EITC ($00)[c]	(1.07)	(0.39)	(0.23)	−(0.65)
State EITC refundable[a]	2.62	1.07	0.51	0.61
	(2.40)	(0.14)	−(1.81)	−(0.88)
Low unemployment rate[a,b]	1.16	1.20	1.11	1.39
	(0.77)	(0.85)	(0.58)	(1.41)
High unemployment rate[a,b]	1.11	1.01	1.10	1.25
	(0.55)	(0.03)	(0.57)	(0.89)
Interview year (base = 1991):				
1993[a]	0.82	2.09	2.17	2.48
	−(0.86)	(2.49)	(3.53)	(2.75)
1994[a]	0.51	1.54	1.68	3.69
	−(1.07)	(0.64)	(0.88)	(1.57)
1995[a]	0.85	2.38	1.38	6.51
	−(0.20)	(0.93)	(0.39)	(1.62)
Region (base = E.N. Central):				
East South Central[a]	0.78	3.35	1.27	0.85
	−(0.59)	(2.46)	(0.62)	−(0.30)
Mid-Atlantic[a]	0.62	0.68	0.40	0.25
	−(1.72)	−(1.18)	−(3.74)	−(3.55)
Mountain[a]	1.92	0.75	0.36	0.47
	(2.08)	−(0.74)	−(3.45)	−(2.02)
New England[a]	0.63	0.60	0.46	0.22
	−(1.03)	−(0.98)	−(1.84)	−(2.44)
Pacific[a]	1.14	0.61	0.35	0.32
	(0.39)	−(1.24)	−(3.27)	−(2.66)

(Continued)

TABLE 5.2
(Continued)

	Work Equation		AFDC Equation	
	Currently Working	School/Job Search	Current AFDC Recipient	Recent AFDC Recipient
Region (base = E.N. Central): *(cont.)*				
South Atlantic[a]	1.16	1.63	1.05	1.19
	(0.54)	(1.48)	(0.18)	(0.47)
West North Central[a]	0.81	0.98	0.90	0.53
	−(0.60)	−(0.04)	−(0.31)	−(1.33)
West South Central[a]	1.29	2.25	1.23	1.12
	(0.74)	(1.87)	(0.63)	(0.26)
N = 2,234	Pseudo R^2 = 0.145		Pseudo R^2 = 0.079	

Note. Z statistics in parentheses. The exponentiated coefficients of dummy independent variables may be interpreted directly as proportional odds. The exponentiated coefficients of continuous independent variables must first be logged to provide the same interpretation. Child-care regulation variables jointly significant at $p = .102$ in current AFDC equation, but insignificant in all other first-stage models.

[a]Dummy variable.

[b]High unemployment = 1 for states above the 75th percentile; low unemployment = 1 for states below the 25th percentile.

[c]Reported in constant 1990 dollars.

[d]State has extended transitional care and/or enhanced earnings disregard.

[e]State has sanctions for JOBS noncompliance and/or age of youngest child work exemption ≤ 12 months for part-time participation.

[f]Federal share of JOBS expenditures as a percent of JOBS allocation.

a negative relationship. In the case of dichotomous (dummy) independent variables, the coefficients indicate the proportional increase in the odds of a given outcome for individuals possessing the characteristic in question (i.e., a coefficient value of 1.5 on a race variable indicates that those of the given race have 50% higher odds of experiencing the outcome than those in the omitted category). For continuous independent variables, the natural log of the coefficients indicates the proportional change in the odds of a given child-care choice from a one-unit change in the variable (i.e., a coefficient value of 3.5 on a continuous variable indicates that the odds of experiencing the outcome are ln[3.5] or 1.25 times higher for each unit increase in the variable).

The analysis of work shows very standard results that mirror the distinctions shown in the means table. Women with older children and fewer younger children are more likely to work. As the economic theory of labor supply predicts, working is less likely for women with higher nonearned income, and the likelihood of work increases with age, but at a decreasing rate.

Child-care policy, cost, and availability variables are included because child care represents a cost to work, and we expect the likelihood of work to be negatively related to the cost of child care. Child-care supply positively and significantly affects work outcomes as evidenced by the odds ratio of 1.25. The child-care regulation variables are difficult to interpret because they reflect both cost of care (negatively related to work) and quality of care (positively related to work).[7] The child-care worker wage is negatively related to both the probability of working and the probability of school or job search (although the coefficient for the choice of working is not significant at conventional levels). Higher paid child-care workers could reflect higher quality. However, because wage compensation is the major component of child-care cost, the negative coefficient on child-care wages is consistent with the argument that higher child-care costs lower work activities.

Our results also show that employment is lower in states with more generous welfare benefits. Notably, work is positively affected by employment-supporting policies, but unaffected by the implementation of stricter eligibility and employment requirements, consistent with the notion that "carrots" appear to be more effective than "sticks" in fostering employment outcomes. In contrast to other studies, we do not find that more generous EITC benefits significantly increase work.[8] However, we do find that state refundable EITC benefits are positively and significantly related to the choice of work. A surprising result is the lack of significant association between the probability of work and the tightness of the labor market. Finally, the steadily increasing year effects mirror the increase in employment over time documented in other data.

With the exception of the size of the welfare guarantee and mother's age, the coefficient estimates for the school/job search choice (Column 2) are generally similar, although slightly smaller in magnitude, to the coefficient estimates for the currently working category. The notable positive impact of AFDC guarantee levels on schooling choice provides some evidence that AFDC may be used by low-income women to subsidize education and/or training. The negative (and marginally significant) effect of mother's age on school choice is not surprising because we expect that education and job search are precursors to employment. Also theory tells us that human capital investment, such as schooling and job search, are most beneficial if undertaken at earlier ages. The differences between working and school/job search are likely to be related to the different number of hours spent in each activity, the schedule of the activity (e.g., traditional vs. nontraditional hours), and the subsequent differences in child-care choice.

---

[7]Center and family day-care regulations are highly correlated within a state. Because of this multicollinearity problem, our regressions only include the family day-care regulations.

[8]Because the primary variation in EITC generosity during this period was over time rather than across states, any effect of increased EITC generosity may already be captured in the year dummies that are included in the regressions.

Columns 3 and 4 of Table 5.2 show the coefficient for the current AFDC recipient and recent AFDC recipient outcomes (the reference category is not current or recent). Most of the economic and demographic relationships are consistent with our expectations. Welfare recipiency falls with mother's education and age and is more likely for Blacks. Having more younger children increases the likelihood of being a current recipient while having more older children decreases it, consistent with the idea that AFDC may be used to subsidize own care of preschool-age children. The negative relationship between nonearned income (and, similarly, number of adult women in the household) and current welfare receipt is likely to be related to welfare rules that count the income of other household members (both related and unrelated) in determining welfare eligibility.

Welfare policy variables are strong predictors of the likelihood of current welfare receipt. An increase of $100 in the maximum benefit guarantee is associated with a 34.6% increase in the odds of welfare receipt (ln[1.441] = .346). Our welfare regressors also include indicators for whether a state had any welfare waiver that expanded welfare eligibility (e.g., increasing the earned income disregard to make it easier to work and be on welfare) and whether a state had a waiver making welfare more restrictive (e.g., work requirements and welfare sanctions for nonwork).[9] Our results indicate that living in a state with a restrictive welfare waiver reduces the odds of being a current recipient by 22.4% (1 − .776 = .224), and living in a state with an expansive welfare waiver increases the probability of welfare receipt by 15.5%. Note, however, that neither coefficient is precisely estimated.

Labor market policies that reward work appear to have some effect on welfare status. In particular, women living in states with a refundable state EITC are less likely to be both current and recent welfare recipients.[10] It is surprising that the business cycle (unemployment rates) does not significantly the probability of current AFDC in our analysis. However, it is possible that variation in unemployment rates across states are not important in predicting welfare receipt, and variation over time in the business cycle is captured by our year indicators. Consistent with other studies, the year dummies show that welfare receipt reached its peak in 1993 and subsequently began to decline.[11]

Many of the predictors of recent welfare receipt are similar to the predictors of current welfare receipt. This is to be expected if individual and state characteristics are correlated over time. Recent welfare receipt is greater for younger women and for those with more young children. Welfare policy variables also have some effect on recent receipt (compared with never or not re-

---

[9]Note that states can have both restrictive and expansive policies.

[10]The federal EITC is refundable, but some states who have an additional state EITC do not make their portion refundable.

[11]Aggregate caseload data show that the peak actually occurred in 1994. In our sample, the SIPP data for 1993 refer to the last quarter of the year.

cent receipt), but the coefficients are generally smaller in magnitude and less precisely estimated. The pattern of year results shows that the probability of being a recent welfare recipient increased steadily from 1993 to 1995. This result is consistent with the steady decline in welfare caseloads caused, in part, by increasing welfare exits.

Regional controls indicate significant variation in welfare behavior, with Mid-Atlantic, Mountain, New England, and Pacific states experiencing lower odds of current and recent recipiency relative to East North Central states. This likely reflects unmeasured differences in both beliefs toward public assistance and regional AFDC policy. Patterns of regional variation in work behavior are less obvious, although significant variation does exist.

Table 5.3 shows the results of the child-care choice equations estimated for the sample of working (including school/job search activity) women. The columns on the left present the results when we include predicted AFDC and work status to account for the problem of endogeneity discussed earlier, and the columns on the right present the model that includes actual AFDC and work status (work vs. searching/school). The predicted values of AFDC and work status are calculated for each individual using the coefficients in Table 5.2. To identify the AFDC effects, we need to find variables that are expected to affect AFDC participation, but only affect child-care choice indirectly through AFDC status. In Table 5.2, we saw that welfare policy variables were strong predictors of AFDC status, and these are unlikely to directly affect the type of child care chosen. Similarly, to identify the work selectivity effect, we need to find variables that will affect the probability of work, but not the type of child care chosen. The EITC and welfare work requirements are reasonable candidates for identifying instruments.

Focusing on the first three columns, our results show that older children are more likely to be in center care ($\ln[1.536] = 1.429$ or a 42.9% increase in odds per year of age), compared with the reference category of parental care. The odds of relative care over parental care are higher in households with more adult females ($\ln[1.583] = 1.459$ or 45.9% higher per additional female). Patterns by race and ethnicity also mirror the results of other studies. Compared with Whites, Blacks and Hispanics are more likely to choose center and relative care over parental care, but not significantly more likely to choose family day care.

Work characteristics are an important predictor of child-care choice. Women who work a traditional day-time schedule are more likely to use center and family day care—modes of child care that are primarily available during day-time hours. Working a traditional schedule more than doubles the odds of center and family day care. This result is important because as current or former welfare recipients have entered the labor force, they more often find jobs with nontraditional schedules, which constrain their child-care choices. An argument that is sometimes made is that work schedule is endogenous and

TABLE 5.3

Second-Stage Child-Care Choice Multinomial Equations

(Base = Parental Care) With Actual and Predicted Work, AFDC Status

(Exponentiated Coefficients, e^β, Presented)

	Predicted AFDC/Work Status			Actual AFDC, Work Status		
	Center Care	Family Home/Sitter	Relative Care	Center Care	Family Home/Sitter	Relative Care
Predicted)/Actual values:						
(Probability of) Current work[a]	0.53	0.43	0.56	0.51	1.38	1.12
	−(0.31)	−(0.39)	−(0.29)	−(1.62)	(0.76)	(0.30)
(Probability of) Search/ school[a]	4.83	1.77	0.21			
	(0.51)	(0.18)	−(0.52)			
(Probability of) Current AFDC[a]	0.02	0.06	0.10	1.89	1.17	1.08
	−(1.65)	−(1.12)	−(0.99)	(1.95)	(0.46)	(0.24)
(Probability of) Recent AFDC[a]	80.44	0.66	1.56	1.82	1.43	1.11
	(1.45)	−(0.13)	(0.15)	(1.69)	(0.98)	(0.31)
Household characteristics:						
Age of child	1.54	0.99	1.08	1.70	0.98	1.09
	(3.08)	−(0.05)	(0.55)	(5.11)	−(0.15)	(0.90)
# of other women > 18 in HH	0.76	1.00	1.58	0.93	1.05	1.73
	−(1.11)	−(0.01)	(1.94)	−(0.32)	(0.20)	(2.59)
# of other women > 65 in HH	1.68	0.34	1.26	1.34	0.30	1.10
	(0.81)	−(1.33)	(0.38)	(0.47)	−(1.48)	(0.17)
Number of children ages 0–4	1.70	1.06	0.84	1.19	0.87	0.73
	(1.52)	(0.15)	−(0.53)	(0.74)	−(0.56)	−(1.35)
Number of children ages 13–18	0.88	0.83	1.06	1.14	1.00	1.13
	−(0.47)	−(0.63)	(0.22)	(0.70)	−(0.01)	(0.69)
Household owns vehicle[b]	1.78	1.67	1.53	1.86	1.38	1.44
	(0.93)	(0.80)	(0.71)	(1.96)	(0.97)	(1.20)
Nonlabor income ($000)[c]	0.961	0.981	0.984	1.007	1.015	1.003
	−(0.73)	−(0.34)	−(0.31)	(0.17)	(0.37)	(0.07)
Mother's characteristics:						
Race = Black non-Hispanic[b]	3.16	1.40	2.56	1.72	1.07	1.84
	(2.62)	(0.73)	(2.17)	(1.75)	(0.22)	(2.03)
Race = Hispanic[b]	2.40	2.15	3.06	2.28	2.11	3.00
	(1.83)	(1.57)	(2.41)	(1.73)	(1.54)	(2.38)
Highest grade completed	0.94	0.89	0.90	1.13	0.96	0.95
	−(0.42)	−(0.81)	−(0.81)	(1.80)	−(0.68)	−(0.80)
Mother's age	1.00	0.99	0.97	0.98	0.99	0.99
	−(0.12)	−(0.38)	−(0.82)	−(0.74)	−(0.61)	−(0.58)
Work characteristics:						
Part time (< 20 hrs/wk)[b]	0.92	0.60	0.73	1.16	0.58	0.71
	−(0.29)	−(1.77)	−(1.16)	(0.47)	−(1.68)	−(1.11)
Traditional schedule[b]	2.13	2.51	1.09	3.41	2.12	1.06
	(2.80)	(3.27)	(0.33)	(3.79)	(2.29)	(0.19)

(Continued)

TABLE 5.3
(Continued)

	Predicted AFDC/Work Status			Actual AFDC, Work Status		
	Center Care	Family Home/Sitter	Relative Care	Center Care	Family Home/Sitter	Relative Care
Child-care regulations:						
Family child:caregiver	0.94	0.91	0.81	0.98	0.95	0.85
ratio (infants)	−(0.61)	−(0.85)	−(2.00)	−(0.19)	−(0.48)	−(1.68)
Family home # of an-	1.16	1.22	0.94	1.44	1.28	1.04
nual inspections	(0.76)	(0.95)	−(0.30)	(2.04)	(1.35)	(0.25)
Family home teacher re-						
quired education ≥ 12	2.39	1.28	1.54	3.43	1.36	1.71
yrs[b]	(1.54)	(0.41)	(0.78)	(2.20)	(0.53)	(0.99)
Immunizations required:	0.28	0.35	0.41	0.17	0.31	0.34
family home[b]	−(1.69)	−(1.33)	−(1.17)	−(2.45)	−(1.54)	−(1.49)
Child-care market/availability:						
Real child-care worker	1.43	1.19	1.07	1.21	1.12	1.02
hourly wage[c]	(2.50)	(1.18)	(0.50)	(1.91)	(1.13)	(0.22)
Centers per 1,000 chil-	1.81	1.17	1.52	2.22	1.25	1.62
dren < 5	(2.29)	(0.58)	(1.64)	(3.36)	(0.90)	(2.10)
State CC spending per						
1,000 children < 5 in	0.78	0.80	0.67	0.76	0.78	0.66
poverty ($000)[c]	−(2.46)	−(2.17)	−(3.89)	−(3.03)	−(2.49)	−(4.43)
Welfare policy:						
Extend transitional CC	0.53	1.07	0.55	0.62	0.97	0.51
benefit[b]	−(1.35)	(0.15)	−(1.31)	−(1.07)	−(0.08)	−(1.58)
JOBS draw down[d]	1.00	1.01	1.00	1.00	1.01	1.00
	−(0.12)	(0.70)	(0.04)	(0.57)	(1.04)	(0.42)
Interview year (base = 1991):						
1993[b]	1.15	1.08	1.43	0.92	0.83	1.07
	(0.27)	(0.14)	(0.73)	−(0.18)	−(0.40)	(0.16)
1994[b]	1.48	0.93	1.79	1.51	0.81	1.56
	(0.79)	−(0.15)	(1.22)	(0.88)	−(0.45)	(0.99)
1995[b]	1.08	1.91	1.76	1.94	1.79	1.66
	(0.10)	(0.84)	(0.77)	(1.12)	(0.97)	(0.87)
$N = 1,173$		Pseudo-R^2 = .119			Pseudo-R^2 =.125	

Note. Z statistics are in parentheses. The exponentiated coefficients of dummy independent variables may be interpreted directly as proportional odds. The exponentiated coefficients of continuous independent variables first must be logged to provide the same interpretation. Child-care regulation variables are jointly significant at $p = .015$ in center care choice model with *actual* AFDC status, but insignificant in all other choice models.

[a]Actual values (Columns 4–6) are dummy variables. Predicted values are calculated from the appropriate regression in Table 5.2, and values range from 0 to 1 inclusive.

[b]Dummy variable.

[c]Measured in constant 1990 dollars.

[d]Federal share of JOBS expenditures as a percentage of JOBS allocation.

should not be included in a reduced form analysis of child-care choice. For example, women may choose their job schedules to facilitate care by the child's father or another relative. However, studies have shown that when mothers are asked why they work a particular schedule, they rarely report that it is because of child-care scheduling concerns. In addition, recent empirical tests for the endogeneity of job schedule fail to reject exogeneity of that variable (Kimmel & Powell, chap. 6, this volume). Finally, welfare work requirements may limit the choices that mothers have about what hours to work. Often the only jobs available to low-skilled workers are during nontraditional hours. This argument supports the idea that changes in the probability of having a traditional schedule are most likely due to exogenous events. Nevertheless, we test the importance of treating work schedule as an endogenous variable by estimating a similar child-care choice model that leaves work schedule out of the regression. Our results are robust to the exclusion of work schedule, so we conclude that the possibility of endogeneity of work schedule is not a serious concern.

The child-care market variables are all significant predictors of center care. The strongest result, and one that is consistent across different specifications, is the effect of the supply of center care. For every increase of one center per 1,000 children less than 5 in the state, the odds of center care increase by 59.3% ($\ln[1.809] = 1.593$). This result is consistent with previous work (Gordon & Chase-Lansdale, 2001), which links choice to availability at the zip code level. It has been argued that this relationship could be due to tastes for center care driving supply rather than the reverse. To examine the empirical significance of this argument, we ran a specification in which we included child-care supply that is lagged 1 year (lagged supply is unlikely to be driven by tastes one period later). Our results are robust to the inclusion of lagged rather than contemporaneous supply, indicating that reverse causation is not an important problem here.

The other two child-care market results are more puzzling. We find that center care is more likely to be chosen in states with higher child-care provider wages. As discussed earlier, higher wages may reflect a mixture of cost and quality, so a priori predictions about the effects of higher wages are uncertain. One possible explanation for this result is that it may reflect reverse causation. If provider wages are higher for center employees than for family day-care providers, then higher observed wages could be a result of a higher propensity to use center care. This question needs further investigation.

We also find that families living in states with greater state child-care spending are less likely to choose center, family day care, and relative/sitter care compared with parental care. If this spending reflects child subsidies that would not be available for parental care, then we would have expected a positive sign on this coefficient. Again reverse causation is a possibility. States with a high prevalence of informal care may increase child-care spending to increase the incentives for formal care. To understand the relationship we find in our data, we need to have a better idea of the priorities and policies of state child-care agencies.

By leveraging the substantial variation in welfare reform policies in the early to mid-1990s, we are able to show clear evidence of endogeneity of AFDC status. For example, comparing the results in Columns 1 and 4, we find that center care is significantly *less* likely for current welfare recipients when we account for endogeneity, but center care is significantly *more* likely for current welfare recipients when we do not control for endogeneity.[12]

How can we account for this result? One possible explanation relies on the fact that welfare recipients who work have historically been a small and probably select sample and, as a result, may have stronger ties to the formal labor market. Perhaps they work because they are able to utilize child-care subsidies that are available for welfare recipients. In the early 1990s, subsidies were almost exclusively used for center care. Thus, this argument would suggest that welfare recipients who work would be more likely to use center care.

The way to interpret the coefficient on predicted AFDC receipt is that this is the effect on child-care choice of increasing the likelihood of AFDC receipt for the average woman at risk of being on welfare. Our pattern of results is consistent with the hypothesis that the average welfare recipient has fewer ties to the labor market (and perhaps lower motivation as well) than working welfare recipients, and that if the average recipient were to work, she would be least likely to use center care over other types of care.

The results on the effect of predicted work reinforce this interpretation, as do models that estimate the joint probability of work and AFDC receipt relative to AFDC receipt without work. The negative coefficients on predicted current work imply that increasing the probability of work will bring women with fewer child-care resources into the labor market. These women will be more likely to rely on parental child care. National statistics from 1995 show that mother care while at work accounts for about 5.4% of the primary child care, whereas father care accounts for 16.6% (Smith, 2000). However, father care falls by one third to one half when the mother is not married to the father (Smith, 2000). Our results suggest that parental child care increases as low-income mothers with young children increasingly enter the labor force, but whether that care is provided by the mother while at work or by the father is a question for further investigation.

---

[12]Note that first-stage models run without the key welfare policy variables—namely, identifiers for restrictive and expansive policy and a continuous variable for the level of the AFDC guarantee—fail to precisely estimate predicted AFDC effects in the second-stage choice model.

CONCLUSIONS AND FUTURE WORK

In this chapter, we address the question of how the welfare-to-work policies and stricter welfare eligibility requirements of the first half of the 1990s affected the welfare, labor supply, and child-care choices of low-income single mothers with young children. We develop a model in which these three outcomes are estimated jointly. We find that welfare decisions are strongly influenced by socioeconomic characteristics, child-care availability, welfare guarantee levels, and labor market policies, and our data mirror the welfare caseload decline that began in 1993. Similarly, labor market choices are affected by socioeconomic characteristics, child-care costs and availability, and supportive (as opposed to punitive) welfare and labor market policies.

Our child-care results highlight the importance of child-care supply and work schedules in the child-care choices that mothers make. In contrast, welfare and labor market policies appear to matter only secondarily through work and welfare decisions. We also find evidence that welfare status is endogenous, and failing to model child-care, welfare, and work choices jointly will bias the estimated effect of AFDC on child-care choice. In the early 1990s, less than 10% of welfare recipients were employed, and our results imply that there is positive selection into the work and welfare status. As stricter welfare-to-work policies are implemented, women with fewer ties to the labor market and worse child-care options are drawn into the labor force. We find that these new entrants are most likely to use parental care as opposed to all other types of care, including center, family day care, and relatives.

ACKNOWLEDGMENTS

The research has been funded, in part, by NICHD grant #HD30944, and the Russell Sage Foundation. We thank Suzann Eshleman, Ann Horvath-Rose, Youngok Lim, Susan Averett, and Laura Paszkiewicz for help in collecting policy data and programming the SIPP files, and we thank V. Joseph Hotz and Rebecca Kilburn for providing access to their data on child-care regulations. Participants at a workshop in the economics department at the University of Massachusetts provided helpful comments on an earlier draft of the chapter.

REFERENCES

Averett, S., Peters, H. E., & Waldman, D. (1997). Tax credits, labor supply, and child care. *The Review of Economics and Statistics, 79*(1), 125–135.
Berger, M. C., & Black, D. A. (1992). Child care subsidies, quality of care, and the labor supply of low income single mothers. *Review of Economics and Statistics, 74*(4), 635–642.

Bishop, J. (1998). *Is welfare reform succeeding?* (Center for Advanced Human Resource Studies Working Paper #98-15). Ithaca, NY: Cornell University School of Industrial and Labor Relations.

Blank, R. M., Card, D., & Robins, P. K. (2000). Financial incentives for increasing work and income among low-income families. In R. M. Blank & D. Card (Eds.), *Finding jobs: Work and welfare reform* (pp. 373–419). New York: Russell Sage Foundation.

Blau, D., & Hagy, A. (1998). The demand for quality in child care. *Journal of Political Economy, 106*(1), 104–146.

Blau, D., & Tekin, E. (2000). Child care subsidies for low-income families. In B. Meyer & G. Duncan (Eds.), *The incentives of government programs and the well-being of families.* http://www.jcpr.org/book/index.html

Blau, D., & Tekin, E. (2001). The determinants and consequences of child care subsidy receipt by low income families. In B. Meyer & G. Duncan (Eds.), *The incentives of government programs and the well-being of families* (chap. 10, pp. 1–34). Chicago: Joint Center for Poverty Research.

Chapman, J., & Bernstein, J. (2003). *Falling through the safety net: Low income single mothers in the jobless recovery* (EPI Issue Brief #191). Washington, DC: Economic Policy Institute.

Council of Economic Advisors. (1997). *Explaining the decline in welfare receipt, 1993–1996: Technical report.* Washington, DC: Executive Office of the President of the United States.

Council of Economic Advisors. (1999). *Economic expansion, welfare reform, and the decline in welfare caseloads: An update: Technical report.* Washington, DC: Executive Office of the President of the United States.

Ficano, C. K. C. (2004). *Market mechanisms in the child care market: Does policy affect the quantity supplied?* Unpublished manuscript.

Figlio, D. N., & Ziliak, J. P. (1999). Welfare reform, the business cycle, and the decline in AFDC caseloads. In S. H. Danziger (Ed.), *Economic conditions and welfare reform* (pp. 17–48). Kalamazoo, MI: W.E. Upjohn Institute for Employment Research.

Gallagher, L. J., Gallagher, M., Perese, K., Schreiber, S., & Watson, K. (1998). *One year after welfare reform: A description of state Temporary Assistance for Needy Families (TANF) decisions as of October, 1997.* The Urban Institute. *Assessing the New Federalism,* Occasional Paper, No. 6.

Gelbach, J. (2002). Public schooling for young children and maternal labor supply. *American Economic Review, 92*(1), 307–322.

Gordon, R., & Chase-Lansdale, P. L. (2001). Availability of child care in the United States: A description and analysis of data sources. *Demography, 38*(2), 299–316.

Harris, K. M. (1996). Work and welfare among single mothers in poverty. *American Journal of Sociology, 99*(2), 317–352.

Hotz, V. J., & Kilburn, M. R. (1991). *The demand for child care and child care costs: Should we ignore families with non-working mothers?* Economics Research Center/NORC Population Research Center Discussion Paper 91-11.

Hotz, V. J., Kilburn, M. R., & Heeb, R. (2000, March). *The effects of state regulations on child care prices and choices.* Paper prepared for the Population Association of America 2000 annual meeting.

Hotz, V. J., Mullin, C., & Scholz, J. K. (2000). The earned income tax credit and labor market participation of families on welfare. In B. Meyer & G. Duncan (Eds.), *The incentives of government programs and the well-being of families.* http://www.jcpr.org/book/index.html

Killingsworth, M. (1983). *Labor supply.* New York: Cambridge University Press.

Meyer, B. D., & Rosenbaum, D. T. (1999, September). *Welfare, the earned income tax credit, and the labor supply of single mothers* (National Bureau of Economic Research Working Paper 7363). Washington, DC: National Bureau of Economic Research.

Meyers, M. K., Heintze, T., & Wolf, D. A. (2002). Child care subsidies and the employment of welfare recipients. *Demography, 39*(1), 165–179.

Moffitt, R. (1998). The effect of welfare on marriage and fertility. In R. Moffitt (Ed.), *Welfare, the family and reproductive behavior* (pp. 50–97). Washington, DC: National Academy Press.

Nada, E., & Lieberman, J. B. (1996). Labor supply response to the earned income tax credit. *Quarterly Journal of Economics, 111*(2), 605–637.

NICHD Early Child Care Research Network. (1999). Child outcomes when childcare center classes meet recommended standards for quality. *American Journal of Public Health, 89,* 1072–1077.

Schoeni, R. F., & Blank, R. M. (2000). *What has welfare reform accomplished? Impacts on welfare participation, employment, income, poverty, and family structure* (National Bureau of Economic Research Working Paper 7627). Washington, DC: National Bureau of Economic Research.

Schumacher, R., & Greenberg, M. (1999). *Childcare after leaving welfare: Early evidence from state studies.* Washington, DC: Center for Law and Social Policy.

Smith, K. (2000). *Who's minding the kids? Child care arrangements: Fall 1995* (Current Population Report, P-70). Washington, DC: U.S. Census Bureau.

U.S. Census Bureau. (various years). *County business patterns.* Washington, DC: U.S. Government Printing Office.

U.S. Department of Health and Human Services. (1997). *Setting the baseline: A report on state welfare waivers.* http://aspe.hhs.gov/hsp/isp/waiver2/title.htm

U.S. Department of Health and Human Services. (2000). *Temporary assistance to needy families program third annual report to Congress.* http://www.acf.dhhs.gov/programs/opre/director.htm

U.S. Department of Health and Human Services. (2001). *Trends in the well-being of America's children and youth.* http://aspe.hhs.gov/hsp/01trends

U.S. General Accounting Office. (1998). *Welfare reform: States' efforts to expand child care programs* (GAO-HEHS-98-27). Washington, DC: Author.

U.S. House of Representatives, Committee on Ways and Means. (1992). *Green Book.* http://aspe.hhs.gov/92gb/

U.S. House of Representatives, Committee on Ways and Means. (1994). *Green Book.* http://aspe.hhs.gov/94gb/

U.S. House of Representatives, Committee on Ways and Means. (1996). *Green Book.* http://aspe.hhs.gov/96gb/

U.S. House of Representatives, Committee on Ways and Means. (1998). *Green Book.* http://aspe.hhs.gov/98gb/

U.S. House of Representatives, Committee on Ways and Means. (2000). *Green Book.* http://aspe.hhs.gov/2000gb/

## CHAPTER SIX

Nonstandard Work and Child-Care Choices: Implications for Welfare Reform

Jean Kimmel
Western Michigan University

Lisa M. Powell
University of Illinois at Chicago

During the 1990s, as a result of a strong economy and ongoing welfare reform, welfare caseloads fell dramatically. In some states, the numbers of welfare recipients fell by over 80%; on average, the decline was approximately 60%. What happens to those welfare leavers and those potential recipients who never joined the rolls in the first place? Although numerous local analyses are underway to answer this broad question, the two major national surveys designed specifically with this question in mind are only now being publicly released.[1] Fortunately, some information about the likely labor force behavior of these new workers can be gleaned from existing evidence concerning single mothers, particularly low-income single mothers. This chapter relies on data from 1994 using the Survey of Income and Program Participation (SIPP) to relate work schedules of single mothers to child-care utilization patterns and then relate these findings to welfare reform.

In light of the massive overhaul of the federal welfare reform program in 1996, the need for research is particularly acute. We offer this study, in part, in response to recent calls for welfare reform research. The Council of Economic Advisors (1997) called for research into the employment and child-care utilization patterns of low-income single mothers. The Joint Center for Poverty Research devoted an issue of their newsletter to calls for welfare reform and

---

[1]The two data sets are the Survey of Program Dynamics (SPD), a Census Bureau extension of the SIPP, and the National Survey of America's Families (NSAF), designed by the Urban Institute and collected by Westat.

child-care research by researchers active in the field of policymaking (see e.g., Divine & Tvedt, 2000).

Historically, less-educated workers have worked disproportionately in off-hours jobs—that is, hours other than the standard Monday through Friday 8 a.m. to 6 p.m. work day. Loprest (1999) found that welfare leavers are entering the workforce at "the low end of the labor market, where they are working in much the same circumstances as near-poor and low-income mothers who have not recently been on welfare" (p. 1). As we move into a new century, more and more poorly educated women will enter the workforce unqualified for the higher paying jobs and face limited choices in low earnings, often non-standard work. This is in part driven by the Personal Responsibility and Work Opportunities Reconciliation Act (PRWORA), the 1996 federal reform of welfare that block-granted welfare dollars to the states and put a 5-year maximum life-time eligibility limit on the receipt of welfare. This increase in the employment rates of single mothers began before PRWORA, however. During the 1990s, the labor force participation rates of single mothers living in poverty or under two times the poverty line rose dramatically—from 44% in 1992 to 57% in 1999—reaching the employment rate of mothers in general (Divine & Tvedt, 2000).

If potential welfare recipients are disproportionately represented in non-standard work hours, then a study of the linkages between such work patterns and child-care choices will help inform the debate concerning the likely outcome of encouraging work for large numbers of unprepared new workers. Working nonstandard hours simply magnifies the difficulty of finding affordable and high-quality child care faced by many working parents (*Child Care Around the Clock*, 1995). Preliminary evidence of recent welfare leavers suggests that, indeed, they are disproportionately likely to hold nonstandard jobs. Loprest (1999) used the National Survey of America's Family to study recent welfare leavers and found that approximately a quarter of recent leavers are working mostly night hours.[2]

This problem was first discussed by Presser and Cox (1997), who stated that the prevalence of shift work and the accompanying child-care problems should be considered when assessing the success or failure of PRWORA. Presser and Cox discussed the work schedules of less-educated women and linked these schedules to welfare reform that will encourage even more less-educated women to enter the workforce. Their primary conclusions are that less-educated mothers are more likely to work a nonstandard schedule than are other women, and the main reason they work such schedules relates to the

---

[2]Georges, Wagmiller, and Lu (2001) discussed this issue in the preliminary draft of their manuscript. Additionally, Tekin (2004) examined the relationship between the availability of child-care subsidies and standard employment and tested to see whether this impact differs for welfare recipients.

occupations in which they work—occupations that are likely to grow in the future. Maynard et al. (1990) examined the child-care challenges facing low-income families and identified child care to accommodate nonstandard work schedules as a special need that serves as a constraint in the child-care markets of low-income areas. Further, The National Study of Child Care for Low-income Families (Collins et al., 2000) revealed that the most frequently reported shortage is in child care during nonstandard work hours. Thus, this special need is surely one of the barriers to work that will be faced by new labor market entrants that policymakers have an interest in addressing.

The purpose of this chapter is to describe and model the impact of nonstandard work schedules on the demand for alternative modes of child care by single mothers. We begin by discussing the patterns of nonstandard work seen in recent years in the United States, and we briefly describe the existing literature on child-care choice demand. Next, we describe our data and then develop an econometric model to examine more formally the relationship between nonstandard work and child-care choices. In particular, we estimate a multinomial choice model to examine the impact of nonstandard work, child-care prices, wages, nonlabor income, and other demographic variables on the child-care choice decisions of single mothers. Finally, we discuss the model results and provide some concluding remarks.

RECENT NONSTANDARD WORK PATTERNS IN THE UNITED STATES

Drawing on data from the May 1997 supplement to the Current Population Survey, Beers (2000) found that 16.8% of all full-time wage and salary workers worked a nonstandard job. Stratifying by sex, 19.5% of full-time employed men and 13.9% of full-time employed women work a schedule other than a regular daytime schedule. Both married men and women are less likely on average to work nonstandard hours, with the percentages at 17.5 and 10.8, respectively. Finally, men with young children in the household are most likely to work a nonstandard schedule—at 19.7%—while women with young children in the household are relatively unlikely to engage in shift work—at 12.9%. These statistics only look at full-time workers, however, and so exclude a fairly significant percentage of nonstandard workers who only work part time. Beers showed that over a third of part-time workers worked a nonstandard primary job, but that the proportion of part timers on alternative shifts fell from 46% in 1991 to 36% in 1997.

For these workers employed on a nonstandard schedule, what is the reason for this work schedule? Beers' data include a self-reported reason for working nonstandard hours. From the range of responses given next, it is clear that both supply and demand factors are at work. The driving force appears to be the nature of the job, with 51% reporting this reason. Approximately 4.2% of nonstandard workers report that better child care was the motivating factor for working this shift, while 2.8% report being motivated by better care for family members. These statistics imply that a fairly large percentage of non-standard workers are working this shift involuntarily, and so are not picking the schedule to benefit child-care choices. In fact this is precisely the finding of the survey underlying the report *Child Care Around the Clock* (1995), in which the majority of workers reports that nonstandard work is not a choice, but rather a consequence of restricted job opportunities. As a consequence, it is likely that procuring child care is a hurdle for a nonstandard worker facing limitations in her child-care choices.[3]

The most important factor in nonstandard work is the occupation. The occupations with the highest prevalence for shift work are protective services at 55%; food service at 42%; and operators, fabricators, and laborers at 27%. Industries are also important, with the most common for shift work eating and drinking places at 47%, transportation at 36%, and the hospital industry at 25.8%. Overall, Beers found that men are more likely than women to engage in shift work due both to occupational and industrial variation in jobs and even after controlling for such differences.

What trends are expected in the future? Beers (2000) cited no increase in the incidence of shift work since the mid-1980s, explaining that it was the increases in service occupations that caused the rate of shift work to stay the same; otherwise it would have fallen. However, Presser and Cox (1997) predicted that nonstandard jobs will increase as the job market experiences growth in the types of jobs most likely to be nonstandard, such as services. In *Child Care Around the Clock: Developing Child Care Resources Before Nine and After Five*, five major trends are described to which continued growth in nonstandard jobs can be attributed. These trends are: structural change toward a service-based economy; increase in job structure variability due to consumer preferences, worker preferences, and pollution-reduction goals; increases in the standard work week beyond the 9 to 5 time frame of a significant portion of the workforce; increases in shift work in manufacturing due to downsizing and economic expansion; and increases in paid work by mothers with young children.

Other than child-care problems, why do we care about nonstandard work? There are likely to be a wide range of problems faced by families (single-parent or two-parent families) with a worker on a nonstandard shift. Staines and Pleck (1983) studied nonstandard work and families extensively. They reviewed literature that examines a potential link between shift work and work/

---

[3]Shapiro (1996) examined the demand factors influencing the number of nonstandard jobs and found a cyclicality to these jobs. That is, shift work tends to grow in expansionary economic times. He found that, "In a typical workweek, one in every four manufacturing production workers in the United States is employed at night. This fraction fluctuates sharply over the business cycle, accounting disproportionately for business cycles changes in employment" (p. 79).

family conflict. Although many studies lack scientific rigor, they extended the existing evidence with their own rigorous studies and concluded that shift workers do experience disproportionate work/family conflict. Additionally, Presser (2000) examined the potential link between nonstandard work and marital instability and found some evidence that couples with one or both partner on a nonstandard schedule are more likely to suffer marital disruption. There are also health problems associated with working nonstandard shifts, particularly as the shift workers adjust their schedules quickly to conform on nonworking days to the regular schedules of family members and society at large. For all these reasons, shift work is likely to impose extra pressure in low-income single-mother families, which are already facing severe stresses.

REVIEW OF THE CHILD-CARE CHOICE LITERATURE

A substantial empirical literature has developed over the last two decades that examines the child-care choice decisions of mothers with young children. Although the results report a broad range of price elasticity estimates for child-care demand, overall there seems to be some consensus that the demand for formal child-care modes are relatively more price elastic compared with informal modes. The bulk of the existing empirical literature focuses on married mothers and does not account for the endogenous effect of the mothers' nonstandard work schedules on the demand across different child-care modes.

The early literature in this area (Cleveland & Hyatt, 1993; Hofferth & Wissoker, 1992; Lehrer, 1989; Leibowitz, Waite, & Witsberger, 1988; Robins & Spiegelman, 1978) examined the determinants of the choice of mode of care conditional on working without accounting for the potential endogeneity of the employment decision. Connelly and Kimmel (2003) examined the demand for alternative modes of child care controlling for the potential endogeneity of the employment decision by including predicted full-time employment as a regressor in their demand model. Only a few articles jointly examined labor supply decisions and the demand for specific modes of child care. This latter work included articles by Blau and Hagy (1998), Michalopoulos and Robins (2000), and Powell (2002).

Little research has examined nonstandard work and child-care modal choices in an econometric framework. Presser (1986, 1988) provided detailed descriptive statistics on marital status, hours of work, shift work, and the mode of child care used by the youngest child in the family. Folk and Beller (1993) examined the effect of variable work schedules for employed mothers on the combination of part-time/full-time employment status and the use of nonmarket (parents and relatives) versus market (sitters and formal settings) child care. Brayfield (1995) and Casper and O'Connell (1998) both examined the impact of nonstandard work schedules on the probability of care by the father in married households. More recently, Chaplin et al. (1999) examined the importance of a nonday job on the child-care choice decisions of mothers among center, sitter, relative, and parent care, finding a significant positive effect of a nonday job on the probability of choosing either relative or parent care versus center care. Each of these latter empirical articles included the nonstandard work schedule variables as direct regressors in their models, and hence failed to account for their potential endogeneity.

DESCRIPTION OF OUR DATA

Our data are a merged file drawn from the 1992 and 1993 panels of the Survey of Income and Program Participation. These interviews overlap the same calendar time, covering the period of July to December 1994. The SIPP data are from a nationally representative survey that collects information on a wide array of employment and income issues.[4] Although post-welfare reform data would be preferred for this project, such data were not available at the time of this chapter's writing. In any event, the richness of the SIPP data makes it the best source at this time for research of this nature.

The following paragraphs provide a brief discussion of the data and key variable definitions. Tables containing extensive descriptive information of the data are available from the authors on request. Each mother in our sample has at least one child under the age of 6 living in her household. Although all model estimation is implemented using our full sample of single mothers, some of our descriptive discussion stratifies our full sample into low-income and non-low-income subsamples due to the connection between income level and the risk of welfare receipt. We define *low income* as having family income at or below twice the poverty threshold. Also, as mentioned earlier, we define *nonstandard work* as any job for which the work is performed outside the standard times of 6 a.m. to 6 p.m. Monday through Friday. This includes anyone reporting regular evening or night-time work, weekend work, irregular schedules, or split shifts. Nonstandard work as defined this way is fairly common, and relatively more common for lesser educated workers. Finally, we break the mode of child care into three categories: center care, sitter care, and relative care.

Our study includes 978 single mothers of whom 714 work. There are 696 low-income single mothers in our low-income subsample, of whom 466 (67%) work. Of these low-income workers, 240 (52%) work a nonstandard schedule. Although demographic characteristics like age and education are similar by work status, the nonstandard workers are more likely to have an ad-

---

[4]Each panel surveyed a sample of individuals nine times over the course of 3 years. We pull our employment and child-care information from the sixth interview of the 1992 panel and the third interview of the 1993 panel. Also, these interviews each contain a special topical module (special set of questions asked only at three of the nine interviews) on child care and nonstandard work.

ditional preschooler in the family, more likely to have other adults in the household, more likely to have a teenager in the household, and less likely to live in the south. There are some fairly substantial differences in occupation and industry by work schedule. For example, nonstandard workers are twice as likely to work in the trade industry (44% vs. 22%) and twice as likely to work in service occupations (45% vs. 23%).

In terms of child-care patterns, only 41% of low-income single mothers working a nonstandard schedule pay for child care versus 59% of those working the standard shift. This is likely due to both the relative unavailability of off-hours child-care arrangements (except by relatives) and differences in preferences for the child's care at different hours of the day. There are also differences in modal choice by work schedule. Nonstandard workers are less likely to choose center care than standard workers (26% vs. 42%), but are considerably more likely to choose relative care (43% vs. 3%). Additionally, nonstandard workers are likely to pay a bit more per hour of care—$1.53 versus $1.48 an hour.

Now how do low-income single mothers compare with their non-low-income counterparts? Our sample contains 282 non-low-income single mothers, which is only 29% of all the single mothers in our study. The non-low-income single mothers are slightly older on average than the low-income single mothers and are better educated. Their youngest child is older, and they are less likely to have a second preschooler in the family. Also, they are more likely to have another adult in the household, and they are less likely to be non-White. Finally, 41% of the non-low-income workers work nonstandard hours, versus 52% of the low-income sample.

Looking at child-care patterns, the non-low-income mothers are more likely to report paying for care (60% vs. 50%), and when paying they pay more per hour for such care ($1.89 vs. $1.50). There are also differences across income-level groups in the mode of care chosen. Forty-seven percent of the non-low-income single mothers choose center care versus 33% of the low-income single mothers, whereas the latter are somewhat more likely to choose each of the other three modes.

The data also provide information regarding the exact type of nonstandard work in which our sample workers engage. For all groups of mothers, working a weekend is quite common—ranging from 60% to 74%. Regarding the particular type of shift work reported, by far the most common across the two samples are regular evening shift and irregular schedule. The latter pattern, in particular, creates difficulties in arranging child care because the care must accommodate a constantly changing schedule. The low-income single mothers are less likely than the non-low-income mothers to work weekends, but more likely to work a regular night shift.

There are notable differences in child-care utilization patterns by work status and income status. Considering first low-income single mothers, while over a half of standard workers rely on center-based care, just over a third of nonstandard workers rely on such care. Regardless of income, nonstandard workers who work a regular night shift are most likely to use relative care. Overall, relative care is quite common for single mothers, but particularly so for nonstandard workers.

CHILD-CARE CHOICE MODEL

This chapter estimates a multinomial logit choice model to examine the importance of nonstandard work schedules in the child-care choice decisions of single mothers with young children. We expect that the employment status of the mother will affect the mode of child care that is used while she works. Hence, this model estimates the impact of nonstandard work status, child-care prices, wages and nonlabor income, and other demographic variables on the modal choice among center, sitter, and relative care for the youngest child in the household.

In the multinomial logit model, the ith mother's utility if she chooses child-care choice state s is given by:

$$V_{is} = \beta_{Cs}C_{is} + \beta_{Ns}N_i + \beta_{Ws}W_i + \beta_{Xs}X_i + \varepsilon_{is} \tag{1}$$

where $s = 1, \ldots, n$; C_{is} are modal child-care prices, N_i is the mother's nonstandard work schedule status, W_i is the mother's wage rate, and X_i is a vector of observed individual/household characteristics and variables relating to the mother's demand for alternative modes of child care.

The mother will choose state V_{is} if $V_{is} > V_{im}$ for all other m possible outcomes, where the probability that state s is chosen by individual i is given by:

$$P_{is} = \text{Prob}(V_{is} > V_{im}) = \frac{\exp(\beta_{Cs}C_{is} + \beta_{Ns}N_i + \beta_{Ws}W_i + \beta_{Xs}X_i)}{\sum_s [\exp(\beta_{Cs}C_{is} + \beta_{Ns}N_i + \beta_{Ws}W_i + \beta_{Xs}X_i)]}. \tag{2}$$

The hourly price of child care of mode s is expected to reduce the probability of using child-care mode s. It is expected that mothers working in a nonstandard job will increase the probability of choosing informal child-care modes, such as relative care, that offer more flexibility compared with formal modes. The presence and ages of children and the presence of another adult in the household, race and education level of the mother, nonlabor income, and urban residence are also expected to affect the mother's child-care choice decisions.

Before we can estimate the multinomial logit model, we must estimate several supporting equations for nonstandard work status, child-care prices, and wages. First, we estimate the probability of nonstandard work for inclusion in our multinomial logit model to account for the potential endogeneity of nonstandard work status and child-care choice decisions. We estimate a bivariate probit model of the probability of nonstandard work and the employment decision with selection. The regressors included in the labor force participation equation include age, education, nonlabor income, and standard demographic variables, whereas the nonstandard work status equation also includes dummy variables for occupation and industry.[5]

Second, we must estimate price equations for each of the three types of child care (center, sitter, and relative) to produce price estimates for each type of care for all mothers in the sample. It is assumed that the price of each mode of child care varies according to a set of family characteristics, state per capita income, and child-care regulation variables. In each of the three price equations to be estimated, *price* is defined as the hourly price of child care for mode s per hour of care used by the youngest child in the family. To account for potential selection bias that those mothers who use a particular mode of care may face lower prices than the population as a whole, we include a sample-selection correction lambda term based on a multinomial logit child-care choice model (see Lee, 1983).

Thus, predicted prices for each mode of care are obtained by the following procedures. First, a reduced form multinomial logit model is estimated. Next, three separate sample-selection correction lambda terms, one for each mode of care, are computed using the results from the reduced form logit model according to Lee's (1983) formula, where in each case the selection is based on choice $= s$ according to the mode of care in question. Each price equation is then estimated by ordinary least squares (OLS), including the appropriate selection term, and the sample-selection-corrected coefficients are used to predict prices for the whole sample.

Third, we estimate wages where an OLS wage equation is specified as a function of age, education, race, health, regional variation, and intermittent work history. We use standard techniques to correct for the labor force participation selection bias by including a Heckit-type correction term (inverse Mills ratio) as a regressor (Maddala, 1983).

Finally, predicted nonstandard work schedule status, predicted wages, and predicted child-care prices for center care, sitter care, and relative care are in-

---

[5]The validity of occupation and industry dummy variables as identifiers can be questioned on the grounds that both are choices and therefore endogenous. However, occupations and industries are choices made more in a lifecycle context, and we would expect more transitions between standard and nonstandard work than across occupations and industries over the immediate time frame considered here. In any event, they are the most appropriate identifiers available to us. Unfortunately, regional controls are not feasible given that the SIPP data are not broken down below the state level.

cluded in the child-care choice model. The multinomial logit child-care choice model is then estimated using maximum likelihood estimation.

ESTIMATION RESULTS

Our model estimation was conducted using our full sample of single mothers. This section of the chapter begins with a brief discussion of the results from our supporting equations, which include the estimation of the probability of nonstandard work, the wage equation, and the child-care price equations.[6] We then present the empirical results from the child-care choice model for single mothers including price elasticities and simulations.

The results from the bivariate probit estimation of the probability of nonstandard work and labor force participation are found in Table 6.1. We find that after controlling for the fact that the number of children in the household significantly reduces the probability of labor force participation, conditional on working an increase in the number of own children increases the probability of nonstandard work. This suggests that, given the decision to work, mothers with more children use nonstandard work as a means of juggling work and family. The remaining key significant variables in the determination of the probability of nonstandard work relate to job occupation and industry. This confirms the descriptive evidence provided by Beers (2000) as described earlier.

The results from the log wage equation are presented in Table 6.2. As expected, the mothers' age and years of education have a significant positive effect on wages. Increases in the number of children in the household, included as a proxy for labor market interruptions, has a significant negative effect on wages. Mothers living in a metropolitan area receive higher wages, whereas mothers living in the south and unhealthy mothers receive lower wages. The sample selection term, *lambda*, is statistically significant, suggesting that whether the mother works significantly affects her potential wage rate.

The results from the child-care price regressions for center, sitter, and relative care are presented in Table 6.3. The results show that if the youngest child is an infant, price is higher for center care, but unaffected for sitter and relative care. Having an additional preschooler increases the price of care for all modes. In all three price equations, mothers with higher levels of unearned income pay significantly more for child care, which suggests that they may be choosing (affording) higher quality care. Living in a metropolitan area significantly increases the price of center and sitter care, but does not significantly affect the cost of care by a relative. Living in the south significantly reduces the

---

[6]The results from the supporting (instrumenting) equations are based on a combined sample of single and married mothers because the single-mother sample is of insufficient size to produce robust instruments.

TABLE 6.1
Marginal Effects From Bivariate Probit Model
of Employment Status and Nonstandard Work

Variable	LFP	Nonstandard Work Schedule
Constant	−0.642***	0.963
Education	0.042**	−0.051
Age	0.042***	−0.073
Age^2	−0.001***	0.001
Education × age	−0.002**	0.002
Education × age^2	3.020E-05*	−8.400E-06
Education^2 × age	3.900E-06	−2.260E-05
Non-White	−0.004	0.028
Unhealthy	−0.048***	0.118
Nonlabor income	−1.000E-05***	7.300E-06
Number of children	−0.039***	0.111*
Presence of children ages 0–2	−0.013**	−0.004
Presence of children ages 3–5	−0.002	−0.003
Presence of children ages 6–12	0.015**	−0.030
Presence of children ages 13–17	0.049***	−0.079
Presence of other adults	0.023***	0.031
Urban residence	0.001	0.003
Southern residence	−0.004	−0.025
Unemployment rate	−0.007***	−0.011
State's regulated child:staff ratio < 10:1	−0.001	−0.004
State regulates center teachers' education	0.013**	0.010
Employers estimated workers' comp. payment by state	−0.001	−0.002
State's per capita personal income	−8.000E-07	6.300E-06
Married	0.016***	−0.006
Industries:		
Manufacturing	—	0.120
Transportation, comm., and other public utilities	—	0.277**
Wholesale trade and retail trade	—	0.478***
Finance, insurance, real estate, business, and repair	—	0.134
Personal, entertainment, and recreation services	—	0.381**
Professional and related services	—	0.234*
Public administration	—	0.101
Occupations:		
Technical, sales and administrative support occupations	—	−0.001
Service	—	0.226***
Farming, forestry, and fishing	—	0.244
Precision production, craft, and repair	—	0.160*
Operators, fabricators, and laborers	—	0.131**
State's average Medicaid expenditure per enrollee	−2.834E-06	—
State's average monthly AFDC payment per family	−4.334E-06	—
Rho	—	−0.412

*Significance at 10% level.
**Significance at 5% level.
***Significance at 1% level.

TABLE 6.2

Determinants of the Probability of Being Employed and the Hourly Wage (Probit Model for Employment and OLS Selection Equation for Hourly Wages; Standard Errors Are in Parentheses)

Variable	LFP	Natural Logarithm of Hourly Wage
Constant	−2.363***	−1.947***
	(0.766)	(0.325)
Education	0.157***	0.107***
	(0.063)	(0.007)
Age	0.154***	0.133***
	(0.048)	(0.019)
Age^2	−0.002***	−0.002***
	(0.001)	(0.000)
Education × age	−0.008*	—
	(0.004)	
Education × age^2	1.103E-04*	—
	(5.855E-05)	
Education^2 × age	1.382E-05	—
	(1.926E-05)	
Non-White	−0.016***	−0.040
	(0.020)	(0.033)
Unhealthy	−0.176***	−0.246***
	(0.029)	(0.062)
Nonlabor income	−3.661E-05	—
	(3.682E-06)	
Number of children	−0.141***	−0.110***
	(0.012)	(0.019)
Presence of children ages 0–2	−0.048**	—
	(0.023)	
Presence of children ages 3–5	−0.008	—
	(0.023)	
Presence of children ages 6–12	0.056**	—
	(0.022)	
Presence of children ages 13–17	0.178***	—
	(0.029)	
Presence of other adults	0.083***	—
	(0.021)	
Urban residence	0.001	0.097***
	(0.017)	(0.027)
Southern residence	−0.018	−0.071***
	(0.025)	(0.025)
Unemployment rate	−0.024***	0.022*
	(0.008)	(0.011)
State's regulated child:staff ratio < 10:1	−0.003	—
	(0.022)	
State regulates center teachers' education	0.047**	—
	(0.019)	
State's average Medicaid expenditure	−1.076E-05	—
	(9.504E-06)	

(Continued)

TABLE 6.2
(Continued)

Variable	LFP	Natural Logarithm of Hourly Wage
State's average monthly AFDC payment	−4.746E-05	—
	(9.685E-05)	
Employers' estimated workers' compensation	−0.001	−0.006
	(0.013)	(0.019)
State's per capita personal income	−2.322E-06	—
	(4.580E-06)	
Married	0.059***	0.060**
	(0.020)	(0.029)
Lambda	—	0.417***
		(0.084)
Adjusted R^2	—	0.292

*Significance at 10% level.
**Significance at 5% level.
***Significance at 1% level.

price of center care. The child-care regulation variables do not significantly affect the price of care. Higher levels of state per capita income, however, significantly increase the price of center and sitter care, reflecting the expectation of corresponding higher wages for child-care workers. Finally, the selection term in each of the child-care price equations accounts for the possibility that those mothers who choose a particular mode of child care may face lower prices than the population as a whole: It is negative and significant for center and sitter care.

We now turn to the estimation results from the child-care choice model, which includes the predicted probability of nonstandard work, predicted wages, and predicted child-care prices. Table 6.4 presents the results based on a choice model across three modes of care that include center care, sitter care, and relative care. Our results reveal that, as expected, the mothers' work patterns play an important role in the decisions regarding the choice of child-care mode. Because the nonstandard work status of the mother is likely to be endogenous to the choice of child-care mode, we include the predicted probability of nonstandard work as a regressor in our choice model. We find that a higher probability of nonstandard work by the mother reduces the likelihood that she uses either center or sitter care (although it is not significant), and it significantly increases the likelihood of using relative care. Thus, single nonstandard working mothers are more likely to rely on relatives for care, but also must search for market child care that is sufficiently flexible to meet their needs.

Turning to child-care prices, the results show that, as expected, the own price of center and sitter care has a significant negative effect on the probability of choosing those respective modes of care. The own price effect for rela-

TABLE 6.3
Determinants of the Amount Paid for Each Child-Care Mode
(Standard Errors Are in Parentheses)

Variable	Center Care (n = 799)	Sitter Care (n = 550)	Relative Care (n = 240)
Constant	−1.593***	−0.775	1.061
	(0.522)	(0.693)	(0.770)
Non-White	−0.329**	−0.168	−0.045
	(0.146)	(0.182)	(0.157)
Nonlabor income	6.296E-05**	2.026E-04***	5.626E-05
	(2.892E-05)	(2.478E-05)	(4.455E-05)
Presence of children ages 0–2	0.442***	0.104	0.082
	(0.171)	(0.154)	(0.156)
Presence of other preschoolers	1.083***	0.743***	0.503***
	(0.128)	(0.117)	(0.149)
Presence of children ages 6–12	−0.113	−0.216*	−0.176
	(0.113)	(0.112)	(0.138)
Presence of children ages 13–17	—	—	−0.074
			(0.280)
Presence of other adults	—	—	−0.029
			(0.187)
Urban residence	0.340***	0.399***	0.133
	(0.120)	(0.120)	(0.148)
Southern residence	−0.218	0.184	−0.407**
	(0.147)	(0.137)	(0.178)
State's regulated child:staff ratio < 10:1	0.022	0.201*	0.123
	(0.135)	(0.119)	(0.171)
State regulates center teachers' education	−0.026	0.069	−0.085
	(0.125)	(0.129)	(0.164)
State's per capita personal income	1.569E-04***	1.117E-04***	−9.433E-06
	(2.583E-05)	(2.567E-05)	(3.170E-05)
Married	0.256*	−0.071	0.123
	(0.132)	(0.134)	(0.174)
Lambda	−0.496*	−0.501*	0.443
	(0.278)	(0.297)	(0.294)
Adjusted R^2	0.225	0.302	0.091

*Significance at 10% level.
**Significance at 5% level.
***Significance at 1% level.

tive care, however, is insignificant. The own price elasticity values for center, sitter, and relative care are −1.1, −4.7, and 0.3, respectively. The insignificant own price effect for relative care may stem from the fact that the potentially constrained size of the relative market for the family plays an important role in the use of such care, compared with the potential size of the markets for the other two modes of care. Note that the presence of a teenager in the household has a significant positive effect on the probability of choosing relative care, although the presence of another adult does not significantly affect this

TABLE 6.4

Partial Derivatives of the Probability of Choosing Among Modes of Child Care
(Standard Errors Are in Parentheses)

Variable	Center Care	Sitter Care	Relative Care
Predicted wage	−0.015	0.116	−0.100
	(0.115)	(0.081)	(0.114)
Predicted price of center care	−0.173***	—	—
	(0.056)		
Predicted price of sitter care	—	−0.336***	—
		(0.128)	
Predicted price of relative care	—	—	0.154
			(0.114)
Predicted probability of nonstandard work	−0.138	−0.088	0.226**
	(0.110)	(0.080)	(0.111)
Education	0.050***	−0.037***	−0.013
	(0.019)	(0.013)	(0.019)
Non-White	−0.062	−0.050	0.112**
	(0.047)	(0.037)	(0.050)
Nonlabor income	−2.220E-05	4.010E-05*	−1.790E-05
	(2.000E-05)	(2.000E-05)	(2.000E-05)
Presence of children ages 0–2	−0.233***	0.033	0.199***
	(0.044)	(0.040)	(0.047)
Presence of other pre-schoolers	0.169**	−0.011	−0.158**
	(0.082)	(0.055)	(0.073)
Presence of children ages 6–12	0.0222	−0.020	−0.002
	(0.047)	(0.037)	(0.051)
Presence of children ages 13–17	−0.120**	−0.048	0.168***
	(0.057)	(0.042)	(0.063)
Presence of other adults	−0.013	−0.025	0.038
	(0.044)	(0.033)	(0.045)
Urban residence	0.065	0.045	−0.110**
	(0.051)	(0.040)	(0.054)

Note. Center care is the excluded category.
*Significance at 10% level.
**Significance at 5% level.
***Significance at 1% level.

choice. The potential reliance on a teenager as the primary mode of care by single mothers has both implications for the quality of care received by the younger children in the household and the school performance of the teenagers responsible for providing such care. Of note here is the fact that low-income single mothers are three times more likely to have a teenager in the household, compared with their non-low-income counterparts.

Controlling for child-care prices, having an infant does not significantly affect the choice of mode of care, whereas the presence of an additional pre-schooler ages 0 to 5 significantly increases the use of center care. With respect to our earned and unearned income variables, we do not find significant effects of the wage rate of single mothers on their child-care choice decisions. With higher levels of nonlabor income, however, single mothers are significantly more likely to use sitter care.

Controlling for the mother's wage rate, we expect the mother's level of education to affect her preferences across different modes of child care. The results show that more educated single mothers are significantly more likely to choose center care and less likely to use care by a sitter or relative. This finding has implications for the choices of low-income single mothers as they have, on average, lower levels of education compared with non-low-income single mothers. Finally, living in an urban versus a rural area significantly reduces the likelihood of using relative care. Non-White single mothers are significantly more likely to use care by a relative.

We now present some simulations to highlight the implied behavioral features of our model. In Table 6.5, we present child-care price simulations to assess the degree to which government subsidies may affect child-care choice decisions, and we present simulations based on the nonstandard work status of the mother to assess the extent of the implications of work patterns on child-care usage. The simulations are performed at the sample means. The baseline probabilities are those predicted by the model with no simulated changes.

Examining the effects of providing conditional subsidies for individual modes of care only, a 10% reduction in the price of care conditional on either one of center, sitter, or relative care increases the probability of working and using center or sitter care, respectively, but has virtually no effect on the use of relative care. The use of center care rises from 37% to approximately 41%, whereas the use of sitter care by single mothers is up to 27% from 17%. When child-care subsidies are provided unconditionally on mode of care (all prices reduced by 10%), there is an increase in the use of center and sitter care by single mothers reflecting a substitution away from the use of relative care.

Finally, we also perform simulations with respect to the nonstandard work status of the mother—we simulate the child-care choices for a nonstandard versus a standard worker. For these mothers, we see that there is almost a 50%

TABLE 6.5
Simulations of Child-Care Choices

Simulation	Center Care	Sitter Care	Relative Care
Baseline	0.374	0.172	0.454
Center price (−10%)	0.412	0.126	0.462
Sitter price (−10%)	0.331	0.268	0.402
Relative price (−10%)	0.383	0.177	0.440
All prices (−10%)	0.385	0.207	0.408
Nonstandard worker	0.299	0.128	0.573
Standard worker	0.435	0.215	0.350

difference in the use across modes of care among the two types of workers: The use of center and sitter care is reduced for nonstandard versus standard workers from 44% to 30% and 22% to 13%, respectively, whereas the use of relative care increases from 35% to 57%.[7] Recall that among single mothers our descriptive statistics showed that the low-income group has a higher rate of nonstandard work. Thus, it is the low-income single mothers who are most likely to face potential difficulties in adjusting their child-care arrangements to accommodate their work schedules.

CONCLUSIONS

Our findings show that the child-care choice decisions of single mothers are affected by not only price, but also the nonstandard work status of the mother. Overall, our results for single mothers speak to the potential child-care problems faced by low-income single mothers given that a substantial proportion of this group holds a nonstandard job.

The problems identified are associated with child care for nonstandard workers and the high incidence of nonstandard work for single mothers most at risk of welfare receipt. What are the potential solutions? Remember that the nonstandard workers are less likely to pay for care, possibly due to the unavailability of off-hours center-based care or insufficient subsidies. Solutions to this problem include public/private ventures to increase the availability of off-hours care and public commitments to increase the subsidy rates for off-hours care. *Child Care Around the Clock* (1995) looked at local programs that work, putting them into three categories: the Single Employer Model (where the employer can make after-hours care available or offer assistance in finding such care), the Employer Consortium Model (several employers work together to accomplish what one alone cannot), and the Community Partnership Model. All models can work under the appropriate local circumstances. Regarding adjustments to child-care subsidies, it can be argued that current reimbursement policies are biased against nonstandard care because the reimbursement structure is not adjusted sufficiently for price differences that prevail for care provided at different times of day. That is, night-time care is more expensive than day-time care. Reallocation of child-care subsidy funds can be justified for this reason.

---

[7]To provide further implications of our empirical results for mothers facing the welfare-to-work transition, we simulate across the full sample of workers and nonworkers assuming that all single mothers must now enter the labor market. Again, we simulate the child-care choices for a nonstandard worker versus a standard worker. Consistent with our simulation results based on the estimation sample of workers presented in Table 6.5, there is approximately a 50% difference in the use across modes of care for nonstandard versus standard workers, respectively: 0.259 versus 0.386 for center care, 0.136 versus 0.235 for sitter care, and 0.605 versus 0.379 for relative care.

Because the 1996 welfare reform legislation transferred the design and implementation of welfare programs to the states, state governments will bear the burden of developing policy responses for child-care problems associated with nonstandard work. Some states are already addressing these problems. Blank et al. (2001) outlined state strategies that deal with the problem they described as *odd-hour care*. Some examples of state strategies include programs in eight states to offer higher child-care reimbursement rates to providers offering off-hours care, coordinating private/public funding cooperatives to underwrite the construction of expanded hours day-care centers in rural communities, and improvements in the availability of state grants to child-care providers who want to expand their hours to off-hours care. This sort of program is likely to ameliorate the problem of unstable child-care arrangements that will be particularly problematic for the children of nonstandard workers. Such unstable arrangements hamper child well-being and child development, and they make it more difficult for single mothers to build the job tenure necessary for promotion to better-paying standard hours jobs.

Another response to this research is to investigate further the consequences of the standard current welfare policy of "work first," which favors pushing unprepared workers into the labor force immediately without any training. It might be that some up-front job training can improve the initial job prospects of these new workers, resulting in first jobs that are somewhat less likely to be nonstandard. Whatever the solution, until attention is paid to the child-care problems faced by nonstandard workers, those workers (disproportionately the lesser educated and low-income single mothers) will continue to face interrupted job tenures and difficulty securing stable, high-quality child care for their children.

ACKNOWLEDGMENTS

Jean Kimmel thanks the W.E. Upjohn Institute for Employment Research for its support during the drafting of the first version of this chapter. We are deeply indebted to Wei-Jang Huang (for superb research assistance), Nancy Mack (for quality secretarial support), and Linda Richer (for library research). Lisa Powell thanks the Economic Research Department at the Federal Reserve Bank of Chicago for hosting her while a draft of this chapter was written. An earlier draft of this chapter was prepared for presentation at the May 17 to 18, 2001 conference *From Welfare to Child Care: What Happens to Infants and Toddlers When Single Mothers Exchange Welfare for Work*. This conference was sponsored by Cornell University School of Industrial and Labor Relations Pierce Memorial Fund, Cornell University Institute for Labor Market Policies, The National Institute of Child Health and Human Development Family and Child Well-Being Network, and the Russell Sage Foundation. We thank

Natasha Cabrera, Elizabeth H. Peters, Ruby Takanishi, and particularly Robert Hutchens for their valuable comments.

REFERENCES

Beers, T. M. (2000, June). Flexible schedules and shift work. *Monthly Labor Review, 123*(6), 33–40.

Blank, H., Behr, A., & Schulman, K. (2001, March). *State developments in child care, early education, and school-age care 2000.* Washington, DC: Children's Defense Fund.

Blau, D. M., & Hagy, A. P. (1998). The demand for quality in child care. *Journal of Political Economy, 106*(1), 104–146.

Brayfield, A. (1995). Juggling jobs and kids: The impact of employment schedules on fathers' caring for children. *Journal of Marriage and the Family, 57*, 321–332.

Casper, L. M., & O'Connell, M. (1998). Work, income, the economy, and married fathers as child-care providers. *Demography, 35*(2), 243–250.

Chaplin, D. D., Robins, P. K., Hofferth, S. L., Wissoker, D. A., & Fronstin, P. (1999). *The price sensitivity of child care demand: A sensitivity analysis.* Unpublished manuscript.

Child Care Around the Clock: Developing Child Care Resources Before Nine and After Five. (1995). U.S. Department of Labor, Women's Bureau. Accessed April 20, 2001, from http://www.dol.gov/dol/wb/public/media/reports/care.htm#

Cleveland, G. H., & Hyatt, D. E. (1993). Determinants of child care choice: A comparison of Ontario and Quebec. *Canadian Journal of Regional Science, 16*(1), 53–67.

Collins, A. M., Layzer, J. I., Kreader, J. L., Werner, A., & Glantz, F. B. (2000). *National study of child care for low-income families: State and community substudy interim report.* Washington, DC: U.S. Department of Health and Human Services, Administration for Children and Families.

Connelly, R., & Kimmel, J. (2003, May). Marital status and full-time/part-time work status in child care choices. *Applied Economics, 35*(7), 761–777.

Council of Economic Advisers. (1997, December). *The economics of child care.* CEA White Paper.

Divine, P. L., & Tvedt, K. (2000). Child care and child wellbeing. *Joint Center for Poverty Research Newsletter, 14*(6).

Folk, K. F., & Beller, A. H. (1993). Part-time work and child care choices for mothers of preschool children. *Journal of Marriage and the Family, 55*, 146–157.

Georges, A., Wagmiller, R. L., Jr., & Lu, H.-H. (2001). *Child care, subsidy receipt and state of residence: Comparisons by age and parent work schedule.* Unpublished manuscript, National Center for Children in Poverty.

Hofferth, S. L., & Wissoker, D. A. (1992). Price, quality, and income in child care choice. *The Journal of Human Resources, 27*(1), 70–111.

Lee, L.-F. (1983). Notes and comments: Generalized econometric models with selectivity. *Econometrica, 51*(2), 507–512.

Lehrer, E. (1989). Preschoolers with working mothers: An analysis of the determinants of child care arrangements. *Journal of Population Economics, 1*, 251–268.

Leibowitz, A., Waite, L. J., & Witsberger, C. (1988). Child care for preschoolers: Differences by child's age. *Demography, 25*(2), 205–220.

Loprest, P. (1999). *Families who left welfare: Who are they and how are they doing?* (Discussion Paper No. 99-02). Washington, DC: Assessing the New Federalism Project, The Urban Institute.

Maddala, G. S. (1983). *Limited-dependent and qualitative variables in econometrics* (Econometric Society Monographs No. 3). Cambridge, MA: Cambridge University Press.

Maynard, R., Kisker, E. E., & Kerachasky, S. (1990). Child care challenges for low-income families. The Minority Female Single Parent Demonstration, *Into the Working World*. New York: Rockefeller Foundation.

Michalopoulos, C., & Robins, P. K. (2000, May). Employment and child-care choices in Canada and the United States. *Canadian Journal of Economics, 33*(2), 435–470.

Powell, L. M. (2002). Joint labor supply and child care choice decisions of married mothers. *Journal of Human Resources, 37*(1), 106–128.

Presser, H. B. (1986). Shift work among American women and child care. *Journal of Marriage and the Family, 48*, 551–563.

Presser, H. B. (1988). Shift work and child care among young dual-earner American parents. *Journal of Marriage and the Family, 50*, 133–148.

Presser, H. B. (2000, February). Nonstandard work schedules and marital instability. *Journal of Marriage and the Family, 62*, 93–110.

Presser, H., & Cox, A. G. (1997). The work schedules of low-educated American women and welfare reform. *Monthly Labor Review*, pp. 25–34.

Robins, P. K., & Spiegelman, R. G. (1978). An econometric model of the demand for child care. *Economic Inquiry, 16*(1), 83–94.

Shapiro, M. D. (1996). Macroeconomic implications of variation in the workweek of capital. In W. C. Brainard & G. L. Perry (Eds.), *Brookings papers on economic activity* (pp. 79–119). Washington, DC: The Brookings Institution.

Staines, G. L., & Pleck, J. H. (1983). *The impact of work schedules on the family*. Ann Arbor: University of Michigan Press.

Tekin, E. (2004). *Single mothers working at night: Standard work, child care subsidies, and implications for welfare reform* (IZA Discussion Paper No. 1014). Bonn, Germany.

## CHAPTER SEVEN

Low-Income Families' Child-Care Experiences: Meeting the Needs of Children and Families

Rebekah Levine Coley
Boston College

Christine P. Li-Grining
University of Chicago

P. Lindsay Chase-Lansdale
Northwestern University

One of the most significant demographic changes in the late 20th century has been the unprecedented rise in maternal employment. In 1940, only 1 out of 10 women with children worked outside of the home; by 1970, this had risen to 1 out of 3; and by 1997 to 2 out of 3 (U.S. Department of Health and Human Services, 1996, 1999). As thousands of mothers have moved from household labor to out-of-home employment, concomitant increases have occurred in the need for child-care and early education programs for young children. The passage of the 1996 welfare reform bill (the Personal Responsibility and Work Opportunity Reconciliation Act [PRWORA]), which mandated time limits and employment for most mothers on welfare, has pushed a substantial new group of very low-income families into the child-care market. Welfare reform also brought increased attention to the central role that high-quality, accessible, and dependable child care plays in supporting employment and self-sufficiency among mothers and healthy development among children.

In this chapter, we provide a rich view of the child-care settings that urban, low-income families are using in the wake of welfare reform, with particular attention to two central aspects of child care. First, we consider whether child-care settings are meeting the needs of mothers—that is, whether mothers are satisfied with the quality of care and its accessibility, flexibility, affordability, and provision of communication. Second, we consider whether the child-care settings are providing low-income preschool children with high-quality care from a developmental perspective—that is, whether care is safe, cognitively stimulating, and provides the support and structure central for young chil-

149

dren's well-being and school preparation. Across these aspects, we focus on what types of child care best meet the needs of families and children.

CHILD CARE AND THE NEEDS OF PARENTS AND FAMILIES

From a family's perspective, finding care that is accessible, dependable, and agrees with one's childrearing values and goals can be an integral support for families as they juggle the competing demands of employment and parenthood. Low-income parents, whether self-sufficient or seeking to exit the welfare system, may face greater barriers than more well-off families in finding acceptable child-care settings for their children due to issues concerning cost, flexibility, access, and preferences. For example, the cost of child care is often prohibitive, especially for families with limited financial resources that tend to pay a greater proportion of their income for child care than do higher income families (Giannarelli & Barsimantov, 2000; Hofferth, 1996). Federal subsidies of child care, through vouchers and other forms of payment, can help alleviate this inequality and support low-income mothers' efforts to gain employment and higher incomes (Blau & Hagy, 1998; NICHD Early Child Care Research Network, 1997). Yet research indicates that only a small percent of children who are eligible for government vouchers actually receive them (Meyers, Heintze, & Wolf, 1999).

Low-income parents may also experience difficulties finding child care that fits their work schedules and transportation needs. Parents with low education and entry-level jobs have a greater likelihood than middle-class parents of working nonstandard hours, such as nights, weekends, and split shifts, when options for formal child care in centers and family day-care homes are limited (Beers, 2000; Presser & Cox, 1997; see also Kimmel & Powell, chap. 6, this volume). Transportation difficulties and a dearth of licensed and high-quality child-care options in low-income neighborhoods can further limit parents' access to child care (Duncan & Brooks-Gunn, 2000). In addition, the time limits and work requirements of welfare reform may push some families into accessing child care they might otherwise have avoided.

The patterns of child-care use by low-income parents may also be driven by personal preferences and beliefs. For example, research has shown that parents who value the developmental characteristics of care tend to use centers, whereas those who value the child–caregiver relationship, hours, location, and cost of care are more likely to use family day care or home care (Johansen, Leibowitz, & Waite, 1996). Parents' goals and beliefs regarding nonparental caregiving may vary systematically—for instance, across cultures or socioeconomic status (Holloway, Fuller, Rambaud, & Eggers-Pierola, 1996; Lamb & Sternberg, 1992; LeVine, 1974). A recent review of research found that Hispanic families most often use relative care, whereas African Americans are more likely to use center care (Brown-Lyons, Robertson, & Layzer, 2001).

However, it is important to keep in mind that trends that appear to be attributable to preferences or cultural beliefs might actually be driven by issues of need, cost, or accessibility. For instance, recent research has found that low-income families, and particularly families that have recently left welfare, most often use relative care (Capizzano, Adams, & Sonenstein, 2000; Schumacher & Greenberg, 1999). This pattern could reflect the challenges of finding accessible and affordable formal child care in low-income neighborhoods, or parents' focus on trust and comfort with the care they choose for their children, and may mask heterogeneity among the preferences of low-income families (Yoshikawa, Rosman, & Hsueh, 2001). Overall, knowledge is still limited regarding parents' preferences and beliefs concerning child care and the settings that they view as best for their children and their families.

CHILD CARE AND THE NEEDS OF CHILDREN

In addition to providing a service to parents and families, child care also serves as a central context for child development. Social science researchers are making significant strides in delineating and measuring the components of high-quality child care that meet the developmental needs of children, as well as in identifying the impacts of child care on children's cognitive and social development. Scientific evidence has accrued concerning a link between the provision of high-quality child care by trained providers and improved school readiness and behavioral functioning in children, both concurrently and over time (NICHD Early Child Care Research Network, 1998, 2000b, 2001; Votruba-Drzal, Coley, & Chase-Lansdale, 2004). Some of the strongest findings have focused on low-income children, supporting the contention that quality child care might be an even more important support for low-income children than for their more well-off counterparts (Barnett, 1995; Cost, Quality, and Outcomes Study Team, 1999; Infant Health and Development Program, 1990; Lamb, 1998; National Research Council and Institute of Medicine, 2000; Yoshikawa, 1995).

Yet just as low-income parents face barriers in accessing child care that meets their needs, they may also face particular difficulty in accessing care that provides high-quality, developmentally appropriate settings for their children. The quality of child care varies widely in the United States (Cost, Quality, and Outcomes Study Team, 1999; NICHD Early Child Care Research Network, 2000a; Whitebook, Howes, & Phillips, 1990), and most parents, irrespective of income and education, are not adept at discriminating developmental quality in child-care settings (Cryer & Burchinal, 1997). High-quality care tends to be more expensive than care of lower quality (Helburn & Howes, 1996). Differences are also found across types of care settings, with center-based care better than relative care or regulated day-care homes at providing developmentally appropriate care for low-income children (NICHD

Early Child Care Research Network, 1997). However, low-income children may gain an advantage in accessing quality child-care programs from government vouchers and programs such as Head Start. Research has found that low-income and high-income children tend to be in care of higher quality than their counterparts in working-class and middle-income households (Phillips, Voran, Kisker, Howes, & Whitebook, 1994). Yet as low-income and welfare families become more self-sufficient, this safety net begins to unravel even though families may still be in relative financial need.

RESEARCH QUESTIONS

This brief review underscores the challenges that low-income parents may face in accessing child care that meets both the needs and preferences of their families and the developmental needs of their children. Given the recent and significant changes driven by the new systems of welfare reform, we know little about low-income families' experiences with child care within the current economic and policy context. In this chapter, we address the following questions using a representative sample of low-income children and families in Boston, Chicago, and San Antonio. What types of child care are low-income families accessing? Do their choices match up with their preferences? Do child-care settings vary systematically by family characteristics? How well do child-care settings fulfill the developmental needs of children? Do they provide appropriately safe, stimulating, and warm environments? How well do they fulfill the needs of parents and families in providing satisfactory, reliable, accessible, and affordable care? Are there certain child-care settings that meet the needs of both children and parents?

METHODS

The data for this chapter are drawn from a subsample of families ($N = 181$) from the first wave of *Welfare, Children, and Families: A Three-City Study*, a longitudinal, multimethod analysis of the well-being of children, families, and communities in the wake of federal welfare reform (see Winston et al., 1999, for a detailed overview of the study design). The main component of the Three-City Study was comprised of a household-based survey with a stratified, random sample of about 2,400 children and their primary caregivers in low-income families living in low-income neighborhoods in Boston, Chicago, and San Antonio. In households with a child ages 0 to 4 or ages 10 to 14 and with incomes below 200% of the federal poverty line, interviewers randomly selected one focal child and interviewed the child and his or her primary female caregiver, which we refer to as the child's mother (as over 90% of caregivers were biological mothers of the focal child). The screening rate for the main survey sample was 90%, and the interview completion rate was 83%, leading to a total response rate of 74%. The first wave of the survey was conducted in 1999, just 3 years after the initial passage of the welfare reform act and 5 to 10 years after many states had implemented waivers to alter the rules of welfare receipt. At the time of the first wave of data collection in 1999, 38% of the families were receiving cash welfare payments, 77% had incomes below the federal poverty line, and 73% were headed by single mothers. The sample was 47% Hispanic, 44% African American, and 9% non-Hispanic White.

All survey families with a focal child between the ages of 2 and 4 years were invited to participate in the Embedded Developmental Study (EDS), designed to capture in much greater detail young children's primary caregiving environments through multiple in-depth methodologies. If mothers reported in the main survey that the focal child was in nonmaternal care for 10 or more hours per week, permission was sought to conduct an observation of the child-care arrangement and to interview the provider. Seventy percent of eligible child-care settings participated ($N = 248$). In addition, 85% of mothers completed an additional EDS interview, which contained extensive questions concerning the focal child's primary nonmaternal care arrangements. The analyses reported here are based on a sample of 181 families for which we have observation, provider report, and maternal report information.[1] All analyses are weighted with probability weights that adjust for the sampling strategy as well as for nonresponse. Hence, our sample can be thought of as representative of children in low-income families in low-income neighborhoods in Boston, Chicago, and San Antonio who were in nonmaternal care for 10 or more hours per week.

Measures

Demographic Characteristics.   Demographic data on children, including age and gender, were reported by mothers during the main survey. Mothers also reported on their own race/ethnicity, education, employment, and welfare status, as well as on household composition and income. Table 7.1 presents demographic information on the sample. Within this group of 181 families, children average 3 years of age, and there is a relatively even split between boys and girls. The families are primarily African American and His-

---

[1]Of the 248 child-care cases, 15 did not have parallel mother EDS interviews, 40 had mother EDS interviews but did not have mother reports on the child-care setting (typically because the child was no longer in child care at the time of the mother EDS interview), 7 cases were missing central demographic data from the main survey interview, and 5 cases were dropped because of administration problems in the observational measures, leading to a sample of 181. Analyses that use the maximum N for each individual analysis (e.g., 248 when considering observational ratings and child-care provider reports only), not reported, do not differ substantially from the results reported here.

TABLE 7.1
Sample Characteristics

Variable	% or Mean (SE)
Child age in years	3.10 (.08)
Gender	
Boy	57%
Girl	43%
Race	
White	6%
African American	56%
Hispanic	31%
Other	6%
Income-to-needs ratio	.86 (.06)
Family structure	
Single	72%
Single with other adult	8%
Married	20%
Maternal education	
Less than high school	27%
High school	58%
Some college or more	15%
Maternal employment	
0–9 hours	31%
10–34 hours	29%
35 & more hours	40%
Welfare status	
On welfare	35%
Recent leavers	18%
Past leavers	20%
Nonentrants	27%

Note. Weighted percentages, means, and standard errors.

panic, and on average they have incomes below the federal poverty line. Twenty percent of the mothers are married, and 85% have relatively low education—a high school diploma or less. Two thirds of the mothers are employed. Regarding welfare experience, one third of the mothers reported receiving welfare at the time of the interview, 18% had received welfare in the 2 years prior to the study (recent leavers), 20% had received welfare at some point prior to that (past leavers), and 27% reported never having received welfare (nonentrants). Some mothers are also combining welfare and work. At the time of the interview, 19% of mothers received welfare only, 16% both worked and received welfare, 52% worked only, and 13% neither worked nor received welfare (data not shown).

Observations of Child Care. Structured observations lasting 2 hours or more were conducted in each child-care setting. The developmental quality of each child-care setting was rated with widely used, well-validated developmental instruments. For children in formal center arrangements, the Early Childhood Environment Rating Scale–Revised (ECERS–R; Harms, Clifford, & Cryer, 1998) was used. Each item on the ECERS–R is given a score of 1 to 7, anchored on the odd numbers by the terms of 1 = *inadequate*, 3 = *minimal*, 5 = *good*, and 7 = *excellent*, through the dichotomous rating of a number of subitems. The first 37 items of the ECERS–R, covering the spheres of space and furnishings, personal care routines, language and reasoning, activities, interactions, and program structure, were combined into a global quality score (alpha = .94, intraclass correlation [ICC] on 15% of the observations, which were independently coded by two coders averaged .90).

Informal care arrangements, including both day-care homes and unregulated home-care settings, were rated using the Family Day Care Rating Scale (FDCRS; Harms & Clifford, 1989), which is organized in a similar way to the ECERS–R. The first 29 items, covering the spheres of space and furnishings for care and learning, basic care, language and reasoning, learning activities, and social development were combined into a global quality scale (alpha = .95, ICC = .98).

For both center and home-based care settings, the Arnett Scale of Provider Sensitivity (Arnett, 1989) was used to tap into the emotional and behavioral relationships between the care providers and the children. The Arnett contains 26 items rated on a 4-point scale, which were combined into one measure, with higher scores indicating care providers who are warm, engaged, and use consistent and appropriate discipline strategies, and low scores indicating providers who are harsh, detached, and use inconsistent or inappropriately strong forms of discipline (alpha = .94, ICC = .81). Finally, the observers also recorded the number of care providers and children present, and a *child–adult ratio* was calculated.

Child-Care Provider Interviews.   Following the observations, care providers completed 1-hour face-to-face interviews, reporting on group size, education (less than high school, high school, some college, or college degree or higher), relationship to child (related or not), the child's time in the care setting (the number of months since they had begun caring for the child), and whether the care was provided in a center, regulated home (the care provider was licensed to provide care), or unregulated home (care provider was not licensed).

Mother Reports on Child Care.   During the EDS mother interviews, mothers reported on various aspects of their child's primary nonmaternal care arrangement. The Emlen (1999) short scale measured mothers' general *Satisfaction* with the care provided to their child. This 15-item measure taps into mothers' views of whether the care setting is a safe, warm, and healthy environment with a caring, involved, and informed care provider. Each question was answered on a Likert scale (1 = *never* to 5 = *always*), with higher scores indicating greater maternal satisfaction (alpha = .83). Two other scales, also adapted from Emlen, measure the level of flexibility and accessibility the mother sees in the child-care situation. *Flexibility* is a 4-item scale (alpha = .84) with items focusing on how flexible the care provider is regarding hours of care and the mothers' work schedule. *Accessibility* (10 items, alpha = .60) reflects whether the mother felt she had choices and options that met her standards, whether she had transportation problems, and whether she felt she had access to reliable and dependable child care and a care provider who shares her values. The items for these scales were answered with a 1 (*strongly disagree*) to 4 (*strongly agree*) Likert scale. A fourth measure, *Mother–Provider Communication*, is a 5-item scale (alpha = .67; 1 = *never* to 5 = *nearly every day*) that assesses the level of communication and emotional support that occurs between the mother and the care provider.

Mothers also reported on their out-of-pocket expenses for the child care, termed *Cost to Mother*. Finally, we asked mothers about their *Preference* for child care, inquiring what type of care they would choose if they had complete freedom. Responses were coded into the categories of center, home care, and regulated day-care home.

RESULTS

What Types of Child Care Are Low-Income Children Attending?

Table 7.2 provides descriptive information on the child-care settings that children attended. Forty-four percent of the children were in formal child-care centers, including nonprofit and for-profit centers and Head Start programs; 10% were in regulated home environments; and 46% were in unregulated homes. Centers had the greatest number of children in the care setting and the highest child–provider ratios, although the average group size and ratio for centers fall within the suggested ranges for children of this age, according to the National Association for the Education of Young Children standards (National Association for the Education of Young Children, 1998). The majority of care providers in unregulated homes were related to the focal child (85%), as were nearly half of the regulated home providers. Providers in centers were much more likely to have education beyond the level of high school, whereas this was quite rare for the home-care providers, particularly for those in regulated home settings. The number of months since the care provider had begun to care for the child was much higher in home-care settings than in centers, although it is possible that care had stopped and restarted within this time period.

TABLE 7.2
Child-Care Characteristics

Variable	Centers 44% % or Mean (SE)	Regulated Homes 10% % or Mean (SE)	Unregulated Homes 46% % or Mean (SE)
Mean number of children	14.71 (.70)[a,b]	5.68 (.57)[a,c]	3.26 (.36)[b,c]
Child:provider ratio	6:1[a,b]	3:1[a,c]	1:1[b,c]
Percentage of relative care	—	45[a]	85[a]
Provider education			
Less than high school	0[a,b]	12[a]	38[b]
High school	15	78	37
Some college	70	10	20
College or more	14	0	5
Time in setting (months)	7.65 (1.23)[a,b]	19.93 (3.45)[a]	24.77 (2.53)[b]
Cost to mother per week	$19.86 (3.48)	$41.77 (14.41)	$24.11 (4.88)

Note. Weighted percentages, means, and standard errors. Adjusted Wald tests were used to test for significant differences, except for % relatives, which used a chi-square test. Shared superscripts across values in a row represent significant differences at $p < .05$.

Turning to the cost of child care, mothers' out-of-pocket expenses were similar in centers ($20 per week) and unregulated homes ($24 per week), but about twice as high in regulated homes ($42 per week). It is important to note, however, that these cost averages mask significant variability. Within the families using centers, 45% of mothers reported receiving free care primarily due to the use of Head Start. Nearly half (48%) of the children in unregulated home care also received free child care, compared with 34% of children in regulated homes. The proportions of mothers paying more than $30 per week for care were 26%, 44%, and 32% for center, regulated home, and unregulated home care, respectively. On average, mothers in our sample paid 19% of their total household income on child care for the focal child.

Do Child-Care Choices Match Up With Maternal Preferences?

We next consider whether the type of child care parents access for their children matches up with their stated preferences, with results presented in Table 7.3. For the group as a whole, the proportions of mothers who reported they would choose centers, homes, and (regulated) day-care homes matched up quite well with the actual prevalence rates shown in Table 7.2. Forty percent of mothers reported they would choose center care, 38% home care, and 6% day-care homes. An additional 17% of mothers reported that they would prefer to provide full-time care themselves. The remainder of the columns in Table 7.3 present mothers' preferences split by the type of care they actually use. Mothers using center-based care and mothers using unregulated home care

TABLE 7.3
Child-Care Preferences

Type of Care Preferred	Total Sample	Mothers Currently Using Centers	Mothers Currently Using Regulated Homes	Mothers Currently Using Unregulated Homes
Mother care preferred	17%	17%	35%	12%
Center care preferred	40%	52%	37%	28%
Home-based care preferred	38%	18%	28%	58%
Day-care home (regulated home) preferred	6%	12%	0%	2%

Note. Numbers represent weighted percentages.

were equally likely to say that they would prefer a different type of care situation than the type they were currently using. In both groups, just over one half of mothers stated that they would choose the same type of care that their child was currently in, about 15% said they would prefer to care for their child themselves full time, and 30% stated that they would prefer a different type of care. In contrast, mothers using regulated home care were twice as likely to state that they would prefer a different type of care setting than the kind they were currently using.

Do Family Characteristics Differ Systematically Across Type of Care?

We next consider whether family characteristics differ systematically across child-care type. Selection processes could be operating, whereby certain types of families are more likely to use a particular type of child care. In this sample of low-income families, however, these processes do not appear to be at work. A series of OLS regression models were run to consider differences in child and family characteristics across the three types of child care. No significant differences were apparent for child gender and age, or mother education, employment status and shift, welfare status, marital status, and race/ethnicity. Children in regulated home care had marginally higher family incomes than children in center [$F(1, 180) = 3.24, p < .10$] or unregulated home care [$F(1, 180) = 3.60, p < .10$].

How Well Are Child-Care Settings Meeting the Developmental Needs of Low-Income Children?

In the next sets of analyses, we consider how well child-care settings are meeting the developmental needs of children through their provision of safe, structured, cognitively stimulating, and emotionally engaging care, with an examination of the ECERS/FDCRS and Arnett scores. Table 7.4 presents a de-

TABLE 7.4
ECERS/FDCRS Developmental Quality Ratings by Type of Care

Variable	Inadequate	Minimal	Good
All child-care settings	24%	32%	43%
Centers	6%	15%	78%
Regulated homes	8%	57%	35%
Unregulated homes	44%	44%	12%

scriptive look at the ECERS/FDCRS scores, broken into the ranges of *inadequate* (1–2.99), *minimal* (3–4.99), and *good* (5–7), for the sample as a whole and separately by type of child care. Results indicate that for the sample as a whole, nearly one quarter of the child-care settings were rated as being inadequate in meeting the basic developmental needs of children, nearly one third were rated as minimally adequate, and 43% were rated as good at meeting the developmental needs of children. These findings are generally comparable to other studies with both nationally representative and low-income samples, which also show that a large proportion of young children are in child care of poor developmental quality (Kontos, Howes, Shinn, & Galinsky, 1997; NICHD Early Child Care Research Network, 2000a; Phillips et al., 1994; see also Fuller & Kagan, 2000). However, different patterns emerge according to the type of care. Over three quarters of child-care centers in our sample received scores in the *good* range of the ECERS. In contrast, only one third of regulated homes were in the *good* range, with more than half rated as *minimal*. In the unregulated home category, only a small percentage (12%) were rated as *good*, whereas substantial proportions fell into the *inadequate* or *minimal* ranges.

OLS regression analyses indicate that these differences in developmental quality by the type of child-care setting are significant for the ECERS/FDCRS scores, as well as for the Arnett scores, as seen in the top panel of Table 7.5. Results indicate that developmental quality is higher in centers than in regulated homes and unregulated homes, and developmental quality is higher in regulated than unregulated homes. For the Arnett measure of provider sensitivity, centers score higher than unregulated homes. These differences, particularly for the ECERS/FDCRS measures, are substantial. For example, the difference in ECERS/FDCRS scores between centers and unregulated homes shows an effect size of 1.36 SDs (.50 SDs for centers vs. regulated homes).

The second panel of Table 7.5 presents multivariate OLS regression models to examine whether differences in developmental quality hold when demographic and socioeconomic characteristics of children and mothers are controlled. Even with a wide range of child and family characteristics controlled, child-care centers show higher ECERS/FDCERS scores than unregulated home settings and marginally higher scores than regulated homes. For

TABLE 7.5

OLS Regression Models of Observational and Mother Report Measures of Child-Care Settings

Bivariate Models

Type of Child Care	ECERS/FDCRS		Arnett		Satisfaction		Accessibility		Flexibility		Communication	
Center	—		—		—		—		—		—	
Regulated home	-0.77[*,a]	(0.30)	0.02	(0.15)	0.02	(0.11)	0.04[c]	(0.10)	0.22[b]	(0.18)	-0.35[a]	(0.25)
Unregulated home	-2.11[**,a]	(0.23)	-.15[*]	(0.08)	0.13[*]	(0.06)	0.23[**,c]	(0.07)	0.61[**,b]	(0.13)	0.76[**,a]	(0.11)

Multivariate Models

	ECERS/FDCRS		Arnett		Satisfaction		Accessibility		Flexibility		Communication	
Type of Child Care												
Center	—		—		—		—		—		—	
Regulated home	-0.63[+,a]	(0.37)	0.00	(0.12)	-0.01	(0.09)	-0.02[b]	(0.10)	0.22[b]	(0.18)	-0.26[a]	(0.25)
Unregulated home	-1.91[**,a]	(0.19)	-0.07	(0.06)	0.13[**]	(0.05)	0.24[**,b]	(0.06)	0.63[**,b]	(0.11)	0.78[**,a]	(0.10)
Child age	0.04	(0.12)	-0.05	(0.04)	-0.01	(0.03)	-0.08[*]	(0.03)	0.00	(0.05)	-0.06	(0.06)
Girl	-0.10	(0.19)	0.03	(0.07)	0.04	(0.06)	-0.02	(0.07)	0.01	(0.12)	0.04	(0.10)
Family Structure												
Single					—		—				—	
Single w/ other adult	-0.23[a]	(0.23)	-0.14[a]	(0.09)	-0.09[+]	(0.05)	-0.17[*]	(0.08)	-0.21	(0.13)	-0.14	(0.11)
Married	0.74[**,a]	(0.27)	0.20[+,a]	(0.10)	-0.08	(0.08)	-0.16[+]	(0.09)	-0.07	(0.19)	0.06	(0.14)

	(1)		(2)		(3)		(4)		(5)		(6)	
Race												
Hispanic	—		—		—		—		—		—	
White	0.57[c]	(0.46)	0.20[c]	(0.12)	-0.16[b]	(0.12)	-0.02	(0.11)	-0.11	(0.20)	-0.18	(0.20)
African American	-0.30[c]	(0.19)	0.02[a]	(0.08)	0.13*,[b]	(0.06)	0.07	(0.07)	0.09	(0.12)	0.08	(0.09)
Other	0.11	(0.28)	0.42**,[ac]	(0.09)	0.07	(0.15)	0.10	(0.15)	0.02	(0.21)	-0.21	(0.24)
Maternal Employment												
0–9 hours	—		—		—		—		—		—	
10–34 hours	-0.44[+]	(0.24)	-0.14[+],[b]	(0.08)	-0.01	(0.06)	0.04	(0.07)	0.07	(0.12)	-0.15	(0.13)
35 & more hours	-0.55*	(0.21)	0.03[b]	(0.07)	-0.02	(0.07)	0.08	(0.07)	0.05	(0.14)	-0.00	(0.12)
Welfare Status												
On welfare	—		—		—		—		—		—	
Recent leaver	-0.28	(0.27)	-0.18*	(0.08)	0.02	(0.08)	-0.22*	(0.10)	-0.10[c]	(0.15)	0.19	(0.12)
Past leaver	-0.06	(0.31)	-0.07	(0.10)	-0.03	(0.07)	-0.10	(0.09)	0.20[cc]	(0.17)	0.12	(0.15)
Nonentrant	-0.34	(0.27)	-0.21[+]	(0.11)	-0.06	(0.07)	-0.09	(0.08)	-0.07[c]	(0.16)	0.04	(0.12)
Income-to-needs ratio	0.46*	(0.20)	0.16*	(0.06)	0.02	(0.04)	0.05	(0.05)	0.02	(0.09)	-0.05	(0.09)
Maternal Education												
Less than high school	-0.11	(0.22)	-0.07	(0.07)	-0.01	(0.07)	-0.02	(0.07)	-0.14	(0.16)	0.01[b]	(0.11)
High school	—		—		—		—		—		—	
Some college or more	0.05	(0.28)	-0.11	(0.10)	0.00	(0.07)	-0.04	(0.10)	-0.09	(0.15)	-0.33**,[b]	(0.12)
R squared	0.54**		0.24**		0.20**		0.22*		0.27**		0.44**	

Note. Dashes indicate omitted variable. Significant differences in comparison to omitted group are indicated by: [+]$p < .10$; *$p < .05$; **$p < .01$. Significant differences between nonomitted groups are indicated by: [c]$p < .10$; [b]$p < .05$; [a]$p < .01$.

Arnett scores, the differences by child-care type become insignificant with the addition of the control variables. In summary, according to the observational assessments, child-care centers appear to best meet the developmental needs of children.

How Well Do Child-Care Settings Fulfill the Needs of Mothers?

The next set of results considers how well child-care settings fulfill the preferences and needs of mothers. The fourth through seventh columns in Table 7.5 present results for the mother report measures of *Satisfaction, Accessibility, Flexibility,* and *Mother–Provider Communication.* Bivariate results indicate a consistent pattern across all of our mother-report measures in which unregulated home settings score significantly higher than child-care centers and often higher than regulated homes as well. Effect sizes for these results are also substantial, ranging from .45 *SD*s for *Satisfaction* to 1.09 *SD*s for *Communication* for differences between unregulated home settings and centers. The second panel indicates that all of these significant differences hold in the multivariate models. Mothers whose children are cared for in more informal arrangements, often with relatives, have less difficulty with transportation or with finding care during their work hours, have care providers who show more understanding of their situation and with whom they share information about their child more regularly, and report that their child care is more reliable and dependable than other mothers in our sample. These mothers also report being more satisfied overall with the care their children receive. In short, unregulated home care appears to be the child-care setting in which mothers feel most comfortable and that best meets family needs.

The multivariate results also indicate the relationships between child and family characteristics and child-care quality. In particular, we draw attention to the findings concerning mothers' financial and human capital characteristics. Family structure, employment, income, and welfare status all relate to child-care measures. Mothers who have recently left welfare report lower accessibility scores, and their children's child-care providers receive lower scores on the Arnett measure of provider sensitivity, as compared with mothers remaining on welfare. In addition, higher family income and married status relate to better developmental quality child care, whereas maternal employment relates to lower quality.

Are There Child-Care Settings That Meet the Needs of Both Children and Mothers?

The previous findings suggest a clear dichotomy, with formal center care providing the most developmentally supportive care for children and unregulated home settings providing care that best meets mothers' needs. But are there care settings that score high on both of these sets of factors? That is, do any children in our sample have child care that meets both their and their mothers' needs? To address this issue, the ECERS/FDCRS and Arnett total scores were each standardized and then averaged to create a total quality score for each child-care setting. The scores on the four mother report measures were similarly combined to create a total mother report score. Each of these totals was split at the median and then combined to create four categories of care: settings that score high on both developmental quality and mother reports (high/high, 19%), settings that score low on both indexes (low/low, 21%), and settings that score either high/low or low/high, which we refer to as mixed settings (60%). Chi-square analyses and OLS regressions were then run to test whether these three categories differed significantly on child, family, and child-care characteristics that were discussed in the earlier analyses.

No differences were found for licensure or relative status of the provider among home-care settings, provider education, time in setting, or cost to the mother. Findings were also insignificant for maternal marital status, employment, work shift, and education, as well as child gender and racial/ethnic group. Significant differences were found for type of center (for-profit, nonprofit, Head Start; $\chi^2 = 17.99$, $p < .05$), child age ($\chi^2 = 19.86$, $p < .05$), mother welfare status ($\chi^2 = 30.21$, $p < .01$), and family income ($F = 3.07$, $p < .10$). Specifically, the high/high category—that is, scoring high on both developmental and maternal ratings—was more likely among higher income families, nonprofit centers, 3-year-olds, and past leavers of welfare, whereas the low/low category was more likely among for-profit centers, older preschoolers (4-year-olds), and recent welfare leavers.

DISCUSSION

Using direct observations of child-care settings and interviews with mothers and child-care providers, drawn from a representative sample of preschoolers in urban, low-income neighborhoods in Boston, Chicago, and San Antonio, our data provide an array of new information on the child-care settings that low-income families access following welfare reform. Results indicate that the majority of child-care settings appear to be meeting only some of the diverse needs of low-income preschool children and their families as they traverse welfare reform. This work represents an important contribution in providing a multifaceted view of low-income preschoolers' nonmaternal care experiences, allowing us to assess child care from a more comprehensive family perspective, rather than from a unidirectional perspective.

Our data show that formal child-care centers and informal, unregulated home arrangements with relatives are the most popular child-care choices for low-income parents. Whereas centers appear to best meet the developmental needs of children, unregulated homes seem to best meet the needs of mothers. Formal centers, including preschools, Head Start programs, and other child-care centers, provided the most developmentally supportive settings for children, the highest levels of safety, greatest cognitive stimulation, most appropriate supervision and control, and greatest warmth and caring. Centers in our sample also had educated staff, had reasonable group sizes and child–staff ratios, and were relatively affordable. However, center care did not match the needs of mothers as well as informal care arrangements.

Regulated home environments, often referred to as family day-care homes, had lower quality scores than centers (although higher than unregulated homes), were more expensive, and had lower provider education than other types of care and, like center care, were rated by mothers to be less accessible, flexible, and communicative than unregulated home-care settings. Mothers also preferred center or more informal home arrangements over regulated day-care homes.

On the other hand, informal unregulated home arrangements, in which care was typically provided by a relative, best fulfilled mothers' needs and goals and provided the most support for their families. Mothers who used unregulated home care reported the highest levels of accessible, flexible, and dependable care and better communication with their care providers, and they were more globally satisfied with the care that their children were receiving. Yet unregulated home settings provided care of the lowest developmental quality of the three types. Indeed 88% of unregulated care settings were rated as providing *inadequate* to *minimal* quality care.

These results suggest that distinct types of care arrangements have different strengths and weaknesses, which have important implications for children and families. Many research studies have shown the importance of high-quality child care, including appropriate cognitive stimulation, warmth, limit setting, and consistent attention to children's health and safety, in supporting children's healthy cognitive and socioemotional development, particularly for low-income children (Barnett, 1995; Cost, Quality, and Outcomes Study Team, 1999; Infant Health and Development Program, 1990; Lamb, 1998; National Research Council and Institute of Medicine, 2000; Votruba-Drzal et al., 2004; Yoshikawa, 1995). However, to juggle the competing demands of parenthood, family responsibilities, and employment, parents need child care that is accommodating to their work schedules and that is affordable, reliable, dependable, and viewed as providing a safe and supportive setting for their children (Blau & Hagy, 1998; Giannarelli & Barsimantov, 2000; Presser & Cox, 1997). Except for safety and supportiveness, observational assessments of child-care quality do not capture these important criteria. In addition, it appears that mothers base their satisfaction with child care on different dimensions from those tapped in structural and process quality measures. These discrepancies may be due to mothers' level of comfort with relatives or neighbors versus professional child-care providers, and to differences in maternal expectations and preferences regarding their children's social and cognitive enrichment. A greater understanding of low-income mothers' views of the importance and availability of cognitive stimulation and learning environments in child-care settings would help in interpreting these discrepancies.

More important, our results also indicate that some characteristics of child-care settings and families were related to the use of child-care settings that were supportive of both child development and family functioning. Higher family incomes and the use of nonprofit centers increased the likelihood of this optimal combination. On the other hand, a recent exit from the welfare system and the use of for-profit centers lowered the likelihood of experiencing child care that meets the needs of both children and families. These findings provide evidence that particularly disadvantaged low-income mothers as well as those who have recently left the welfare rolls use child care that is both less developmentally supportive of children and also less supportive of mothers. Still the lack of significant associations between other family characteristics and child-care measures support the contention that many of the experiences and challenges of child care are shared by all low-income women and children. It is also important to acknowledge that our data were collected only from families who were using regular child care. It is possible, indeed even likely, that some families had even greater difficulty accessing child care that met their needs and preferences—so much difficulty that their children were not in child care at the time of the study and thus were not included in the sample.

The results of this study provide a notable addition to the knowledge base on low-income families' use of child care in the era of welfare reform and are buttressed by the strengths of the study's design. First, the sample was drawn from a representative sample of low-income preschoolers in Boston, Chicago, and San Antonio, allowing conclusions to be extended to disadvantaged families both in and outside of the welfare system. Second, the data encompass a wide array of measures of child care, including structural characteristics, process measures, and mothers' perspectives on dimensions of child care, providing a multidimensional view of the strengths and weakness of child care settings used by low-income families. Third, the results can help to move the literature base forward by placing child care within the context of low-income families and communities. Although research on child-care quality and mothers' reports of quality has grown substantially in recent years (e.g., Cryer & Burchinal, 1997), understanding low-income mothers' perspectives of how child care fits their families' needs has been an underdeveloped area of study (Holloway & Fuller, 1999).

This research also has limitations, including a small sample size and correlational data from only one time point, as well as a lack of information on mothers' views of the developmental aspects of child care. In addition, our use of the FDCRS measure in informal, unregulated home settings extends this measure from its original intent—assessment of family day-care homes—and thus suggests caution in the interpretation of results. Finally, our analyses, unlike much previous research, did not indicate that families were selecting into certain types of child care (although a sophisticated analysis of selection is beyond the scope of the current work; Burchinal & Nelson, 2000; Duncan & Gibson, 2001). This may be due to the relatively homogeneous nature of our sample, comprised solely of low-income families in low-income urban communities.

CONCLUSIONS AND POLICY OPTIONS

The importance of child care for supporting both the self-sufficiency of low-income mothers as well as the healthy development of children lend urgency to the need for better information on the child-care preferences, choices, and experiences of low-income families. Improved information on the types of child-care settings that low-income families access, and on how well these settings fulfill the needs of both parents and children, will help inform policy efforts aimed at targeting financial and informational child-care resources and at increasing the availability and accessibility of quality child care for all families.

The strengths and weaknesses found in center, regulated home, and unregulated home child care are instructive and support a variety of policy and programmatic options. First, our results suggest the need to improve the flexibility, accessibility, and relationships with parents provided by centers and regulated family day-care homes. Many low-income mothers are employed evenings, nights, or weekends, or on rotating shifts, and they do not have access to reliable and affordable transportation (Beers, 2000; Presser & Cox, 1997). Flexible and accessible child care is a central support for low-income working families, and centers and regulated care settings are sometimes deficient in these arenas. Increasing the accessibility and flexibility of child care could be sought through multiple steps, including an expansion of full-time, full-year Head Start programs; increases in child-care centers located in low-income neighborhoods and at low-income workers' places of employment; and improvements in the availability of sick-child and off-hours child-care centers. Programmatic efforts to increase the engagement and comfort of parents and child-care providers could also be enhanced.

Second, the observational findings indicate that the quality of care provided by informal child-care arrangements, particularly unregulated care, is uneven and, indeed, often alarmingly low, with 44% of unregulated home-care settings rated as *inadequate*. Basic safety precautions are often missing; cognitively enriching activities such as reading, number and word games, and pretend play are sometimes sparse; and some providers do not use appropriate disciplinary strategies or provide warm, attentive care. These are qualities of child care that have been shown to increase children's school readiness, social skills, and health and well-being (National Research Council and Institute of Medicine, 2000). These findings suggest the need for increased training opportunities and resources for home-care providers geared particularly toward improving the safety, developmental appropriateness, and cognitive as well as social enrichment of the care they provide. Further efforts should be developed to extend these resources to unregulated and unlicensed as well as regulated child-care providers.

Third, our results indicate that over half of low-income preschool children in our sample were in child care that was rated as inadequate or minimally adequate at meeting their developmental needs, and many of the mothers reported having at least some difficulty with the level of flexibility and accessibility their child care provided. These findings underscore the challenges that all low-income parents face in accessing child care that meets all of the needs and preferences of themselves and their children in their efforts to balance parenting and employment. In addition to multipronged efforts to increase the availability of quality child care and early childhood education, mechanisms are needed to increase parents' knowledge and options concerning the care their children receive. With increased information and insight regarding child development and the impacts of high-quality child care, parents could become better consumers of the child-care market. Both research and programmatic efforts could also be increased to better understand low-income parents' needs and preferences regarding the aspects of child care that they find most important for the health and well-being of their children, their families, and themselves.

Finally, we also saw some evidence that parents with very low incomes and those who have recently left welfare are particularly likely to access child care that is unsupportive in multiple dimensions, both for children and families. This suggests the need for further supports to the most disadvantaged children and to families who are making the transition from welfare to employment. This might be accomplished through increasing the income and time limits of government subsidies for child care, and by providing more resource and referral services linked to welfare offices and other social service agencies to aid families in locating child care.

As the United States moves toward an era in which the vast majority of mothers with young children are employed outside of the home, the need grows for an adequate supply of affordable, accessible, reliable, and high-quality child care in a variety of settings. Different families have distinct needs and preferences, and one particular type of child care is not right for all children and families. Policy and programmatic choices that address these diverse needs and preferences can support family functioning and healthy child development, especially for those in the most vulnerable families.

ACKNOWLEDGMENTS

We gratefully acknowledge the support of the following organizations: National Institute of Child Health and Human Development (RO1 HD36093 "Welfare Reform and the Well-Being of Children"), Office of the Assistant Secretary of Planning and Evaluation, Administration on Developmental Disabilities, Administration for Children and Families, Social Security Administration, and National Institute of Mental Health; The Boston Foundation, The Annie E. Casey Foundation, The Edna McConnell Clark Foundation, The Lloyd A. Fry Foundation, The Hogg Foundation for Mental Health, The Robert Wood Johnson Foundation, The Joyce Foundation, The Henry J. Kaiser Family Foundation, The W.K. Kellogg Foundation, The Kronkosky Charitable Foundation, The John D. and Catherine T. MacArthur Foundation, The Charles Stewart Mott Foundation, The David and Lucile Packard Foundation, The Searle Fund for Policy Research, and The Woods Fund of Chicago. A special thank you is also extended to the families that participated in the Three-City Study.

REFERENCES

Arnett, J. (1989). Caregivers in day-care centers: Does training matter? *Journal of Applied Developmental Psychology, 10*, 541–552.

Barnett, W. S. (1995). Long-term effects of early childhood programs on cognitive and school outcomes. *The Future of Children, 5*(3), 25–50.

Beers, T. M. (2000). Flexible schedules and shift work: Replacing the "9-to-5" workday? *Monthly Labor Review, 123*(6), 33–40.

Blau, D. M., & Hagy, A. P. (1998). The demand for quality child care. *Journal of Political Economy, 106*(1), 104–146.

Brown-Lyons, M., Robertson, A., & Layzer, J. (2001). *Kith and kin—Informal child care: Highlights from recent research.* New York: Columbia University, National Center for Children in Poverty.

Burchinal, M. R., & Nelson, L. (2000). Family selection and child care experiences: Implications for studies of child outcomes. *Early Childhood Research Quarterly, 15*(3), 385–411.

Capizzano, J., Adams, G., & Sonenstein, F. (2000). Child care arrangements for children under five: Variation across states. *New Federalism: National Survey of America's Families* Series, Number B-7. Washington, DC: Urban Institute.

Cost, Quality, and Outcomes Study Team. (1999). *The children of the cost, quality, and outcomes study go to school* (Tech. Rep.). Chapel Hill: Frank Porter Graham Child Development Center, University of North Carolina at Chapel Hill.

Cryer, D., & Burchinal, M. (1997). Parents as child care consumers. *Early Childhood Research Quarterly, 12*, 35–58.

Duncan, G. J., & Brooks-Gunn, J. (2000). Family poverty, welfare reform, and child development. *Child Development, 71*(1), 188–196.

Duncan, G. J., & Gibson, C. (2001, November). *Selection and attrition in the NICHD childcare study's analyses of the impacts of childcare quality on child outcomes.* Paper at the meetings of the Association for Public Policy Analysis and Management, Washington, DC.

Emlen, A. C. (1999). *From a parent's point of view: Measuring the quality of child care.* Portland, OR: Portland State University and Oregon Child Care Research Partnership.

Fuller, B., & Kagan, S. L. (2000). *Remember the children: Mothers balance work and child care under welfare reform.* Berkeley, CA: University of California at Berkeley, Growing Up in Poverty Project.

Giannarelli, L., & Barsimantov, J. (2000). *Child care expenses of America's families.* Washington, DC: Urban Institute.

Harms, T., & Clifford, R. M. (1989). *The family day care rating scale.* New York: Teachers College Press.

Harms, T., Clifford, R. M., & Cryer, D. (1998). *Early childhood environment rating scale–revised.* New York: Teachers College Press.

Helburn, S. W., & Howes, C. (1996). Child care cost and quality. *The Future of Children, 6*(2), 62–82.

Hofferth, S. L. (1996). Child care in the United States today. *Future of Children, 6*(2), 41–61.

Holloway, S. D., & Fuller, B. (1999). Families and child care: Divergent viewpoints. *The Annals of the American Academy of Political and Social Science, 563*, 98–115.

Holloway, S., Fuller, B., Rambaud, M. F., & Eggers-Pierola, C. (1996). *Through my own eyes: Single mothers and the cultures of poverty.* Cambridge, MA: Harvard University Press.

Infant Health and Development Program. (1990). Enhancing the outcomes of low-birthweight, premature infants: A multisite, randomized trial. *Journal of the American Medical Association, 263*(22), 3035–3042.

Johansen, A. S., Leibowitz, A., & Waite, L. J. (1996). The importance of child-care characteristics to choice of care. *Journal of Marriage and the Family, 58*(3), 759–772.

Kontos, S., Howes, C., Shinn, M., & Galinsky, E. (1997). Children's experiences in family child care and relative care as a function of family income and ethnicity. *Merrill-Palmer Quarterly, 43*(3), 386–403.

Lamb, M. E. (1998). Nonparental child care: Context, quality, correlates, and consequences. In W. Damon, I. E. Sigel, & K. A. Renninger (Eds.), *Handbook of child psychology: Vol. 4. Child psychology in practice* (5th ed.). New York: Wiley.

Lamb, M. E., & Sternberg, K. J. (1992). Sociocultural perspectives on nonparental child care. In M. E. Lamb & K. J. Sternberg (Eds.), *Child care in context: Cross-cultural perspectives.* Hillsdale, NJ: Lawrence Erlbaum Associates.

LeVine, R. A. (1974). Parental goals: A cross-cultural view. *Teachers College Record, 76*(2), 226–239.

Meyers, M. K., Heintze, T., & Wolf, D. A. (1999). *Child care subsidies and the employment of welfare recipients* (UC-Data Archive and Technical Assistance Working Paper #15). Berkeley: University of California.

National Association for the Education of Young Children. (1998). *Accreditation criteria and procedures of the National Association for the Education of Young Children—1998 edition.* Washington, DC: Author.

NICHD Early Child Care Research Network. (1997). Poverty and patterns of child care. In G. J. Duncan & J. Brooks-Gunn (Eds.), *Consequences of growing up poor.* New York: Russell Sage.

NICHD Early Child Care Research Network. (1998). Early child care and self-control, compliance, and problem behavior at 24 and 36 months. *Child Development, 69*(4), 1145–1170.

NICHD Early Child Care Research Network. (2000a). Characteristics and quality of child care for toddlers and preschoolers. *Applied Developmental Science, 4*(3), 116–135.

NICHD Early Child Care Research Network. (2000b). The relation of child care to cognitive and language development. *Child Development, 71*(4), 960–980.

NICHD Early Child Care Research Network. (2001). Child care and children's peer interaction at 24 and 36 months: The NICHD study of early child care. *Child Development, 72*(5), 1478–1500.

National Research Council and Institute of Medicine. (2000). Growing up in child care. In J. P. Shonkoff & D. A. Phillips (Eds.), *From neurons to neighborhoods: The science of early childhood development*. Washington, DC: National Academy Press.

Phillips, D. A., Voran, M., Kisker, E., Howes, C., & Whitebook, M. (1994). Child care for children in poverty: Opportunity or inequity? *Child Development, 65*(2), 472–492.

Presser, H., & Cox, A. G. (1997). The work schedules of low-educated American women and welfare reform. *Monthly Labor Review, 20*(4), 25–34.

Schumacher, R., & Greenberg, M. (1999). *Child care after leaving welfare: Early evidence from state studies*. Washington, DC: Center for Law and Social Policy.

U.S. Department of Health and Human Services. (1996). *Trends in the well-being of America's children and youth: 1996*. Hyattsville, MD: Author.

U.S. Department of Health and Human Services. (1999). *Access to child care for low-income working families*. Washington, DC: Author.

Votruba-Drzal, E., Coley, R. L., & Chase-Lansdale, P. L. (2004). Child care and low-income children's development: Direct and moderated effects. *Child Development, 75*, 1–17.

Whitebook, M., Howes, C., & Phillips, D. A. (1990). *Who cares? Child care teachers and the quality of care in America* (Final Report of the National Child Care Staffing Study). Oakland, CA: Child Care Employee Project.

Winston, P., Angel, R. J., Burton, L. M., Chase-Lansdale, P. L., Cherlin, A. J., Moffitt, R. A., & Wilson, W. J. (1999). *Welfare, children, and families: Overview and design*. Baltimore: Johns Hopkins University Press.

Yoshikawa, H. (1995). Long-term effects of early childhood programs on social outcomes and delinquency. *The Future of Children, 5*(3), 51–75.

Yoshikawa, H., Rosman, E. A., & Hsueh, J. (2001). Variation in teenage mothers' experiences of child care and other components of welfare reform: Selection processes and developmental consequences. *Child Development, 72*(1), 299–317.

PART THREE

Government Subsidies and
the Nature of Child Care

CHAPTER EIGHT

The Dynamics of Child-Care Subsidy Use: A Collaborative Study of Five States

Marcia K. Meyers
University of Washington

Laura R. Peck
Arizona State University

Elizabeth E. Davis
University of Minnesota

Ann Collins
Abt Associates Inc.

J. Lee Kreader
Annie Georges
Columbia University

Roberta Weber
Linn-Benton Community College

Deanna Schexnayder
Daniel Schroeder
Jerry A. Olson
University of Texas at Austin

The federal welfare reform legislation enacted in 1996, the Personal Responsibility and Work Opportunity Reconciliation Act (PRWORA), gave states and communities new challenges and opportunities for meeting the needs of low-income families and children. The intensity of these challenges and the importance of these opportunities are especially striking in policies for subsidized child care. In developing subsidy policies, both federal and state policy officials have had to act in the absence of good information about subsidy use among low-income families. Although some (but not all) states are able to use administrative data to obtain basic information about the population using subsidies at a point in time, they have been unable to extend these analyses to examine in great depth the characteristics of families or their patterns of child-care use.

Of particular importance, cross-sectional data have not provided information about the dynamics of subsidy use. Given persistent low earnings, parents leaving welfare (and other low-income working parents) are likely to need child-care assistance for a relatively long period. At the same time, however, their participation in short-term employment preparation activities, turnover in employment, and variable earnings may make it difficult for these families to remain continuously eligible for subsidy assistance. As described in Adams and Snyder (chap. 9, this volume), burdensome application and recertification processes may create additional barriers to continuous subsidy receipt. For parents, instability in subsidy receipt may mean the difference between keeping and losing a job and, for those employed, between self-sufficiency and poverty. For children, instability in subsidy receipt may contribute to instability in care arrangements, which developmental experts identify as a risk to healthy socioemotional development. Thus, the stability or continuity of subsidy assistance has two-generational implications: for the employment stability and self-sufficiency of families and for the healthy development of children.

In addition to reforming the federal cash assistance program, the welfare reform legislation enacted in 1996 combined four categorical federal child-care subsidy programs into a new Child Care and Development Fund (CCDF) block grant. The block grant removed most federal rules for child-care subsidy assistance and gave states both a larger pool of federal funding and greater flexibility in deciding how to spend these funds. States, which already exercised substantial control over child-care services and regulation, were given new authority to design and deliver child-care assistance to low-income families. States now set policy governing which families are eligible for services, along with their traditional role in determining what families need to do to secure and retain assistance, what services families receive, how generously these services are funded, and how heavily they are regulated. States set these policies in the broader context of other policies, most notably welfare and training assistance, which also have been devolved to the state level.

Child-care and welfare policies may influence the dynamics of child-care subsidy use through a number of mechanisms. High co-payments or low provider reimbursements, for example, may reduce incentives for participation and shorten the length of subsidy receipt. Policies that prioritize assistance for TANF recipients may direct subsidies to families with less stable employment and shorter spells of child care and subsidy use. Policies that influence the choice of care arrangements may also contribute to the duration of subsidy use by increasing the use of more or less stable forms of care. Although there is reason to expect that state policies such as these may affect the duration of subsidy assistance, there has been little empirical study of these issues.

To advance knowledge and understanding about the dynamic use of child-care subsidies, this study uses administrative data from the child-care subsidy systems in five states (Illinois, Maryland, Massachusetts, Oregon, and Texas) to address the following questions about subsidy use and cross-state variation: (a) What are the characteristics of children and families who receive subsidies? (b) What assistance do these children and families receive? (c) How long do spells of subsidy receipt last? (d) How likely is it that children who end a spell of subsidy receipt subsequently begin another? and (e) How *stable* are children's care arrangements while they are in the subsidy system?

In the next section, we describe the data and methods for the study. We then consider the policy context for the analyses by briefly summarizing policies governing child-care subsidies and TANF in the five states, which varied in their child-care and TANF policies. The following section presents the empirical results of our analyses of the characteristics, services, and dynamics of subsidy assistance. We conclude by summarizing these findings, relating them to aspects of state policy, and suggesting policy implications.

DATA AND METHODS

This study used data collected and analyzed by a team of policy and methodological experts brought together through the Child Care Policy Research Consortium. University-based researchers studying child care in each of the states collected policy data by reviewing documents and interviewing key informants in each state. They obtained administrative data from state childcare subsidy payment systems with the cooperation of the relevant state agency officials. Researchers from each of the state teams constructed and analyzed state-specific data. The team at Columbia University then synthesized the state-level analytic findings.

Raw data from the states' subsidy payment files were obtained for 24 calendar months from each state, covering the period of July 1997 through June 1999.[1] For the five states in the study, the data include all (or a significant portion) of the child-care subsidy assistance that was delivered through each state's voucher program. In Maryland and Texas, this corresponded to the universe of families assisted through the subsidy system because all assistance was provided through vouchers. In the remaining states, the data did not include the portion of the population assisted through contracted care (i.e., child care that was paid for through a direct contract with a provider). This excluded approximately 5% of all subsidized families in Oregon, approximately 20% in Illinois, and approximately 50% in Massachusetts. In addition, data for Massachusetts were available for only part of the state, capturing an estimated 50% of all voucher-based assistance, and are weighted heavily toward TANF-

---

[1]Data for Oregon cover the period of October 1997 through September 1999; data for Massachusetts cover October 1996 through September 1998.

related users.[2] The findings from this study can be generalized only to voucher-based subsidy assistance.

The administrative data for each state were cleaned and transformed to a family-level sample by randomly selecting one child from each family that received any subsidy assistance during the 24-month observation period. Results are interpreted as the experience of families that served in the subsidy system, with equal representation of families regardless of the number of children who received subsidies. The sample was further restricted by excluding cases receiving a subsidy during the first month of the observation period (i.e., if the spell was left censored). This restriction excluded between 24% and 36% of observations in various states. The exclusion of these cases could bias results by eliminating cases with the longest duration of receipt. Because the large majority of all spells are short, this bias is expected to be minimal. State-level analysis samples ranged from 15,202 observations (person-months) in the smallest sample to 130,112 in the largest.

Measures of child/family characteristics (age of the child, activity status of the parent, and family income) and service characteristics (type of care, value of subsidy, and size of co-payment) in each of the five states were constructed directly from the administrative data. The length of subsidy receipt was measured in spells, with a *spell* defined as one or more consecutive months of subsidy receipt that were preceded and followed by 1 or more months of nonreceipt. Because the monthly data corresponded to service receipt (i.e., the month in which the child received care), even a 1-month break indicated a break in the continuity of subsidized care. The data reflected the month in which the family received assistance (rather than the month in which the provider was paid, if different).[3] For the descriptive analyses, measures of child/family and service characteristics were constructed for the first month of the first observed spell of subsidy receipt for the randomly selected child. Analyses were conducted on those spells of subsidy receipt that started during the observation period.

Our measures of family, child, and service characteristics, which are constructed from the 2-year data, will differ from measures constructed from a

---

[2]Data were available for the city of Boston, the diverse suburbs west of the city (e.g., Cambridge, Chelsea, and Somerville), number of smaller metropolitan areas (i.e., Springfield/Chicopee/Holyoke, Lowell, and New Bedford/Fall River), as well as the rural areas of Hampden, Bristol, and Plymouth counties. Implications for interpretation of the results of the differing levels of coverage across the states are discussed in a later section.

[3]To test whether the use of a 1-month break to define spells impacted our results, we calculated median spell lengths in two states using both a 1- and 2-month break to define spells. The median spell lengths were not substantially different. Because the data reflect actual service month, not payment month, a 1-month break represents a true interruption in subsidized care, not an administrative error such as a delayed payment. In this, administrative data for child-care subsidies differ from those used in studies of cash assistance; these studies often use a longer break in service to avoid confounding administrative errors with exits from assistance.

point in time such as 1 month's caseload. For example, the proportion of children who are a certain age will differ between our study and a point-in-time study if older children have longer spells of subsidy receipt. These differences arise because families with longer spells of subsidy receipt make up a larger share of all families participating at a point in time. The measures presented in this report represent the experience of all families participating in the subsidy program over a 2-year period regardless of the length of receipt.

As a measure of the *continuity* of subsidy assistance, we calculated the median length of continuous spells of subsidy receipt for the randomly selected child. Given a relatively short 24-month observation window, an unadjusted estimate of average spell length was likely to be biased by the lack of data on spells that began before the observation period (i.e., left censored) and those that were in process at the end of the period (i.e., right censored). To avoid problems of left censoring, the analysis samples were restricted to periods of subsidy receipt that began during the 24-month observation period. To correct for right censoring, we used the Kaplan–Meier procedure to estimate spell length. This statistical procedure estimates the conditional survival rate at each month (the proportion of cases that continue to the observed month, given that they survived to the prior month), using spells for which data are available in the observed month (correcting for right censoring of spells that extended beyond the observation window). Median spell lengths across the states are compared using the first observed (nonleft censored) spell for the randomly selected child.

Given a relatively short observation period (2 years), accurate estimates of children's total time in the subsidy systems were difficult to obtain. Considering whether children who exited the subsidy system returned for subsequent spell(s) of assistance provides a sense of the total duration of assistance. Using the first spell of new entrants during the observation period, we calculated the proportion of those ending a subsidy spell that returned to the subsidy system within 3, 6, 9, and 12 months. For this analysis, the sample was restricted to spells with a sufficient number of months of data to calculate the reentry rate (e.g., to be included in the calculation of the rate of reentry within 12 months, there must be at least 12 months of data following the end of the subsidy spell). Obviously, those with longer first spells will be less likely to be included in the reentry rate (because of insufficient follow-up data), which may bias the results.

Finally, to examine the *stability* of children's care arrangements, we calculated the number of providers that children had during their time in the subsidy system. Because the data for this analysis included only months during which children received subsidies, it was impossible to measure the *total* length of time children spent in a single arrangement (because children may have been in the same arrangement before or after the period of subsidization). Instead, the data were used to measure the stability of providers for each child during the entire period of subsidization. As a measure of the stability of arrangement within periods of subsidy receipt, we calculated a primary provider ratio. The *primary provider* was defined as the provider with the most months of care for that child (while on subsidy). The primary provider ratio was calculated as the number of months during which the child was cared for by this provider relative to the total number of months that the child was in subsidized care during the 24-month observation period. A primary provider ratio of 1 is interpreted to mean that all of the months of subsidized care were spent with the primary provider. We compare across the states the percentage of children who stay with the same provider during all months of subsidy receipt.

CONTEXT: STATE CHILD CARE AND TANF POLICIES

As shown in several other chapters in this volume, state child care and TANF policies influence both the characteristics of families served in the state subsidy system and the assistance that families are provided. These policies may also influence the length of assistance, both directly (by restricting the period of assistance or creating barriers to continuous assistance) and indirectly (through their influence on the characteristics of the subsidized population and subsidized services). The states involved in this project varied in their administrative structures and philosophies, approaches to welfare reform, subsidy delivery systems, and local child-care and labor markets. Key aspects of the states' TANF and child-care subsidy policies are summarized in Table 8.1 (see Ross & Kirby, chap. 2, this volume, for a description of these policies for a different subset of states).

Illinois was the only state of the five to formally extend a subsidy guarantee to all families that met income and other eligibility guidelines. Relatively high TANF benefits and earnings disregards supported employment and the mixing of welfare with work. Although the state had adopted a broad child-care entitlement and supported parental employment, the income threshold for initial and continued subsidy eligibility (as a share of the state median income) was among the lowest of the five states. Maximum allowable payments to providers (as a share of the prevailing market rate) were also low relative to those of other states. Few families were exempted from co-payments, but co-payment levels were generally lower than co-payments among the other four states. Retaining eligibility was relatively less burdensome for Illinois families than it was for those in the other states; families were required to recertify their eligibility every 6 months.

Maryland's welfare reforms also emphasized employment and gave priority for subsidies to parents in job preparation activities or postwelfare employment. Although non-TANF, working families were eligible for subsidy assistance, the income thresholds for initial and continuing eligibility (as a share of

TABLE 8.1

Selected Elements of State Child-Care Subsidy and TANF Policies (1997–1999)

	Illinois	Maryland	Massachusetts	Oregon	Texas
		Eligibility Rules (Child Care Subsidies)			
Income eligibility threshold per month as % of state 1998 median income (for family of three, 1998)	48% ($1,818)	36% ($1,534) at application and 44% ($1,872) for continued services	47% ($1,931) at application and 67% ($2,771) for continued services	65% ($2,088)	74% of SMI ($2,278) and 92% of SMI ($2,824) for continued services
Co-payment rules (for families with co-payment)	Adjusted for income, family size and, from 10/97, number of children in care	Adjusted for income, family size, number of children in care and local costs	Adjusted for income and family size	Minimum of $25 and increased with family income	Nine percent of gross income for one child and 11 percent for two or more children
Co-payment exemptions	Child-only TANF cases	TANF and SSI recipients	TANF cases and some child-protective cases	Participants in JOBS employment programs, and Unemployment Insurance or Food Stamps recipients	TANF, SSI, Food Stamps Employment and Training, child protective services clients
Service rationing	Commitment to serve all eligible families	Waiting lists until October 1997, with no waiting lists after that date	Waiting lists for non-TANF families	Waiting lists only for participants in postsecondary education	Varied; waiting lists maintained by some local agencies during some parts of study period

(Continued)

TABLE 8.1
(Continued)

	Illinois	Maryland	Massachusetts	Oregon	Texas
TANF Policy (1998)					
Maximum TANF grant for a one-parent family of three	$377	$377	$579	$460	$188
Earning disregard policies for TANF eligibility	Disregard 67% for all months	Disregard 26% for all months	Disregard first $120 and 50% of remainder for all months	Disregard 50% for all months	Disregard first $120 and 33% of remainder for first 4 months; first $120 for next 8 months; first $90 after that
Age of youngest child that exempts parent from TANF work requirements	1 year	1 year	School-age[a]	3 months	5 years until 10/97, 4 years thereafter during study period

[a]Parents with children under school age were exempt from work requirements, but not time limits. Also, 2-year time limits began when children turned 2 years old.

the state median income) were low in comparison with those of other states. The state exempted TANF and SSI recipient families from co-payments, but imposed relatively high co-payments on other families. Provider payments were low, relative to prevailing market rates, at the beginning of the study period. By the end of the 24-month period, however, the state had raised payment rates for market care to about the 75th percentile of market rates. Although families could be certified for subsidy eligibility for up to 1 year, the actual period of eligibility averaged 3 months for TANF clients and 6 months for non-TANF clients; practices at local offices varied, but the norm was a 3- or 6-month recertification period.

Massachusetts provided the highest TANF benefits among the five states, along with generous earnings disregards (see Witte & Queralt, chap. 3, this volume, for data on another dimension of subsidy use in Massachusetts). The state exempted parents from work requirements until their children reached school age (although 2-year time limits began when children reached age 2). The state used child-care subsidies primarily to help TANF families achieve and maintain employment; former TANF families in Massachusetts had priority for assistance among the income-eligible families. Families that were receiving and exiting welfare were served primarily through the voucher system; working, non-TANF families were more likely to receive assistance from a provider who contracted directly with the state. The state exempted TANF recipient families from co-payments, but imposed relatively high co-payments on higher income families. The state had the highest rate of payment, among the five states, for center-based care; payments for family child care, relative, and in-home care were all substantially lower. Families were required to redetermine their eligibility for assistance every 1 to 6 months depending on their TANF and employment status.

Oregon's welfare reform policies emphasized both initial deterrence from welfare and rapid employment among TANF recipients, who were required to participate in work activities as soon as their youngest child reached the age of 3 months. Child-care subsidies were also available to working, non-TANF families, but these were not widely advertised. In comparison with the other states in the study, Oregon set an eligibility threshold that was reasonably high (as a share of the state median income). However, provider payments were below the 75th percentile of market rates for market-based care. Oregon was also distinguished by unusually high parental co-payments. Most employed families receiving means-tested benefits were exempted from co-payments. Among those that were not exempt, however, the minimum co-payment was $25 per month and rose very steeply with family income above the poverty line. Maintaining subsidy eligibility was relatively burdensome for Oregon families. Although caseworkers had the option of scheduling redeterminations as infrequently as once per year, most subsidy recipients were required to recertify their eligibility every 3 months.

Texas subsidy policies were characterized by a combination of high provider payments, family co-payments that were low (relative to other states) and increased at a constant rate with income, and the highest income eligibility threshold (relative to state median income) among the five states. In contrast, TANF benefits and income disregards were the lowest across the five states. The state's welfare reform goals emphasized rapid employment and welfare deterrence and strongly discouraged mixing welfare and work. TANF families preparing for employment through the CHOICES program were given priority for subsidy assistance, although benefits were extended to more working, non-TANF families later in the study period. The redetermination burden was relatively low for most families. Non-TANF, working families were required to recertify their subsidy eligibility every 6 months; TANF families remained eligible as long they were actively engaged in the CHOICES program.

RESULTS: POPULATIONS SERVED, ASSISTANCE PROVIDED, AND DYNAMICS OF ASSISTANCE

Populations Served

Incomes of Subsidy Recipients.   Although all states served families with low initial incomes, the median incomes (considering TANF and earnings) of subsidized families at the start of the child's subsidy spell varied from $363 in Texas to $920 in Illinois (Table 8.2).[4] Illinois also served families at the highest income level relative to all families in the state; families at the middle of the distribution of incomes in the subsidy population had incomes at 24% of the state median. Subsidized families in Massachusetts and Texas were the poorest, relative to other families in their states, with median incomes of only 11% to 12% of state median income.

To examine how actual family incomes corresponded to the states' eligibility thresholds, Fig. 8.1 compares the median incomes among subsidy recipients (at the start of the spell) to the relevant state thresholds for initial and continuing eligibility. Median incomes among subsidized families in Illinois and Maryland were close to half of the initial threshold; in Oregon and Texas, the incomes of families in the subsidy system appeared to be substantially lower than state eligibility thresholds. This suggests that in Texas and Oregon, the

---

[4]Income measures varied across the states due to differences in data availability. Income in Illinois and Maryland is measured as household earnings and income as well as public assistance payments. Income in Massachusetts is measured as the sum of individual earnings and an imputed public assistance payment. Income in Oregon is measured as the sum of household earnings and income and an imputed public assistance payment. Income in Texas is the sum of individual earnings and actual public assistance payments.

TABLE 8.2

Characteristics of Families Receiving Subsidies (First Month of First Observed Spells Starting During Observation Period), by State

Characteristic	Illinois	Maryland	Massachusetts	Oregon	Texas
Recipients' median income as share of state median income	24%	17%	11%	18%	12%
Recipients' median income as share initial threshold	51%	48%	24%	27%	16%
Recipients' median income as share continuing threshold	51%	39%	17%	27%	13%
Activity status of parent with child in subsidy					
Working	85%	66%	36%	50%	72%
Not receiving TANF	15%	32%	10%	45%	55%
Receiving TANF	71%	34%	26%	5%	16%
Not working	15%	34%	64%	50%	28%
Receiving TANF	14%	30%	48%	33%	14%
Not receiving TANF	1%	4%	15%	17%	14%
Age of child in subsidy (randomly selected child)					
Infants, 0–23 months	30%	30%	31%	36%	40%
Preschool, 24–47 months	24%	27%	27%	22%	25%
School transition, 48–71 months	19%	18%	18%	17%	17%
School age, 72 months and older	27%	25%	24%	25%	18%

Note. The observation period in Illinois, Maryland, and Texas is July 1997 through June 1999; the observation period in Oregon is October 1997 through September 1999; and the observation period in Massachusetts is October 1996 through September 1998. Income in Illinois and Maryland is measured as household earnings and income as well as public assistance payments. Income in Massachusetts is measured as the sum of individual earnings and an imputed public assistance payment. Income in Oregon is measured as the sum of household earnings and income and an imputed public assistance payment. Income in Texas is the sum of individual earnings and actual public assistance payment. Data for Massachusetts do not include contracted care arrangements (an estimated 50% of all subsidized arrangements in the state) and include voucher recipients for only a portion of the state (approximately 50% of all voucher recipients). Because working poor families were more likely to use contracted care arrangements, the data for this study reflect the experiences of TANF-related subsidy users. Due to left censoring and exclusion of very long subsidy spells, the analysis sample may be biased toward families with younger children. Because the large majority of all spells are short, this bias is expected to be minimal.

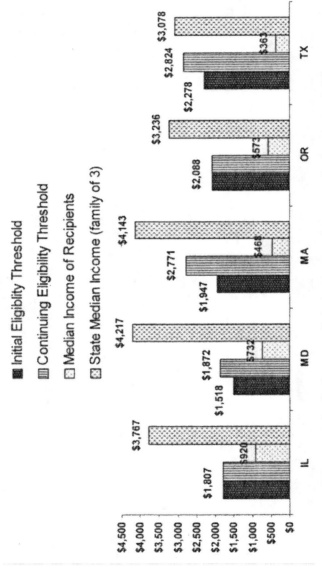

FIG. 8.1. Median family income of subsidy recipients relative to initial and continuing eligibility thresholds (1998).

population of families served was substantially more disadvantaged than the potentially eligible population. This may reflect state policies that gave priority to current and recent TANF recipients, who were likely to have lower incomes than working families. It is difficult to interpret income information for the fifth state, Massachusetts, because the sample excluded families that were using contracted care, and these families were more likely to be higher income, working families.

Activity Status of Subsidy Recipients.   Cross-state variation in parents' initial TANF and employment status (derived from income measures during the first month of subsidy receipt) was substantial and largely consistent with states' welfare rules and reform goals. In Oregon and Texas, states that strongly discouraged TANF receipt through initial diversion and/or low benefits, about one half of subsidy recipient families were employed families not receiving TANF (Table 8.2). In contrast, 71% of recipients were mixing welfare with work in Illinois, a state with liberal earnings disregards and TANF benefits. In Maryland, about two thirds of families were working, equally divided between those who were and were not receiving TANF. In Massachusetts, the largest single group of subsidized families was TANF recipients who were not employed. This is explained, in large part, by the exclusion of the large system of contracted care from the sample, which served primarily working, non-TANF families.

Age of Children Receiving Subsidies.   Despite large differences in state policies regarding work exemptions relating to children's ages, the five states were similar in the ages of children during their first month of subsidy receipt (Table 8.2). Between one fifth and one sixth of children in the subsidy system of all states were school age (ages 6–13). Between one third and one half of children were under age 3, with the highest proportion of very young children (under age 1) in the subsidy systems of Oregon and Texas. This result is not surprising in Oregon given that the work exemption was lowest there (3 months). In Texas, however, a relatively high *age of youngest child* work exemption (4–5 years old) exempted a relatively larger proportion of TANF clients from employment activities.

Assistance Provided

Type of Care Used by Children Receiving Subsidies.   To compare the type of care used by families, we identified the care arrangement of the randomly selected child during the first month of subsidy receipt during the observation period (Table 8.3). In both Massachusetts and Texas, most subsidized care was provided in regulated settings and most was center based. At the opposite extreme, families in Oregon were more likely than not to be in

TABLE 8.3

Characteristics of Services Received by Families
(First Month of First Observed Spells Starting During Observation Period), by State

Characteristic	Illinois	Maryland	Massachusetts	Oregon	Texas
Care arrangement (randomly selected child)					
Center care	31%	33%	53%	18%	79%
Family child care (nonrelative)	17%	32%	23%	58%	7%
In-home care (nonrelative)	20%	7%	15%	4%	0%
Relative care	32%	27%	10%	19%	14%
Regulation status of care arrangement					
Regulated	42%	65%	90%	38%	86%
Unregulated	58%	35%	10%	62%	14%
Provider payments					
Monthly payment to provider, family level					
Median value ($)	$248	$297	$363	$195	$190
Family co-payments					
Share of families with no co-payment (%)	10%	48%	85%	59%	55%
Monthly co-payment, family level					
Among all families					
Median co-payment ($)	$35	$2	$0	$0	$0
Among families with co-payment only					
Median co-payment ($)	$43	$29	$62	$67	$35

Note. The observation period in Illinois, Maryland, and Texas is July 1997 through June 1999; the observation period in Oregon is October 1997 through September 1999; and the observation period in Massachusetts is October 1996 through September 1998. Data for Massachusetts do not include contracted care arrangements (an estimated 50% of all subsidized arrangements in the state) and include voucher recipients for only a portion of the state (approximately 50% of all voucher recipients). Because working poor families were more likely to use contracted care arrangements, the data for this study reflect the experiences of TANF-related subsidy users.

unregulated care and in a family child-care setting.[5] Care arrangements in Illinois and Maryland were distributed more evenly across care types, with about one third each in relative, nonrelative, and center care. As discussed later, differences in care types reflect both state policies concerning which providers are eligible and maximum provider payment rates and differences in local child-care markets.

Provider Payments.   The value of subsidies at the family level was measured as the total of monthly payments to all providers for all children in the family receiving subsidies during the first observed month of subsidy receipt (Table 8.3). The median value of monthly subsidy payments varied by more than $150 per month across the states. Despite the heavy reliance on center-based and regulated care in Texas, and relatively high payments in comparison with market rates, the median payments to providers in Texas were the lowest among the five states ($190); monthly payments were about the same ($195) in Oregon. At the high end, the median monthly payment in Massachusetts was $363.

Family Co-Payments.   To compare co-payments at the family level, we calculated the average total monthly co-payment for the family during the first month of subsidy receipt, considering all children in subsidized care (Table 8.3). The share of families making any co-payment varied markedly. Consistent with state policies that exempted few Illinois families from co-payment, about 90% of families in that state made a co-payment. At the opposite extreme, in Massachusetts, where voucher recipients were primarily TANF recipients, 85% of families had no co-payment. In the remaining states, between 48% and 59% of families did not have a co-payment.

Considering only families that incurred a co-payment, median co-payments ranged from $29 in Maryland to $67 in Oregon. When exemptions and average payments are considered jointly (i.e., the average co-payment across all families), only Illinois, which excluded few families from co-payments, had a relatively high ($34) median co-payment. In three of the states, median co-payments were zero because more than half of families were exempt from any co-payment.

Dynamics of Subsidy Use

Continuity.   To estimate the continuity of subsidy use, we used survival analysis techniques to estimate the number of months by which 25%, 50%, and 75% of children, respectively, had left the subsidy system. In all five states,

---

[5]Because child-care regulations varied across the states, regulated care does not denote a consistent category in all states. For example, states differ in the number of children that a provider can care for without being subject to regulation.

the length of subsidy receipt was short (Table 8.4). For 25% of children, sub-sidy spells ended within 3 months. Spell length also varied by state. Within 3 months, subsidy receipt ended for one half of the children who had started a spell in Oregon; within 7 months, spells ended for 75% of all children. In Mary-land and Massachusetts, half of spells ended within 4 to 5 months and 75% of spells within 8 to 11 months. Spells were longer in Illinois and Texas. One half of children in these states received subsidies for 6 to 7 months or less, and 25% of children had spells longer than 14 or 15 months.

The probability that children exited subsidies was very high in all states dur-ing the first few months of receipt. By 6 months, more than half of subsidy spells had ended in Maryland, Massachusetts, and Oregon, and nearly half had ended in Illinois and Texas as well. Although most spells ended quickly in all states, variation in the survival rate across states is clear (Fig. 8.2). Exits were most rapid in Oregon and slower in both Texas and Illinois. By the 1-year point, about 30% of spells were continuing in Illinois and Texas, in contrast to fewer than 15% of spells in Oregon.

These estimates suggest little continuity in children's receipt of subsidy as-sistance. It is possible, however, that continuity increases over time for fami-lies and children. This might be the case if, for example, parents are likely to be in employment-preparation activities during their first spell of subsidy receipt and more likely to be employed, and to have more stable child-care arrange-ments, in later spells of receipt. To consider whether subsequent spells of sub-sidy receipt were longer for children who had multiple spells during the obser-vation period, we compared the length of first observed spell to that of the second spell in the two states with the longest and shortest subsidy spells. In Texas, where children had the longest or most continuous spells of subsidy re-ceipt, the median length second spells of receipt were 1 month longer than first spells. In Oregon, where children had the shortest spells, there was no dif-ference in the median length of first and second spells. These analyses suggest that the continuity of children's subsidy receipt did not increase much with families' time in the subsidy system.

Continuity of subsidy receipt varied by family characteristics in similar pat-terns across the five states. Working, non-TANF families had the longest me-dian spells of receipt in all states other than Illinois, and nonworking families (re-ceiving TANF or not) generally had the shortest spells (Table 8.4). (In Illinois, median spell length were similar across groups.) For TANF-recipient families, subsidy exits were notably rapid during the first 2 months of assistance; in three of the states (Texas, Maryland, and Oregon), about one half of the children in these families had exited the subsidy system within 3 to 4 months. Although spell lengths differed across families within states, the pattern of cross-state vari-ation was nearly the same for each subgroup of families.

The length of spells did not differ much by child age in three of the states (Table 8.4). Spells were 1 to 2 months shorter for the oldest children (school

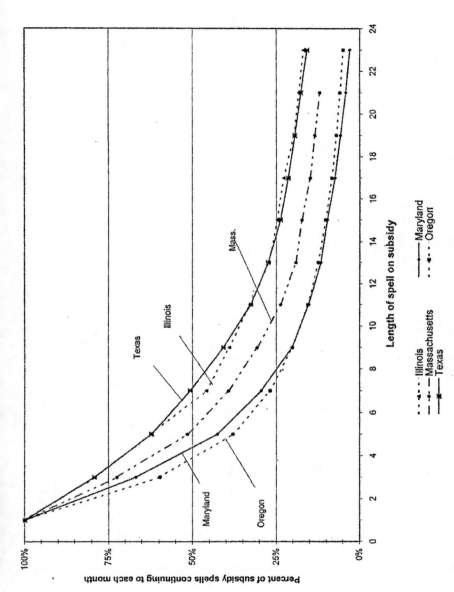

FIG. 8.2. Survival rate—first observed spell starting during observation period.

189

TABLE 8.4

Kaplan–Meier Estimates of Duration of Subsidy Receipt in Months
(First Observed Spell Starting During Observation Period), by State

Characteristic	Illinois	Maryland	Massachusetts	Oregon	Texas
All families					
25th percentile	3	2	3	2	3
Median	6	4	5	3	7
75th percentile	14	8	11	7	14
Families by work and TANF status					
Working, not receiving TANF	5	5	7	4	8
Working, receiving TANF	6	4	5	3	5
Not working, receiving TANF	5	4	5	3	4
Not working, not receiving TANF	6	3	5	2	6
Families by age of child in subsidy					
Infants, 0–23 months	6	4	5	4	7
Preschool, 24–47 months	6	4	6	3	7
School transition, 48–71 months	6	4	6	3	6
School age, 72 months and older	6	4	4	3	5
Families by care arrangement for child in subsidy					
Center care	5	4	6	3	7
Family child care (nonrelative)	7	4	5	3	7
In-home care (nonrelative)	6	3	4	4	NA
Relative care	6	3	5	3	6

Note. The observation period in Illinois, Maryland, and Texas is July 1997 through June 1999; the observation period in Oregon is October 1997 through September 1999; and the observation period in Massachusetts is October 1996 through September 1998. The Kaplan–Meier method adjusts estimates of duration for incompletely observed or right-censored spells of subsidy receipt. Data for Massachusetts do not include contracted care arrangements (an estimated 50% of all subsidized arrangements in the state) and include voucher recipients for only a portion of the state (approximately 50% of all voucher recipients). Because working poor families were more likely to use contracted care arrangements, the data for this study reflect the experiences of TANF-related subsidy users.

age) in Texas and Massachusetts. When spell lengths are compared across states within groups of families with children of various ages, the ranking of the states by length of spell remained the same: Spells were longest in Texas and Illinois and shortest in Oregon for all age groups. Within states, median spell length varied only modestly—by 1 to 2 months at most for children starting in different forms of care (Table 8.4). There was no consistent pattern, across states, in which type of care was associated with longer spells.

Reentry to the Subsidy System. The length of a single, continuous spell of subsidy receipt provides one indicator of the continuity of assistance. But if children cycle in and out of subsidy spells over time, it will not provide a good indicator of the total duration of children's subsidy assistance. The 24-month observation period for this study limited options for estimating the duration of subsidy assistance for children and their families over a long period of time. Some indication of this duration is provided by the rate at which children reentered the system for a subsequent spell of subsidy assistance within 12 months after the end of a subsidy spell (for all children for whom a full 12 months of data were available).

Return to subsidy receipt was common in all states, but the rate varied across the five states (Table 8.5). Among those with completed spells during the observation period, between one fifth (in Texas) and almost one half (in Maryland) of children returned to subsidy receipt within 3 months of the ending of their spell. Over a 12-month period, one third or more of children in all five states began another spell of subsidy receipt, and as many as 50% to 60% returned in Illinois and Maryland. These analyses suggest that the length of a single spell of subsidy receipt does not capture the total duration of subsidy assistance for many children. For one third to one half of children, the duration of assistance was greater than the length of a single, continuous spell.

Stability of Care Arrangements.   Patterns of exit from and reentry to the subsidy system capture two aspects of child-care stability. From the standpoint of children's experience of care, as well as the reliability of care for parents, it is equally important to consider the stability of the child–caregiver relationship. The research team compared the stability of children's care within spells of subsidy receipt by considering the proportion of the total time in sub-

TABLE 8.5
Cumulative Percent of Children Exiting Subsidy Spell
Who Return Within 3, 6, 9, and 12 Months, by State

Interval	Illinois	Maryland	Massachusetts	Oregon	Texas
3 month	32%	46%	28%	24%	20%
6 month	43%	56%	36%	34%	27%
9 month	49%	60%	38%	39%	32%
12 month	50%	58%	40%	40%	35%

Note.   The observation period in Illinois, Maryland, and Texas is July 1997 through June 1999; the observation period in Oregon is October 1997 through September 1999; and the observation period in Massachusetts is October 1996 through September 1998. Data for Massachusetts do not include contracted care arrangements (an estimated 50% of all subsidized arrangements in the state) and include voucher recipients for only a portion of the state (approximately 50% of all voucher recipients). Because working poor families were more likely to use contracted care arrangements, the data for this study reflect the experiences of TANF-related subsidy users.

TABLE 8.6
Stability of Provider–Child Relationships, by State

Cumulative Duration of Subsidy Receipt (Months)	Percent Remaining With Primary Provider for Entire Subsidy Period (PPR = 1)				
	Illinois	Maryland	Massachusetts	Oregon	Texas
3	93%	76%	87%	76%	90%
6	83%	64%	72%	52%	73%
9	69%	62%	61%	43%	67%
12	60%	53%	57%	36%	57%
18	54%	52%	58%	29%	53%

Note. The primary provider ratio is the number of months with the longest provider divided by the total observed months of subsidy receipt. Data for Massachusetts do not include contracted care arrangements (an estimated 50% of all subsidized arrangements in the state) and include voucher recipients for only a portion of the state (approximately 50% of all voucher recipients). Because working poor families were more likely to use contracted care arrangements, the data for this study reflect the experiences of TANF-related subsidy users.

sidies that children remained with the primary provider (the most common provider during the months of subsidy receipt).[6]

Most children on subsidy in these states remained with the primary provider during all the months they received subsidies (Table 8.6). This may be due, in large part, to the fact that the length of subsidy spells is short. Within this overall pattern, variation is evident across the states. Provider stability was low in Oregon, where only about half of children who received subsidies for 6 months remained with the same provider and less than 30% of those receiving subsidies for 18 months were with the same person. In contrast, from 73% to 83% of children who received subsidies for 6 months in Texas and Illinois, respectively, stayed with the same provider, and over half of children receiving subsidies for as long as 18 months were with the same person. Provider stability is higher in the states with longer median spells, suggesting that children with multiple short spells are less likely to remain with the same provider.

These data suggest that while care arrangements were relatively stable for children who remained in the subsidy system for a short time, the stability of providers declined sharply in all states as the cumulative months of subsidy receipt increased. Because many subsidy spells ended within a few months, provider stability may not appear to pose a significant problem. If the end of subsidy receipt leads to the end of the care arrangement, however, children have

---

[6]This is likely to overestimate stability for some children because the provider was defined as the billing entity. Children who were in center-based arrangements may have experienced multiple individual providers while they were in one setting. Children may also experience multiple providers because they are in multiple-care arrangement.

experienced greater turnover in arrangements than can be observed in these data. Stability appears to be low for the one third to nearly one half of children who received subsidies for a cumulative period of more than 6 months.

SUMMARY: STATE POLICIES AND SUBSIDY PATTERNS

The diversity of the populations served and the diversity of the assistance provided across the five states are two of the most striking findings of this study. The devolution of already highly decentralized child-care subsidy programs in the 1990s increased opportunities for state policymakers to determine who receives subsidies, what types of providers are subsidized, how much providers are paid, and what portion of costs are paid by families. These policy choices have interacted, sometimes in unexpected ways, with other state policy decisions about welfare benefits and client obligations.

One consequence of these policy choices and interactions is that states serve very different populations of families in their subsidy systems. In Illinois, for example, employed families, many of whom also received TANF, dominated the subsidy system; this reflected Illinois' welfare policies, which encouraged mixing welfare and work through relatively high TANF benefits and income disregards. In contrast, in Oregon, only about one half of subsidized families were working, and a relatively large share were neither working nor receiving TANF. Many of these families were provided child-care assistance as part of Oregon's short-term, welfare deterrence service strategy. In Texas, the very low TANF benefits and earnings disregards in the state made it difficult for families to retain welfare benefits once they started working, so relatively few of the subsidy families are working and receiving TANF.

Subsidized families differed across the states in terms of income levels as well as employment and TANF status. In Illinois, the median incomes of subsidized families were about one quarter of the state median income, whereas in Texas they were only 12% of the state median income. Higher income levels among subsidy recipients in Illinois reflect both the state's formal and explicit commitment to serve all families who met eligibility guidelines and policies that encouraged employment with and without TANF receipt. Very low incomes among subsidy recipients in Texas, despite the highest initial and continuing eligibility thresholds among the five states, are consistent with state policies that encouraged rapid welfare exits while rationing assistance to working, nonrecipient families (particularly in the earlier periods of the study). Given the heavy concentration of TANF families in the Massachusetts sample, it is not surprising that the median incomes of subsidy recipients were low relative both to the incomes of all families in the state and to the maximum income eligibility thresholds for subsidy assistance. In Oregon, the incomes of families in the subsidy system were low relative to the state median income and well below the eligibility threshold for subsidy assistance. Again this is consistent with state policy that prioritized subsidy assistance as a form of upfront welfare deterrence.

Co-payment levels and exemptions varied across the states, which may explain in part the differences in the characteristics of families served by the programs. For example, it is possible that higher income families in Oregon were not represented in the subsidized population because they were deterred by high co-payment rates. More than half of subsidized families in Oregon had no co-payment, but among those who did monthly co-payments were the highest observed in the five states. Maryland exempted about one half of subsidy recipients from co-payments, but also had relatively high co-payments for those who did have a co-payment. In Illinois, nearly all families had a co-payment, and this co-payment averaged $56; in Massachusetts, nearly all voucher families were exempt from co-payment, but those who paid had an average payment of $82. In Texas, family co-payments rose steadily with income, whereas in Oregon, they remained low until families had incomes of around $1,500 per month and then began to climb steeply. Depending on their state of residence, families with similar income levels could pay very different co-payments because of these different state policies.

The services received by families—in particular, the type of care being subsidized—also varied considerably across the five states. These differences may be explained, in part, by state policy choices related to provider payment rates, as well as to differences in local child-care markets. In Texas, for example, nearly 80% of children were in center care, in contrast to 18% of children in Oregon. Payments to providers in Oregon were also among the lowest across the five states, and payments were relatively similar for alternative forms of care. This, along with the large share of families in short-term employment preparation activities, may help explain the heavy use of unregulated care by subsidized families. Provider payments in Texas were also considerably lower than those of other states, but they were generous in comparison to local market rates and similar across forms of care. Although relative care in Texas was reimbursed at nearly the same rate as market care, weak regulation of nonmarket forms of care and prohibition of in-home nonrelative care may help explain the very large proportion of Texas children who were enrolled in center care.

Use of center care was also high in the Massachusetts sample (53%), and Massachusetts reimbursed center care at the highest rate among the five states. Although the Massachusetts payment rate for center care was low in relation to the state's market rates, payments were much lower for other forms of care, which may have created incentives for parents to select center care.

About one third of subsidized children in Illinois and Maryland were in center care, although the proportion in family and in-home care differed between these two states. In Illinois, provider payments were low in comparison with market rates and were particularly low for care provided in home or by relatives. As explicit state policy, Maryland's provider payment rates were raised by 1997 to approximately the 75th percentile of market rates for center and family child care. Payment rates for relative caregivers, however, were less than half of the rate for market forms of care. This may help explain why nearly two thirds of children were in market forms of care (either center or family child care).

SUMMARY: STATE POLICIES AND SUBSIDY DYNAMICS

The question of how state policies influence subsidy assistance was a primary motivating question for this study. Unfortunately, the administrative data were not appropriate for microanalyses of policy impacts. Qualitative comparisons of the variation of subsidy spells and state policies suggested some preliminary insights about how state policies influenced the populations served and the assistance provided. Given complex interactions among welfare and child-care policies, it is difficult to draw generalized conclusions. Perhaps the most striking conclusion is the very complexity of these policy interactions.

One common characteristic across these states was the low level of continuity in subsidy assistance. Within 7 months, subsidy assistance ended for one half of children in all five states. Many children also reentered the subsidy system, although the rate of reentry varied and did not exceed 50% in any state. For these children, the total duration of assistance was longer than that observed for a single spell. Because subsequent spells of receipt were about the same length as the first observed spell, however, the continuity of the assistance was probably no greater either. Due to the nature of the data, only limited observations can be made about the stability of children's care arrangements. When children were receiving subsidies, they had a good chance of remaining with one provider, especially if their spell of subsidy receipt was short. Among children who received subsidies for a full year, however, the proportion cared for by the same primary provider ranged from 36% to 60%.

Despite similarities in the low level of continuity and provider stability, the duration and stability of subsidy assistance varied considerably across the five states. Oregon was notable for having both the shortest spell lengths and the least stable provider arrangements for children receiving subsidies. Median subsidy spells lasted about twice as long in both Illinois and Texas than they did in Oregon, and rates of provider stability were generally higher as well. These dynamics are likely to be interrelated in that children with multiple short spells are less likely to remain with the same provider. Somewhat surprisingly, the median length of children's spells in each state was not consistently associated with the rate at which children reentered the state's subsidy system.

Subsidy spells were among the longest in Illinois. This cannot easily be explained by the relative generosity of benefits. It may be due in part to relatively less burdensome recertification procedures and to very high proportion of families mixing welfare and work; these families may have had both more stable child-care needs and longer periods of continuous eligibility. Once exiting the system, families in Illinois were also among the most likely to reenter, consistent with Illinois' explicit guarantee of assistance to all income-eligible families. Provider stability was also high in this state, which may be related to both the longer periods of assistance and the high levels of employment among subsidized parents.

Despite many exemptions from co-payments and higher levels of employment among subsidy recipients, spells of subsidy receipt and provider stability were relatively short in Maryland and differed little between families that were and were not employed. Families that exited the system were more likely to reenter in this state, however, than in other states.

Data for Massachusetts must be interpreted cautiously in that it captures the experience of less than one half of all subsidy recipients in the state. In particular, families that used contracted care are not included in the sample, and non-TANF, employed families were more heavily represented in this excluded population. Extensive use of center care and a high rate of exemptions from co-payment may explain why provider stability was relatively high in Massachusetts, but it did not translate into long spells of subsidy receipt. Relatively short subsidy spells in Massachusetts may have had more to do with the mix of clients; two thirds of families receiving vouchers were TANF recipients and were likely to have been engaged in short-term job preparation activities. In part, this reflected Massachusetts' use of child-care vouchers to help TANF families transition to employment. Reentry rates following the end of spell were relatively low, however, suggesting that transitions between programs serving TANF and non-TANF clients may have inhibited returns to assistance.

Spells of subsidy receipt and provider stability were longer in Texas than in most states. This may have been due to the high proportion of employed, non-TANF families in the subsidy caseload; spells of subsidy receipt were notably long for working families. In Texas, both welfare and child-care policies were in transition during the study period. Although priority for child-care subsidies was given to TANF families in employment preparation during the observation period, only about one third of all families served during this period were receiving TANF when they started receiving subsidies. The large majority of families were working and not receiving TANF. This may reflect the very low TANF benefits and earnings disregards in the state, which made it difficult for families to retain welfare benefits once they started working. Once families left the subsidy system in Texas, reentry rates were much lower than in other states. Although all families participating in the TANF Choices program in Texas were guaranteed a child-care subsidy, income-eligible families outside the TANF system were routinely placed on waiting lists until December 1998.

Relatively high co-payments in Oregon, for those families required to pay, and relatively burdensome recertification procedures may have contributed to subsidy spells that were the shortest observed. Short spells of receipt are also consistent with the mix of clients in the system; one half of subsidy recipients were not working and were likely to be cycling through short-term job-readiness activities. Even among working, non-TANF families, however, median spells were shorter than in all other states. Provider stability and reentry to the subsidy system were also lower in Oregon than in most states.

Because the data for this study did not reveal why children left the subsidy system, it is difficult to interpret these findings. Short subsidy spells and churning in and out of the system may be due to the episodic nature of parents' employment activities or to problems associated with child-care or subsidy arrangements. Regardless of the reason, the lack of continuity and short duration of subsidy assistance is of concern. It is unlikely that parents who were poor enough to qualify for subsidies had achieved a level of self-sufficiency such that they no longer needed subsidies within the few months that their children received assistance. Indeed, the fact that as many as one half of children returned for a subsequent spell of subsidy assistance within 1 year suggests that many parents remained eligible for assistance.

IMPLICATIONS FOR POLICY

The results of this study do not provide specific lessons for the development of child-care subsidy policy. The sample of five states was too small and the administrative data sets were too limited for the study team to identify policies that hinder or support families' use of subsidies. The results do suggest, however, two areas of concern for future policy.

The first concern relates to equity. Social policy devolution is often praised as a mechanism for increasing local political control and responsiveness. It is just as often criticized because it eliminates national standards and due process protections for applicants and clients who are often socially and economically vulnerable. This tension is apparent in child-care subsidy policies. The consolidation of categorical federal child-care programs into the CCDF and TANF block grants has given states and localities new opportunities to develop child-care systems that are responsive to local needs and local markets. At the same time, it has contributed to increasing variability in child-care programs. As these results suggest, essentially similar families have different likelihoods of receiving assistance depending on the state in which they live. Once they are in the system, families have different service options and face different costs and benefits depending on where they live. This raises important questions about whether the public child-care subsidy system is providing assistance equitably to needy families.

The second concern relates to the specific dynamics observed in this study. This study suggests that, once they obtain subsidies, low-income families may be having trouble retaining that assistance. One of the clearest conclusions from decades of research on welfare dynamics and the employment of low-educated workers is that mothers in the low-wage job sector experience both high levels of job instability and low levels of earnings growth over time. This suggests that low-income families exiting welfare, and other working poor families, are likely to need child-care subsidy assistance for a long period of time. The results of this study suggest that, currently, the assistance families receive is not very continuous, does not last very long, and may be associated with substantial turnover in their children's care arrangements. These dynamics do not bode well either for families' economic security or for children's healthy socioemotional development.

ACKNOWLEDGMENTS

This project was supported, in part, under grant #90XP0006 by the Child Care Bureau, Administration for Children, Youth and Families, Administration for Children and Families, Department of Health and Human Services.

## CHAPTER NINE

Child-Care Subsidies and Low-Income Parents—Policies and Practices That Affect Access and Retention

Gina Adams
Kathleen Snyder
and Analysis Team*
Urban Institute

Child-care subsidies for low-income families are critical to support work. Yet a relatively small proportion of eligible low-income families receive subsidies. This research examines policy-related factors that might explain this pattern. Using qualitative data from a comparative multisite case study in 1999, it suggests that two kinds of subsidy policies are likely to affect subsidy use: (a) policies—usually related to limited funding—that affect which families are eligible, know about the program, and can receive a subsidy if they apply; and (b) policies and practices that affect the ease/difficulty of applying for and keeping a subsidy. It discusses the possible implications of these issues and provides practical suggestions of policies that could better support subsidy use.

SETTING THE CONTEXT

Helping low-income families afford child care has become a major social policy concern over the last decade, spurred in large part by the recognition of the critical role that child care plays in helping low-income families work. As a consequence, child-care subsidies have been a cornerstone of federal and state efforts to reform welfare, and public funding for such assistance has risen significantly in the last decade.

---

*Jeffrey Capizzano, Deborah Montgomery, and Jodi Sandfort.

Despite these increases, a relatively small proportion of eligible families receive child-care assistance (Collins, Layzer, Kreader, Werner, & Glantz, 2000). Although this is primarily because there are insufficient funds to serve all eligible families, recent research suggests that additional factors may be at play. In particular, subsidy usage patterns are low even in states with relatively more resources (U.S. Department of Health and Human Services, 2000) and among high-priority groups that should be the most likely to receive subsidies (Meyers, Heintze, & Wolf, 1999; Schumacher & Greenberg, 1999). These findings highlight the importance of looking beyond funding and eligibility issues to what additional factors might affect access and retention of subsidies.

There are many different factors that could affect subsidy utilization patterns, including individual and family characteristics, characteristics of the child-care market, and characteristics of the subsidy system, such as child-care subsidy policies, funding, and administration (Meyers, 2001). The research presented here focuses on these latter issues—the characteristics of the child-care subsidy system that can affect utilization. These issues are relatively unexplored and are most directly under the control of state and local subsidy agencies, and therefore can be addressed through policy strategies.

As described in greater depth later, our findings come from qualitative data collected in 12 states/17 sites across the country in 1999. In presenting these data, we seek to describe subsidy policies and practices, and how parents experienced them, with a focus on those issues that could affect subsidy utilization. There are other points of view that are also important to consider when examining these issues, such as the perspectives of the subsidy agency and child-care providers. These perspectives are included in the more in-depth reports on which this chapter is based (Adams & Rohacek, 2002; Adams, Snyder, & Sandfort, 2002).

We first describe our research approach and data. We then discuss our findings in two areas: (a) those policies that directly affect who can access subsidies, and (b) those policies and practices that affect the relative ease of applying for and retaining subsidies. We conclude with a discussion of the implications of these findings.

DATA AND RESEARCH METHODS

This research was part of the case study/policy research component of the Urban Institute's Assessing the New Federalism (ANF) project. This study utilized a comparative, case-study design to explore the implementation of state child-care subsidy programs in the aftermath of national welfare reform. Data

TABLE 9.1
Data-Collection Approach and Study Respondents

Respondent Type	Approach to Data Collection	Number Conducted	Number of Respondents (Approximate)
State-level agency administrators	Semistructured interview	14	14
State-level policy experts	Semistructured interview	12	12
Local agency administrators	Semistructured interview	18	18
Local experts	Semistructured interview	15	15
Caseworkers (separate for TANF and non-TANF where appropriate)	Focus group	27	190
Parents receiving subsidies (usually separate for TANF and non-TANF)	Focus group	33	200
Providers serving subsidized families	Focus group	18	150

were collected from 17 sites in 12 of the 13 ANF states between June 1999 and March 2000.[1]

Because many of the issues we examined were affected by how subsidy policies were implemented at the local level, the research team focused on one to three local sites within these states.[2] As shown in Table 9.1, data were collected through semistructured interviews with state and local child-care administrators and key experts; focus groups with caseworkers, parents, and providers involved with the subsidy system; and document analysis. Because the experiences of parents on the Temporary Assistance for Needy Families (TANF) cash assistance program were different, we often held separate focus groups for those parents and, where relevant, for caseworkers who were responsible for working with child care and TANF. Eight semistructured interview and focus group protocols were used to standardize data collection across different respondents and across specific state contexts.[3]

---

[1] The sites/states were Alabama (Birmingham), California (Los Angeles, Oakland, San Diego), Colorado (Denver), Florida (Miami and Tampa), Massachusetts (Boston), Michigan (Detroit), Minnesota (Minneapolis), New Jersey (Jersey City), New York (Buffalo and New York City), Texas (El Paso and Houston), Washington (Seattle), and Wisconsin (Milwaukee). Mississippi, an Assessing New Federalism (ANF) state, was not included in the second round of case studies. These states were chosen for the larger ANF study because they include a large proportion of the nation's population and represent a range of geography, fiscal capacity, citizens' needs, and traditions of providing government services. They also contain over 50% of the U.S. population and, thus, represent the social services provision encountered by most Americans. The Urban Institute also gathered data about child-care subsidy systems in these same states during late 1996 and early 1997 (Long et al., 1998).

[2] Multiple localities were investigated in California, Florida, New York, and Texas because of the size of these states.

[3] For more information on the methodology and data-collection methods of this study, see the full reports from which this chapter was drawn (Adams, Snyder, & Sandfort, 2002).

This research approach allowed us to document the voices and unique perspectives of those on the front line—parents, providers, and caseworkers—which are perspectives that are essential, but have been underrepresented in subsidy research. It is also based on information from multiple levels and perspectives, as well as from different states and sites, which is an essential approach given the devolution of child-care policies and practices.[4] However, this approach has a number of implications:

1. Because much of this research focused on local implementation and the experiences of parents, providers, and caseworkers, a number of our findings are specific to the agencies and/or localities that we visited and, in some cases, specific to the individuals with whom we talked. As a consequence, it is not appropriate to generalize from these data to identify any particular state, site, or agency as particularly exemplary or problematic.

2. The focus group nature of much of our data means that we cannot provide quantitative measures of the extent to which particular issues occurred among our respondents or information on the characteristics of respondents that reported specific experiences. Instead we highlight those findings that were identified by a number of respondents across a number of sites because they are the most likely to reflect common issues as well as be relevant to other sites.

3. This research design focused on understanding the experiences of families and providers who were currently in the subsidy system. We did not talk to those families and providers who were *not* participating, which means that some of the challenges to participation identified by our respondents may actually underestimate the actual scope of the problem.[5]

Also note that these findings reflect the period during which this research was conducted—specifically, 1999 to 2000. This period was unusual in that it was preceded by a significant increase in public funding for child care stemming from the welfare reform legislation of 1996. This not only meant that many of the subsidy systems we visited had recently grown rapidly, but also that some of the issues identified in this study might be somewhat different in a period where funding was either stagnant or being cut back (such as is true as this chapter is going to press).

---

[4]Child-care subsidy systems have always been decentralized and have varied across states. For example, our sites varied in the number of programs that were in place, the levels of funding, the extent to which policies were devolved to the local level, and the child-care policies they had in place.

[5]Also, note that our parent and provider focus groups more often reflected center-based or family child-care settings than relative or in-home care. In addition, we primarily examined the operation of the state subsidy program that operated through vouchers at the local level—as a result, issues around the operation of subsidy programs funded through contracts (as is seen in our California sites, Jersey City, New York City, and Boston) are not generally included.

FINDINGS

There are a number of complex issues in child-care subsidy funding, policy, and practice that can affect whether low-income parents use subsidies. These fall into two broad categories, each of which are described in more detail next:

1. Policies and practices that directly affect who can access subsidies—specifically, which families are eligible for subsidies, which eligible families can get them if they apply, and which families know that they can get child-care assistance. These policies are often, although not always, set at the state level and are closely related to funding.

2. Policies and practices that affect how easy it is for those families who can access subsidies to be able to apply for and retain subsidies. These include overarching administrative and structural factors that affect how a family experiences *any* interaction with the subsidy program and what parents must do to get and retain subsidies. These issues are generally the result of a complex interaction of state and local policy, funding, administration, and implementation.

Factors That Directly Affect Who Can Access Subsidies

There are two interrelated issues that determine whether and how a family is able to initially obtain a subsidy. First, there are policies that determine which families are eligible, as well as which eligible families are able to get a subsidy if they apply. The second issue is whether families are likely to know that subsidies are available.

Factors Affecting Which Low-Income Families Can Get Subsidies. Although discussions of access to child-care assistance often focus narrowly on state eligibility policies, a low-income parent's ability to get a subsidy is actually the cumulative impact of several different policies and practices, which in turn are related to the relative adequacy of state funding levels.

State eligibility policies are the first set of policies that determine access, as they effectively provide an eligibility ceiling that determines the broadest group of families that would be able to obtain services *if* sufficient funds are available. Generally, families must meet both income eligibility criteria and categorical criteria to be eligible for child-care subsidies. Specifically:

• States are required to set their income eligibility cutoff for child-care subsidies within the maximum allowable under federal law, which is 85% of the state median income (SMI). At the time of our site visits, all of the ANF states had set their statewide cutoffs *below* this level—with the statewide ceilings ranging from 45% to 75% of SMI (Blank & Poersch, 2000)—although in Texas, local jurisdictions were allowed to set their eligibility levels up to 85% of SMI.

• Categorical criteria define additional conditions that income-eligible families must meet to be eligible for subsidies. For example, in our focal states, parents had to either be working or (depending on the state and whether the parent was on welfare) be involved in an approved work-related activity (education, training, or job search) for a specified number of hours per week. In addition, their child had to fall within specified age ranges—generally, the federally eligible age range of birth to 12 years. Other categorical criteria used by some states included being in the foster care system, being a teen parent, or having a child with special needs.[6]

The second issue that shapes the ability to get assistance is whether the state has adequate resources to serve all of the families that meet these criteria and who apply for service. In 1999, at the time of our site visits, 8 of our 12 states did not have adequate resources to serve all eligible applicants. As a result, some families were put on waiting lists for subsidies.[7] (This did not reflect national patterns of that time period, where approximately one third of states had waiting lists or had frozen intake as of March 2000 [Schulman, Blank, & Ewen 2001]. The number of states with waiting lists or frozen intake has grown slightly since that time due to the subsequent economic downturn [Schulman & Blank, 2004].) The other four states were able to serve all eligible applicants at the time of our visit.

This leads to a third issue that shapes access, which is how states and localities prioritize among those eligible families that apply. Because of the inadequacy of funds to serve all eligible applicants, most—10 out of 12—of our focal states had to prioritize which families would be served first.[8] In the ANF states with priority systems, families that were working to get off cash assistance (TANF) were consistently a top priority, as were families transitioning off welfare. This finding is not surprising due to concerns about moving families from welfare to work and because of the incentives to serve families on welfare to avoid sanctions under the work participation requirements of

---

[6]Most states also allowed families that need child care for other special circumstances to be eligible as well (e.g., families with foster children, children in protective services, children with special needs, and/or teen parents). Families with these special circumstances may be exempt from the other requirements, such as being of low-income or having children below age 12.

[7]Alabama, California, Florida, Massachusetts, Minnesota, New Jersey, New York, and Texas.

[8]The two states without priorities—Washington and Wisconsin—did not need to set priorities as they reported being able to serve all eligible families that applied. Although Michigan and Colorado also reported being able to serve all eligible families that applied, these states continued to have priority groups for child-care subsidies. Respondents in Michigan reported that the state had established priority groups in case they did not have enough money to serve all families in the future.

TANF. It was also common for states to have other priorities, such as children in high-risk situations (e.g., those served through child protective services, children with special needs, and families receiving SSI) and very low-income families. Generally, low-income working families that had *not* been on welfare were the lowest priority for service and were put on waiting lists for assistance.

Factors Affecting Whether Low-Income Families Know About Subsidies. In addition to these issues, access to subsidies is shaped by whether families *know* that they can get child-care assistance. Although there was some variation across our sites, respondents fairly consistently reported that there were eligible families that did not know they could get assistance, particularly among nonwelfare families. This issue is one of the key differences between TANF and non-TANF families in their experience of the subsidy system.

Respondents reported that TANF families were likely to hear about subsidies from their TANF caseworkers (although there were other sources of this information as well). Although TANF agencies varied in when and under what circumstances they told TANF families about the availability of subsidies, local administrative staff across sites consistently reported that there was a stage in the TANF application/employment activity process when families were supposed to be told about subsidies. Furthermore, in some sites, the TANF/employment caseworkers would actually facilitate the parent accessing the child-care subsidy system (e.g., by helping them fill out the subsidy application, sending the application to the child-care agency for them, etc.). This is not surprising given the incentive that states have to help TANF families obtain child care so they can meet the work participation requirements under the TANF program. However, despite that TANF parents were more likely to be told, some respondents noted that some TANF families may not have received this information.

In contrast, non-TANF parents were less likely to hear about subsidies overall. A range of respondents—from parents to state administrators—across many of our sites reported that there were eligible working non-TANF families that did not know they would be able to get help. Also, those non-TANF families that did learn about subsidies were likely to report having heard about the availability of child-care assistance via word of mouth, from their child providers, and through the efforts of nongovernmental organizations such as Child Care Resource and Referral agencies (CCR&Rs).[9] These findings are not surprising for several reasons. First, these families are less likely to be in touch with state agencies that might inform them of their eligi-

---

[9]CCR&Rs appeared to play a key role in conducting outreach in the ANF states. In Massachusetts, for example, CCR&Rs conducted outreach for both TANF and non-TANF families by going to different venues to distribute information about the availability of child care.

bility, which means that states/localities would have to undertake broader outreach efforts to inform them of the availability of the service. Second, respondents across many of our sites reported that agencies did not undertake such outreach efforts (although there were some exceptions). This is related to the lack of adequate resources to serve all families because many administrators felt it was illogical to conduct outreach efforts to inform non-TANF families about child care if there was no money to provide them with subsidies. Third, some respondents reported that low-income working families did not realize that subsidies were available to families that were not on welfare and/or had heard about waiting lists so did not bother to apply.

What This Means for Who Can Access Subsidies. The net impact of the policies and practices described in this section is that, across all of our sites, funding levels meant there were low-income families that were not getting subsidies due to a combination of eligibility restrictions, prioritizing policies, and limited outreach. Furthermore, respondents agreed that TANF families working to get off welfare were more likely to access subsidies than low-income non-TANF families. In the few sites with sufficient resources, this was primarily because they were more likely to know that they were eligible. However, in those sites with inadequate resources, this was compounded by a more explicit priority for assistance to TANF families.

As a consequence, eligibility criteria—the most easily identified policy that determines access—is only a small part of the policies and practices that determine which families are able to get subsidies. The end result can be that there is a significant discrepancy between who is theoretically eligible and who is actually able to get help if they apply. In California, for example, although income eligibility limits were set at 75% of the SMI, one California respondent estimated that inadequate funding meant that the majority of subsidy recipients were either on TANF or were non-TANF families with incomes below 25% to 30% of SMI.

Factors That Affect the Ease of Applying for and Retaining Child-Care Subsidies

Qualifying for subsidies, knowing about them, and being able to actually receive them if you apply are only the first components of using a subsidy. Once eligible parents make it to the stage of actually applying for a subsidy, there are a number of factors that shape how easy it is for them to get and keep child-care assistance. These include:

- overarching administrative and structural factors that affect every interaction the parent has with the subsidy agency;
- factors that affect the ease of the application process; and

- factors that affect the ease of retaining subsidies once you receive them.

These differ from those described in the preceding section because they generally stem from a combination of state policy, funding, and administrative approaches, as well as local agency implementation and leadership. Furthermore, the role played by each of these issues differs across different agencies, sites, and states, making it difficult to clearly disentangle which are more significant in affecting access and retention.

Overarching Factors Affect Every Interaction With the Subsidy Program. When talking to respondents about specific policies or practices (such as the application process or what parents had to do to redetermine their eligibility), we often found that parents, providers, and caseworkers talked as much about how the services were delivered as about the specifics of any particular policy requirement. For example, parents discussed in depth about how many caseworkers they had to see, how they were treated, whether their caseworker(s) were able to help them, whether they experienced delays, and so forth.

In listening to parents, it became clear that these fundamental issues can play a critical—although often overlooked—role in affecting child-care utilization. They affect the ease or difficulty of *every* interaction that parents have with the subsidy system and, as such, contribute to whether families are easily able to comply with requirements. For example, the relative ease with which parents can contact their caseworker (and the quality of that interaction) affects the likelihood that they will successfully understand *and* be able to comply with the requirements necessary to either initially obtain or subsequently retain their subsidy. Consequently, these broader factors provide an essential context for all of the specific interactions that families have with the subsidy agency, which are described later in this chapter.

Parents' comments were often framed in terms of their own personal experiences and generally fell into one of three overlapping areas—interactions with caseworkers, general office practices, and the number of agencies they had to deal with. As discussed later, parents' seemingly individual problems can often be linked to underlying structural and/or administrative issues.

Parental Concerns About Caseworkers Were Often Related to Structural Factors. Caseworkers play a critical role in shaping the experiences that families have with the subsidy system. They are responsible for translating policy into practice, communicating details of policies to parents and helping them with forms, and processing paperwork and claims.

The central importance of the caseworkers' role was clear as we talked with parents, who described in depth the quality of their interactions and how they were treated. In some cases, parents described how caseworkers helped them resolve a problem and how they were responsive and helpful. For example, some parents speaking about one subsidy office in Los Angeles noted that "caseworkers respect us as individuals" and were "helpful with getting the documents needed by families—even birth certificates." However, in a number of other cases, parents described serious concerns about being treated disrespectfully, having to wait for long periods of time, being given misinformation, or having paperwork lost.

In some cases, these problems were no doubt the fault of the parent or related to a normal level of complaints. However, it would be a mistake to dismiss all of these concerns this way, as many of their concerns were corroborated by other respondents. In addition, further exploration reveals that many of these issues may have their roots in more fundamental structural and administrative issues. Respondents in a number of our sites reported that their subsidy agencies were dealing with changing caseworker responsibilities, growing caseloads and high turnover rates among staff, and/or inadequate training and computer systems. As one respondent noted,

> The [caseworkers] were supposed to only have something like 60 cases . . . and they ended up with maybe 100 and then they weren't really trained to do the job. So in a lot of district offices, there were tremendous complaints. Kids were being kicked out of day care, people were losing jobs because their applications were several months old and had not been processed.

Consequently, these issues are closely related to overall resources and funding levels, as well as to administrative decisions about where to allocate resources and how much to invest in administrative systems. (Note that some of these issues may also be related to the timing of our site visits—as noted earlier, 1999 to 2000 was the end of a period of significant expansion in subsidies, which may have caused the systems to be in more flux than would be the case now.)

The effect of these problems on parents, in those sites where they occurred, was very real and appeared likely to affect their ability to use subsidies. For example, parents in Denver and Houston described having to call caseworkers repeatedly without being able to get through, which was particularly challenging during work hours when employers did not appreciate them being away from their jobs. Parents in Oakland and Seattle described giving up and finally taking time off work to go into the office, with a Seattle mother saying "it is pointless to call, you have to go in." Issues such as these can present real barriers to families that are facing multiple challenges and working to balance entry-level jobs with the often stressful lives associated with poverty.

General Office Practices and Accessibility Also Affected the Ease of Interacting With the Agency. In addition to issues that affected parent–caseworker interactions, parents and other local respondents described general office practices that affected the ease of client access. One of the most common issues discussed by parents was whether they had to come into the office to deal with the various interactions required by the state (e.g., application, redetermination, etc.). Although face-to-face meetings can help caseworkers build a relationship with the parent and ensure they understand the program requirements, they can also present a burden when they occur frequently or unnecessarily.

Our sites varied in the extent to which parents had to come into the office. In some sites, parents dealt with most interactions by mail, phone, or fax. This could be relatively easy for parents—for example, one parent in discussing her experience with contacting the agency to change providers noted, "It was just a matter of a phone call and they asked what the person's [new provider's] name was. They [the subsidy agency] just did it over the phone." In other sites, however, parents went to the office in person for some or all interactions, although the reasons behind the visits varied. Some local agencies required parents to come into the office in person. In some other local agencies that had alternative mechanisms (such as mail, phone, or fax), parents reportedly came into the office even though the policy did not require them to do so. Although sometimes this was due to parent error or choice, in other cases this occurred because the caseworker would require parents to come in, the parents could not get through to the caseworker by other means, or they did not trust the agency to appropriately process the paperwork. For example, despite one site's explicit policy that everything could be done by phone or fax, one mother described how she not only felt she had to come into the office, but she would ask her caseworkers to stamp her paperwork to prove they received it, "otherwise they say, 'I never saw you, I never signed anything', . . . they pretend they never saw you."

Although often difficult in and of themselves, the burden of in-person visits was further affected by other factors—for example, whether the local office served parents on a first-come, first-served basis or through appointments. The former approach worked well when the agencies were staffed so as to be able to see parents promptly when they came in. However, it was more difficult for parents if this were not the case—a mother in Tampa reported having to visit the agency 2 days in a row (and wait almost the entire day each time) before she was able to be seen. Furthermore, although appointments were a good alternative, they appeared to be most effective in those sites that were able to see parents on a timely basis and were flexible in their scheduling. However, in some of our sites, parents had to wait for weeks or months to get an appointment, whereas in other sites, backlogs and agency management practices meant that parents waited for several hours after their appointment time. Some sites also gave parents little or no flexibility in determining the appointment time.

A related issue that affected the ease of access for families was the office hours of the local agency. A number of parents described the challenge of having to deal with the subsidy office during the agency's office hours, which often coincided with the hours they worked. Interestingly, we sometimes heard about the challenge of taking time off work from parents who were served by agencies with only slightly extended office hours, suggesting that these schedules did not recognize the realities that parents face in coordinating a visit to the office (e.g., dealing with transportation and traffic and having to pick up their child from child care). However, we heard very few complaints about this problem from parents who were served by a Los Angeles agency, which was open until 7:00 p.m. during the week and open on Saturdays.

Many local respondents described the resulting challenges for parents who had to take time away from their job—for example, the difficulty of asking for time off from a new employer, losing a full day of pay because they did not have leave, and their concern about how missing work reflected on their performance and how it was perceived by their employers. These problems are particularly striking given that the focus of child-care subsidies is to support low-income parents in the workforce. As a Florida mother commented: "[It is] almost like you have to be unemployed to be able to apply for all of these benefits, because if you were employed there would be absolutely no way the nicest employer would excuse all that time."

All of these issues—the extent to which policies and practices necessitate that parents come into the office, and the relative ease of such visits (e.g., whether parents can be seen promptly and whether they can come in outside of work hours)—affect the ease with which parents can meet the reporting requirements described later in this chapter. They can also act as a deterrent for eligible families that might otherwise want to apply.

Although important in and of themselves, office practices are also related to the extent to which local agencies focused on client service and efficiency. For example, some local agencies appeared to have client services as a priority, were conscious of how the services were experienced from the parents' perspective, and were working to improve service delivery. In one site, administrators tested the quality of the service delivery—for example, whether parents were able to get through when they called. However, there were also some agencies that seemed unaware of the challenges that their policies and practices presented for parents. Furthermore, we saw variation on this spectrum across agencies *within* sites, as a respondent in one site said:

> I have been in a number of [local subsidy agencies]. Some are very orderly, people get in on time, have appointments. Others are just zoos, with hundreds of people milling around, you overhear conversations that their [parents'] caseworkers are running 2–3 hours behind, there are children everywhere.

This variation shows that these issues are not solely dependent on state funding or resources—although these are also important—but that they are also closely linked to local agency leadership and management.

Administrative Approaches Sometimes Required Families to Deal With Multiple Agencies. The number of agencies or divisions a family had to deal with to obtain and/or retain their subsidy also could present additional challenges for parents—particularly for families receiving TANF—because it often added to the complexity of what they were required to do each time they needed to interact with the subsidy agency. We found that it was fairly common for TANF families to have to interact with more than one agency (or part of an agency) because their eligibility for child care was dependent on their eligibility for/compliance with TANF requirements. Thus, families had to deal with both the TANF and child-care agencies for many of the interactions described next.

The extent to which dealing with multiple agencies was a problem depended significantly on how subsidy systems were implemented. Some agencies facilitated the communication between the two agencies, thus minimizing the burden on families (e.g., in some sites, the TANF caseworkers did much of the legwork for parents in terms of obtaining and retaining child care). In other sites, however, families had to navigate between the two agencies and systems, taking paperwork back and forth and dealing with conflicting and/or duplicative requirements. In a Florida site, for example, a mother on welfare carefully drew us a diagram of the four caseworkers she had to notify whenever she experienced a change in her employment situation. Another respondent in Florida described the recertification process for TANF families as follows:

> A WAGES [Florida's TANF program] family, they go to their AFDC worker [the worker that handles Food Stamps and other services] because they're misinformed, but that is the wrong worker. So they have to make another appointment, because even though they are already in the welfare office, they are with the wrong person. So they have to make another appointment with their WAGES worker to get a referral. Then you have to make another appointment with child care to get the day care.
>
> So they [parents] say it is too much . . . and then, not only that, but if they are in training, then they have to make an appointment to go down to where this training is at . . . then they have to take off another day to get their bus card. If they are lucky enough to get a job, they have to keep on taking time off [to get their eligibility redetermined] . . . that is the purpose of the WAGES program, to get parents a job so they can get off welfare, but . . . a lot of times they get fired, lose their job.

(Note that the Urban Institute child-care research team has conducted an in-depth follow-up study to examine the intersection of the child-care and TANF welfare-to-work systems in greater depth to explore how states and localities approach the challenge of connecting these two essential service areas [see e.g., Adams, Holcomb, Snyder, Koralek, & Capizzano, 2005].)

Factors That Affect the Ease of Initial Application.   What parents have
to do to apply for subsidies can also play an important role in affecting utilization of subsidies. The process of entering the child-care subsidy system varied
in the ANF sites, although it generally involved an initial application (often in
person), dealing with paperwork, finding a provider, and getting the provider
approved. Generally, parents across our sites were required to fill out an application form and provide documentation to verify their income, identity, and
relationship to the child. However, the burden of this process varied widely,
both in how it was supposed to occur in policy as well as in how it functioned
in practice.

Looking first at the application process, the majority of our sites (12 of 17)
required at least some families to appear in person at the subsidy agency to
deal with at least some part of the application process,[10] although these requirements sometimes varied by whether the family was on TANF.[11] Some
sites required families to come into the office multiple times as they dealt with
the application process and getting their provider approved. Only five sites allowed parents to deal with the entire process by phone or fax.[12] As noted earlier, in-person visits can be difficult for families, and particularly for working
parents.

Similarly, the amount and types of eligibility documents required for the
application process varied. For example, in one site, in addition to filling out
an application, non-TANF working parents only needed to provide 1 month
of pay stubs and a child support statement. In contrast, in another site, parents
were required to provide eight different types of documents (proof of residence, social security cards, birth certificates, 1 month of pay stubs, food
stamp/Medicaid eligibility letter, proof of child support, proof of any other income, and school attendance verification for each child under 18).

The extent to which a particular policy/practice was burdensome on a
family was dependent on many of the implementation issues discussed earlier, such as the training and knowledge of the caseworkers, the extent to
which parents trusted their caseworker, the efficiency and client service focus
of the local office, and so forth. A seemingly difficult process could be made
easier by a helpful caseworker (e.g., in being flexible if the parent was missing
one pay stub, or in helping parents deal with the multiple systems that were
sometimes involved). However, a seemingly simple process could be made
much more difficult—for example, as noted earlier, parents in some sites with
easier application processes were unable to get through by phone or fax, and
thus had to take time off work to come into the office. Again, for families on

---

[10]Birmingham, Los Angeles, Oakland, San Diego, Denver, Miami, Tampa, Boston, Jersey City,
Buffalo, New York City, and Milwaukee.

[11]In five sites—Denver, Jersey City, Boston, Buffalo, and New York City—these requirements
varied by TANF status.

[12]Detroit, Minneapolis, El Paso, Houston, and Seattle.

welfare, there could be an additional layer to the entry process because they sometimes had to deal with the requirements of two systems.

The net result of these policies and practices is that the ease of the application process varied significantly across sites, across agencies within sites, and across TANF and non-TANF families. In one site, parents could be determined eligible over the phone and mail in the paperwork. In contrast, another site required parents to make multiple visits to the subsidy agency and/or welfare agencies to complete all steps of the application process.

Factors That Affect the Ease of Retaining Subsidies.

The requirements that families have to fulfill to *retain* subsidies once they get them have generally not been explored, but are critical in affecting utilization patterns. Our research shows that families must do far more to keep their subsidies than has generally been recognized, which may help explain recent research in five states that found that average subsidy spells lasted only 3 to 7 months (Meyers et al., 2002). Here we describe three different kinds of situations where families must do something to retain subsidies.

Families Needed to Prove Eligibility on a Regular Basis. Although there is a perception that families are able to retain their subsidy until they become ineligible, in actuality they are given a time-limited authorization for subsidy, which expires unless the family proves that it is still eligible for assistance. Consequently, once families enter the child-care system, they are required to regularly prove to the state that they have remained eligible for child-care subsidies; if they fail to do so, their subsidy is terminated. This reauthorization or recertification process is therefore central to parents' ability to retain their child-care subsidy.

Local subsidy agencies differed in what families needed to do to recertify—in policy, half the sites allowed families to recertify by mail, phone, or fax, and eight sites required some families to visit the subsidy office to recertify.[13] Again there were situations where parents would come into the office even if not required to do so. Given the severity of the consequence if paperwork did get lost, which is that parents risked losing their subsidy, it is not surprising that some parents were not willing to take this chance. As a result, face-to-face meetings were a reality for at least some families even in sites that did not require them. Eligibility redetermination also requires parents to submit certain documentation to prove that they are still eligible. In most of the ANF sites, parents had to fill out a form and document their income, which often meant

---

[13]In nine sites (Denver, Detroit, Minneapolis, Jersey City, El Paso, Houston, Seattle, Milwaukee, and Boston), all parents could recertify by mail, phone, or fax. In the remaining sites (Birmingham, Los Angeles, Oakland, San Diego, Miami, Tampa, Boston, and New York City), at least some families were required to visit the subsidy office to recertify.

providing a number of pay stubs. However, in some sites, the process was more complex, requiring families to take additional steps, such as completing an employment verification form, providing verification about child support, or (in at least one site) providing the parent's social security card and the children's birth certificate each time they saw a worker. (As was the case with the application process, families on TANF can face an extra layer of requirements because their eligibility for child care is dependent on their continuing eligibility for TANF and compliance with TANF work-related requirements, although this depended on whether the agency facilitated this process.)

In addition to what families have to do during recertification, it is also important to consider *how often* they have to go through this process. Frequent recertification can ultimately become a barrier for families that need childcare assistance, particularly if it means taking time off from work to go to the subsidy office. In our ANF sites, there was often a significant difference between the reported policies on the length of the recertification period—often set at the state level—and how they were implemented. From the *policy* perspective, the maximum recertification period in the ANF sites ranged from every 3 months to every 12 months, with the majority of the sites requiring redetermination at least every 6 months. In *practice*, however, respondents across ANF sites indicated that families may have to recertify more often if the family experienced frequent changes in circumstances and/or did not regularly report changes in circumstances. Caseworkers often played an important role in determining the recertification period because they determine whether the family's situation is less stable and needs to be tracked more closely. Given these factors, although it may seem the family needs to recertify once or twice a year, in practice a number of families experience shorter recertification periods. For example, families on welfare may have to redetermine eligibility more often given the transitory nature of their activities. In Jersey City, TANF families needed to recertify at the end of each work/training activity, which meant that these parents could have to recertify on a monthly basis.

Families Needed to Prove They Were Still Eligible Whenever They Experienced a Change That Could Affect Their Eligibility. In addition to recertification, families need to re-prove their eligibility each time they experience a change in their situation—such as a change in income, job, work schedule, or child-care provider—because these changes can affect their subsidies. For example, a change in income can make a family ineligible for subsidy, change the parent's co-payment amount, and/or change how much the state will pay as a reimbursement (the reimbursement rate). Such changes can happen frequently in the lives of low-income families, which can mean that they need to interact with the subsidy agency on a more frequent basis than is indicated by the standard recertification periods. Here we focus on what families have to do around changes in employment (e.g., schedule change, change in pay, change in job)—more information on this transition and others can be found in other analyses described earlier.

Changes in employment situation are common for low-income workers. The employment patterns of low-income families can be very dynamic—entry-level and low-wage workers tend to experience frequent job turnover (Lane, 2000), and welfare recipients in particular are more likely to have jobs with changing schedules or that involve irregular work patterns (Rangarajan, Schochet, & Chu, 1998). Although there was some variation across sites, generally parents were required to notify the subsidy agency of any changes in their employment, income, and work schedule. In most sites, parents were able to notify the subsidy agency by phone or mail (at least in policy), but in 4 of the 17 sites[14] some or all families had to make an in-person visit to notify the agency of changes in job hours or income.

Although policies required that families report these changes when they happen, agency staff across many of our sites reported that a number of parents actually waited until their eligibility redetermination for this change to be reported. Agency staff varied in how they dealt with this issue. In most of the sites where this was reported to be an issue, staff relied on the redetermination to identify changes in employment if parents failed to report this earlier. Caseworkers, however, were attentive to any indication of actual fraud and had strategies to address this problem, such as having the parent recertify more often or terminating the case. In a few sites, parents could be sanctioned for failing to report changes.

Families Often Needed to Do Something to Retain Their Subsidies When They Left Welfare. One of the important transitions unique to TANF families is the transition off welfare. How and whether states help families retain subsidies through this transition is critical to the success of welfare reform because leaving welfare is a time of both great potential and great risk for parents. At a minimum, families leaving welfare are coping with the loss of cash assistance and having to manage a household budget without the safety net of welfare. Helping families retain subsidies during this transition can help ease their transition off welfare and support their employment (see Adams, Koralek, & Martinson, 2005, for a more in-depth discussion of this issue).

Although most states used language of *guarantee* or *automatic eligibility* when referring to families leaving welfare, the process of retaining subsidies when leaving welfare appeared to be seldom automatic for families. Only two sites—Minneapolis and Seattle—allowed families to continue to get assistance without having to do something when they left welfare. In the remaining sites, families may need to come to the office in person (as was true in the 6

---

[14]Miami, Tampa, Jersey City, and New York City.

of 12 sites[15] where we have data), reapply/ recertify for subsidies, and/or move to a new agency. As a consequence, the process of retaining subsidies when transitioning off welfare could be more burdensome for families than is suggested by this language, although the extent to which this is true depended on what was required from families, whether the process was facilitated, and so forth.

Also, although most of our states gave transitional families higher priority for a limited period (from 1–3 years),[16] they varied in whether families were able to continue to get child-care assistance at the *end* of this transitional period. Although some sites continued to see these families as a high priority, three sites were already putting these families on waiting lists due to limited funds,[17] and another four sites said they would only be able to continue to serve these families if funds were available.[18] (Again, note that this was in 1999–2000, prior to the economic downturn that followed.)

IMPLICATIONS FOR SUPPORTING SUBSIDY ACCESS AND RETENTION

This research explores several of the ways in which the characteristics of the child-care subsidy system can affect use of subsidies. It shows that there are several ways in which subsidy funding, policies, and practices can either limit or support subsidy utilization. Although it is beyond the scope of the study to document the level of impact of any particular issue, it suggests that these subsidy system characteristics could at least partially explain the utilization and turnover patterns described earlier. Key themes are summarized as follows.

1. Inadequate Funds Limit Access to Subsidies.   Resources are clearly a predominant factor in affecting whether low-income families have access to subsidies. In most of our sites, inadequate funds placed a limit on the extent to which low-income families could get subsidies and created the need for a series of direct rationing tools (such as low eligibility cutoffs, prioritizing criteria, and wait lists) that were used to allocate scarce resources, as well as indirect ra-

---

[15]Birmingham, Miami, Tampa, Boston, Jersey City, and Milwaukee. A respondent from Boston noted that, although parents are required to visit the TANF/employment office to get an authorization for child-care subsidies, the child-care agency may issue a voucher by mail in some instances. We did not collect data on this issue in El Paso. California sites are not included here as the state's system is sufficiently different from that of other states so it cannot be described in a comparable way in this section. See Adams, Snyder, and Sandfort (2002) for more information.

[16]Colorado, Michigan, Washington, and Wisconsin did not have a transitional period. These states were also serving all eligible families that applied for service.

[17]Jersey City, New York City, and Houston. In Jersey City and Houston, these families were given priority on the waiting list over low-income families that had not been on welfare.

[18]Los Angeles, Oakland, San Diego, and Tampa.

tioning mechanisms (such as limited outreach) that effectively contain demand for services. These policies played a major role in limiting access to subsidies among low-income families overall, and particularly for low-income working families not on welfare. Furthermore, although not examined directly in this chapter, funding levels are also related to many of the administrative and structural issues that could make the *process* of accessing and retaining subsidies more difficult for low-income families. In particular, issues such as caseworker caseloads, training, and technology all require agencies to have the resources to invest in infrastructure.

2. Subsidies Can Be Complex to Access and Retain for Those Families That Are Eligible and Apply.

The process of applying for and retaining child-care subsidies can range from relatively easy to quite complex. Despite a common belief and language that suggests that "Once you are in you stay in," there are a number of steps that parents must take to get and keep subsidies. Although in some sites this process was not difficult, in others it could require parents to repeatedly visit the agency and provide documentation. Given that low-income working parents are particularly likely to face a number of changes of circumstance that require them to contact the state, such as in changes in their employment, income, residence, and/or child-care provider, the cumulative impact of these requirements can place a significant burden on families.

As illustration, Fig. 9.1 provides an example of what might be required of a hypothetical mother "Leslie" who applies for and receives subsidies. During a period of less than a year, Leslie experiences a number of transitions that are common for low-income families, including getting a small raise, changing her job hours, changing providers, and getting laid off. This figure illustrates what she would be required to do in two contrasting sites—one with relatively easier policies/practices around access and retention, and the other with more difficult policies and practices. (Note that these strategies are drawn from the sites that we visited, although they do not reflect any particular site. Most of the sites fell somewhere in between these two examples.) The cumulative impact of the more difficult scenario is evident: For Leslie to comply with program requirements, she would have to take time off work nine or more times over a period of less than 8 months, along with providing duplicative paperwork and spending a lot of time trying to reach caseworkers.

It is clear that more challenging requirements are not only stressful for families and can jeopardize their employment if it requires them to take time off work, but can also create more opportunities for parents to be out of compliance with program rules. As a consequence, these demands appear likely to affect whether families access and retain subsidies and deter some parents from applying in the first place. The root cause of these demands on parents can range from state policy requirements, to local agency implementation practices, to caseworker discretion, or some combination of these.

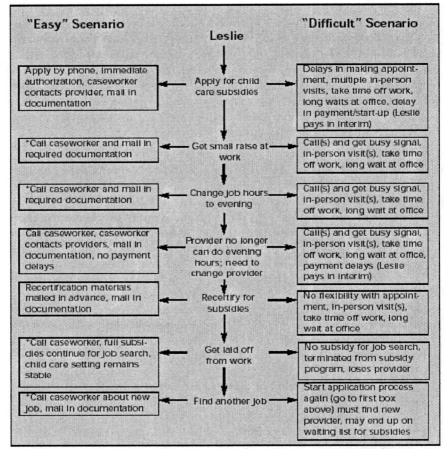

FIG. 9.1.   What Leslie might have to do to get and keep her child-care subsidy.

Barriers to subsidy access and retention can be particularly problematic for specific types of parents. For example:

• Parents on TANF face a unique situation because, although they had better access to subsidies because they were a top priority for services in all of our sites, they also could face additional challenges because they had to deal with multiple agencies. This was not a significant problem for parents living in sites where the agencies facilitated the process, but it was challenging for parents in sites where this was not the case.

• Parents whose lives are more chaotic and who experience many changes in short periods of time appear to be more likely to experience more demands for reporting to the agency. Unfortunately, these requirements may inadvertently contribute further to the instability of employment and child-care situations for these families, rather than providing the support needed to stabilize their situation.

• Parents who face other challenges, such as barriers due to language, literacy, disability, or transportation, may also have difficulty complying with these requirements.

Although we did not collect information on the extent to which parents faced these various problems, examining the particular challenges faced by these families is important because these parents are often the focus of efforts to reform welfare. Such research might suggest ways to better design subsidy policies and local practices to help achieve the larger goals of welfare reform, and to better support these highly vulnerable populations.

3. Subsidy Policies and Practices May Inadvertently Undercut the Goal of Supporting Work.   If implemented well, subsidy policies and practices can be a strong support service that helps families work. However, this research also shows that subsidy policies can sometimes operate at cross-purposes with the larger goal of helping low-income parents become established in the workforce. For example, parents in some sites reported having to repeatedly take time off from their entry-level jobs to deal with agency requirements to access and/or retain subsidies. Parents were clear that this was difficult for them—it jeopardized their ability to perform well in their jobs and affected how their employers perceived them. Some parents described the challenge of choosing between their work and doing what was needed to retain their subsidy. As a mother on TANF in Buffalo commented, "When . . . [my recertification] is in two weeks, I sit there puzzled thinking, I got to work that day. How do I tell my boss that I need off when I know we [her place of employment] are in high demand right now."

These problems are particularly striking given the focus of child-care subsidies on supporting work. In some sites, the system did not appear to recognize the realities facing the low-income working (and often single) parent population that it serves.

4. Subsidy Policies and Practices May Inadvertently Undercut the Stability of Child-Care Arrangements.   Although the focus of subsidy policies is usually on supporting parental work, subsidy policies are likely to have an effect on children as well. Barriers to subsidy retention seem likely to contribute to the short subsidy spells mentioned earlier. This may in turn contribute to unstable child-care situations among subsidized children, who may have to leave their child-care program when their parent loses their eligibility for subsidy (unless the provider chooses to continue to serve the child at a loss). This is problematic given that research suggests that continuity of care and the development of a stable relationship with a nurturing caregiver is one of the most critical aspects of child-care quality and can have a major impact on children's development (NICHD Early Child Care Research Network, 1997).

5. Subsidy Policies and Practices Can Support Access and Retention. This research not only identified various barriers to access and retention, but also a number of strategies that state and local agencies are taking (or can take) to support subsidy use. Although there is not a single easy answer, given that the root cause of the barriers varies from site to site, some of the key strategies include:

• Increase resources for subsidies. This would allow more families to access subsidies, as has been observed in recent years with the increased state and federal investments in child care. Eligibility limitations, prioritizing criteria and wait lists, and limited outreach are all related to insufficient funding to serve all eligible families.

• Focus on client service and accessibility. Basic issues such as whether the phones are answered, whether caseworkers provide good information, what the agency office hours are, how long families must wait to be seen, and so forth are key in shaping whether families can access and use subsidies. These issues can be in part due to resources and funding, but are also related to local agency leadership and management.

• Assess how easy or difficult it is for parents to access and retain subsidies. Looking at what parents must do to get and retain subsidies is a key step in assessing the relative accessibility of any subsidy system. Identifying what they must do at each step, as well as cumulatively, and the cause of any unnecessary steps or burdens, can allow agencies to identify strategies to minimize the burden on parents.

• Examine the application policies and practices. Issues such as the complexity of forms, level of paperwork required, and extent to which parents must come into the office can play a major role in whether families are deterred from applying for subsidies or are unable to comply with the requirements.

• Assess what families have to do to retain subsidies. Examining what parents have to do (whether due to policy or local implementation) to recertify eligibility, leave welfare, or report changes in jobs, income, and providers can provide important insights to the relative ease of retaining subsidies. In examining this, it is important to not only examine what the families must do for each of these steps, but also to assess how often they occur—the combination of these factors determines the *cumulative* impact of these requirements for families.

• Assess the termination process to minimize inappropriate terminations. Protections such as notification procedures, grace periods before termination, and appeal processes can minimize the extent to which parents are inadvertently leaving the system due to the challenges of meeting state / local reporting requirements (rather than because they are no longer eligible).

• Explore the extent to which TANF and child-care systems work together. Taking steps to increase the coordination and communication across agencies and to minimize the burden on parents can help families navigate between these two systems to obtain and retain their subsidies.

One of the challenges in implementing these strategies is the balance between monitoring eligibility and fraud versus supporting families' access to child care. On the one hand, there are often good reasons that subsidy agencies feel the need to closely monitor parents' work and income status—in terms of ensuring the accuracy of the subsidy level and eligibility of the parent—particularly when there are inadequate resources to serve all eligible families. On the other hand, it would be useful to examine the larger costs and benefits of so closely monitoring eligibility. It seems likely that the impact of these requirements on parents and their ability to work, on the resulting workload for caseworkers, and on the high turnover rates among families may make this approach less cost-effective than it otherwise appears. Addressing these issues could result in a subsidy system that is focused on helping families easily access and retain their subsidies, supporting their employment, and maintaining stable child-care situations for their children.

CONCLUSION

This chapter outlines a series of child-care subsidy policies and practices that can affect subsidy use among low-income families. Yet improving subsidy use faces some important challenges. In particular, the current funding context places a fundamental limit on the ability of policy strategies to improve access to subsidies because limited funds mean that eligible low-income applicants are already not getting assistance in a number of states, and other states are making other cuts in services (Schulman & Blank, 2004). Furthermore focused efforts to make it easier for parents to apply for and retain subsidies may simply result in increasing the number of eligible parents who end up on waiting lists or not being served because subsidy slots would not turn over as rapidly if eligible parents found it easier to retain subsidies.

Yet there are also important reasons why these issues should be considered. First and foremost, the declines in the TANF caseloads in recent years, time limits for welfare, and other factors have significantly increased awareness about the importance of supporting employment and preventing welfare among low-income working parents. This has led to a growing interest in designing social service systems to better support working families. Although additional research is needed, the research presented here suggests that supporting access and retention of subsidies could be a key component of this effort. It also seems likely that these strategies could result in more stable settings for low-income children, which could better support their development.

It is also notable that all of the strategies highlighted in this chapter were actually in operation in the study sites, and therefore are realistic and possible. Furthermore, an in-depth analysis of these issues found that states and localities can address almost all of the issues highlighted here because most are not regulated at the federal level (Greenberg, Schumacher, & Mezey, 2001). Nonetheless, there is more information needed to help states and localities implement these strategies on a broader level. For example, it would be useful to examine the effectiveness, trade-offs, and cost implications of different strategies, such as: Are there administrative cost savings associated with reducing the number of unnecessary subsidy terminations? Can states ease reporting requirements without increasing fraud? Are there strategies that are particularly effective for vulnerable populations? (The Urban Institute is currently involved in research designed to begin to answer some of these questions.)

In conclusion, although there are clearly a number of real barriers to fundamentally changing the subsidy usage patterns of low-income families, most notably limited funding, there are also a number of strategies that states and localities can use (and indeed are already using) to make it easier for families to access and retain subsidies. This suggests that even within the current funding context, there are real opportunities to better support low-income working families and their children.

ACKNOWLEDGMENTS

The research presented in this chapter is based on the site visits, data collection, and analysis of a larger team of researchers, which included the authors along with Jeffrey Capizzano, Patricia McMahon, Deborah Montgomery, Jodi Sandfort, Stefanie Schmidt, Freya Sonenstein, Kathryn Tout, and James Barsimantov. The authors are also grateful for the assistance of Matthew Stagner, Monica Rohacek, and Sarah Adelman. This chapter received direct funding from the John D. and Catherine T. MacArthur Foundation under the Assessing the New Federalism project (ANF). The ANF project is supported by the Annie E. Casey Foundation, the W.K. Kellogg Foundation, the Robert Wood Johnson Foundation, the Henry J. Kaiser Family Foundation, the Ford

Foundation, the David and Lucile Packard Foundation, the Charles Stewart Mott Foundation, the McKnight Foundation, the Commonwealth Fund, the Stuart Foundation, the Weingart Foundation, the Fund for New Jersey, the Lynde and Harry Bradley Foundation, the Joyce Foundation, and the Rockefeller Foundation.

REFERENCES

Adams, G., Holcomb, P., Snyder, K., Koralek, R., & Capizzano, J. (2005). *Child care subsidies for TANF families: The nexus of systems and policies.* Washington, DC: The Urban Institute.

Adams, G., Koralek, R., & Martinson, K. (2005). *Child care subsidies and leaving welfare: Policy issues and strategies.* Washington, DC: The Urban Institute.

Adams, G., & Rohacek, M. (2002). Child care and welfare reform. In A. Weil & K. Finegold (Eds.), *Welfare reform: The next act* (pp. 121–141). Washington, DC: The Urban Institute Press.

Adams, G., Snyder, K., & Sandfort, J. (2002). *Getting and retaining child care assistance: How policy and practice influence families' experiences.* Washington, DC: The Urban Institute.

Blank, H., & Poersch, N. O. (2000). *State developments in child care and early education.* Washington, DC: Children's Defense Fund.

Collins, A. M., Layzer, J. I., Kreader, J. L., Werner, A., & Glantz, F. B. (2000). *National study of child care for low-income families: State and community substudy interim report.* Washington, DC: Abt Associates Inc.

Greenberg, M., Schumacher, R., & Mezey, J. (2001). *The southern regional task force on child care action plan to improve access to child care assistance for low-income families in the south: An analysis of legal issues.* Washington, DC: Center for Law and Social Policy.

Lane, J. (2000). The role of job turnover in the low-wage labor market. In K. Kaye & D. S. Nightingale (Eds.), *The low-wage labor market: Challenges and opportunities for economic self-sufficiency* (pp. 185–198). Washington, DC: The Urban Institute.

Long, S. G., Kirby, G., Kurka, R., & Waters, S. (1998). *Child care assistance under welfare reform: Early responses by the states* (Assessing the New Federalism Occasional Paper No. 15). Washington, DC: The Urban Institute.

Meyers, M. K. (2001). *The use of child care subsidies: A conceptual model.* Unpublished manuscript. New York: Columbia University.

Meyers, M. K., Heintze, T., & Wolf, D. A. (1999). *Child care subsidies and the employment of welfare recipients.* Berkeley: University of California Berkeley.

Meyers, M. K., Peck, L. R., Davis, E. E., Collins, A., Kreader, J. L., Georges, A., Weber, R., Schexnayder, D., Schroeder, D., & Olson, J. A. (2002). *The dynamics of child care subsidy use: A collaborative study of five states.* New York: National Center on Children in Poverty, Columbia University.

NICHD Early Child Care Research Network. (1997). The effects of infant child care on infant–mother attachment security: Results of the NICHD Study of Early Child Care. *Child Development, 68*(5), 860–879.

Rangarajan, A., Schochet, P., & Chu, D. (1998). *Employment experiences of welfare recipients who find jobs: Is targeting possible?* Princeton: Mathematica Policy Research.

Schulman, K., & Blank, H. (2004). *Child care assistance policies 2001–2004: Families struggling to move forward, states moving backward* (Issue Brief). Washington, DC: National Women's Law Center.

Schulman, K., Blank, H., & Ewen, D. (2001). *A fragile foundation: Child care assistance policies*. Washington, DC: Children's Defense Fund.

Schumacher, R., & Greenberg, M. (1999). *Child care after leaving welfare: Early evidence from state studies*. Washington, DC: Center for Law and Social Policy.

U.S. Department of Health and Human Services. (2000). New statistics show only small percentage of eligible families receive child care help. Press release from Web site, www .acf.dhhs.gov/news/ccstudy.htm

## CHAPTER TEN

Child-Care Subsidies and the Transition From Welfare to Work

Sandra K. Danziger
University of Michigan

Elizabeth Oltmans Ananat
Massachusetts Institute of Technology

Kimberly G. Browning
High/Scope Educational Research Foundation

We address how child-care subsidies help in the welfare-to-work transition relative to other factors. We examine how the policy operates, whether child-care problems differ by subsidy receipt, and the effect of subsidy on work. Data are from a random sample panel study of welfare recipients after 1996. Findings show that subsidy receipt reduces costs, but not parenting stress or problems with care. It predicts earnings and work duration net of other factors. Increased use of subsidies by eligible families and greater funding for child care would help meet the demand for this important support for working poor families.

CHILD-CARE SUBSIDIES AND THE TRANSITION FROM WELFARE TO WORK

Access to subsidized child care is an important concern for many women moving from welfare to work. Because access to a subsidy program varies by state, we here describe the policy context in Michigan, where the study was conducted. We examine whether demographic characteristics and other factors that may affect work differ by child-care use and subsidy receipt. We assess whether subsidies reduce child-care problems and increase a woman's percent of months worked and monthly earnings. Using data from the Women's Employment Study (WES), a random sample panel survey of women who received welfare, we draw policy and program implications regarding how child-care financial assistance can better promote the welfare reform objective of self-sufficiency through employment.

BACKGROUND

Policies that help families find and pay for nonparental child care can facilitate the employment of women, especially single mothers. All else being equal, mothers facing lower child-care costs are more likely to be employed, particularly low-income or single mothers (Meyers, Han, Waldfogel, & Garfinkel, 2001). Low-income, single mothers also report being more likely to work when care is more available (Mason & Kuhlthau, 1992) and when they are more satisfied with the quality of care (Meyers, 1993). Problems with child care can lead single mothers to leave jobs and also can adversely affect attendance, work hours, and career advancement (Henly & Lyons, 2000). In theory, subsidies can reduce both child-care costs and child-care problems and thereby promote work. As such, subsidies are one policy strategy that can help address the child-care needs of low-income, working families.

In addition to child-care problems and child-care costs, many factors can affect the transition from welfare to work. Previous research has identified a wide range of factors that can potentially increase or hinder the success of low-income mothers in the labor force, including the women's physical or mental health status, their children's health, the women's human capital (her education and training), their personal and social or family problems, and access to transportation.

High rates of health and mental health problems among welfare recipients have been identified (Danziger, Kalil, & Anderson, 2000; Ensminger, 1995; Loprest & Acs, 1996; Olson & Pavetti, 1996; Zedlewski & Alderson, 2001). Some studies found employment effects for low-income or welfare-recipient mothers who had one or more of these barriers, such as depression (Lennon, Blome, & English, 2001). Previous work with the WES found that child health problems, maternal health, and mental health problems reduced work outcomes (Danziger et al., 2000). Analyses with these data also showed reduced work outcomes among women with less than a high school degree relative to women with more education and among those who lacked access to a car or driver's license (Danziger et al., 2000).

Findings on the work effects of social or familial factors are more mixed, such as the effects of domestic violence for welfare and work outcomes (Tolman & Raphael, 2000) and the effects of having social support (Henly, 2000; Newman, 1999). Domestic violence victims can have high rates of health and mental health problems that reduce work, but they also may be highly motivated to work as they seek financial independence from their abusive partners (Tolman & Rosen, 2001). In contrast, social support from relatives and friends in poor families may be insufficient to result in increases in employment (Edin & Lein, 1997).

A sense of personal mastery, a measure of self-efficacy that promotes coping (Pearlin, Lieberman, Menaghan, & Mullan, 1981), may be an important trait that is positively related to moving into work among welfare recipients. Controls for the effects of social support and mastery may be important as personal and social resources that could help women succeed in the transition to work, whereas the effects and direction of domestic violence on work are less clear in the literature. Having personal, health, educational, transportation, and child health problems are likely to constrain work outcomes. Analyses aimed at addressing policy and program effects such as financial assistance for child care would be underspecified if these other conditions and characteristics of the woman and her family situation were not taken into consideration.

CHILD-CARE ASSISTANCE POLICY AND WELFARE REFORM

The federal government and states have greatly expanded spending on child care since the Personal Responsibility and Work Opportunity Reconciliation Act (PRWORA) was enacted in August 1996. The Act consolidated federal funding into a child-care and development block grant (CCDBG); $20 billion was allocated for the period 1997 to 2002, reflecting a 25% increase (an additional $4 billion) over the spending provided under prior legislation (U.S. House of Representatives, Committee on Ways and Means, 1998). States were also given the ability to increase spending further by shifting federal funds out of their Temporary Assistance to Needy Families (TANF) block grants. Additionally, states were given new flexibility in designing subsidy systems. Michigan blended its CCDBG and TANF funds to expend $400 million in child care in FY 1999, up from $128 million in FY 1996 (Seefeldt, Leos-Urbel, McMahon, & Snyder, 2001).

Every state sets its own policies for child-care subsidies. Typically, states set eligibility criteria that include a family income cutoff, expressed as an amount in dollars or a percentage of the poverty line or of the state's median income. They also require that the parent be working or participating in education or training. The states provide subsidies to a subset of eligible families depending on the availability of funds. Prior to 1996, welfare recipients or former welfare recipients had priority, but this is no longer required under the federal law (although it is still often the case in practice).

Work requirements in TANF are presumed to increase the need for child care. Although there were many individuals exempted from work requirements in the Aid to Families with Dependent Children (AFDC) program, nearly all TANF recipients must become engaged in work activities within 2 years of receiving assistance. By federal policy, states are allowed to exempt parents with children less than 12 months of age, and they are allowed to create other categories of exemptions.

Michigan is rather strict in its exemptions. It is 1 of 19 states that requires work participation by the time a recipient's youngest child reaches 12 weeks of age. Thus, welfare mothers with very young children have to find child care to comply with work requirements. The only other reasons the state defers recipients from work participation are for disability, caregiving to a disabled family member age 65 or older, or adolescent parents attending secondary school.

Michigan subsidizes child care after families arrange it with state-contracted providers. Parents can choose a child-care center, family care home, group care home, or relative or nonrelative in-home child-care provider provided they have appropriate licensure or registration and accept state TANF clients.

Types of Child Care

In 1998, there were approximately 4,600 licensed child-care centers in Michigan. Family and group child care both operate in private residences, but family child-care homes care for six or less children at any one time and need only register by attesting to meeting state regulations, providing personal references, and being cleared for criminal records, child protective services, and tuberculosis. In 1998, there were about 15,000 family child-care homes and 1,700 group care homes in the state (Public Sector Consultants, 1998).

Group child care operated in homes provides care for 7 to 12 children at once and must meet licensing requirements, which include maintaining staff–child ratios (1:6) and age requirements for enrollment (no more than four children may be under 30 months and only two may be under 18 months). Like a family child-care home, the provider must also undergo registration screening procedures.

The other care option that can be subsidized is an in-home caregiver (e.g., babysitter, grandparent, friend, or neighbor). Although not regulated by the state, the caregiver must enroll with the state welfare agency by providing documentation of willingness to provide care and permission for a background check. Once both caregiver and family make an agreement, the state may authorize child-care payments for up to 30 calendar days prior to application if the caregiver is found eligible. The state is required to determine eligibility for the assistance of both the caregiver and the family within 45 days of receiving the application.

The majority of the subsidies in Michigan pay for in-home care. In-home care provided by a relative accounted for nearly half (46%) of the settings receiving subsidies in 1998. The next most common was center-based (18%) and in-home care by nonrelatives (16%). Another 11% of providers the state supported were family child-care homes, and 9% were family group homes (Public Sector Consultants, 1998).

Gaps in Subsidies

The Michigan Community Coordinated Child Care Association (4C) reported that in 1998 there were licensed slots to accommodate only 78% of all children in child care in Michigan (Public Sector Consultants, 1998). Not all providers in the state accept children whose families receive subsidies; others limit their enrollment when the state reimbursement rates are lower than their prices—only 47% of the centers, 54% of the family child-care homes, and 53% of group homes accept subsidies (U.S. Department of Health and Human Services, 1999). To increase the capacity and quality of care, the state awarded grants in FY 2001 to licensed or registered providers who served children from low-income or TANF families and awarded start-up grants to initiate new child-care centers, family homes, and group homes (Michigan Family Independence Agency, 2001)

Over calendar years 1995 to 1997, in Michigan, 375,000 children met the state's child-care subsidy income eligibility guidelines (U.S. Department of Health and Human Services, 1999). To be eligible, a family of three must receive TANF or have an income below $26,064, or 59% of state median income. The number of children eligible would be much higher (545,000) if the state raised the income eligibility limits to 85% of the state median income, the maximum level allowed under federal law (U.S. Department of Health and Human Services, 1999). In an average month during 1998, 95,800 children (26% of the estimated eligible children) were subsidized.

Income-eligible families must pay a portion of their child-care costs, from 5% to 70%, based on the type of care selected, the area in which the care is used, and the age of the child. The percentage paid by the state is based on the predetermined state maximum rate or the provider's charge, whichever is less. The maximum rate is set at the 75th percentile of the local market rate for six regions in the state. However, although a market survey of child-care costs was completed in 1999, the state's reimbursement rates for children over age 2.5 were based on the 1995 to 1996 market rate (Seefeldt et al., 2001). For children under age 2.5, the 1999 market rate is used. If the cost of the child care is lower than the maximum rate, the rate of the child care is used. If the rate of the child care is higher than maximum rates, the agency maximum is used.

For the lowest income families, the state will pay 95% of either the cost of care or the maximum. As a family's gross income rises, the subsidy falls; for example, a single mother with one child is no longer eligible if her gross monthly income exceeds $1,758. Any child-care charge above the percentage allowed is the responsibility of the parent.

An example of the subsidy policy for respondents in the survey county is given in Table 10.1. If a family of three with a yearly income of $15,000 does not use a child-care subsidy (although eligible) and enrolls an infant full time in an average-priced center, they spend approximately $559 per month. This amounts to spending about 45% of their monthly income on care. Likewise, if they enroll a preschool-age child full time in an average-priced center, they spend approximately $516 on child care, or 41.3% of their income. These expenditures are slightly lower for family or group home care and considerably lower for in-home care (which does not vary by age of the child).

With subsidies, the percentage of monthly income spent on center-based infant care (the difference between the market price and the maximum state subsidy) drops to $28, or only 2.2% of family income; for center-based care of a preschooler, it drops to $76 per month, or 6.1% of the family income. Subsidies meet the average cost of in-home care fairly well, leaving little out-of-pocket expenditures ($14 or .01%) for the family. Thus, subsidies can reduce costs and may encourage parents to use particular types of care. Whether they help families with child-care problems and increase employment, especially net of other factors related to the welfare-to-work transition, has not been assessed. To fill this gap, we control for a wide range of problems that can impede low-income women's employment success and test for bias in the relationship between subsidy receipt and work.

STUDY DESIGN AND MEASURES

Data to assess the effects of subsidy receipt on child-care problems and employment came from the first three waves of the Women's Employment Study (WES), a multiwave survey of welfare recipients in an urban Michigan county. A simple random sample was systematically selected from an ordered list of 8,875 eligible women who received welfare in the county in February 1997.

The original list sample included single mothers between the ages of 18 and 54 who were residents of the county, which is largely a medium-sized "rust belt" midwestern city. Criteria for inclusion were limited to being White or Black, and U.S. citizens. (Noncitizens and other ethnic/racial groups comprised a very small proportion of the overall caseload and would be of insufficient number to allow examination of these groups in detail.)

In fall 1997, trained interviewers conducted in-home face-to-face interviews lasting about 1 hour with 753 women. The state's TANF agency provided names and addresses of all single-parent cases, and the women were sent letters asking them to participate in a study of how women combine work and family life. Respondents were reinterviewed in home in fall 1998 and fall 1999 for about 90 minutes. Information was collected on a broad and comprehensive set of indicators of economic and psychosocial well-being,

TABLE 10.1

Child-Care Prices and Co-Payments for Hypothetical Sample Family of Three Earning $15,000 With One Child in Full-Time Care

Child Care	Without Subsidy		Maximum Subsidy Rate	With Subsidy	
	Average Monthly Prices For Full-Time Care in Sample County	% of Income		Average Monthly Difference Between Price and Subsidy	% of Income
Infant (age 1)					
Center based	$559	45	$531	$28	2.2
Family or group care home	$537	43	$510	$27	2.2
In-home care	$282	23	$268	$14	.01
Preschooler (age 4)					
Center based	$516	41	$440	$76	6.1
Family or group care home	$494	40	$399	$95	7.6
In-home care	$282	23	$268	$14	.01

Source. Local market estimates provided by the local Michigan Community Coordinated Child Care Association.

physical and mental health, demographic characteristics, income, current/ most recent job, current welfare status, work and welfare histories, and child care.

The response rate was 86.2% (753 of 874) for Wave 1, 92% (693 of 753) for Wave 2, and 91% (632 of 693) for Wave 3. Overall, the participation rate for all 3 waves was 72% (632 of 874). Comparisons of the interview sample and population on race, age, and welfare and administrative data showed no systematic bias. For the analysis reported here, the sample size was limited to those women in Wave 3 who had at least one child ages 14 or younger (561 of 632) because subsidies are limited in the state to children ages 13 or less—or up to age 14 if the child is disabled. We also restricted the sample to families that were income eligible for Michigan's subsidies (529 of 561). This resulted in a subsample of 83.7% of the total sample, but it represents all families in the sample for whom state-subsidized child care was relevant.

Comparisons of characteristics of the respondents in our subsidy-eligible group with the overall sample of current and former recipients showed that the subsidy-eligible sample ($n = 529$) was 56.7% African American, compared with 55.5% of the WES sample at Wave 3 ($n = 632$). Of subsidy eligible, 68.2% had a high school diploma or equivalent (or more education), compared with 72.6% of the overall sample; 33.7% lived with a husband or partner, compared with 36.6% overall. Those who were subsidy eligible had a mean age of 31.8 years, whereas the sample averaged age 30.0. The subsidy eligible had on average 2.5 children, compared with 2.3 children for the sample. Thus, overall, the subset of families was fairly representative of the total sample.

Measures

The third wave of the survey asked many questions about child care to 59.7% of the respondents. These women had a child less than age 14 in the household and had (a) used child care since Wave 2 (on average 14 months before the Wave 3 interview), and (b) indicated that the primary reason they needed care was to work, look for work, or go to school.

Respondents reported whether, in a typical week over the period since the last interview, any of their children had been cared for by (a) a day-care center, nursery, preschool, or before- or after-school program; (b) Head Start; (c) the child's father; (d) a relative besides the child's father; or (e) a nonrelative. For all types of care eligible for state subsidies (center or other program care, nonfather relative care, and nonrelative care), they were asked whether the state agency had helped to pay for that care. If a respondent reported that she had received state help paying for at least one of her care arrangements, she was coded as having received a subsidy. In this sample, center or other program care was the type most likely to be subsidized: 57.5% of those who had used centers reported state help to pay for it, whereas 49.8% of those who used relative care and 42.1% of those who used nonrelative care reported that the state helped in paying for those arrangements.

In addition, the survey included questions about out-of-pocket child-care payments and problems with child care over the period since the last interview. Respondents reported how much they paid for care in a typical week over the time frame. Problems with child care were measured by whether respondents had experienced any work disruption due to a problem with child care since the last wave. Work disruptions included: (a) ever had been unable to look for work or participate in training; (b) ever turned down a job offer; (c) was ever late to or absent from work, school, or training; or (d) had quit or been fired from a job because of child care. Respondents who answered positively to any one or more of these experiences were coded as having work disruption due to child care.

A second possible child-care problem was whether respondents had ever stopped using child care over the time frame for any reason. A third problem that could be a reflection of child-care difficulties was a measure of parenting stress. Parenting stress included a seven-item index asking the degree of stress or irritation the mother perceives in relation to her interactions with her child. Thus, it explores mothers' subjective sense of difficulty with regard to their parenting role and, in previous research, has been related to child maltreatment (Abidin, 1990). Items for this scale were taken from Abidin's (1990) Parenting Stress Index (PSI) and adapted as in the New Chance Study (Zaslow & Eldred, 1998). A sample item was, "I find that being a mother is much more work than pleasure." Items are measured on a 5-point scale and responses range from *never* (1) to *almost always* (5). A composite score is calculated, and higher scores indicate greater parenting stress. The Cronbach's α for the WES respondents in these analyses was .75.

Family Income

Family income was calculated to determine whether the respondent was eligible for the child-care subsidy. It was the sum of the amount of income from all sources reported in the month before the Wave 3 interview. Included were reports of income from the respondent or other members of her "legal family" (i.e., the respondent, her spouse if married, and her children) from earnings, TANF, food stamps, child support, SSI and Social Security, unemployment insurance, money from family and friends, and any other source not specifically mentioned. Respondents reported income that accrued to any household member, not just to legal family members, some of which would not be included in the state's calculations of subsidy eligibility. Thus, we imputed the amount of income received by the legal family. This included imputing a respondent's own earnings and all TANF, food stamps, and child support as belonging to the family unit. SSI or Social Security was counted as belonging to the family unit only if the respondent reported that she or her child received it. Otherwise we included that income only if she was married. Similarly, unemployment insurance and other household members' earnings were imputed only if the respondent was married. Family income in conjunction with the state's income eligibility guidelines, which are based on family size and income, was estimated to compute whether the respondent was income eligible for at least some child-care subsidization.

Using regression analyses, we examined two work-related outcomes that could be affected by the availability and affordability of child care. First, the proportion of calendar months between the interviews in which the respondent reported that she had worked for pay (the total number of months between waves ranges from 8–19, but averages about 14) was estimated in a Tobit regression. The natural logarithm (ln) of respondents' earnings in the month before the interview was the second dependent variable in an ordinary least squares (OLS) regression.

In the regression analyses, we controlled for several other factors identified in previous studies as relevant for low-income mothers' employment: demographic differences, social support, and sense of mastery. The models also included potential barriers to work: whether the respondent reported a physical health problem, a mental health problem, a child health problem, or recent experience of domestic violence at Wave 3; whether the respondent had a human capital barrier (e.g., lacks education); and whether the respondent lacked a driver's license or access to a car.

Specifically, we included race and mother's age. Also, marital status was coded to compare single mothers with those who had married or cohabited with a partner. The number of children ages 0 to 2, 3 to 5, and 6 to 10 (age categories that typically require demanding but different levels of parental monitoring and supervision) was measured.

A respondent was coded as having a physical health problem if she both described her general health as *fair* or *poor* and scored in the bottom quartile of a physical functioning scale derived from the SF-36 Health Survey (Ware, Snow, & Kosinski, 1993). A respondent was coded as having a mental health problem if she met the Diagnostic and Statistical Manual, Third Edition Revised (*DSM–III–R*) diagnostic screening criteria for major depression, social phobia, generalized anxiety disorder, posttraumatic stress disorder, alcohol dependence, or drug dependence, as measured by the Composite International Diagnostic Interview–Short Form (CIDI–SF; Kessler et al., 1994). She was coded as having a child health problem if at least one child for whom she is the primary caregiver had a physical, learning, or emotional problem that limited his or her activity, a question used in national studies such as the National Longitudinal Survey of Youth (NLSY). She was coded as having a transportation problem if she lacked a driver's license or access to a car.

Domestic violence was assessed with a modified version of the Conflict Tactics Scale (CTS; Straus, 1979). Consistent with previous studies, a 6-item severe physical violence score was constructed as a dummy variable. Respondents were coded as 1 if in the last 12 months the woman had experienced any one of six types of partner violence: been hit with a fist or object; been beaten, choked, or threatened with a weapon; or been forced into sexual activity (Tolman & Rosen, 2001).

Human capital measures included whether the woman lacked a high school diploma or equivalent and whether she read below a fifth-grade level. Reading ability was assessed using the Wide Range of Achievement Test 3 (WRAT3); this test of an individual's ability to learn reading and spelling is correlated with results of the California Achievement Test and the SAT (Wilkinson, 1993).

Social support was measured with seven items that indicate perceived availability of support, part of the Social Relationship Scale (O'Brien, Wortman, Kessler, & Joseph, 1993). Such measures have been used in studies to assess whether having support mediates the effects of stress on health and mental health. The items tap a respondent's hypothetical access to people who can help with personal problems, medical emergencies, advice, information, small loans of money, and so forth, all of which can affect a person's contacts in employment networks and her ability to respond to the crises and burdens of home–work conflicts (Henly, 2000). Scores range from 1 to 5 on each item, with responses ranging from *would definitely not* to *yes, definitely* to indicate whether she would have someone to turn to for help. Scores were standardized to range between 0 and 1, and the Cronbach's α was .88.

Mastery was assessed with the Pearlin Mastery Scale (Pearlin et al., 1981), a 7-item scale of the extent to which the respondents feel efficacious and in control of life. Representative items from the mastery scale include "I can do anything I set my mind to" and "What happens in the future depends on me." Items were scored on a 4-point scale, where 1 indicates *strongly disagree* and 4 indicates *strongly agree*. The theoretical range of the scale is 7 to 28, and higher scores indicate greater mastery (Chronbach's $\alpha = .81$). Mastery scores were standardized to range between 0 and 1.

RESULTS

We first addressed the question of whether, among respondents who are eligible to receive the subsidy (by age of children and income level) and who had used child care, the costs or problems of child care differed by subsidy receipt. Only 30.9% ($n = 68$) of those with a subsidy reported out-of-pocket costs in a typical week, whereas 42.7% ($n = 67$) of families who used care but did not get a subsidy had out-of-pocket costs, χ^2 ($df = 1$, $n = 377$) = 5.52, $p = .019$. However, among those who had out-of-pocket costs, the dollars paid for child care and the percentage of family income that went to child care did not differ significantly by subsidy receipt. Specifically, those without subsidies who had costs paid on average $68.76 per week, or 39.6% of family income. Similarly, one third of those who received subsidies and had costs paid $60.47 per week on average, or 31.1% of family income.

Of the several potential care-related problems measured, only one differed by subsidy receipt: 20.5% ($n = 45$) of subsidy users had stopped using child care in the last year, compared with 35.8% ($n = 56$) of those without a subsidy, χ^2 ($df = 1$, $n = 377$) $= 10.81$, $p = .001$. Work disruptions of several kinds that were due to a child-care problem did not differ across the two groups. These included whether in the last year the respondent was ever fired or quit a job or training program, was unable to accept a job or training program, was unable to look for a job or training, or was late or absent from a job or training program because of child care. Approximately one third of each group reported at least one of these problems occurred because of child care. Parenting stress scores did not statistically differ across the two groups—the mean for those with and without subsidies was 22. Thus, the lack of difference on these measures suggests that care-related problems persisted regardless of subsidy receipt. We cannot assess whether the subsidy was insufficient to secure more stable care, or whether, when child care was disrupted, it was difficult to maintain the subsidy.

Table 10.2 reports descriptive information for our sample of low-income families with children ages of less than 14 on demographics, control measures, and work outcomes by subsidy receipt and use of child care. The columns compare respondents who had not used child care since the last interview with those who used care but did not receive a subsidy and those who used subsidized care. Just 41.6% reported having received a subsidy for at least one type of care since the last interview ($n = 220$), whereas 29.7% ($n = 157$) reported having relied on unsubsidized care. The other 28.7% ($n = 152$) did not use care in this period.

Those who had not used care had a racial composition of 55.9% African American, highly similar to that of the WES sample in general (55.5% African American). However, among those who used care, those who received a subsidy were more often African American (66.4%), whereas those who had not were more likely to be White (66%). Among all care users, African Americans had a significantly lower average income-to-needs ratio than Whites (0.87 vs. 1.09, not shown in table). Thus, on average, African Americans may have been more motivated by financial strain to navigate the system to secure a subsidy.

Those who received a subsidy were less often married or cohabiting with a partner and had the highest average number of children and of preschoolers relative to the other groups. Not having a spouse or partner and having more children may have made them more likely to need child care to go to work and less likely to have access to (free) parental care. Thus, these characteristics raised the demand for subsidies.

TABLE 10.2
Sample Characteristics by Use of Care and Subsidy Receipt

	Have Not Used Care	Have Used Care, But No Subsidy	Have Used Care With a Subsidy
Among income-eligible respondents with a child under 14 ($N = 529$)	28.7%, $n = 152$	29.7%, $n = 157$	41.6%, $n = 220$
Demographics			
% African American[a,b,c]	55.9%	44.0%	66.4%
Mean age[a,b]	34.9	29.9	29.3
	(7.69)	(6.35)	(5.86)
% Married or cohabiting[b,c]	39.5%	45.2%	21.4%
Number of care-given children ages 0–2[b]	0.2	0.3	0.4
	(0.51)	(0.50)	(0.63)
Number of care-given children ages 3–5[a,b]	0.4	0.6	0.7
	(0.65)	(0.66)	(0.71)
Number of care-given children ages 6–10[b]	0.9	0.9	1.0
	(0.89)	(0.86)	(0.90)
Advantages for work			
Social support (1 = *lowest* to 5 = *highest*)[a]	4.2	4.4	4.3
	(0.86)	(0.70)	(0.86)
Sense of mastery (1 = *lowest* to 4 = *highest*)[a,b]	3.0	3.2	3.2
	(0.48)	(0.46)	(0.47)
Barriers to work			
% Experiencing domestic violence	10.5%	14.1%	11.8%
% With no high school diploma[a,b]	42.1%	30.6%	25.5%
% With no car or license[b]	37.5%	27.4%	27.2%
% With a physical health problem[a,b]	35.5%	18.7%	11.9%
% With a mental health problem	39.5%	34.6%	31.4%
% Caring for a child with a health problem[b]	20.4%	15.3%	12.3%
% Reading below fifth-grade level[a,b]	27.0%	14.0%	18.2%
Work outcomes			
Mean % of months worked between fall 1998 and fall 1999[a,b,c]	40.4%	74.6%	85.1%
	(0.42)	(0.29)	(0.25)
% Respondents with earnings in month prior to fall 1999 interview[a,b]	41.5%	79.6%	86.8%
Mean earnings in month prior to fall 1999 interview (nonzeroes)	$833	$884	$966
	(682.16)	(551.17)	(580.85)

[a]Those who have not used child care differ from those who have used care but without subsidy at $p < .05$.

[b]Those who have not used child care differ from those with a subsidy at $p < .05$.

[c]Those who have used care but without a subsidy differ from those with a subsidy at $p < .05$.

Standard deviations in parentheses.

Those who did not use care were older and had significantly fewer young children than women in the other groups. They had lower average levels of social support and sense of mastery. They more often faced barriers to work, including lack of a high school diploma, lack of car or drivers' license, reported high number of physical health problems, responsibility for a child with a health problem, and a low reading level.

This profile suggests three plausible explanations for the nonuse of child care among low-income families with young children. The fact that many of these respondents were older, and that fewer of them had a preschooler, suggests that some of them may not have needed child care to work. However, the fact that they had higher rates of barriers to work suggests that some may not have used care because they could not go to work even if they were to find care. Alternatively, it may be that these barriers prevented them from successfully securing care or from successfully navigating the subsidy system to acquire the financial means to secure care. This hypothesis is tested in the regression analysis.

Those who had not used care had the poorest work outcomes. On average, they worked in only 40.4% of the months since the fall 1998 interview, and just 41.5% of them worked in the month prior to the fall 1999 interview. Among those who used care, those who received a subsidy worked in more of the months since the previous wave than those who relied on unsubsidized care (85.1% vs. 74.6%). For mean monthly earnings (among earners), the pattern of best outcomes for the subsidized ($966) and worst outcomes for those who did not use care ($833) persisted, but the differences were not significant.

Single-Stage Regression Results

All regressions examined the predictive role of the child-care subsidy for work outcomes. Use of child care and use of a subsidy may be jointly determined— that is, one may find care and seek out a subsidy to pay for it, or one may learn of the availability of subsidies and, therefore, seek out care. Thus, these regressions include all respondents who made up the eligible population (were income eligible and had an age-eligible child), rather than only those who used care or only those who used a subsidy-eligible type of care. We then contrasted those who received a subsidy with all others—both those who used unsubsidized care and those who did not use care at all. The coefficients on subsidy use represent the effect of the joint decision to use both subsidy-eligible care and a subsidy relative to any other possible care decision.

The results of the first regression, presented in the first column of Table 10.3, have the natural logarithm (ln) of earnings in the month prior to the interview as the dependent variable. If a respondent had no earnings, she is recoded as having $15 in earnings (the lowest amount earned by a respondent with nonzero earnings) to create a valid logarithm. We use the logarithmic transformation because earnings are known to be skewed and are better approximated by a lognormal distribution. The logarithm transforms income into an approximately linear variable with a lower bound of 2.7, ln (15), for which we use a Tobit regression.

The results of the second regression presented in Table 10.3 have the proportion of months worked between waves as the dependent variable (a continuous outcome with values ranging only between 0 and 1). This required a linear transformation on the proportion of months worked, P, and used as the dependent variable the natural logarithm of P divided by the quantity 1-P. We performed an OLS regression on this linear and unbounded variable, an econometric procedure known as a grouped logit regression.

In addition, we controlled for demographic differences and advantages and barriers to work in these analyses. Demographic characteristics including age, race, and number of children ages 3 to 5 and 6 to 10 were not significant in predicting work outcomes after we controlled for subsidy receipt and advantages and barriers to work. Among these respondents, the number of children ages 2 years or younger was significant in predicting earnings when controlling for subsidy status as well as other explanatory characteristics. All else being equal, a woman with an additional child under 2 earned 43% less in the month before the interview.

A greater sense of mastery significantly predicted both higher earnings and a higher percentage of months worked. Lack of transportation and physical health problems also remained significant when controlling for child-care subsidy. Mental health, domestic violence, education, and child health problems were not significant in these analyses of work outcomes.

Taken together, these results show that receipt of a child-care subsidy predicts better work outcomes. Among otherwise similar respondents with a child under age 14, those who had a state child-care subsidy at some point between Waves 2 and 3 had on average worked in more months during the past year and also earned more at Wave 3. The size of the effect of the subsidy depends on the proportion of months that a woman was predicted to work if she did not receive a subsidy, $B*P*(1-P)$. We calculated that, on average, a child-care subsidy increased the total proportion of months that a respondent worked by eight points. However, for a respondent who without a subsidy worked in half the months between interviews, a subsidy is predicted to increase work participation to over three quarters of months. In addition, having a subsidy increased respondents' monthly earnings by 105% (B coefficient in Table 10.3).

Two-Stage Regression Results

Although these findings are quite strong, they are clouded by concerns about the direction of the relationship, or possible endogeneity, between work and subsidy receipt. It could be that the characteristics—both measured and un-

TABLE 10.3

Single-Stage Regressions Predicting Work Outcomes
Among Income-Eligible Respondents With a Child Under 14

	Natural Log (Last Month's Earnings)		Natural Log (% of Months Worked Since W2 / 1 − % of Months Worked Since W2)	
	Tobit		OLS	
	B	Std. Error	B	Std. Error
Receiving child-care subsidy	1.047***	0.221	1.058***	0.170
Demographic controls				
Age	−0.022	0.017	−0.0457***	0.013
Race (1 if African American, 0 if White)	0.007	0.217	0.040	0.166
Married/cohabiting	−0.213	0.232	0.161	0.177
Number of care-given children ages 0–2	−0.434*	0.193	−0.226	0.147
Number of care-given children ages 3–5	−0.132	0.160	−0.085	0.121
Number of care-given children ages 6–10	0.015	0.119	−0.172	0.091
Advantages for work				
Social support (1 = *lowest* to 5 = *highest*)	−0.001	0.139	0.014	0.104
Sense of mastery (1 = *lowest* to 4 = *highest*)	0.827***	0.235	0.443*	0.179
Barriers to work				
Domestic violence	0.146	0.319	0.050	0.241
No high school diploma	−0.433	0.233	−0.285	0.177
Lack of car or license	−0.818***	0.232	−0.366*	0.176
Physical health problem	−1.421***	0.283	−0.633**	0.208
Mental health problem	−0.202	0.223	−0.104	0.170
Child health problem	−0.359	0.292	0.167	0.219
Reads below fifth-grade level	−0.399	0.269	−0.097	0.203
Constant	3.884***	1.139	−1.839*	0.866
N	521[a]		521[a]	
R squared			0.216	
Pseudo R squared for Tobit regression	0.251			

[a]Eight respondents with missing data are excluded from the analysis.

*p < .05.

**p < .01.

***p < .001.

measured—that make a woman more likely to navigate the state system successfully and secure a subsidy are the same characteristics that make a woman
more likely to be successful in work. To the extent that relevant characteristics
are unmeasured, a woman's receipt or nonreceipt of a subsidy is correlated
with the error term that is left after controlling for measured characteristics in
predicting work outcomes. This results in biased coefficients and could lead to
exaggerated estimates of the influence of subsidies on work.

In an ideal research arrangement, one would use a randomized experiment to resolve this problem. If subsidy receipt were randomly assigned, it would not be correlated with unmeasured characteristics of the respondent, and one could be confident that the estimate of the effect of subsidy receipt on work was unbiased. Subsidies are not randomly distributed to the population, so we did not have access to such an arrangement. However, the instrumental variable regression technique is an econometric method that allows researchers to approximate a randomized experiment (Greene, 2000).

The treatment effects regression is a two-stage model. In the first stage, it uses relevant characteristics to generate a prediction of subsidy receipt. In the second stage, it uses the expected value of subsidy receipt, rather than actual receipt/nonreceipt, to estimate the effect of subsidy receipt on work. The predicted value is uncorrelated with the error term in the second equation (and produces an unbiased estimate) only when one of the variables used to create the predicted value is exogenous, or unlikely to cause the outcome of interest. This variable thus acts as an instrument, in effect, like partial random assignment—that is, it must be a factor that affects subsidy receipt, but does not plausibly affect work outcomes directly. Moreover, it must not be self-selected by the respondent in a way that suggests it could be driven by respondent characteristics that also affect work.

In this study, the welfare district office to which a respondent was assigned served as an instrument because of how the welfare, work, and child-care subsidy policies were implemented. In the sample county, the welfare population is concentrated near the city center and is divided into quadrants. The district offices for the quadrants are located near each other within downtown; because of the geographic concentration, travel time from the sectors to the district offices does not differ by quadrant. Applicants for welfare and child-care subsidies were assigned to district office by zip code, and these assignments shifted according to application rates from one office to another.

Employment search services programs, to which recipients were sent to carry out work requirements, were administered outside of the district offices. These employment service agencies were also centrally located, and they all served the same general local labor market of the county. In addition, the referral of cases from district offices to these employment service agencies shifted over time. Because employment assistance was handled by different organizations than those that processed child-care assistance, work outcomes should not depend in any direct way on the district office that processed the child-care assistance. In fact when district office administrative data were examined, we found that, controlling for respondent characteristics, one welfare office had a higher rate of subsidy assignment than that of the other three offices. Given recent literature on differences in subsidy administration between locations (Adams & Rohacek, 2002), such variation is not specific to Michigan, but rather common across states. It was fortuitous for the purpose of this analysis because the welfare district office could be treated as an exogenous factor that affects subsidy receipt, but is unlikely to directly affect work outcomes.

Table 10.4 presents the results of the two-stage analyses of earnings and percent of months worked. In general, the estimates do not look much different with this added layer of statistical precision. The coefficients on expected subsidy in the second stage, although larger than the coefficients on subsidy in the single-stage equations (Table 10.3), are not significantly different when the standard errors are taken into account. Moreover, the likelihood ratio test of the first and second stages does not reject independence, suggesting that the instrument approach is unnecessary. Thus, the cross-sectional relationship of recent subsidy use and work shown in Table 10.3 is representative of the true relationship. This suggests that the treatment effect of a policy change that exclusively increased overall subsidy use (but did not target directly employment of the parents) would be at least as large as the coefficient of subsidy receipt on work would suggest—more than doubling earnings and substantially increasing months worked.

DISCUSSION

Forty-two percent of respondents who were income eligible and had a child under age 14 reported receiving a child-care subsidy for care used during a typical week over the 14-month survey period. Nearly a third of these families also reported out-of-pocket expenses for care during a typical week. These costs (about $60 per week) reflected, on average, 31% of the family income. Yet subsidy users were no less likely to report parenting stress and experienced no fewer work-related child-care problems compared to respondents without this assistance. However, they were less likely to have stopped using care and had worked in a higher proportion of months.

Public expenditures on child care and use of subsidies have grown across the nation since the policy changes of 1996. However, demand for care also has increased with increases in maternal employment. Mezey, Schumacher, Greenberg, Lombardi, and Hutchins (2002) reported that the 1.8 million children receiving subsidies represented only 12% to 18% of income-eligible children whose parents worked or were in training for work. Michigan's estimates of percentage served were higher (26%), and the number served in the study sample was even higher (42%). However, subsidy receipt is defined in this study as a "yes" rather than "no" to having received state financial help during a typical period of child-care use within a 14-month period, which may result in higher estimates of subsidy receipt than would other measures. One five-state study found that the average length of time of subsidy receipt was 3 to 7 months (Adams & Rohacek, 2002).

Despite this limitation in the measure of subsidy, the relationships between subsidy receipt and employment held in our multivariate models, suggesting

TABLE 10.4

Two-Stage Treatment Effect Regressions Predicting Work Outcomes Among Income-Eligible Respondents With a Child Under 14

	Stage 1 Treatment Selection Equation: Subsidy Receipt		Stage 2 Main equation: ln (Last Month's Earnings)		Stage 1 Treatment Selection Equation: Subsidy Receipt		Stage 2 Main Equation: ln (% of Months Worked Since W2 / 1 – % of Months Worked Since W2)	
	B	Std. Error	B	Std. Error	B	Std. Error	B	Std. Error
Receiving child-care subsidy	—	—	2.500***	0.708	—	—	1.828***	0.600
Instrument: District office 2	0.252*	0.125	—	—	0.263	0.136	—	—
Demographic controls								
Age	−0.028**	0.010	0.002	0.015	−0.030*	0.010	−0.039**	0.014
Race (1 if African American, 0 if White)	0.239	0.129	−0.093	0.179	0.239	0.130	−0.015	0.172
Married/cohabitating	−0.804***	0.138	0.303	0.258	−0.807***	0.139	0.365	0.234
Number of care-given children ages 0–2	0.320**	0.115	−0.468**	0.166	0.296**	0.114	−0.300	0.157
Number of care-given children ages 3–5	0.290**	0.092	−0.283*	0.143	0.284**	0.094	−0.161	0.134
Number of care-given children ages 6–10	0.233**	0.072	−0.121	0.110	0.244**	0.072	−0.234*	0.103
Advantages for work								
Social support	−0.019	0.079	0.042	0.109	−0.046	0.081	0.029	0.105
Sense of mastery	0.089	0.140	0.520**	0.187	0.099	0.141	0.414*	0.181

(Continued)

TABLE 10.4
(Continued)

	Stage 1 Treatment Selection Equation: Subsidy Receipt		Stage 2 Main equation: ln (Last Month's Earnings)		Stage 1 Treatment Selection Equation: Subsidy Receipt		Stage 2 Main Equation: ln (% of Months Worked Since W2 / 1 − % of Months Worked Since W2)	
	B	Std. Error	B	Std. Error	B	Std. Error	B	Std. Error
Barriers to work								
Domestic violence	−0.018	0.186	0.116	0.251	−0.053	0.188	0.060	0.242
No high school diploma	−0.426**	0.138	−0.063	0.209	−0.426**	0.140	−0.171	0.196
Lack of car or license	−0.069	0.137	−0.544**	0.183	−0.083	0.138	−0.347	0.177
Physical health problem	−0.411*	0.164	−0.731**	0.232	−0.403*	0.167	−0.537*	0.221
Mental health problem	0.041	0.133	−0.201	0.177	0.040	0.134	−0.118	0.171
Child health problem	−0.213	0.172	−0.117	0.233	−0.204	0.175	0.223	0.224
Reads below fifth-grade level	−0.126	0.158	−0.208	0.213	−0.156	0.160	−0.063	0.205
Constant	0.422	0.654	3.396	1.005	0.510	0.666	−2.345*	0.947
Wald chi-square (16)	135.97***				108.45***			
Likelihood ratio test of independent equations chi-square (1)	2.53				0.65			
N = 521[a]								

[a]Eight respondents with missing data are excluded from the analysis.

*$p < .05$.
**$p < .01$.
***$p < .001$.

that all else being equal, subsidies have a strong impact on work outcomes. Few other studies have examined the role of subsidies in the transition from welfare to work, but a previous study showed results consistent with our findings. Meyers, Heintze, and Wolf (2002) found strong subsidy effects on work among a sample of California welfare recipients prior to 1996. Subsidy receipt was quite low in their study, and few other barriers to work were included as control measures.

In our study, we can rule out that having a subsidy is merely a proxy for other factors (e.g., number of children, good mental health, or access to transportation). Rather, controlling for demographics and other factors shown generally to affect the work outcomes of women who have been on welfare, subsidy receipt is a significant predictor of earnings and employment duration. These findings suggest that the lack of a child-care subsidy is a significant barrier to work for the population of mothers in the present study. The same can be said for lack of transportation and physical health problems and, for some outcomes, age of mother and number of young children.

Finally, when effects of child-care subsidies on work are examined, some factors previously identified as barriers to work were not significant, such as mother's mental health, her education, and child's health (Danziger et al., 2000). These barriers may nonetheless be important for women who do not have children of child-care age. Further, of the two advantages for work controlled for in this study, a higher mastery score remained significant for a mother's employment duration and earnings. Future studies should include controls for both barriers and resources in women's lives that can affect the transition from welfare to work.

POLICY AND PROGRAM IMPLICATIONS

The child-care subsidy is an important component of welfare reform despite that rates of receipt of subsidies among those eligible for them (take-up rates) are low across the nation (Meyers et al., 2001). In our sample of current and former welfare recipients, the majority of families eligible for the subsidy did not receive one, and many subsidized respondents reported continuing and high expenses for child care. Further, receiving a subsidy did not significantly reduce the frequency of work-related child-care problems. These findings suggest that current reimbursement rates, set below market rates for care, do not fully remove the burden on low-income families and may affect the choices of care they make. Subsidies in Michigan are predominantly used for in-home care that is less regulated than other types of child-care services. Advocates and child-care policy analysts should monitor these trends in how many eligible families receive subsidies, how much of the cost of child care is allayed by these subsidies, and, beyond the scope of the present study, the quality of care in subsidized services. They should try to assess reasons for low take-up rates in their communities and seek policy solutions to increase access to these benefit programs. For example, the complexity of the application process may contribute to low take-up rates, as could lack of awareness of the subsidy, knowledge of one's eligibility status, or inadequate outreach by service providers (Adams & Rohacek, 2002). However, some income-eligible families may indeed be able to find and prefer unpaid care and, therefore, will not apply for financial assistance.

The rates of low take-up among eligible families and high reported child-care costs, combined with the positive effects of subsidies on employment success, suggest that outreach efforts must be targeted broadly to families inside and outside of welfare systems. It may be that those who leave welfare for work jeopardize their access to child-care subsidies in addition to losing access to other supports for which they may still be eligible, such as Medicaid and Food Stamps.

If child-care funding does not increase, and if simplified procedures do not allow more of those who qualify to obtain subsidies, demand for child-care assistance will continue to outstrip supply. Although helpful for families, these policies will continue to constrain the child-care and employment choices of low-income parents. The political prospects of expansions in child-care support are not promising; instead cuts in such benefits are more likely in the current political climate (Parrott & Mezey, 2003). Recent debates and proposals for welfare reform reauthorization in Congress explicitly maintained budget-neutrality, despite calls in the Senate to increase child-care funding. Further, many states are facing large budget shortfalls that may bring about cuts in programs for low-income families. For example, a news story in Michigan (Manolatos, *Detroit News*, July 18, 2003) reported that the state budget to take effect in October 2003 called for restricting eligibility for child-care subsidies to families at 150% of the poverty line or below instead of at or below 200% of poverty. More than 3,000 families could lose this critical source of support. Budget savings in child care could result in added state welfare costs if some parents who cannot manage work and pay their child-care bills end up returning to welfare.

ACKNOWLEDGMENTS

A previous version of this chapter was presented at the conference "From Welfare to Child Care: What Happens to Infants and Toddlers When Single Mothers Exchange Welfare for Work?" on May 17, 2001, in Washington, DC and published in *Family Relations*, Vol. 53, No. 2, 2004, 219–228. Support for the Women's Employment Study at the University of Michigan was provided by the Joyce Foundation, the Charles Stewart Mott Foundation, the John D. and Catherine T. MacArthur Foundation, the Office of the Vice President for Research, University of Michigan, and the National Institute of Mental Health

(R24-MH51363). The authors wish to thank Sheldon Danziger, Deborah Curry, Peter Gottschalk, Charles Overbey, Elizabeth Peters, Kristin Seefeldt, Karen Tvedt, Hui-Chen Wang, and anonymous reviewers for comments on a previous draft.

REFERENCES

Abidin, R. R. (1990). *Parenting Stress Index Short Form: Test manual (36-item version)*. Charlottesville, VA: University of Virginia.

Adams, G., & Rohacek, M. (2002, February). *Child care and welfare reform* (Welfare Reform and Beyond Policy Brief No. 14). Washington, DC: Brookings Institution.

American Psychiatric Association (APA). (1987). *Diagnostic and Statistical Manual of Mental Disorders* (3rd ed. rev.). Washington, DC: Author.

Danziger, S. K., Corcoran, M., Danziger, S., Heflin, C., Kalil, A., Levine, J., Rosen, D., Seefeldt, K., Siefert, K., & Tolman, R. (2000). Barriers to the employment of welfare recipients. In R. Cherry & W. Rodgers (Eds.), *Prosperity for all? The economic boom and African Americans* (pp. 245–278). New York: Russell Sage Foundation.

Danziger, S. K., Kalil, A., & Anderson, N. J. (2000). Human capital, physical health, and mental health of welfare recipients: Co-occurrence and correlates. *Journal of Social Issues, 56*, 635–654.

Edin, K., & Lein, L. (1997). *Making ends meet: How single mothers survive welfare and low-wage work*. New York: Russell Sage Foundation.

Ensminger, M. (1995). Welfare and psychological distress: A longitudinal study of African American urban mothers. *Journal of Health and Social Behavior, 36*, 346–359.

Greene, W. H. (2000). *Econometric analysis* (4th ed.). Englewood Cliffs, NJ: Prentice-Hall.

Henly, J. R. (2000). Matching and mismatch in the low-wage labor market: Job search perspective. In K. Kaye & D. S. Nightingale (Eds.), *The low-wage labor market: Challenges and opportunities for economic self-sufficiency* (pp. 145–167). Washington, DC: The Urban Institute.

Henly, J., & Lyons, S. (2000). The negotiation of child care and employment demands among low-income parents. *Journal of Social Issues, 56*, 683–705.

Kessler, R. C., McGonagle, K. A., Zhao, S., Nelson, C. B., Hughes, M., Eshleman, S., Wittchen, H. U., & Kendler, K. S. (1994). Lifetime and 12-month prevalence of DSM–III–R psychiatric disorders in the United States: Results from the National Comorbidity Survey. *Archives of General Psychiatry, 51*, 8–19.

Lennon, M. C., Blome, J., & English, K. (2001, March). *Depression and low-income women: Challenges for TANF and welfare-to-work policies and programs*. New York: Columbia University Research Forum on Children, Families, and the New Federalism. Retrieved October 21, 2003, from http://www.researchforum.org

Loprest, P., & Acs, G. (1996). *Profile of disability among families on AFDC*. Washington, DC: The Urban Institute.

Manolatos, T. (2003, July 18). Day care cuts strap poor: Jeopardize welfare-to-work [Electronic version]. *The Detroit News*. Retrieved July 18, 2003, from http://www.detnews.com/2003/politics/0307/18/a01-221142.htm

Mason, K., & Kuhlthau, K. (1992). The perceived impact of child care costs on women's labor supply and fertility. *Demography, 29*, 523–543.

Meyers, M. K. (1993). Child care in JOBS employment and training program: What difference does quality make? *Journal of Marriage and the Family, 55*, 767–783.

Meyers, M. K., Han, W., Waldfogel, J., &.Garfinkel, I. (2001). Child care in the wake of welfare reform: The impact of government subsidies on the economic well-being of single-mother families. *Social Service Review, 75,* 29–59.

Meyers, M. K., Heintze, T., & Wolf, D. (2002). Child care subsidies and the employment of welfare recipients. *Demography, 39,* 165–179.

Mezey, J., Schumacher, R., Greenberg, M., Lombardi, J., & Hutchins, J. (2002, March). *Unfinished agenda: Child care for low-income families since 1996. Implications for federal and state policy.* Washington, DC: Center for Law and Social Policy.

Michigan Family Independence Agency. (2001, March 19). *News release: $578,100 in new child care grants.* Lansing, MI: Author. Retrieved October 16, 2003, from http://www.mfia.state.mi.us/RELEASES/current/news031901.htm

Newman, K. (1999). *No shame in my game.* New York: Russell Sage Foundation.

O'Brien, K., Wortman, C. B., Kessler, R. C., & Joseph, J. G. (1993). Social relationships of men at risk for AIDS. *Social Science and Medicine, 36,* 1161–1167.

Olson, K., & Pavetti, L. (1996). *Personal and family challenges to the successful transition from welfare to work.* Washington, DC: The Urban Institute.

Parrott, S., & Mezey, J. (2003, July). *New child care resources are needed to prevent the loss of child care assistance for hundreds of thousands of children in working families.* Washington, DC: Center for Law and Social Policy and Center on Budget and Policy Priorities. Retrieved July 15, 2003, from http://www.clasp.org/DMS/Documents/1058295869.52/7-15-03tanf.pdf

Pearlin, L., Lieberman M., Menaghan, E., & Mullan, J. (1981). The stress process. *Journal of Health and Social Behavior, 22,* 337–356.

Public Sector Consultants. (1998). *Michigan in brief 1998–1999* (6th ed.). Lansing, MI: Author.

Seefeldt, K. S., Leos-Urbel, J., McMahon, P., & Snyder, K. (2001, July). *Recent changes in Michigan welfare and work, child care, and child welfare systems* (New Federalism State Update No. 4). Washington, DC: The Urban Institute.

Straus, M. A. (1979). Measuring intrafamily conflict and violence: The Conflict Tactics (CTS) Scales. *Journal of Marriage and the Family, 41,* 75–88.

Tolman, R. M., & Raphael, J. (2000). A review of research on domestic violence and welfare. *Journal of Social Issues, 56,* 655–682.

Tolman, R. M., & Rosen, D. (2001). Domestic violence in the lives of women receiving welfare: Health, mental health, and well-being. *Violence Against Women, 7,* 126–140.

U.S. Department of Health and Human Services. (1999, December). *State child care reports.* Retrieved May 31, 2002, from http://aspe.hhs.gov/hsp/Child-Care99/mi-rpt.pdf

U.S. House of Representatives, Committee on Ways and Means. (1998). *1998 Green book: Background material and data on programs within the jurisdiction of the Committee on Ways and Means.* Washington, DC: U.S. Government Printing Office.

Ware, J. E., Snow, K. K., & Kosinski, M. (1993). *SF-36 Health Survey: Manual and interpretation guide.* Boston: The Health Institute, New England Medical Center.

Wilkinson, G. (1993). *Wide Range Achievement Test 3.* Wilmington, DE: Jastak Associates.

Zaslow, M., & Eldred, C. (1998). *Parenting behavior in a sample of young mothers.* New York: Manpower Demonstration Research Corporation.

Zedlewski, S. R., & Alderson, D. W. (2001). *Before and after welfare reform: How have families changed?* Washington, DC: Urban Institute New Federalism Series B-32.

PART FOUR

Implications and Future Directions

Child Care as Risk or Protection in the Context of Welfare Reform

Deborah Phillips
Georgetown University

Prior to the welfare reform legislation of 1996, child care had been cast as a necessary, but regrettable, add on to efforts to encourage employment among welfare recipients—on a par with work uniforms and transportation costs. Among the many ways in which the 1996 law departed from the incremental reform efforts of the past was the central role it assigned to child care as a cornerstone of welfare reform. Child care was portrayed as an integral component of incentivizing work. Subsidies to offset family expenditures on care were justified as essential to reducing poverty or "making work pay." Federal and state spending on child care increased substantially, and virtually every state reorganized their child-care funding streams to better accommodate the provisions of the welfare law. The chapters in this volume explore the adequacy of these federal and state child-care policies insofar as they are supporting or undermining the fundamental goals of welfare reform.

It is heartening that the editors and authors define these goals in a two-generational framework that lends equal significance to outcomes for adults and their children. This is not always the case. Welfare policies are based in economic thinking and emphasize impacts on adult welfare dependence, employment, income, and family structure. Impacts on children are not central and are primarily viewed in terms of the child's worth as a future adult citizen for whom we want to avoid welfare dependency (Huston, 2002). To the extent that children's current well-being is considered, the benchmark is avoidance of harm rather than the promotion of beneficial development. Child-care benefits tied to welfare reform are viewed as work supports, not as support for child development. This, in turn, fosters an emphasis on the supply and cost of care—dimensions that are central to supporting work effort—and a deemphasis on the stability and quality of care—dimensions that foster child development.

The results of the research summarized in this volume reflect these priorities. Parents seem to be finding child care that enables them to transition into paid employment, and those who avail themselves of government subsidies are more likely to purchase relatively more expensive forms of care (Cochi Ficano & Peters, chap. 5, this volume; Witte & Queralt, chap. 3, this volume). Yet subsidy spells are frequently interrupted with potentially detrimental effects on stability of care, and on-site assessments of the quality of care reveal that the majority of children are in mediocre to poor quality environments. The combined effects on children will likely derive from complex interactions between the cumulative impacts on their home environments and on the environments they experience when not in the care of their parents, as also emphasized by Blau (2001).

AN ECOLOGICAL FRAMEWORK FOR SYNTHESIS

Research on the developmental consequences of child care has increasingly relied on ecological models that place child-care influences in the context of other influences deriving from the home environment, characteristics of the child (e.g., age, gender, temperament), and the broader societal-cultural-political context within which transactions among the child, family, and child-care providers occur (McCartney & Galanpoulis, 1990; Phillips, Howes, & Whitebook, 1992). The somewhat unsatisfying conclusion that has emerged from this literature is that child care sometimes confers risk to young children, sometimes confers substantial protection and benefits, and often plays a neutral role in the context of other more powerful influences on development. Within this framework, the central question posed to welfare reform initiatives is where the child care being provided to families making the transition from welfare to paid employment falls on this spectrum from risk to protection. Although the prevailing goal may be one of avoidance of risk, a developmental perspective emphasizes the need to ensure protection and the value of conferring benefits.

Figure 11.1 offers a schematic for synthesizing the research that is presented in this volume as it fits within the broader ecological literature on child care.

Within the home environment, welfare reform and efforts to support working poor families are designed to affect income and material resources and, to a lesser extent, human capital in the form of parental education and literacy. Potential indirect effects on children's home environments include a higher standard of living (e.g., sufficient food, improved housing, more learning materials, and improved safety), improved parenting practices (affection,

HOME ENVIRONMENT

CHILD-CARE ENVIRONMENT	Risk	Protection
Risk	Double Jeopardy	Lost Resources
Protection	Compensatory Care	Double Protection

FIG. 11.1.   Framework for synthesis.

stimulation, supervision), the provision of positive role models, and improved parental well-being (e.g., mental health, self-confidence). Each of these factors adds to the protective value of the home environment. Their absence aggravates risk.

Within the child-care environment, welfare policy emphasizes access to care and, to a much lesser extent, quality and stability of care (through a quality set aside and consolidation of funding streams). Effects on children will derive from the quantity, type, quality, and consistency of care. Higher quality and more consistent care confers protection on young children. Although less consistent, research is also suggesting that smaller amounts of care overall during the earliest years of life and relatively more time in center-based care also confer protection. Lower quality and inconsistent care are associated with risks for social and intellectual development, large amounts of care may compromise social development for some children, and access to center-based care and preschool appears to confer benefits for cognitive and language development (see reviews by Lamb, 1998; NICHD Early Child Care Research Network, 2005; Vandell & Wolfe, 2000; Yoshikawa, 1999; Zaslow et al., 1999).

Implicit in this framework is the well-established fact that neither child-care nor home environments are inherently beneficial or detrimental for child development. Rather, they can confer risk or protection depending on their features, their synergistic effects, and the surrounding environments (including public policies) that impinge on them. Policies that aim to promote children's development need to ensure that children are doubly protected by positive home and child-care environments. Child-care policies, specifically, should strive to provide compensation for children in less-than-optimal home environments and to avoid detracting from the protection offered by a positive home environment.

CHILD CARE AS RISK AND PROTECTION:
EVIDENCE FROM THE CHAPTERS

We can now turn to the research presented in this volume and consider its implications for children's environments. How has child care supported through welfare reform contributed to the protection of child development and how has it conferred risk? Given that research in this area is in its infancy, the answers offered in this commentary are stated as hypotheses that warrant substantial additional investigation.

Hypothesis 1. *The structure of subsidies, notably the application and recertification processes required to obtain and sustain financial support, contributes to substantial instability in children's child-care arrangements.* The chapters by Meyers et al. (chap. 8, this volume) and Adams and Snyder (chap. 9, this volume) illustrate the many hurdles that families face to receive subsidized child care and the substantial churning in benefits and child-care arrangements that ensues. Within 7 months, subsidy assistance ended for one half of the children in each of five states studied by Meyers and her colleagues. Many reapplied, but at most only 60% reentered the subsidy system within a year. This turbulence in subsidy receipt is undoubtedly among a number of factors, including unstable employment or changes in work hours and disruptions in child care not precipitated by changes in subsidy status, that fueled disturbingly unstable child care among the families studied. Even among children who received subsidies for a continuous 12 months, only 36% to 60% remained with the same primary child-care provider. Regardless of the combination of factors that is fueling this extent of turnover, it is clear from the developmental literature that child-care instability constitutes a risk factor within this environment for young children.

Hypothesis 2. *Nonstandard work hours of many low-income parents, combined with the absence of explicit supports that enable parents to use formal, regulated arrangements, constitute a barrier to use of center-based care.* Several authors in this volume document the disproportionate reliance on informal care among families working their way off welfare (Giannarelli et al., chap. 1, this volume; see also Capizzano, Adams, & Sonenstein, 2000) and link these patterns to nontraditional work schedules (Cochi Ficano & Peters, chap. 5, this volume; Kimmel & Powell, chap. 6, this volume). Data from the National Early Head Start Evaluation reveal that parents working nonstandard hours faced serious hurdles to enrolling their children in this early intervention program for infants and toddlers. Data from the National Survey of American Families from 1997 to 1999 further reveals a general decline in reliance on center-based care among families in poverty with employed mothers (Giannarelli et al., chap. 1, this volume). Gennetian et al. (chap. 4, this volume), using experimental data, provide evidence that these patterns of child care arise, in part, from the absence of policies that support reliance on center-based care. Experimental welfare-to-work programs that included, for example, direct payments to providers, on-site child care, and case management to help parents with their child-care arrangements increased the use of center-based care. These expanded forms of assistance, according to Gennetian and colleagues, offer parents a wider range of choices and, in effect, make center-based care a viable option.

These findings are significant in light of two major findings from developmental research on child care. First, the observed quality of care received by low-income children is consistently poorer than that received by higher income children except among those using center-based arrangements (NICHD Early Child Care Research Network, 1997; Phillips et al., 1994). The chapter in this volume by Coley and colleagues (Coley, Li-Grining, & Chase-Lansdale, chap. 7, this volume) confirms that the majority of child-care centers used by low-income children in the Three City Study provided developmentally beneficial child care, whereas only one third of the home-based arrangements met this standard of care. Second, children who experience more time in center-based arrangements prior to school entry perform better on measures of cognitive and language development than do their counterparts who receive home-based care of comparable quality (NICHD Early Child Care Research Network, 2000; Zaslow et al., 1999). The evidence presented in this volume suggests that, absent explicit policies to support parents' use of center-based care—perhaps particularly in the context of nonstandard work schedules—the compensatory benefits of center-based care will be beyond the reach of growing numbers of very young children living in poverty who are now experiencing child care as a result of welfare reform.

Hypothesis 3. *Reimbursement rates and shortages of care, among other factors, are sustaining, if not aggravating, exposure to low-quality child care among low-income infants and toddlers.* The chapters in this volume by Witte, Coley, and their colleagues document the inadequate environments in which many children receive child care while their mothers are working to meet the requirements of welfare reform and / or to improve their family's economic circumstances outside the context of welfare reform. When combined with evidence of long hours of care, which may pose risk to young children's socioemotional development, this evidence regarding quality of care is cause for concern.

As has been found in research not focused on welfare reform, low-income children in home-based arrangements—both regulated and informal—receive lower quality care than those in center-based arrangements (Coley et al., chap. 7, this volume; Phillips et al., 1997; NICHD Early Child Care Research

Network, 1997). Even when these children receive center-based care, Witte and Queralt (chap. 3, this volume) present evidence that the educational attainments of the adults who care for them are widening to include more providers with less than a high school education and more with AA and BA degrees. Toddlers in subsidized centers are less likely to be cared for by adults with high levels of formal education than are toddlers in nonsubsidized centers, and family care providers who accept vouchers for infants and toddlers are less likely to have a BA degree than those who do not accept vouchers. Between 1996 to 1999, Witte and colleagues also documented a decline in the quality of care for infants and toddlers in their Florida programs.

As noted by Burchinal (chap. 12, this volume), observational measures of child-care quality consistently demonstrate positive associations with virtually all dimensions of early child development for both middle- and low-income children. For low-income children, however, variation in child-care quality appears to have relatively greater developmental consequences (McCartney, Dearing, & Taylor, 2003; Peisner-Feinberg et al., 2001). The chapters in this volume indicating that welfare-linked child care is typically of mediocre or poor quality, and thus unlikely to support child development and school readiness, offer some of the strongest evidence that current policies are likely to be placing children in environments that pose risk far more so than they are likely to offer protection.

IMPLICATIONS FOR CHILDREN

These three hypotheses, as they map onto the broader context of care illustrated in Fig. 11.1, suggest that welfare-linked child care is unlikely to afford protection to young children and may, in some circumstances, actually pose risks to their development. The chapters in this volume did not focus on children's home environments, although the emerging literature is presenting a mixed picture of positive (i.e., increased income, optimism about the future) and negative (i.e., no reductions in maternal depression or perceived hardship, less parental monitoring, few impacts on parent–child interactions) repercussions (Bos et al., 1999; Chase-Lansdale, 2003; Huston & Gennetian, 2003; Huston et al., 2001; Zaslow et al., 2001). McGroder, Zaslow, Papillo, Ahluwalia, and Brooks (2001) present a troubling portrait of home environments characterized by low parental literacy levels and high levels of depression among families affected by welfare reform. It remains to be seen, therefore, if the risks that may accompany child care linked to welfare reform place children in a situation of "lost resources," in which detrimental child care detracts from benefits and resources provided to children's families by welfare reform (i.e., improved income, better role models) or in a situation of "double jeopardy," in which lack of improvements in children's home environments are compounded by child care that compromises their development.

IMPLICATIONS FOR PUBLIC POLICY

The chapters in this volume also offer promising directions for public policy and a framework within which to consider their impacts on both parents and children, illustrated in Fig. 11.2. Specifically, the chapters that address the processes that confront parents seeking child-care assistance (e.g., Meyers et al., chap. 8; Adams & Snyder, chap. 9), the contribution of parental work schedules (e.g., Cochi Ficano & Peters, chap. 5; Kimmel & Powell, chap. 6), and the role of enhanced child-care supports point to the fundamental need to align employment and child-care policies so that parental needs to work and children's needs for developmentally advantageous child care are not set against each other in a zero-sum equation (see also Burchinal, chap. 12, this volume).

Relevant policies would promote standard work hours and enhanced child-care supports that range from case management services for finding, paying for, and sustaining continuity in child care to incentives built into child-care subsidies for use of higher quality care and more formal care, both of which foster positive developmental outcomes. By removing a work-related barrier that restricts access to formal child care and intervention options, as well as enhancing parents' knowledge about child care, providing them with supports for stability of care, and increasing the affordability of care, we would expect to see more children in stable, higher quality, formal child-care arrangements. Potential effects on adults include increased income, reduced child-care problems and associated stress, and sustained employment related to reduced interference from child-care problems (see Huston & Gennetian, 2003). Potential effects on young children include improved achievement, motivation to learn, and enhanced friendships (Casey, Ripke, & Huston, 2002; Gennetian et al., 2002; Laird, Bates, & Dodge, 1997; Posner & Vandell, 1994; Vandell & Ramanan, 1991). For adolescents, an additional outcome to consider is decreased time spent supervising younger siblings, which has been proposed as an explanatory factor for the negative adolescent outcomes emerging from welfare reform experiments (Brooks, Hair, & Zaslow, 2001). Moreover, research conducted within this explicitly two-generation framework holds the potential to reframe the public debate about child care provided in the context of welfare reform toward more inclusive consideration of affordability, access, quality, and stability of care.

POLICY MECHANISMS	CHILD-CARE SELECTION	CHILD-CARE ENVIRONMENTS	ADULT OUTCOMES	CHILD OUTCOMES
Restrict nonstandard work hours	Parental knowledge	Quality of care	Increased income	Learning/achievement
	Access to wider options	Stability of care	Reduced child-care	motivation
Enhanced child-care supports	Support for stability	More formal care	problems	Social relations
• Case management	Enhanced affordability		Sustained employment	Adolescent time use
• Subsidies tied to quality/type				
• Efficient reimbursement				
• Streamlined recertification for subsidies				

FIG. 11.2.   Framework for policy effects on children.

REFERENCES

Chase-Lansdale, P. L., Moffitt, R. A., Lohman, B. J., Chjerlin, A. J., Coley, R. L., Pittman, L. D., Roff, J., & Votruba-Drzal, E. (2003, March 7). Mothers' transition from welfare to work and the well-being of preschoolers and adolescents. *Science, 299*, 1548–1552.

Gennetian, L. A., Duncan, G. J., Knox, V. W., Vargas, W. G., Clark-Dauffman, E., & London, A. (2002). *How welfare and work policies for parents affect adolescent: A synthesis of research.* New York: Manpower Development Research Corporation.

Huston, A. C. (2002). Reforms and child development. *The Future of Children, 12*(1), 59–77.

Huston, A. C., Duncan, G. J., McLoyd, V. C., Crosby, D. A., Ripke, M. N., Weisner, T. S., et al. (2005). Impacts on children of a policy to promote employment and reduce poverty for low-income parents: New hope after five years. *Developmental Psychology, 41.*

Lamb, M. (1998). Nonparental child care: Context, quality, correlates, and consequences. In I. Sigel & K. A. Renninger (Eds.), *Handbook of child psychology: Vol. 5. Child psychology in practice* (pp. 73–134). New York: Wiley.

McCartney, K., & Galanpoulos, A. (1988). Child care and attachment: A new frontier the second time around. *American Journal of Orthopsychiatry, 58*, 16–24.

McGroder, S. M., Zaslow, M. J., Moore, K. A., Hair, E. D., & Ahluwalia, S. K. (2001). The role of parenting in shaping the impact of welfare-to-work programs on children. In J. G. Borkowski, S. Landesman, & M. Bristol-Powers (Eds.), *Parenting and the child's world: Influences on academic, intellectual, and social-emotional development* (pp. 283–310). Mahwah, NJ: Lawrence Erlbaum Associates.

Morris, P. A. (2002). The effects of welfare reform policies on children. *Social Policy Report of the Society for Research in Child Development, XVI*(1), 4–18.

NICHD Early Child Care Research Network. (1997). Poverty and patterns of child care. In G. J. Duncan & J. Brooks-Gunn (Eds.), *Consequences of growing up poor* (pp. 100–131). New York: Russell Sage.

NICHD Early Child Care Research Network. (2000). The relation of child care to cognitive and language development. *Child Development, 71*, 960–980.

NICHD Early Child Care Research Network. (2005). Structure>Process>Outcome: Direct and indirect effects of caregiving quality on young children's development. *Psychological Science.*

Phillips, D. A., Howes, C., & Whitebook, M. (1992). The social policy context of child care: Effects on quality. *American Journal of Community Psychology, 20*(1), 25–51.

Phillips, D., Voran, M., Kisker, E., Howes, C., & Whitebook, M. (1997). Child care for children in poverty: Opportunity or inequity? *Child Development, 65*, 472–492.

Posner, J. K., & Vandell, D. L. (1994). Low-income children's after-school care: Are there beneficial effects of after-school programs? *Child Development, 65*, 440–456.

Yoshikawa, H. (1999). Welfare dynamics, support services, mothers' earnings, and child cognitive development: Implications for contemporary welfare reform. *Child Development, 70*, 779–801.

Zaslow, M. J., McGroder, S. M., Cave, G., & Mariner, C. L. (1999). Maternal employment and measures of children's health and development among families with some history of welfare receipt. In R. Hodson & T. L. Parcel (Eds.), *Research in the sociology of work: Vol. 7. Work and family* (pp. 233–259). Stamford, CT: JAI.

Zaslow, M. J., Moore, K. A., Brooks, J. L., Morris, P. A., Tout, K., Redd, Z. A., & Emig, C. A. (2002). Experimental studies of welfare reform and children. *The Future of Children, 12*(1), 79–96.

## CHAPTER TWELVE

Child-Care Subsidies, Quality, and Preferences Among Low-Income Families

Margaret Burchinal
University of North Carolina at Chapel Hill

This NICHD-sponsored conference yielded a wealth of information about low-income families and how they negotiate work and child care. Many of the leading researchers in developmental psychology, economics, social work, and education presented results from ongoing studies or secondary data analysis of extant databases that describes the work and child-care experiences of these families. Both the variety of projects and the amount of information these projects were able to generate was astounding. All of the presenters should be commended for their timely contributions to this growing literature regarding the impact of welfare reform on these vulnerable women and young children. All of the studies provided valuable information about the degree to which low-income mothers are working and/or receiving cash, medical, or child-care subsidies. The studies followed diverse samples and employed a wide variety of analytic methods. Chapters provided new information about issues such as which mothers are most likely to be employed, which infants experience child care, what kinds and how much, and whether families eligible for child-care subsidies are receiving them. Other issues addressed included to what extent are factors that influence children's development related to working and welfare? Which of those factors predict child outcomes? What kinds of child-care settings do low-income parents prefer? Along with addressing diverse issues, a wide variety of analytic approaches were used to address these questions. Both quantitative and qualitative data were presented. The source of information ranged from secondary data analysis of national representative surveys to primary analysis of data from multisite research projects. Regardless of the type of project or analysis, all studies documented the many obstacles facing these families as they attempt to negotiate the work and child-care systems. The introduction to this volume highlights the major conclusions from these studies. In this commentary, I address two issues: (a) the effect of public policies that are linked to child-care quality on maternal employment and child outcomes, and (b) the directions for future research.

The papers presented at the conference sparked a debate about the cost and quality child care that should be available to low-income children. Econometric analyses indicate that cost and availability of child care were linked to maternal employment. They found fewer mothers were employed when child-care costs were higher and fewer child-care options were available. Low reimbursement rates led to out-of-pocket expenses for many families with subsidies. In addition, considerable evidence from intervention and observational studies suggests that high-quality care promotes cognitive and social skills, especially among low-income children (see Lamb, 1998, for review). Loeb and colleagues provided further evidence by demonstrating that maternal work was not directly linked to child outcomes, but that child-care experiences were. It appears that policies that increase reimbursement rates and link subsidies to child-care quality could further two goals: increasing maternal employment and enhancing child outcomes.

This conclusion, however, was not universally accepted. Some economists have challenged the studies linking child-care quality and child outcomes as overestimating the effects of child care due to family selection bias. Smaller associations between quality and outcomes have been obtained when econometric methods have been applied. There are several reasons for these discrepancies between analyses by psychologists and economists. First, the measures of quality used by the economists (e.g., maternal report of group size) are not always universally accepted as direct measures of quality by psychologists. Psychologists prefer direct observations of child-care settings to more distal factors. Unfortunately, standardized measures are not often available in survey studies, and use of other indicators of quality such as mother report of adult–child ratios is questionable because of their modest to moderate associations with observed quality (Lamb, 1998).

Second, the statistical methods used by psychologists are likely too liberal in estimating effects when applied to observational studies, whereas the methods used by economists are likely too conservative. Both disciplines recognize that family selection of child care biases parameter estimates of the quality–outcome association, but each discipline has approached the problem differently. The psychologists acknowledge that observational data are unlikely to be able to yield unbiased estimates because the true underlying statistical model is unknown, so they fit regression models that include relevant measured family characteristics. The economists acknowledge that unmeasured variables can bias estimated and use methods that adjust for omitted variable bias. These methods make stringent assumptions about the model, such as the absence of interactions among measured and unmeasured if not explicitly included in the model and appropriate allocation of shared variance across parameter estimates. The consequence is almost certainly underestimation of child-care effects by the economists when examining observational data because those stringent assumptions are unlikely to be met completely. The best statistical solution to these problems, instrumental variable approaches, is not possible because of the lack of useful instruments. As a psychologist, I would prefer to see a range of estimates to describe the likely association between child-care quality and child outcomes in observational studies, including both estimates that we know are likely too liberal and estimates we suspect are too conservative.

Finally, economists worry that costs of high-quality care are too high for the benefits associated with such care, even when the benefits were demonstrated with experimental studies. They point to published costs for Head Start, and especially for the most successful early intervention programs such as the Abecedarian Project. It is clear that further work is needed to provide accurate cost data. Projects such as Abecedarian involved costs linked to being a research project, and that would not be included if those programs were implemented as policy. For example, Abecedarian Project's costs included salaries linked to pay scales that would never be implemented outside a university demonstration child-care program. Further work is needed to document benefits as well as costs. For example, high-quality child care is linked to less retention in grade, use of special services, and unemployment as adults (Campbell et al., 2001), so early investment may save tax payers money across the lifetime of the child.

As a developmental psychologist, it seems clear to me that policies should promote the placement of low-income children in child-care settings with higher observed quality because it is observed quality that is linked to child outcomes, and preparing low-income children to enter school ready to learn is a national priority. I believe a major objective for providing tax dollars for child care should be to enhance these children's development to deter the transmission of intergenerational poverty. High-quality child-care experiences increase the likelihood that low-income children are ready to learn when they enter school and are successful in school and as adults (Campbell et al., 2001; Lazar & Darlington, 1982; Peisner-Feinberg et al., 2001). The papers presented at this workshop and the child-care literature suggests that low-income children are unlikely to receive high-quality care unless placed in federal or state programs such as Head Start (Lamb, 1998). Current reimbursement rates for child-care subsidies are unlikely to allow parents to select high-quality care if that was their preference or ensure that the child will remain in that setting after the subsidy is acquired. The transfer of child-care subsidies to block grants eliminated guarantee that tax dollars, except for dollars spent on programs like Head Start, were purchasing the quality care needed to help low-income children enter school ready to learn. This is especially unfortunate because only child-care interventions, not family-oriented interventions, have demonstrated efficacy (St. Pierre, Layzer, & Barnes, 1995).

To accomplish the policy goal of ensuring that tax dollars for child-care subsidies are spent on settings that promote child development, we need to address issues regarding what is meant by quality and how quality can be assessed. The only definition of *quality* that consistently relates to child outcomes involves warmth and stimulating caregiving by adults. States such as North Carolina have moved to a multitiered accreditation system in which centers that meet criteria when assessed with standard measures of quality are recognized and higher reimbursement rates are provided for those centers. Caregiver education and training are most consistently linked to observed quality, and perhaps could be used as a surrogate. We can hope that such a multitiered system would encourage more child-care settings to provide and document higher quality care. The ability of such a system to both provide sufficient high-quality care and ensure that that care is available to low-income income children should be explored.

Both the federal government and many state governments are spending growing amounts of money to provide high-quality center-based care to low-income families, but these programs tend to be part-day programs for preschoolers. Head Start is available throughout the country, and public pre-kindergarten programs are now available in many states. However, neither program usually offers the opportunity for low-income families to place their child in full-day high-quality programs for preschoolers or either part- or full-day programs for infants and toddlers. Thus, these programs are unlikely to meet the other objective of providing child care to low-income families, allowing the mother to work. This is really unfortunate because only full-day high-quality child-care programs have demonstrated effectiveness in improving child outcomes.

In terms of future directions for research, we need to achieve design research projects that can obtain consensus between psychologists and economists regarding the role of cost and availability of child care linked to maternal employment and quality of child care linked to enhancing school readiness. Cost–benefit analyses are needed that attend to costs to the state and families when states subsidy child care of varying quality for low-income families and its subsequent impact on children's cognitive and social development. Greater emphasis on ensuring that low-income children enter school ready to learn under No-Child-Left-Behind Legislation has led to massive state and federal funding on pre-kindergarten programs with little attention to the quality of care children receive either in these programs or other child-care programs. To achieve this goal, we need to agree on how costs and benefits to families and government can be quantified. Comprehensive longitudinal data sets can be carefully examined to determine the extent to which families benefit from maternal employment made possible through child-care subsidies, and whether children benefit or are harmed by their child-care experiences. Careful use of econometric methods such as propensity score analysis for linking costs and benefits to both child-care subsidies and child-care quality will likely result in greater consensus between economists and psychologists because both disciplines appear to be embracing these types of analytic methods. Collaborations across disciplines are becoming more common (e.g., Dearing, McCartney, & Taylor, 2001; Huston et al., 2001; NICHD Early Child Care Research Network, & Duncan, 2003), and future collaborations are clearly needed to address these important policy questions.

In addition, there are several other issues I believe we should consider as research on child care, especially for low-income children, moves forward. First, we need to disaggregate our analyses to see whether our conclusions are appropriate. For example, there is growing evidence that center child care promotes cognitive development for preschoolers (NICHD Early Child Care Research Network, 2001), but less is known about center care for infants and toddlers. The few studies that examined center child care for infants and toddlers reveal a disturbing pattern of lower quality care for both infants and preschooler. There was a hint that centers subsidize infant-toddler center care to attract and keep the more lucrative preschoolers at lower quality center (Phillipsen et al., 1997). Similarly, it is clear that smaller group sizes and better child–adult ratios reflect better quality center care (Lamb, 1998), but it is less clear that group size or ratios are indicators of quality in child-care homes or relative care where group sizes are almost always very small. Indeed some evidence suggests that group sizes were negatively, not positively, related to child-care quality in home-based care for low-income children (Kontos et al., 1996). Second, we need to ask about parental preferences, but much more work is needed to ensure the measures accurately reflect parents' values and preferences. We need to distinguish between satisfaction and quality with child care because there is extensive evidence that parents too often believe their child care is high quality. Third, we need frank discussion regarding child-care policies and the extent to which those policies should strive to promote child outcomes as well as maternal employment.

In conclusion, research has documented many obstacles facing low-income women with young children as they enter the job market. This research identified personal, community, job market, and policy characteristics that promote employment, child-care choice, and child outcomes. There is some disagreement regarding the interpretation of these findings into policy recommendations, reflecting discipline differences in emphasis on free markets or child development.

REFERENCES

Campbell, F. A., Pungello, E. P., Miller-Johnson, S., Burchinal, M. R., & Ramey, C. (2001). The development of cognitive and academic abilities: Growth curves from an early intervention educational experiment. *Developmental Psychology, 37*, 231–242.

Dearing, E., McCartney, K., & Taylor, B. (2001). Change in family income to needs matters more for children with less income. *Child Development, 72*, 1779–1793.

Huston, A., Duncan, G., Granger, R., McLoyd, V., Mistry, R., Crosby, D., Gibson, C., Magnuson, K., Romich, J., & Ventura, A. (2001). Work-based antipoverty programs for parents can enhance the school performance and social behavior of children. *Child-Development, 72*, 318–336.

Kontos, S., Howes, C., Shinn, M., & Galinsky, E. (1995). *Quality in family child care and relative care*. New York: Teachers College Press.

Lamb, M. E. (1998). Nonparental child care: Context, quality, correlates. In W. Damon, I. E. Sigel, & K. A. Renninger (Eds.), *Handbook of child psychology: Vol. 4. Child psychology in practice* (5th ed., pp. 73–134). New York: Wiley.

Lazar, I., & Darlington, R. (1982). Lasting effects of early education: A report from the Consortium for Longitudinal Studies. *Monographs of the Society for Research in Child Development, 47*(2–3, Serial No. 195).

NICHD Early Child Care Research Network. (2001, April 19). Overview of early child care effects at 4.5 years. In J. Belsky (chair), *Early childcare and children's development prior to school entry*. Symposium presented at the biennial meeting of the Society for Research in Child Development, Minneapolis, MN.

NICHD Early Child Care Research Network, & Duncan, G. J. (2003). Modeling the impacts of child care quality on children's preschool cognitive development. *Child Development, 74*, 1454–1475.

Peisner-Feinberg, E. S., Burchinal, M. R., Clifford, R. M., Culkin, M. L., Howes, C., Kagan, S. L., & Yazejiam, N. (2001). The relation of preschool child care quality to children's cognitive and social developmental trajectories through second grade. *Child Development, 72*, 1534–1553.

Phillipsen, L. C., Burchinal, M. R., Howes, C., & Cryer, D. (1997). The prediction of process quality from structural features of child care. *Early Childhood Research Quarterly, 12*, 281–303.

Author Index

Note: Page numbers in *italic* refer to reference pages; those followed by "n" refer to footnotes.

A

Abidin, R. R., 233, *247*
Acs, G., 226, *247*
Adams, G., *xxvii*, 34, 37, 48, 80, 89, 98, 151, 168, 200, 201n, 211, 215, *223*, 241, 242, 246, *247*, 254
Administration on Children and Families, *xxvii*
Ahluwalia, S. K., 256, *259*
Alderson, D. W., 226, *248*
American Academy of Pediatrics, 21, *48*
American Psychiatric Association, *247*
Anderson, N. J., 226, *247*
Angel, R. J., 152, *170*
Arnett, J., 155, *168*
Averett, S. L., *xxvii*, 104, *125*
Ayelet, T., 45, *49*

B

Barnes, 264
Barnett, W. S., 151, 164, *168*
Barsimantov, J., 150, 164, *169*
Bates, 257
Baydar, N., *xxvii*
Beckwith, L., 21, *48*

Beers, T. M., 131, 132, 138, *147*, 150, 166, *168*
Behr, A., 146, *147*
Beller, A. H., 133, *147*
Berger, M. C., *xxvii*, 104, *125*
Berlin, L. J., 21, *48*
Bernstein, J., 103, *126*
Bianchi, S. M., *xxvii*
Bishop, J., 102, *126*
Black, D. A., *xxvii*, 104, *125*
Blank, H., 36, 36n, *50*, 146, *147*, 204, 221, *223*
Blank, R. M., 101, 102, 103, 104, *126*, *127*
Blank, S., 82, 97, *99*
Blau, D. M., *xxvii*, 82, 97, 104, 105, 109, *126*, 133, *147*, 150, 164, *168*, 252
Blau, F. D., *xxvii*
Blome, J., 226, *247*
Bloom, D., 79, 83, *97*
Bos, J. M., 83, 97, *100*, 256
Brayfield, A., 133, *147*
Broberg, A., 81, *98*
Brock, T., 83, *97*
Brooks, J. L., 256, *259*
Brooks-Gunn, J., *xxvii*, 150, *169*
Brown-Lyons, M., 150, *168*
Burchinal, M. R., *xxviii*, 151, 165, 166, *168*, 256, 263, 265, 266
Burton, L. M., 152, *170*
Byers, C., 21, *50*

C

Campbell, F. A., 263, *266*
Cancian, M., 30, *49*
Capizzano, J., *xxvii*, 80, *98*, 151, *168*, 211, *223*, 254
Card, D., 84, *99*, 101, 103, *126*
Carol, B., 80, *99*
Carrol, B., *xxvii*
Casey, _, 257
Caspary, G. L., 80, *98*
Casper, L., 82, *98*
Casper, L. M., 133, *147*
Cassidy, J., 21, *48*
Cave, G., 81, *100*, 253, 255, *259*
Chang, Y., 82, 87, 95, *98*, *99*
Chaplin, D. D., 82, *98*, 133, *147*
Chapman, J., 103, *126*
Chase-Lansdale, P. L., *xxvii*, 79, 80, *98*, 123, *126*, 151, 152, 164, *170*, 256, *259*
Cherlin, A. J., 152, *170*
Child Care Around the Clock, 130, 132, 145, *147*
Child Care Bureau, *xxvii*
Chjerlin, A. J., 256, *259*
Choong, Y., 34, *49*
Chu, D., 215, *223*
Clark-Dauffman, E., 257, *259*
Cleveland, G. H., 133, *147*
Clifford, R. M., *xxviii*, 155, *169*, 256, 263, *266*
Coley, R. L., 79, 80, *98*, 151, 164, *170*, 256, *259*
Collins, A. M., 34, 36, *49*, 81, *98*, 131, *147*, 200, 213, *223*
Connelly, R., *xxvii*, 104, 133, *147*
Coonerty, C., 34, *49*
Corcoran, M., 245, *247*
Cost, Quality, and Child Outcomes Study Team, *xxvii*, 21, *49*, 151, 164, *168*
Council of Economic Advisors, 82, *98*, 102, 104, *126*, 129, *147*
Cox, A. G., 21, *49*, 130, 132, *148*, 150, 164, 166, *170*
Crosby, D. A., 87, 95, *98*, *259*, 265, *266*
Cryer, D., 151, 155, 165, *168*, *169*, 265, *266*
Culkin, M. L., *xxviii*, 256, 263, *266*

D

Danziger, S. K., 226, 245, *247*
Darlington, R., 263, *266*

Davis, E. E., 34, 36, *49*, 213, *223*
Dearing, E., *xxvii*, 256, 265, *266*
Desai, S., *xxvii*
Divine, P. L., 130, *147*
Dodge, _, 257
Dowsett, C., *98*
Duncan, G. J., 79, 83, 97, *99*, 150, 166, *169*, 257, *259*, 265, *266*
Dunn, L., 81, *99*

E

Earle, A., 21, *49*
Edin, K., 82, *100*, 227, *247*
Eggers-Pierola, C., 150, *169*
Ehrle, J., 89, *98*
Eldred, C., 233, *248*
Elixhauser, A., 21, *49*
Emig, C. A., 256, *259*
Emlen, A. C., 40, *49*, 82, *98*, 155, *169*
English, K., 226, *247*
Engstrom, D., 78, *98*
Ensminger, M., 226, *247*
Eshleman, S., 234, *247*
Ewen, D., 204, *223*

F

Fenichel, E., 21, *49*
Ficano, C. K. C., 103, *126*
Figlio, D. N., 102, 104, *126*
Fleck, M. B., 21, *49*
Folk, K. F., 133, *147*
Fronstin, P., 82, *98*, 133, *147*
Fuller, B., *xxvii*, 34, *49*, 80, *98*, *99*, 150, 159, 165, *169*

G

Galanpoulis, A., 252, *259*
Galinsky, E., 159, *169*, 265, *266*
Gallagher, L. J., *49*, 107n, *126*
Gallagher, M., *49*, 107n, *126*
Garfinkel, I., *xxviii*, 226, 245, *248*
Gasman-Pines, A., 87, *98*
Gauthier, C. A., 80, *98*
Geis, S., 96, *99*

Gelbach, J., 104, *126*
Gennetian, L. A., *xxviii*, 82, 84, 87, *95*, *98*, *99*, *256*, *257*, *259*
Georges, A., 34, 36, *49*, 130n, *147*, 213, *223*
Giannarelli, L., 150, 164, *169*
Gibson, C., 166, *169*, *265*, *266*
Glantz, F. B., 81, *98*, 131, *147*, 200, *223*
Glazewski, B., 21, *49*
Gordon, R., 123, *126*
Granger, R., *97*, *265*, *266*
Greenberg, M., *xxviii*, 30, *49*, 78, 79, *98*, *99*, 100, 104, *127*, 151, *170*, 200, 222, *223*, 224, 242, *248*
Green Book, 107n
Greene, W. H., 241, *247*
Griesinger, H., *xxviii*, 54n, 56, 70, *73*
Griffin, A., 21, *49*
Grossberg, A., *xxvii*
Guerra, N., 21, *50*

H

Hagy, A. P., 104, *126*, 133, *147*, 150, 164, *168*
Hair, E. D., 257, *259*
Han, W., 226, 245. *248*
Harknett, K., 84, *99*
Harms, T., 155, *169*
Harris, K. M., *126*
Heckman, _, 104
Heeb, R., 104, *126*
Heflin, C., 245, *247*
Heintze, T., *xxvii*, 104, *127*, 150, *169*, 200, *223*, 245, *248*
Helburn, S. W., 151, *169*
Henderson, C. R., 45, *49*
Hendra, R., 83, *97*
Henly, J. R., 226, 235, *247*
Heymann, J., 21, *49*
Hiatt, S., 45, *49*
Hofferth, S. L., 82, *98*, 133, *147*, 150, *169*
Holcomb, P., 211, *223*
Holloway, S. D., 150, 165, *169*
Hotz, V. J., 102, 104, 106n, *126*
Howes, C., *xxviii*, 21, *49*, 81, *98*, *99*, 151, 152, 159, *169*, *170*, 252, 255, 256, *259*, 263, *265*, *266*
Hsu, H., 81, *99*
Hsueh, J., 151, *170*
Hughes, M., 234, *247*
Hurst, A., 96, *100*

Huston, A., 82, 83, 87, *95*, *96*, *97*, *98*, *99*, 251, 256, 257, *265*, *266*
Huston, A. C., *259*
Huston, R. Q., 78, *98*
Hutchins, J., 242, *248*
Hwang, C. P., 81, *98*
Hyatt, D. E., 133, *147*

I

Infant Health and Development Program, 151, 164, *169*

J

Johansen, A. S., 150, *169*
Joseph, J. G., 235, *248*

K

Kagan, S. L., *xxvii*, *xxviii*, 80, *98*, *99*, 159, *169*, 256, 263, *266*
Kalil, A., 226, 245, *247*
Kalmanson, B., 21, *4* ⟩
Kass, B., 21, *49*
Kemple, J. J., 83, *97*
Kendler, K. S., 234, *247*
Kerachasky, S., 131, *148*
Kessler, R. C., 234, 235, *247*, *248*
Kilburn, M. R., 104, 106n, *126*
Killingsworth, M., 112, *126*
Kimmel, J., 133, *147*
Kipnis, F., 34, *49*
Kirby, G., *49*, 201n, *223*
Kisker, E. E., *xxviii*, 21, *49*, 131, *148*, 152, 159, *170*, 255, *259*
Knox, V. W., *xxviii*, 82, *97*, *99*, 257, *259*
Kontos, S., 81, *99*, 159, *169*, *265*, *266*
Koralek, R., 211, 215, *223*
Koren, P. E., 40, *49*, 82, *98*
Korfmacher, J., 45, *49*
Kosinski, M., 234, *248*
Kreader, J. L., 34, 36, *49*, 81, *98*, 131, *147*, 200, 213, *223*
Kuhlthau, K., 226, *247*
Kurka, R., 201n, *223*

L

Laird, 257
Lally, J. R., 21, 49
Lamb, M. E., 78, 81, 98, 99, 150, 151, 164,
    169, 253, 259, 262, 263, 265, 266
Lane, J., 215, 223
Layzer, J. I., 81, 98, 131, 147, 150, 168, 200,
    223, 264
Lazar, I., 263, 266
Lee, L.-F., 137, 147
Lehrer, E., 133, 147
Leibowitz, A., 133, 147, 150, 169
Lein, L., 227, 247
Lemke, R. J., xxvii, 72
Lennon, M. C., 226, 247
Leos-Urbel, J., 227, 229, 248
Levine, J., 245, 247
LeVine, R. A., 150, 169
Levin-Epstein, J., 78, 98
Lieberman, J. B., 102, 104, 127
Lieberman, M., 227, 235, 248
Li-Grining, C. P., 79, 80, 98
Loeb, S., xxvii, 80, 99
Lohman, B. J., 256, 259
Lombardi, J., 242, 248
London, A., 82, 96, 97, 99, 100, 257, 259
Long, S. G., 201n, 223
Loprest, P., 29, 50, 130, 147, 226, 247
Lowe, E. D., 82, 83, 87, 96, 97, 99
Lowe, T., 95, 98
Lu, H.-H., 130n, 147
Luckey, D. W., 45, 49
Lyons, S., 226, 247

M

Maddala, G. S., 137, 147
Magnuson, K., 265, 266
Manolatos, T., 246, 247
Mariner, C. L., 81, 100, 253, 255, 259
Martinson, K., 215, 223
Mason, K., 226, 247
Maynard, R., 131, 148
Mazelis, J., 82, 100
McCartney, K., xxvii, 252, 256, 259, 265, 266
McCormick, M. C., 21, 49
McCune, L., 21, 49
McGonagle, K. A., 234, 247
McGroder, S. M., 81, 100, 253, 255, 256, 259

McLoyd, V. C., 83, 97, 259, 265, 266
McMahon, P., 227, 229, 248
Melton, L., 83, 97
Menaghan, E., 227, 235, 248
Meyer, B. D., 102, 104, 126
Meyers, M. K., xxvii, 104, 127, 150, 169, 200,
    213, 223, 226, 245, 247, 248
Mezey, J., 78, 99, 222, 223, 242, 246, 248
Michael, R. T., xxvii
Michalopoulos, C., xxviii, 79, 83, 84, 95, 97,
    98, 99, 133, 148
Michigan Family Independence Agency,
    229, 248
Miller-Johnson, S., 263, 266
Mistry, R., 265, 266
Moffitt, R. A., 105n, 127, 152, 170, 256, 259
Moore, K. A., 256, 259
Morris, P. A., xxviii, 83, 97, 256, 259
Mullan, J., 227, 235, 248
Mullin, C., 102, 104, 126
Myers, M., 34, 36, 49

N

Nada, E., 102, 104, 127
National Association for the Education of
    Young Children, 156, 169
National Research Council and Institute of
    Medicine, 151, 164, 167, 170
Nelson, C. B., 234, 247
Nelson, L., 166, 168
Newman, K., 226, 248
Ng, R. K., 45, 49
NICHD Early Child Care Research Net-
    work, xxviii, 21, 49, 78, 79, 80, 81, 99,
    109, 127, 150, 151–152, 159, 169, 170,
    220, 223, 253, 255, 259, 265, 266

O

O'Brien, K., 235, 248
O'Brien, R., 45, 49
O'Connell, M., 133, 147
Olds, D. L., 45, 49
Olson, J. A., 34, 36, 49, 213, 223
Olson, K., 226, 248
Ooms, T. J., 78, 98

P

Papillo, 256
Parrott, S., 246, *248*
Pavetti, L., 226, *248*
Pearlin, L., 227, 235, *248*
Peck, L. R., 34, 36, *49*, 213, *223*
Peisner-Feinberg, E. S., *xxviii*, 256, 263, *266*
Perese, K., *49*, 107n, *126*
Peters, H. E., *xxvii*, 104, *125*
Pettitt, L. M., 45, *49*
Phillips, D. A., *xxviii*, 21, *49*, *50*, 82, 99, 151, 152, 159, *170*, 252, 255, *259*
Phillipsen, L. C., 265, *266*
Pittman, L. D., 256, *259*
Pleck, J. H., 132, *148*
Poersch, N. O., *223*
Polit, D. F., 83, *100*
Posner, J. K., 257, *259*
Powell, L. M., 133, *148*
Presser, H. B., 21, *49*, 130, 132, 133, *148*, 150, 164, 166, *170*
Public Sector Consultants, 228, 229, *248*
Puffer, L., *49*
Pungello, E. P., 263, *266*

Q

Queralt, M., *xxvii*, *xxviii*, 54n, 56, 70, *72*, *73*
Quint, J. C., 83, *100*

R

Raikes, H., 21, *49*, 78, *100*
Ramanan, J., *xxviii*, 257
Rambaud, M. F., 150, *169*
Ramey, C., 263, *266*
Rangarajan, A., 215, *223*
Raphael, J., 226, *248*
Redd, Z. A., 256, *259*
Ribar, D. C., *xxviii*, 104
Ripke, M. N., 257, *259*
Robertson, A., 150, *168*
Robins, P. K., *xxvii*, *xxviii*, 82, 84, 98, 99, 101, 103, 104, *126*, 133, *147*, *148*
Robinson, J., 45, *49*
Roff, J., 256, *259*
Rohacek, M., 34, 37, *48*, 200, *223*, 241, 242, 246, *247*
Romich, J., 265, *266*

Rosen, D., 226, 235, 245, *247*, *248*
Rosenbaum, D. T., 102, 104, *126*
Rosman, E. A., 151, *170*
Ross, C., 37, *49*

S

Sandfort, J., 34, 48, 200, 201n, *223*
Savner, S., 30, *49*
Schexnayder, D., 34, 36, *49*, 213, *223*
Schochet, P., 215, *223*
Schoeni, R. F., 102, 103, 104, *127*
Scholz, J. K., 102, 104, *126*
Schreiber, S., *49*, 107n, *126*
Schroeder, D., 34, 36, *49*, 213, *223*
Schulman, K., 36, 36n, *50*, 146, *147*, 204, 221, *223*
Schultze, K. H., 40, *49*, 82, 98
Schumacher, R., *xxviii*, 78, 79, 98, 99, *100*, 104, *127*, 151, *170*, 200, 222, *223*, 224, 242, *248*
Scott, E. K., 82, 96, 97, 99, *100*
Scrivener, S., 83, 97
Seefeldt, K., 245, *247*
Seefeldt, K. S., 227, 229, *248*
Segal, M., 21, *49*
Shapiro, M. D., 132n, *148*
Sheff, K. L., 45, *49*
Shinn, M., 159, *169*, 265, *266*
Shonkoff, J. P., 21, *50*
Siefert, K., 245, *247*
Sillari, J., 21, *49*
Simpson, L., 21, *49*
Smith, K., *xxviii*, 82, *100*, 103, 124, *127*
Snow, K. K., 234, *248*
Snyder, K., 34, 36, 48, 200, 201n, 211, *223*, 227, 229, *248*
Sonenstein, F., *xxvii*, 80, 98, 151, 168, 254
Spiegelman, R. G., 133, *148*
St. Pierre, 264
Staines, G. L., 132, *148*
State Policy Documentation Project, 40, *50*
Sternberg, K. J., 150, *169*
Straus, M. A., 235, *248*
Szanton, E., 21, *49*

T

Taylor, B. A., *xxvii*, 256, 265, *266*
Tekin, E., 104, 105, 109, *126*, 130n, *148*

Thompson, J., 21, *49*
Tolman, R. M., 226, 235, 245, *247, 248*
Tout, K., 89, *98*, 256, *259*
Turetsky, V., 78, *98*
Tvedt, K., 130, *147*

U

U.S. Census Bureau, 52, 53, *73*, 107n, *127*
U.S. Department of Health and Human Services, *xxviii*, 26n, 27n, 50, *50*, 82, *100*, 102, 103, 104, 107n, *127*, 149, *170*, 200, *224, 229, 248*
U.S. General Accounting Office, *xxviii*, 78, 82, *100*, 108, *127*
U.S. House of Representatives, *xxviii*, 77, *100*, 103, *127*, 227, *248*

V

Vandell, D. L., *xxviii*, 68, *73*, 253, 257, *259*
Vargas, W. G., 257, *259*
Ventura, A., 265, *266*
Verma, N., 83, *97*
Voran, M., *xxviii*, 21, *49*, 152, 159, *170*, 255, *259*
Votruba-Drzal, E., 151, 164, *170*, 256, *259*

W

Wagmiller, R. L., Jr., 130n, *147*
Waite, L. J., 133, *147*, 150, *169*
Wald, E. R., 21, *50*
Waldfogel, J., 226, 245, *248*
Waldman, D. M., *xxvii*, 104, *125*
Walker, J., *xxviii*

Walter, J., 83, *97*
Ware, J. E., 234, *248*
Waters, S., 201n, *223*
Watson, K., *49*, 107n, *126*
Weber, R., 34, 36, *49*, 213, *223*
Weisner, T. S., 82, 83, 96, 97, *99, 259*
Weissbourd, B., 21, *49*
Werner, A., 81, *98*, 131, *147*, 200, *223*
Wessels, H., 81, *98*
Whitebook, M., *xxviii*, 21, *49*, 151, 152, 159, *170, 252, 255, 259*
Wilkinson, G., 235, *248*
Wilson, W. J., 152, *170*
Winston, P., 152, *170*
Wissoker, D. A., 82, *98*, 133, *147*
Witsberger, C., 133, *147*
Witt, R., *xxvii, xxviii*, 54n, 70, 72, *73*
Wittchen, H. U., 234, *247*
Witte, A. D., *xxvii, xxviii*, 54n, 56, 70, 72, *73*
Wolf, D. A., *xxvii*, 104, *127*, 150, *169*, 200, *223, 245, 248*
Wolfe, B., 68, *73*, 253
Wortman, C. B., 235, *248*

Y

Yazejian, N., *xxviii*, 256, 263, *266*
Yoshikawa, H., 81, *100*, 151, 164, *170*, 253, *259*

Z

Zaslow, M. J., 81, *100*, 233, *248*, 253, 255, 256, 257, *259*
Zedlewski, S. R., 29, *50*, 226, *248*
Zhao, S., 234, *247*
Ziliak, J. P., 102, 104, *126*

Subject Index

Note: Page numbers in *italic* refer to figures; those in **boldface** refer to tables.

A

AFDC benefits, 112, *112*, 114, *114*
AFDC status
  child-care arrangements and, 124
  child-care subsidies and, 109
  as data sample, 108–109
  demographics and economics of, 109–112,
    110–111, **115–117**, 119–120
  education and, **115–117**, 118
  government policies and, **115–117**, 119–120
  labor force participation and, 109–117,
    110–111, **115–117**
Age of child
  child-care arrangements and, 8, **8**
  child-care subsidies and, **13**, 14, **183**, 185,
    188, 204
Aid to Families with Dependent Children
  (AFDC). *See* AFDC benefits; AFDC
  status
Arnett Scale of Provider Sensitivity, 155
Assessing the New Federalism (ANF), 4,
  200–201

B

Babysitters
  cost effect on, 141–144, **144**

education level of mother and, 144
nonstandard work hours and, 141, **143**,
  144–145
use by all family types and incomes, 5, *6*
use by low-income families, 6–8, *7*, **8**, *9*, *10*

C

The Canadian Self-Sufficiency Program
  (SSP)
  impacts of
    child-care type, 92–94, *93*, **94**
    child-care use, 89–92, *90*, *91*
  study description, 83–88, **88**
Caregiver-to-child ratio standards, 58
Caseworker relations, 207–208
Center-based care
  AFDC status and, 109
  availability and choice of, 123
  child-care subsidies and, 185–187, **186**,
    194, 228–229
  child development and, 80–81, 158–159,
    159, **160–161**, 255
  costs and, 141–144, **144**
  education levels of mother and, 144
  illness and, 81
  increases in, 78, 103, 112–114, *113*
  for infants, 42, **43**

Center-based care *(cont.)*
  labor market participation and, 82,
      120–123, **121–122**
  nonstandard work hours and, 135, 141,
      143, 144–145
  parental needs and preferences and,
      157–158, **158**, **160–161**, 162
  policy effects on, 92–97, *93*, **94**, 219
  provider wages and choice of, 123
  use by all family types and incomes, 5, *6*
  use by low-income families, 6–8, 7, **8**, *9*,
      10, 156–157, **157**
Child Care and Development Fund (CCDF)
  effects of, 78, 108, 174, 227
  family copayments and, 37
  funds consolidated under, xvii–xviii, 20
Child-care arrangements
  for all family types and incomes, 5–6, *6*
  availability of, 166–167
  child-care subsidies and
      care options, in Michigan, 228–229
      effects on choice, 123–124, 144, **144**,
          185–187, 194
      stability of care and, 191–193, **192**,
          219–220, 254
      subsidy continuity and, 195–197
  child development and, 80–81, 151–152,
      158–159, **159**, **160–161**, 162–165, 167,
      253–256
  future research on, 264–265
  labor force participation and, 81–82,
      105–108, 120–123, **121–122**
  for low-income families, 6–8, 7, **8**, *9*, *10*,
      156–158, **157**
  nonstandard work hours and
      choice model of, 137–138
      literature review of, 133–134
      parental choices in, 82, 120–123, 141,
          143, 144–145, 150
      SIPP data on, 134–136
      solutions to, 145–146
  parental needs and preferences and,
      150–151, 157–158, **158**, **160–161**,
      162–165
  for parents of infants, 40–42, **43**
  policy effects on, 92–97, *93*, **94**
  TANF penalty exception and, 40–41
  welfare reform and, xvi–xvii, *xvii*, 59–63,
      60, *62*
Child-care costs. *See also* Child-care subsidies
  factors affecting, 138–141, **142**

  labor force participation and, 104, 117–118
  nonstandard work hours and, 135
  as percent of income, xvii, 11, **11**, 82, 157,
      230, **231**
  subsidy receipts and, 235–236
  welfare reform and, 66–70, *67*, **69**
Child-care demands, welfare reform and, 81,
      103
Child-care providers
  minimum standards for, 57–58
  quality of, 63–66, 166–167
  reimbursement rates for, 37–40, 56–57, 67,
      186, 187, 194–195
  subsidized, 55–56, 228–229
  wages of and child-care choices, 123
Child Care Resource and Referral agencies
      (CCR&Rs), 205
Child-care subsidies
  access to, 203–206, 216–219, *218*
  AFDC status and, 109
  applying for, 207–213
  child-care arrangements and, 123–124,
      144, **144**, 185–187, 219–220
  child-care use and, 89–92, **90**, *91*, *95*,
      236–238, *237*
  continuity of, 174, 187–191, *189*, **190**, *191*,
      195–198, 254
  devolution to state level, 174, 197–198,
      227–228
  eligibility for, 54–55, 203–204
  gaps in, in Michigan, 229–230
  increases in, xvii–xviii, 78, 103, 112–114, *113*
  labor force participation and, 226,
      238–245, **240**, **243–244**
  NSAF data on families receiving, 11–16,
      13, 15
  for parents of infants, 34–40, **35**, **38**
  policy effects on, 174, 220–222
  populations served by, 182–185, **183**, *184*,
      193–194
  providers of, 55–56
  retaining, 213–219, *218*
  study descriptions
      access and retention study, 200–202,
          201
      use dynamics study, 175–178
      welfare to work transition study,
          230–235
  take-up rates for, xviii, 245–246
  TANF policies and, 34–40, **35**, **38**,
      178–182, **179–180**

welfare reform and, 53–54, 59–63, *60, 62*
Child development
  child-care arrangements and, 80–81,
     151–152, 158–159, **159, 160–161,**
     162–165, 167, 253–256
  early intervention services for, 44–45
  risks and protections for, 252–253, *253*
Conflict Tactics Scale, 235
Connecticut's Jobs-First Program
  impacts of
    child-care type, 92–94, *93, 94*
    child-care use, 89–92, **90,** *91*
  study description, 83–88, **88**
Copayments, for child-care, 36–37, **38, 186,**
  187, 194, 229–230, **231**
Credentials, for child-care providers, 57–58,
  63–65

D

Demographic differences
  AFDC status and, 109–112, **110–111,**
    115–117
  child-care choices and, 120, **121–122**
  in labor market participation, **115–117**
Domestic violence, 226–227, 235, 239

E

Early Childhood Environment Rating
  Scale–Revised, 155
Early intervention programs, for parents of
  infants, 30, 44–45
Earned Income Tax Credit (EITC)
  increases in, 112, *113*
  labor force participation and, 103–104, 118
Economists, versus psychologists, 262–264
Education
  AFDC status and, **115–117,** 118
  child-care arrangements and, 144
  labor force participation and, 235, 245
  nonstandard work hours and, 130–131
  as work requirement activity, 33
Embedded Developmental Study (EDS), 153
Emlen scale, 155–156
Employment. *See* Labor force participation

F

Family and Medical Leave Act, 22
Family child care
  use by all family types and incomes, 5, *6*
  use by low-income families, 6–8, *7,* **8,** *9, 10*
Family structure
  child-care arrangements and, 6, 7, 158
  child-care subsidies and, **13,** 14
  nonstandard work hours and, 138, **139**
Family Support Act of 1988, 77–78
Financial assistance. *See* Child-care subsidies
Florida, in cross-state study
  child-care costs in, 66–70, *67, 69*
  child-care quality in, 63–66
  child-care use in, *60, 62,* 69–63
  government policies of, 53–58
  socioeconomics of, 52–53
Florida's Family Transition Program (FTP)
  impacts of
    child-care type, 92–94, *93,* **94**
    child-care use, 89–92, **90,** *91*
  study description, 83–88, **88**
Funding, for child-care subsidies, 204,
  216–217

G

Gender differences, in nonstandard work
  hours, 131–132
Gold Seal Quality Care program, 56, 66
Government policy effects. *See also specific*
  policies or programs
  AFDC status, **115–117,** 119–120
  child-care arrangements, 92–97, *93,* **94,** 219
  child-care subsidy use, 174, 220–222
  child-care use, 89–92, **90,** *91*
  child development, 257, *258,* 262–264
  future research on, 264–265
  infant and toddler care, 53–58
  labor market participation, 89–92, **90, 91,**
    226, 257, *258,* 262
  work goals, 219

H

Health problems
  center-based care and, 81
  as work barrier, 226, 234, 239, 245

Home-based care
    child-care subsidies and, 185–187, **186**,
        228–229
    child development and, 80–81, 158–159,
        159, **160–161**
    for infants, 42, **43**
    labor market participation and, 82
    parental needs and preferences and,
        157–158, **158**, **160–161**, 162
    policy effects on, 92–97, *93*, **94**
    use by low-income families, 156–157, **157**
Home environments, risks and protections
    in, 252–253, *253*, 256–257

I

Illinois, in child-care subsidy study
    assistance provided by, 185–187, **186**, 194
    child care and TANF policies of, 178,
        179–180
    continuity of care arrangements in,
        191–193, **192**, 195–196
    continuity of subsidies in, 187–191, *189*,
        190, **191**, 195–196
    populations served by, 182–185, **183**, *184*,
        193
Illness
    center-based care and, 81
    as work barrier, 226, 234, *239*, 245
Income
    of child-care subsidy recipients, 182–185,
        183, *184*
    determinants of, 138, **140–141**
    percent used for child-care costs, 11, **11**,
        82, 157
    as study measure, 233–234
Infant and toddler care. *See also* Parents of
        infants
    child development and, 255–256
    cross-state study of
        child-care cost findings in, 66–70, *67*, **69**
        child-care quality findings in, 63–66
        child-care use findings in, 59–63, *60*, *62*
        data sources for, 58–59
        government policies in, 53–58
        socioeconomics in, 52–53
    difficulties in finding, 78
    requirements for, 21

J

Jobs-First. *See* Connecticut's Jobs-First Pro-
    gram

L

Labor force participation. *See also* Nonstan-
        dard work hours; Work disruptions
    AFDC status and, 109–117, **110–111**,
        115–117
    child-care arrangements and, 81–82,
        105–108, 120–123, **121–122**
    child-care costs and, 104, 117–118
    child-care subsidies and, 185, 188, 193,
        204, 214–215, 238–245, **240**, **243–244**
    factors affecting, 226–227
    increases in, xv, 101–104, 130, 149
    policy effects on, 89–92, **90**, **91**, 226, 257,
        258, 262
    welfare benefits and, 118
Licensing and accreditation, of child-care
    providers, 56, 65–66

M

Maryland, in child-care subsidy study
    assistance provided by, 185–187, **186**, 195
    child care and TANF policies of, 178,
        179–180
    continuity of care arrangements in,
        191–193, **192**, 196
    continuity of subsidies in, 187–191, *189*,
        190, **191**, 196
    populations served by, 182–185, **183**, *184*
Massachusetts
    in child-care subsidy study
        assistance provided by, 185–187, **186**,
            194
        child-care and TANF policies of,
            179–180, 181
        continuity of care arrangements in,
            191–193, **192**, 196
        continuity of subsidies in, 187–191, *189*,
            190, **191**, 196
        populations served by, 182–185, **183**,
            184, 193
    in infant and toddler care study
        child-care costs in, 66–70, *67*, **69**

child-care quality in, 63–66
child-care use in, 60, 62, 69–63
government policies of, 54–58
socioeconomics of, 53
Mastery, labor force participation and, 227, 235, 239, 245
Mental health problems, 226, 234, 239
Milwaukee's New Hope program
    impacts of
        child-care type, 92–94, 93, 94
        child-care use, 89–92, 90, 91
    study description, 83–88, 88
Minimum standards regulations, for child-care providers, 57–58

N

Nannies
    use by all family types and incomes, 5, 6
    use by low-income families, 6–8, 7, 8, 9, 10
National Survey of America's Families (NSAF), 3–4, 11–16, 13, 15, 129n
The New Chance Program
    impacts of
        child-care type, 92–94, 93, 94
        child-care use, 89–92, 90, 91
    study description, 83–88, 88
New Hope. See Milwaukee's New Hope program
Nonstandard work hours
    child-care arrangements and
        child development and, 254–255
        choice model of, 137–138
        literature review of, 133–134
        parental choices in, 82, 120–123, 141, 143, 144–145, 150
        SIPP data on, 134–136
        solutions to, 145–146
        trends in, 130–133, 138, 139

O

Oregon, in child-care subsidy study
    assistance provided by, 185–187, 186, 194
    child care and TANF policies of, 179–180, 181
    continuity of care arrangements in, 191–193, 192, 195, 197

continuity of subsidies in, 187–191, 189, 190, 191, 195, 197
populations served by, 182–185, 183, 184, 193
Outreach
    in child-care selection, 41–42
    in subsidy availability, 205–206

P

Parenting skills support, 44–45
Parenting stress, 233, 236
Parenting Stress Index (PSI), 233
Parent/other care
    child-care subsidies and, 123–124
    labor force participation and, 121–122, 124
    use by all family types and incomes, 5, 6
    use by low-income families, 6–8, 7, 8, 9, 10
Parents of infants
    child-care arrangements of, 40–42, 43
    child-care subsidies for, 34–40, 35, 38
    early intervention programs for, 30, 44–45
    future research on, 47
    study description of, 26–29, 27
    work requirements for
        exemptions for, 22–26, 23–25, 40–41
        local implementation of, 29–30, 31–32
        parents' view of, 30–33
        support for teenage parents, 33
Part-time work
    nonstandard work hours and, 131
    for parents of infants, 29–30
Pearlin Mastery Scale, 235
Personal mastery. See Mastery
Personal Responsibility and Work Opportunity Reconciliation Act (PRWORA)
    described, xv, 20, 77–78, 227
    results of, 130, 149
Psychologists, versus economists, 262–264

R

Racial and ethnic differences
    in AFDC status, 109–112, 110–111, 115
    in child-care choices, 120, 121–122, 150–151
    in child-care use and subsidy receipt, 236
    in labor market participation, 115

Relative care
child-care subsidies and, 185–187, **186**, 194
costs and, 141–144, **144**
education level of mother and, 144
nonstandard work hours and, 135–136,
141, **143**, 144–145
use by all family types and incomes, 5, *6*
use by low-income families, 6–8, *7*, **8**, *9*, *10*

S

School requirement exemptions, 22–26,
23–25. *See also* Education
Self-efficacy. *See* Mastery
Shift work. *See* Nonstandard work hours
Single parents. *See* Family structure
Social Relationship Scale, 235
Social support, 226–227, 235
State of residence. *See also specific states*
child-care arrangements and, 8, *9*
child-care subsidies and, 15, 22
welfare benefits and, 112, *112*, *113*, *114*
work and school exemptions and, 22–26,
23–25
Support services. *See* Early intervention pro-
grams
Survey of Income and Program Participa-
tion (SIPP) data, 107–108, 134–136
Survey of Program Dynamics (SPD), 129n

T

Teenage parents
early intervention programs for, 44
school requirements for
exemptions from, 22–26, **23–25**
parent's view of, 33–34
support for, 33
Teenagers, as caregivers, 142–143
Temporary Assistance for Needy Families
(TANF). *See also* Work requirements
child-care arrangements and, 40–42
child-care subsidies and
access to, 34–36, **35**, 205–206
applying for, 212, 218
benefit and employment status and,
185, 188, 193
copayments for, 36–40, **38**

cross-state comparison of, 178–182,
179–180
retaining, 213–216, 218
described, xv
Texas, in child-care subsidy study
assistance provided by, 185–187, **186**, 194
child care and TANF policies of, **179–180**,
182
continuity of care arrangements in,
191–193, **192**, 195–196
continuity of subsidies in, 187–191, *189*,
190, **191**, 195–196
populations served by, 182–185, **183**, *184*,
193
Three-City Study
conclusions of, 166–168
limitations of, 165–166
results of
child-care arrangements, 156–157, **157**
child-care costs, 157
child development needs, 158–162, **159**,
162–165
parental needs and preferences,
157–158, **158**, 162–165
study description, 152–156, **154**
Time limits, 54
Time period differences
in child-care arrangements, 8, *10*
in child-care subsidies, 16
Transportation problems, 234, 239

U

Unemployment. *See* Labor force participation

W

Wages. *See* Income
Welfare benefits. *See also specific benefits or
programs*
labor force participation and, 118
state of residence and, 112, *112*, *113*, *114*
Welfare caseload decrease, 102–104
Welfare reform. *See also* Work requirements
child-care costs and, 66–70, *67*, **69**
child-care needs and, 81, 103
child-care quality and, 63–66
overview of, xv–xviii, 103–104, 227

subsidized care enrollment and, 53–54,
59–63, *60*, *62*
Women's Employment Study (WES), 225,
230
Work disruptions, 210, 219, 233, 236
Work goals, policy effects on, 219
Work requirements
Family Support Act guidelines, xv–xvi,
77–78

for parents of infants
exemptions for, 22–26, **23–25**, 40–41
local implementation of, 29–30,
31–32
parents' view of, 30–33
study description of, 26–29, **27**
support for teenage parents, 33
PRWORA guidelines, 20, 77–78
TANF guidelines, xvi, 227–228